THE POMP OF YESTERDAY

The Defence of India
and the Suez Canal

1798–1918

THE POMP OF YESTERDAY

The Defence of India and the Suez Canal

1798–1918

———

WILLIAM JACKSON

BRASSEY'S
London • Washington

First English edition 1995

UK editorial offices: Brassey's, 33 John Street, London WC1N 2AT
UK orders: Marston Book Services, PO Box 87, Oxford OX2 ODT

North American Orders: Brassey's Inc,
PO Box 960, Herndon, VA 22070, USA

The Author has asserted his moral right to be identified as
author of this work.

Library of Congress Cataloging in Publication Data
available

British Library Cataloging in Publication Data
A catalogue record for this book is available from the British Library

ISBN 1 85753 008 X Hardcover

Typeset by M Rules
Printed in Great Britain by
Bookcraft (Bath) Limited

*To my grandson, John Reid,
an outstanding young musician
and an avid reader of history.*

CONTENTS

List of Maps   ix

PROLOGUE   THE POMP OF YESTERDAY   1

CHAPTER 1   THE FORERUNNERS *Nelson, Sidney Smith and*
Abercromby 1798–1802   5

CHAPTER 2   THE EASTERN QUESTION AND THE GREAT
GAME *The Dardanelles, Alexandria, the 1st Afghan*
War, and the Lebanon 1802–1850   29

CHAPTER 3   THE END OF THE GREAT GAME *The 1st Gulf*
War and the 2nd Afghan War, 1850–1881   66

CHAPTER 4   SEIZING THE WORLD'S STRATEGIC
CROSSROADS *The British Occupation of Egypt*
and Conquest of the Sudan 1882–1898   93

CHAPTER 5   THE NEAR SUCCESS OF THE TURCO-
GERMAN *JIHAD The Start of the Palestine and*
Mesopotamian Campaigns 1900–1916   123

CHAPTER 6   THE LOSS OF KUT AND THE ARAB REVOLT
Townshend, Murray and TE Lawrence 1916   160

CHAPTER 7   LLOYD GEORGE'S POLITICO-MILITARY
TARGETS *Baghdad, Jerusalem and Damascus 1917*   194

CHAPTER 8   DESTROYING THE OTTOMAN EMPIRE
Allenby's Megiddo 1918   227

EPILOGUE   'THE COCKPIT OF THE MOSLEM WORLD'   250

References   252
Bibliography   256
Index   259

LIST OF MAPS

1. The Middle East at the end of the 18th Century 4
2. Egypt and the Levant Coast in 1798–9 10
3. The Battle of Alexandria: 21 March 1801 22
4. The Playing-Field of the Great Game: 1800–81 33
5. Russian Imperial Expansion in the 19th Century 37
6. The First Anglo-Afghan War: 1839–42 40
7. The Retreat from Kabul: January 1842 56
8. The Syrian Campaign: 1840–41 61
9. The Persian Gulf Campaign of 1856–57 68
10. The Battle of Kush-ab; 8 February 1857 72
11. The Battle for Mohammerah: 26 March 1857 74
12. The Second Afghan War: 1878–81 82
13. The Occupation of Egypt 97
14. The Sudan Campaigns of 1885 and 1898 105
15. The Battle of Omdurman: 2 September 1898 115
16. The Turkish Theatre of War: 1914–18 124
17. The Turkish Advance on the Suez Canal: January 1915 131
18. Mesopotamia: 1914–15 133
19. The Turkish Counter-Offensive: Spring 1915 138
20. The First Battle of Kut: 28 September 1915 151
21. The Battle of Ctesiphon: 22 November 1915 156
22. The Sinai Front: 1916 164
23. Operations for the Relief of Kut: 1916 167
24. The Defences of Kut: January 1916 170
25. The Battle of Es Sinn: 7–8 March 1916 178
26. The Beginning of the Arab Revolt: June 1916 187
27. The Battle of Romani: 4 August 1916 190
28. The Recapture of Kut: December 1916–February 1917 196
29. Maude's Capture of Baghdad: 5–11 March 1917 203
30. Southern Palestine: 1916–17 206

31. The 1st and 2nd Battles of Gaza: 26 March and
      17 April 1917   210
32. The 3rd Battle of Gaza and Beersheba:
      27 October–7 November 1917   218
33. British Operations in North-West Persia: 1918   228
34. Northern Palestine before the Battle of Megiddo
      in September 1918   233
35. British Operations on the Caspian Sea:
      June–October 1918   235
36. The Battle of Megiddo: 17–22 September 1918   237
37. The Advance on Damascus, Beirut and Aleppo:
      October 1918   243
38. The Upper Tigris: October 1918   246

PROLOGUE

THE POMP
OF YESTERDAY

Lo, all our pomp of yesterday
Is one with Nineveh and Tyre!
Judge of the nations, spare us yet
Lest we forget; lest we forget.

Kipling's Recessional, 1897

Soon after midday on 1 August 1798, the lookouts in Nelson's leading ships-of-the-line, HMS *Goliath* and HMS *Zealous*, saw the masts of Napoleon's fleet at anchor in Aboukir Bay eleven miles east of Alexandria. By dawn next day the decisive Battle of the Nile had been fought and won by Nelson, and Napoleon's Army of the East, with which he intended to invade India, was trapped, unable to advance eastwards or return to France.

Nelson's victory marked the start of Britain's military involvement in the Middle East, which was to last for 200 years and continues to this day. The story of the blood, sweat and treasure expended by Britain in the deserts, marshes and mountains of the Moslem heartlands is told in this book, *The Pomp of Yesterday: The Defence of India and the Suez Canal; 1798–1918*, and its sequel, *With Nineveh and Tyre: Britain's Triumph and Decline in the Middle East; 1919–1992*. As Kipling put it, 'Lest we forget; lest we forget'.

This first volume covers the first century from the Battle of the Nile in 1798 to Allenby's delivery of the *coup de grâce* to the crumbling Ottoman Empire at the Battle of Megiddo in 1918. British strategic policy throughout the period was centred upon blocking all attempts by other European powers to reach India over land to seize 'The Jewel in the Crown'. Revolutionary France, Tsarist Russia, the Ottoman Empire and Imperial Germany all tried and were, in the end, always worsted by British and Indian fighting men, sometimes at very great cost. The many campaigns fought to defend India, and latterly the new route to India through the Suez Canal, may have been bungled at times, but by November 1918, Britain was the paramount power in the Middle East, hoping to bring independence to the Arab peoples and other ethnic groups, and an era of

1

peace and prosperity to former Ottoman lands. Thoughts of 'Nineveh and Tyre' were far from anyone's mind amidst the 'Pomp' engendered by Britain's decisive victories in 1918.

The second volume, *With Nineveh and Tyre*, will cover the second century. It will tell a very different tale of great endeavour and new triumphs, but eventual eclipse. After reshaping the political map of the Middle East and decisively defeating predatory Fascist Italy and Nazi Germany, the dragon's teeth of conflicting promises made to Arabs and Jews by Britain during the First World War started to germinate. Arab and Jewish nationalism became unbridled; the United States entered the fray; and Whitehall was forced by political and economic decline to surrender paramountcy to Washington. 'All our Yesterdays' in the Middle East have, indeed, become as 'One with Nineveh and Tyre'.

WGFJ
West Stowell

THE POMP OF YESTERDAY

The Defence of India
and the Suez Canal

1798–1918

———

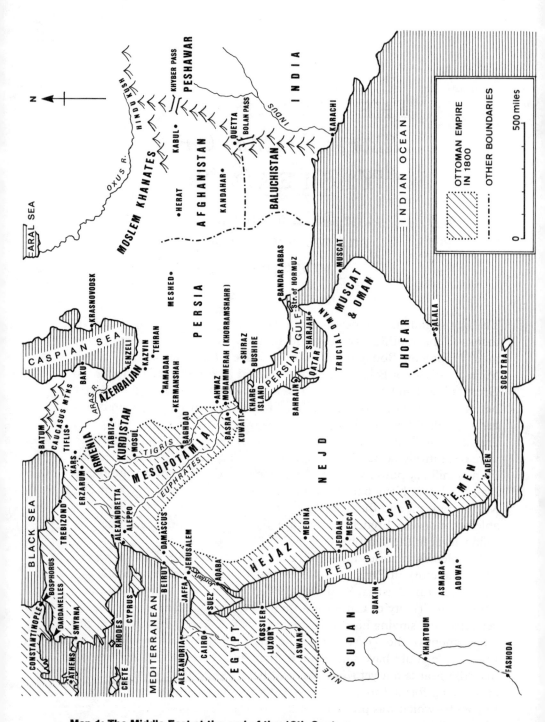

Map 1: The Middle East at the end of the 18th Century

CHAPTER 1

THE FORERUNNERS
Nelson, Sidney Smith and Abercromby 1798–1802

Had I been master of the sea, I would have been lord of the Orient.

Napoleon to the Directory in 1798[1]

The British military connection with the Middle East began prematurely, thanks to the youthful fantasies and subsequent ambitions of one young man: Napoleon Bonaparte. Since his days as a cadet at the French Military School of Brienne, he had dreamed of emulating Alexander the Great rather than Charlemagne. The fates ultimately decided the reverse, but in 1798 the vision of a great French Empire in the Orient, won by his genius, still fascinated him. Nevertheless, dreams – even Napoleonic dreams – rarely come true unless conditions are right, and in 1798 they were deceptively favourable. The Ottoman Empire was in steep decline; French military power was in the ascendant, spurred on by revolutionary zeal; the Royal Navy had been forced to withdraw completely from the Mediterranean; and the only British troops, who might have been available to oppose a French descent on Egypt, were being decimated by yellow fever in the Caribbean.

Napoleon's victories in Italy had made him a political danger to the timid Directory in Paris when he returned there in the autumn of 1797 after subjecting Austria, Sardinia, the Papacy and Venice to the humiliations of the Treaty of Campo Formio. The five Directors knew that his veterans were singing his praises in every village, and were calling for the replacement of the 'lawyers' by their 'little corporal' as the new king of France. He could have seized power then and there, but wisely decided that 'the pear is not yet ripe'[2]. Instead he accepted the command of the army being formed to carry the war across the Channel – the Army of England – which was proffered to him by the Directory to keep him out of the political arena.

Napoleon had little intention of invading England in 1798. He made a play of inspecting military preparations on the Channel coast, but his

5

mind was already set on acquiring his real glory in the East. The wish was father to Napoleon's thought: he was quick to persuade the Directory, with Talleyrand's help, that since the proposed invasion of England was too risky, the British should be challenged by threatening their position in India with an overland advance from Egypt, thus circumventing their command of the seas. The Directory's secret decree, issued on 12 April 1798, instructed him to take Egypt, to drive the English from all their oriental possessions, and to dig a canal through the isthmus of Suez.

Napoleon's plan was less impracticable than it may seem at first sight. Although the French position in India had deteriorated since Clive's victory at Plassey, Frenchmen still wielded considerable power amongst the many independent Indian rulers who had not yet submitted to British rule. France was providing European military cadres to modernise their armies, and financial subsidies for the likes of Tippoo Sahib of Mysore to embarrass the British and to keep French influence alive on the sub-continent. In an advance from Egypt through today's Syria, Iraq, Iran and Afghanistan, the French could expect to acquire anti-British allies on the way, and be able to recruit local forces to protect their lines of communication, as Alexander the Great had done. Sea communications would eventually be established by digging a canal across the isthmus of Suez as ordered by the Directory. The British certainly felt that such an operation was feasible. As early as 1796, London was warning the East India Company at Bombay and Calcutta that a French advance on India via the Middle East was a possibility.

Napoleon managed to convert the Army of England into his Egyptian expeditionary force in ten weeks, and he kept the secret of its destination from the British until well after he had sailed from Toulon on 19 May 1798. Surprisingly, none of the many English spies in France, who were well aware of preparations for some major overseas expedition, managed to pick up definitive clues as to its actual destination.

Across the Channel in London, the vacillations of the French Directory were well matched by the performance of the younger Pitt as Prime Minister and Henry Dundas, his close personal friend and political ally, as War Minister. Neither had any military experience or vestige of strategic sense; both failed to understand the military need for concentration of effort; and each, in his turn, tried the patience of the very experienced British commanders at sea and, even more so, on land.

Ten days before Napoleon left Paris on 3 May 1798 for Toulon to embark in Admiral Brueys's flagship, *L'Orient*, a British naval officer, who had been held prisoner in the Temple in Paris, escaped 'with the assistance of Colonel Phélypeaux, an officer in the old royal army of France, and aided, it was supposed, by a feminine intrigue'[3]. De Bourrienne, Napoleon's private secretary, ruefully comments:

An escape so unimportant in itself afterwards caused the failure of the most gigantic projects and daring conceptions. This escape was pregnant with future events; a false order of the Minister of Police prevented the revolution of the East![4]

The escaper was Sir Sidney Smith, who, more than anyone else, was to thwart Napoleon's dreams of empire in the Middle East. He was a restless, egocentric and highly articulate naval officer, who, like Nelson, was always chasing the fantasy of 'his glory'; but, unlike Nelson, sought fame as a loner in politico-military operations and had few friends amongst his more orthodox naval colleagues. Nelson, for one, could not stand him. In his teens, Sidney Smith had seen several naval actions during the war of American Independence; and during the short peace before the French Revolution threw Europe into disarray, he had lived in Caen, learning French and exploring the French coast clandestinely! In 1788, he tried to involve himself in the affairs of the Barbary coast, but when the Admiralty decided otherwise, he took leave and went off in high dudgeon – and on half pay – to serve as an unofficial naval adviser to the King of Sweden. He was largely responsible for the Swedish success against the Russians in the Baltic in 1790, for which he was knighted by King Gustavus III.

Sidney Smith's younger brother, Charles, was appointed British Ambassador to the Porte, so off Sidney went to Constantinople to volunteer for service with the Turks, but when France declared war on Britain in 1793, he tried to return to England. He only got as far as Toulon, arriving at the moment when the young Napoleon's gunnery was forcing Admiral Hood to withdraw the Anglo-Spanish blockading fleet. Smith volunteered at once to lead incendiary parties to burn the captured French ships, which Hood had decided must be abandoned. It was not Smith's fault that 15 ships-of-the-line escaped destruction. The Spanish Admiral Langara, with an eye to Spain changing sides in the near future, obstructed him, deeming 'that it might be for the interest of England to burn the French Fleet but it was by no means the interest of Spain.'[5] Those 15 un-burnt ships enabled the French to rebuild their Mediterranean Fleet, which was to carry Napoleon to Egypt.

Smith's efforts at Toulon may not have increased his popularity in the Navy, but he was soon displaying his aptitude for partisan style naval warfare by harassing French shipping with considerable success in the North Sea and Channel in command of the *Diamond* frigate and a flotilla of small raiding craft. In April 1796, he went one step too far: he was captured, trying to cut out a French privateer at Le Havre, and ended up in the Temple prison in Paris.

While Smith was making his escape from the Temple in the spring of 1798, their Lordships in the Admiralty and Admiral Jervis, now Earl of St

Vincent, in command of the British fleet off Cadiz, were trying to fathom the purpose of the large French force assembling at Toulon. Egypt did not enter into their calculations. Lord Spencer, the First Lord of the Admiralty, writing to St Vincent, surmised that the obvious destination was Naples, but went on to suggest that Portugal or Ireland might be possibilities. 'Whatever its destination' he wrote, 'its defeat would surely be a great object for this country'. He went on to suggest sending a detachment back into the Mediterranean for the first time since 1796, to watch Toulon. He ended by saying:

> If you determine to send a detachment into the Mediterranean, I think it almost unnecessary to suggest to you the propriety of putting it under the command of Sir H. Nelson.[6]

And so began the first major British military involvement in the Middle East since the Crusades. It was quite unpremeditated and had nothing whatsoever to do with British ambitions in the Levant or the strategic need to protect the land route to India. The British Government was intent on destroying Napoleon's amphibious force wherever it might be heading. It was Napoleon who led Nelson to Egypt and the Battle of the Nile; and it was the stranding of his Army of the East by Nelson's destruction of his fleet in Aboukir Bay which led three years later to the British Army taking a hand in expelling the French from Egypt.

Between the beginning of May and the end of July 1798, Nelson suffered all the frustrations, and Napoleon enjoyed all the luck. Nelson re-entered the Mediterranean on 2 May, flying his flag in *Vanguard*, a fast 74, in company with Sir James Saumarez in *Orion* and Captain Ball in *Alexander*, both 74s but slower ships. He had two frigates and a sloop with him for reconnaissance and communication. He was to be reinforced with ten more of the newest 74s and an older 50 from the blockading force off Cadiz as soon as St Vincent received replacements from England. Knowing the importance of Nelson's sortie, St Vincent selected the best ships from the inshore squadron, which Nelson had been commanding before his ill-fated raid on Tenerife, which had cost him his arm. Their very experienced captains – 'choice fellows of the inshore squadron' – were all known to him and belonged to his 'band of brothers' in whom he had the greatest confidence and they in him. When concentrated, his squadron would be the finest force of 74s ever assembled, but it could not be brought together off Toulon earlier than the first week of June even under the most favourable circumstances.

The circumstances were far from favourable. A near hurricane drove Nelson's three 74s away from Toulon, and dismasted *Vanguard*. She would have been driven ashore had it not been for the heroic efforts of Captain Ball, who managed to tow her clear with *Alexander*. The same storm delayed Napoleon's sailing, but the wind eased sufficiently to let him slip away from Toulon unseen on 19 May, while *Vanguard* was being repaired off Sardinia with spare masts carried in the other British ships. Regrettably, Nelson's two frigates, anticipating that the squadron would have to return to Gibraltar for repairs, withdrew on their own initiative and never managed to rejoin him.

By the time Nelson was off Toulon again with his complete squadron of 13 ships-of-the-line, but no precious frigates, Napoleon had taken Malta on 11 June and had set sail again on the 19th for Alexandria on a course that took him close to and along the south coast of Crete. Nelson set off in pursuit, reaching Naples on the 17th, where he heard that Napoleon was thought to be at Malta. He sailed on through the Strait of Messina, heading for the island, and was off Cape Passaro, the south-eastern tip of Sicily, when reports reached him that the French had been seen leaving Malta on an easterly course. He sent a questionnaire to his captains asking for their views on Napoleon's most likely destination. The consensus pointed to Alexandria. Crowding on sail, his squadron took the shortest possible route well south of Crete; and, as luck would have it, he passed his quarry during the night of 22 June without knowing it. He reached Alexandria on 28 June, three days ahead of the French. Finding no sign of them there, and lamenting his lack of frigates to widen his search, he turned north up the Levant coast towards Alexandretta, thinking that Napoleon might have decided to advance on India via Syria. Three weeks later, on 19 July, he was back at Syracuse, still baffled as to Napoleon's whereabouts. Re-victualled and watered, he set off eastwards again, at last gaining firm intelligence on 28 July off Greece that the French had, indeed, reached Alexandria.

Meanwhile much had happened in Egypt. Like all would-be conquerors, Napoleon looked first to the morale and conduct of his own troops, and secondly to winning the support of the Egyptians by dividing them from their current rulers, the Mamelukes. In his proclamation to his troops he said:

> Soldiers – You are about to undertake a conquest the effects of which on civilisation and commerce are incalculable. The blow you are about to give England will be the best aimed and the most sensibly felt, she can receive until the time arrives when you can give her her deathblow . . .[7]

This was all good stuff, but masked the reality. Any ideas that Napoleon's veterans may have had of the Nile Delta being comparable to the rich plains of Italy were soon to be swept away like mirages in the heat, sand, flies and poverty of disease-ridden Egypt. Many British and American soldiers were to echo French sentiments about the squalor of life in the Middle East over the next two centuries, but they expected it: the French

Map 2: Egypt and the Levant Coast in 1798–9

did not, and began to suffer a resentful homesickness as the truth began
to dawn upon them.

Napoleon's letter to the 'Pasha of Egypt' had just as unfortunate an
effect as his proclamation to his troops. Egypt, as a province of the
Ottoman Empire, was nominally ruled by the Porte's viceroy, but real
power lay with the military Mameluke Beys – an aristocracy descended
from the Circassian slave soldiers, who had ruled and corrupted Egypt
since 1250. In 1798, their power still rested upon their gorgeously accoutred Mameluke cavalry, who, like their Cossack forebears, were fine
horsemen and reputed to be some of the finest cavalry in the world.
Addressing the Ottoman governor, Napoleon aimed to drive wedges
between the Porte and the Mamelukes, and between the Mamelukes and
the impoverished Egyptian people, but he failed to realise that they were

all followers of Islam and would unite against infidel intrusion into their affairs.

The French fleet had reached Alexandria in the late afternoon of 1 July. A heavy sea was running, but, hearing from the French consul that Nelson had been there only three days before, Napoleon overrode Admiral Brueys's protests and ordered immediate disembarkation on the Marabut beach, a few miles west of Alexandria, saying 'Fortune gives me three days: if I do not profit by them we are lost'.[8]

Many men were drowned during the landing, but by three o'clock in the morning Napoleon was heading an advance by three divisions on Alexandria, which was soon his, and his troops had their first experience not of an Egyptian city steeped in gold and classical history, but of one reeking of poverty and medieval squalor.

During the next few days, the French columns, advancing eastwards to the Nile, experienced heat, sand, thirst, dysentery and, as yet, only apathetic local Egyptian hostility. Villages consisted of a few mud huts of little use to the French, who were accustomed to feeding off the land as they advanced. The Army of the East was soon in a potentially mutinous state.

After reaching the Nile and organising a flotilla of local craft to support his advance on Cairo, Napoleon, fearing the disintegration of his army, tried to bring the Mameluke commanders, Murad Bey and Ibrahim Bey, to a decisive action as soon as possible. The Beys were equally keen to destroy the infidel French. The first major action was fought at Shubra Khit on 14 July. Mameluke gunboats had some success against the ill-equipped French flotilla, but Murad Bey's whirlwind cavalry charges against Napoleon's main body were decimated by French fire power.

A week later, the two Beys tried to challenge Napoleon as he approached Cairo. Unwisely they divided their forces. Murad faced Napoleon, who was advancing up the west bank of the Nile, while Ibrahim stood in reserve on the east bank. The battle, known in history as the Battle of the Pyramids, was fought in the heat of the afternoon of 21 July in scrubland and melon fields. The French formed mutually supporting squares when the Mameluke cavalry struck and again destroyed them with efficient musketry and cannon fire. The rest of Murad's army was driven to its destruction on the banks of the bridgeless Nile. All was over in about two hours, the French losing barely 40 dead amongst their 200 casualties. Ibrahim played no part in the battle and withdrew eastwards into Sinai to fight more successfully another day. Murad gathered what was left of his Mamelukes and disappeared southwards into Upper Egypt. Napoleon entered Cairo on 25 July.

Exactly a week later, in the early afternoon of 1 August, the lookouts in Nelson's leading ships, *Goliath* and *Zealous*, spotted the masts of Admiral Brueys's fleet anchored in Aboukir Bay. Nelson's hunt was over, and the first British military action in the Middle East since medieval times – albeit naval – was about to begin.

The two fleets were almost equal, but Brueys had the tactical advantage of being anchored in a strong defensive position of his own choosing. Alexandria's harbour was too shallow for his warships, so Napoleon had given him the option of putting to sea after the landings were completed, but he had elected to stay in close support of the army in Aboukir Bay, just 11 miles east of the city. He had anchored his ships in line across the bay with the western end covered by guns that he had placed on Aboukir Island, and the eastern end protected by shoal water. As this flank lacked gun support from the shore, he placed his heavier ships, including *L'Orient*, in the eastern half of his line. But he had made a major tactical error: he stationed his ships-of-the-line two to three hundred yards apart to give them room to swing safely on their bow anchors. He would have been wiser to have anchored them fore and aft, and closer to the shore, allowing no room for an opponent to penetrate his line or to sail in between it and the shore.

During his long search for Brueys's fleet, Nelson had rehearsed with his 'band of brothers' the tactics they would use for every conceivable combination of circumstances when the two fleets met. The common denominator was immediate attack, and the principal tactic was to sandwich each French ship in succession between the broadsides of two British ships. To do this at Aboukir, half of Nelson's ships had either to manoeuvre round the end of the French line, or sail through it. Only the very experienced eyes of Nelson's leading captains showed that Brueys's line was vulnerable to both forms of attack.

Brueys made a second, but more understandable, mistake. By the time the British fleet was fully in sight, it was mid-afternoon. It did not seem conceivable that Nelson would attack without careful reconnaissance, which would consume what was left of the daylight. Most of the French ships were undermanned with parties ashore searching for food and digging wells for water. Local Egyptian hostility was already such that each foraging and digging party had to be protected by 20 or so armed sailors. In the ships, guns on the inshore side were not run out and were encumbered with piles of material being used for repair and maintenance work. In *L'Orient*, for instance, repainting was in progress with drums of highly inflammable paint stacked on the top gun deck!

Nelson attacked the western end of Brueys' line, in army parlance 'off the line of march' with barcly a pause. His leading ships, *Goliath* and *Zealous*, which were well ahead of the main body of his fleet, profited by *Culloden*'s grounding when navigating round the Aboukir Island shoals. None of his ships had accurate charts of the bay, so they had to sound their way in. It was Captain Thomas Foley in *Goliath* who saw that he could pass between the Aboukir shoals and the French van; and it was he who led the first five British ships into the attack along the unmanned inshore side of the French Line. Nelson in *Vanguard* led the rest of his fleet into the attack along the seaward side.

The action lasted well into the night as the British ships forced the French ships, one by one, to strike their colours. The fiercest fighting was around the powerful *L'Orient*, which disabled *Bellerophon* before being set on fire by *Swiftsure* and *Alexander*. The drums of paint on her deck added to the conflagration, and she blew up at quarter to eleven, taking the loot of Malta with her. By then Brueys was dead. He had had both legs shot away, but insisted on continuing to command, seated in a chair with tourniquets around his stumps! He died soon after a cannon-ball from *Swiftsure* almost cut him in two.

Nelson too was wounded during a fierce engagement between *Vanguard* and *Le Spartiate*. A piece of metal ripped his forehead, blinding him temporarily with a flap of skin that dropped down over his one good eye. He thought that he had been killed, but the surgeon soon reassured him that the wound, though messy and painful, was only superficial. He remained in command throughout the battle, and issued a stream of orders for exploiting success after *L'Orient* blew up. Only two of the most easterly of the French ships-of-the-line and two frigates had not struck by next morning and escaped out to sea.

Apart from stranding Napoleon in Egypt, Nelson's annihilation of the French Mediterranean Fleet had four far-reaching repercussions: it removed the immediate threat to India; it gave new heart to the anti-French powers, bringing Austria, Russia and Turkey into the field on Britain's side; it reduced the low morale of Napoleon's troops in Egypt still further; and it gave encouragement to the Moslem opposition to Napoleon's colonising efforts.

After the battle, Nelson wrote to the Governor of Bombay to relieve anxieties in India and to encourage the dispatch of Indian-based naval forces to deal with any French attempt to interfere with British Red Sea trade. With Ottoman agreement, the Governor despatched a small force, which established a forward operating base temporarily at Aden in January 1799, and occupied the island of Perim to block the southern exit from the Red Sea. The British Government supplemented these moves by dispatching a small naval squadron under Commodore John Blankett on a 10-month voyage from England to the Red Sea via the Cape. Blankett, variously described as 'a coarse-mannered blockhead' or 'an accomplished and amiable gentleman, notwithstanding a certain irritability induced by gout', arrived in August 1799, and, despite acute discomfort from heat combined with the pain of his gout, effectively put paid to any ideas Napoleon might have had of clearing British traders out of the Red Sea ports.

The formation of the Second Coalition of Britain, Austria, Russia and

Turkey against France led indirectly to the re-entry of Sir Sidney Smith into Middle Eastern affairs. After his escape from the Temple, Lord Spencer, the First Lord of the Admiralty, appointed him to command the 80 gun *Tigre*. In October 1798, he was sent out in *Tigre* to join St Vincent's fleet at Gibraltar, but with a special commission from the Foreign Office, appointing him joint plenipotentiary with his brother, the Ambassador, to the Porte in Constantinople; and instructing St Vincent to send him to the Levant to help organise Turkish opposition to the French in Egypt. Unfortunately, St Vincent did not see fit to place him under Nelson's command, and even more unfortunately Sir Sidney assumed the airs of an independent commander and hoisted the broad pennant of a commodore within Nelson's sea area. The ensuing row ended in Smith accepting subordination to Nelson as Senior Naval Officer, Levant, and putting all his very considerable energies into helping the Turks to expel Napoleon from Egypt without the help of British troops.

Napoleon was at first dejected by the loss of his fleet, but this did not last long. Egypt had still to be pacified and turned into a French colony. Ibrahim Bey had taken his Mamelukes back to El Arish on the Levant coast halfway to Jaffa and presented no immediate threat, but Murad Bey had retired only a short distance up the Nile and would have to be dealt with before he could become the focus of anti-French resistance. Napoleon gave the task of defeating him to Desaix.

Desaix's campaign in Upper Egypt was one of extraordinary endurance and frustration, such as several British columns were to experience in the years to come. It was a hide-and-seek type of campaign, fought along the Nile and in its surrounding deserts. Murad, with his few thousand Mamelukes, played 'Will-o'-the-Wisp' as the French trudged ever southwards, many of them half blinded by trachoma that filled their eyes with pus. Dysentery, and virulent Egyptian strains of gonorrhoea and syphilis, took their toll as well; and logistic problems created conditions of terrible want, many units becoming shoeless and having to march barefoot through the hot sand.

In the engagements that did take place, Murad showed that he had learned nothing from his earlier encounters with the French. He would throw his cavalry into reckless charges at the wretched, but nevertheless steady, French squares with the same disastrous results every time. After each defeat, he disappeared into the desert only to return to try his luck again a month or two later as Desaix pushed on southwards. After the last engagement, which took place near Aswan in October 1799, Murad agreed to submit to French rule, but never came in to make his submission: he just vanished as far as the French were concerned.

Back in Cairo, all Napoleon's efforts to portray himself as a supporter of Islam in debates with the Moslem clerics at al Azhar University, and as the destroyer of the hated Mamelukes, were brought to nothing by the high-handed and often barbaric behaviour of his disillusioned troops and civilian administrators. On 20 October, a secret signal for revolt was passed through the bazaar grape-vine and in the muezzins' evening calls to prayer. Next day all shops were shut; French occupied property and barracks came under attack by the Cairo mob; and the French Military Governor was killed by a lance thrust into his back when he arrived to deal with the trouble. Napoleon with his experience of similar insurrections in the Paris streets, soon gripped the situation and had no hesitation in using cannon: a 'whiff of grapeshot' in the streets, and round shot against the great al Azhar Mosque cooled Moslem dissent. Even so, it took three days to quell the uprising. French rule was re-established with brutal reprisals.

Meanwhile, the repercussions of the Battle of the Nile were reverberating through the capitals of Europe and the Middle East, and nowhere more so than in Constantinople where the Smith brothers were having some success in propelling the Sublime Porte into attempting the expulsion of the French from all Ottoman domains. Two concentrations of Turkish troops were being built up: one on the island of Rhodes for amphibious operations against Alexandria in conjunction with Sidney Smith's squadron, and the other in Palestine under Djezzar Pasha, supported by Ibrahim Bey from El Arish. Djezzar Pasha was a fearsome Bosnian, nick-named 'the Butcher', who was reputed to strangle opponents with his own bare hands. Napoleon was well aware of these concentrations, but decided to advance on Suez first before dealing with the Turkish threat so that work could start on the Canal Project.

Blankett's Red Sea squadron had no troops embarked to oppose the French occupation of Suez, so he made no attempt to do so. Having visited Suez in person, Napoleon set about planning his overland advance on India via Syria and Persia. He ascertained through agents that the Shah of Persia would, subject to payment in advance, be willing to grant a right of passage through his realms and the establishment of depots along the chosen route.

The prerequisite for any successful advance through Syria was the defeat of the British backed Djezzar Pasha and Ibrahim Bey in Palestine. Napoleon tried to subvert them, but without success. Reporting to the Directory on 10 February 1799, he wrote:

> Djezzar Pasha, an old man 70 years of age is a ferocious person, who has unbounded hatred of the French. He has treated with disdain the friendly advances which I made . . .
> I sent him a letter; he had the messenger's head chopped off . . .
> There was therefore no choice. I was challenged; I promptly decided to carry the war into the enemy's country.[9]

Napoleon left the Nile delta on 11 February for his advance into Syria with some 12,000 men. Winter temperatures made marching easier, but rain could turn the desert tracks into quagmires so Napoleon took the risk of shipping his artillery in small craft along the coast. The Turkish garrison of El Arish surrendered after a short 10 day siege and its men were released on parole. Ominously, plague was found amongst them. It was to be a very different story when Napoleon reached Jaffa on 3 March. The town refused to surrender to its French 'liberators'. It was stormed on the 7th and sacked with a brutality that even Napoleon's hardened generals felt went beyond acceptable limits. As if by Allah's divine intervention, plague broke out amongst Napoleon's troops. It was to cost him almost 1000 men during the campaign.

As the French advance guards reached Mount Carmel on 17 March, expecting to make equally short work of Djezzar's main base in the dilapidated and neglected old Crusader fortress and town of St Jean d'Acre, they saw in the bay below them two British ships-of-the-line, the 80 gun *Tigre*, flying the broad pennant of Commodore Sir Sidney Smith, and the 74 gun *Theseus* commanded by Captain Ralph Miller.

A fortnight earlier on 3 March, despite Nelson's qualms about him, Smith had been given command of all British naval forces blockading the French in Egypt. His task was to escort the Turkish amphibious force assembling at Rhodes under command of Hassan Bey for the planned attack on Alexandria. That same evening, he had heard that Napoleon was in front of Jaffa. He had sailed at once for Acre to put some spirit and naval muscle into Djezzar's defence of Syria. With him he took his old friend, the former French Colonel of Engineers, de Phélypeaux, who had helped him to escape from Paris. Phélypeaux had been in the same class as Napoleon at Brienne, passing out with first-class honours and well above the Corsican. The two men hated each other: de Phélypeaux, an ardent royalist, had old scores to settle with the republican Napoleon. Djezzar accepted de Phélypeaux as his engineer with authority to strengthen the ramshackle fortifications as best he could while Captain Miller of *Theseus* crewed gunboats to harass the French from the sea, and provided marines and bluejackets as reinforcements ashore. Smith himself assumed overall command and set about organising the dispatch of Turkish reinforcements and supplies from Rhodes.

Napoleon laid siege to Acre on 18 March. Things went wrong from the very start. Smith captured the convoy of small craft carrying the French siege guns and ammunition, and left the French with only light field guns and very little ammunition with which to try breaching Acre's walls. He organised the hauling of the captured French guns into Acre and their positioning in the fortifications, from which his naval gun crews kept the French besiegers under constant harassing fire. Napoleon was reduced to offering his troops and local inhabitants 20 sous for every spent cannonball recovered.

The siege was to last two and a half months. Napoleon managed to drag a few siege guns overland from Jaffa, which made breaching the walls practicable. He launched no less than nine major assaults, getting into the city but never managing to break into the citadel. While shortage of artillery was Napoleon's main worry, French mining operations were Smith's. Like all British commanders before and since, Smith was determined to dominate no-man's land, launching frequent sorties to destroy French saps and mines. One raid did seriously disrupt work on the main French mine, and subsequent British counter-mining resulted in it being only partially successful when it was eventually fired during the last French assault. Napoleon's diary for 14 April records:

> The siege progresses. We have run a gallery . . . which is now only 18 feet from the wall. We have not fired a shot for two weeks; the enemy blazes away like mad, and we merely pick up their cannon-balls humbly, pay 20 sous for them, and pile them up so that we already have about 4,000. That will be enough to pour in hot fire for 24 hours and to batter a breach.[10]

On 7 May, Hassan Bey's ships, coming from Rhodes with reinforcements, were sighted off Acre. Napoleon knew it was now or never, and accelerated plans for what was to be his last despairing effort. By this time a practical breach had been made, and on 9 May the final assault was delivered. Infuriatingly, from Smith's point of view, Hassan Bey's ships were becalmed and his landing delayed. Gathering all available men from his ships and arming them with pikes, Smith rushed with them to the breach, arriving just in time to help Djezzar's men hold off the assault until the arrival of Hassan Bey's reinforcements. Napoleon's diary for the following day reads:

> We have carried the principal parts of the wall, but the enemy have built a second wall abutting Djezzar's palace. We shall have to sap through the town . . . and to lose more lives than I am willing to lose. In any case, the season is too far spent. My object is accomplished: Egypt calls me.[11]

With his object far from accomplished, but with his propagandists blaring the success of French arms in stopping Djezzar's invasion of Egypt, the Army of the East started its painful withdrawal back to the Nile 12 days later, abandoning sick and wounded at every stage, and in Jaffa, putting them out of their misery with over-doses of opium before abandoning the city.

Many of the Syrian factions had been sitting on the fence before deciding where their best interests lay. After Acre no one sided with the French. Smith had worsted Napoleon and put an end to any attempt to march on

India via Syria. Sadly neither de Phélypeaux nor Miller survived to share his triumph. The former is said to have died of fever, but more probably from plague; and the latter was killed in an ammunition accident in *Theseus*.

Smith's victory brought him the thanks of both Houses of Parliament and a pension of £1,000 a year, but his luck did not last. Two months after saving Acre, he escorted a reassembled Turkish amphibious force from Rhodes, now commanded by the ageing Mustapha Pasha, to Aboukir Bay for the long planned assault on the French in Alexandria. The landing took place on 14 July 1799 without much opposition. As so often happens in amphibious landings, Mustapha gave priority to building up his forces and their supplies ashore before advancing on the city. Napoleon, who after his return to Cairo, had marched south to support Desaix in Upper Egypt, turned in his tracks and in one of his extraordinary bursts of energy concentrated a striking force which dealt with the Turks within 10 days of their landing. Murad's cavalry led the counteroffensive and had cut great swathes through the Turkish ranks before the French infantry came up and routed them. Smith did his best to rescue those who tried to swim out to his ships. Pitifully few escaped, and by the end of the day Mustapha's force had ceased to exist.

A month after defeating this Turkish landing, Napoleon slipped secretly back to France, leaving a disgruntled Kléber in command of a desperately home-sick Army of the East. Smith was not entirely surprised when he received a friendly letter from Kléber, suggesting that he, Smith, should act as an intermediary between the French and the Turks, who had advanced once more to El Arish. Smith, fancying himself as an astute diplomatist, was delighted to receive Desaix and the head of the French civilian administration in *Tigre* for negotiations. They stayed three weeks on board with Smith acting as mediator between the representatives of the Ottoman Grand Vizier, Yussef, and Kléber.

Smith, by this time, was very much the old hand in Middle Eastern affairs. His local political and military superiors were all new: Lord Elgin – the preserver of the Elgin Marbles – had relieved Smith's brother as British Ambassador in Constantinople; Admiral Lord Keith had taken over from St Vincent; and Nelson was back in England. Both Elgin and Keith encouraged Smith to pursue his negotiations, which ended in the Turks and French signing the Convention of El Arish on 24 January 1800 on board *Tigre*. French troops would leave Cairo within 40 days and would be shipped back to France through Alexandria and other Nile Delta ports at Turkish expense. In order to ensure that these disgruntled soldiers spread as much disaffection in France as possible, Smith insisted that they should not travel as a formed body and should be landed at widely dispersed French ports, from which they were to be sent straight home.

Poor Smith had every right to feel aggrieved when the Government refused to ratify the Convention on the grounds that he had exceeded his powers in not insisting on unconditional surrender. He had enjoyed both Elgin's and Keith's support, and with instructions from Whitehall often taking over two months to reach him, it was reasonable to assume the man on the spot was the best judge of what was practicable in the circumstances. The British Government, however, was struggling to hold the Second Coalition together, and had no wish to see 30,000 troops sent back to France, however mutinous they might be. It was a stupid mistake, which was to lead to British troops having to intervene in Egypt a year later to drive the French into accepting almost exactly the same terms which Smith had negotiated for them.

Kléber, however, did not have long to live: on 14 June he was murdered by a young Moslem fanatic – rough justice for a man whom the Egyptians had come to revere as a *Just Sultan* for the fairness of his administration.[12] Kléber had always opposed Napoleon's plans for colonising Egypt. Menou, who replaced him, was an imperialist fanatic. He has been described as looking like a seedy waiter of a third class restaurant. He had made himself the laughingstock of the French Army and Egyptians alike by taking a Moslem wife and accepting conversion to Islam, including circumcision! Such was the man whom the British Army was to face in eight months time, calling himself Abdullah Menou.

★ ★ ★

Pitt and Dundas's handling of British military operations in 1799-1800 had been little short of pathetic. Fortescue in his definitive history of the British Army aptly quotes the words of Lord Cornwallis, the Master-General of Ordnance:

> What a disgraceful and expensive campaign we made! 22,000 men, a large proportion not soldiers, floating round the greater part of Europe, the scorn and laughing stock of friends and foes![13]

As the driving force behind the Second Coalition, Pitt had landed a scratch force of some 30,000 partially trained troops under the Duke of York near Den Helder at the entrance to the Zuider Zee in August 1799, to help the Prussians liberate Holland from French occupation. The very experienced General Sir Ralph Abercromby was his principal field commander with Major-General John Moore (later Sir John, who was to win undying fame at Corunna in 1809) as one of the brigade commanders. The two men had served together in the Caribbean and in Ireland, and had a great respect for each other. After a shambolic landing, followed by some initial success on land, which brought them within a few miles of Amsterdam, the autumn weather, coupled with the gross administrative incompetence of Dundas's ministry, persuaded the Duke to accept very lenient terms offered by the French for an unimpeded British evacuation. Unknown to the French, the British had only two days' supply of bread left when they withdrew in October 1799!

Abercromby and Moore advocated holding their now battle-experienced force together when it returned to England, and retraining it properly for whatever campaigns were envisaged for 1800. Nothing of the sort happened: Dundas's penny-packetting operations continued under the all too pervasive influence of the Admiralty. Operations against Belleisle, Tenerife, Ferrol, Vigo and Cadiz were planned for small British amphibious forces, but none proved practicable. Fortescue explains why:

> One and all had their origin in the counsels of naval officers, which were not wholly un-influenced by the question of prize money.[14]

The only saving grace was the appointment of wise and loyal old Abercromby (he was 66) as the Army's Commander-in-Chief in the Mediterranean in May 1800 with the unpopular and uncouth Hely-Hutchinson as second-in-command, and with John Moore again as one of his trusted subordinates in command of the 'Reserve' or, in today's parlance, 'Striking Force'. Minorca was to be his main base where he was to concentrate the many detachments of British troops scattered around the Mediterranean for a descent upon the Ligurian coast to help the Austrians drive the French out of Italy. But Napoleon pre-empted the Coalition's plans with his epic march over the Alps and his decisive victory over the Austrian armies at Marengo in the spring of 1800. There could be no question of British troops intervening on the Continent for the time being. Abercromby was, therefore, directed to co-operate with Lord Keith in taking Cadiz. Much to the Navy's annoyance, Abercromby vetoed the operation when he arrived off the port. He discovered that Keith's ships would have no secure anchorage and might leave him and his troops stranded in Spain if the weather turned foul. He withdrew his troops to Gibraltar where they suffered the misery of being cooped up in their transports for weeks while awaiting fresh orders.

★ ★ ★

In Whitehall there had been a marked change of outlook. With Napoleon in the ascendant once more, the British Cabinet feared a renewed threat to India. The mad Tsar Paul of Russia had fallen out with the Austrians and was veering towards an alliance with France against Britain. The combination of the unprincipled French dictator with the remnants of his Army of the East still trapped in Egypt, and the insane autocrat of all the Russias with ambitions in the Middle East, was a worrying prospect.

For once Pitt and Dundas reacted sensibly, setting in hand a strategic concentration to round up the French in Egypt with thrusts from the East as well as the West. Abercromby was to sail at once towards Egypt to link up with the Turks at El Arish for a combined offensive to re-take Alexandria and Cairo on behalf of the Porte. The Governor of Bombay was to provide a force of British and Indian troops to land at Suez, supported by Blankett's Red Sea squadron and reinforced by British troops sent from Cape Town. Dundas hoped that Abercromby would reach Egypt by December, but the forces coming from India and South Africa could not possibly arrive before April 1801. Sidney Smith, who was to support Abercromby with his Levant squadron, must have smiled wryly. None of this would have been necessary if the Cabinet had been prepared to ratify his El Arish Convention instead of demanding a French unconditional surrender.

By mid-November 1800, Abercromby had managed to concentrate his forces at Malta, the French garrison of which had capitulated on 5 September, having been reduced to eating cats and dogs by the closeness of the British naval blockade. He had but 16,000 men fit for duty and 1,200 sick in his transports when he sailed from Malta for the Levant on 13 December. He sent Moore ahead to El Arish, and his Quartermaster-General to Rhodes to concert plans with the Grand Vizier, Yussef, and Sidney Smith. Moore found that the British Commissioner with the Turks at El Arish had died of plague and the Turkish troops there were 'an indisciplined mob with their ranks never wholly free of plague'.[15]

Things were even worse at Rhodes. Elgin and Smith had received all kinds of promises from the Porte, but Ottoman lethargy, and perhaps fear of Russia, had frustrated their combined efforts to prepare for Abercromby's arrival. No small craft suitable for landing operations had been collected; the Turkish gunboats were unmanned; no food had been stockpiled; and no horses or wagons had been requisitioned. Even the Turkish Fleet had withdrawn to Constantinople and showed no sign of cooperating. It was clear that Abercromby would have to go it alone with minimal Turkish help.[16]

Having experienced the chaotic landing at Den Helder in 1799, caused by a lack of understanding of each others' problems between the Navy and the Army, Abercromby rehearsed and rehearsed landing techniques on the Turkish coast north of Rhodes while waiting for the Turks to provide for his most urgent needs, and for further British reinforcements to arrive.

By this time, Abercromby's force consisted of six infantry brigades and a cavalry brigade, nominally 1,000 strong but only half could be mounted. His artillery consisted of 58 field guns and 78 heavier siege guns and mortars. Elgin's attempts to persuade the Turks to provide horses for the cavalry and artillery had not been very successful, and horse transport ships, hired in Smyrna, were late in arriving. Another worry was water supply for the troops once they were ashore. All ships' tanks were topped up and extra water storage was provided in them, but landing it was going to be difficult.

Sidney Smith reckoned – accurately as it turned out – that the French had about 30,000 troops in Egypt, but Abercromby deemed this to be an exaggeration, and estimated that Menou would not be able to concentrate more than 10,000 men to oppose a British landing at Aboukir Bay. Nevertheless, as he had only enough boats to land 6,000 of his 15,000 fit troops at a time, and as he would have no transport or draught animals for some days, the risks were high. A promised force of 4,000 Janissaries from Rhodes under Capitan Pasha was not likely to be much help, even if it were to arrive in time, which seemed highly unlikely.

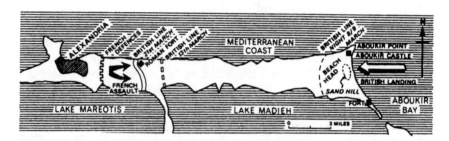

Map 3: The Battle of Alexandria: 21 March 1801

Lord Keith's main fleet and Sidney Smith's squadron escorted Abercromby's transports from Rhodes on 22 February 1801 and reached Alexandria on 1 March, but storms delayed the landing in Aboukir Bay until the night of 7/8 March. Moore, who had carefully reconnoitred the beaches with Abercromby from a cutter soon after their arrival, was in command of the landing, which was to be made on a mile long stretch of beach at the western end of the bay. The approach to Alexandria, which was some 11 miles away, would be along the narrow isthmus between the sea and Lake Madieh. The beach was just in range of French guns in Aboukir Castle to the north and in a redoubt at the entrance to Lake Madieh to the south. There was a prominent sand-hill overlooking the beach, which Moore thought must be the centre of the French position, although he could not see any fortifications on it. He made it his objective: its capture would clear rifle fire off the chosen landing area.

Meanwhile in Cairo, Abdullah Menou, who was certainly no Napoleon, had heard on 4 March of the appearance of Keith's fleet off Alexandria. Despite the urgings of his own subordinates, he did little more than dispatch some 600 men to reinforce General Friant, the French garrison commander in Alexandria. Friant was made of sterner stuff. He deployed most of his 1,600 infantry, 200 cavalry and 15 guns to cover the Aboukir beaches, concealing most of them in the dunes out of sight of the British warships.

After dark on 7 March, two marker-boats were anchored off the beaches as guides for the landing-craft coxswains. Loading the assault craft and cutters started at 2 am, and by dawn the flotilla was formed up for the run-in. In the assault wave, there were 58 flat-boats each with about 50 soldiers 'burdened with three days' provisions and 60 rounds of ammunition, sitting patiently with their firelocks between their knees, blinking at the fierce glare of the low morning sun'.[17] Then came 84 cutters packed with the reserves, and behind them 51 launches, containing the gunners with 14 field guns and naval landing parties of some 500 seamen under the personal command of Sidney Smith, who was determined to be in on the fight ashore. On both flanks, there were gunboats and bomb-ships, and three of the lighter ships-of-the-line came in as close as they could to provide support with their broadsides.

Friant's men and guns concealed in the dunes, and the guns in the fort and redoubt, gave the approaching flotilla all they had. The sea 'seethed under the tempest of iron. and the men were drenched to the skin but the bluejackets rowed steadily on'.[18] As the boats touched down, losses began to mount. Some boats were hit and grapeshot and musketry fire swept the beach. Moore was quickly ashore and assaulted the central sand-hill with the 40th, 23rd and 28th of Foot in line. The hill was much steeper and more strongly held than they expected, but they rushed it and routed the French demi-brigade on its crest with the bayonet, capturing their four guns. On Moore's flanks the 42nd Highlanders, who had suffered some loss during the run-in, beat off Friant's cavalry and captured three more of his guns; and the Coldstream Guards, who had suffered most in the boats, were equally successful. In a mere 20 minutes, Moore with 2,500 men had secured the key to the British beachhead, and within another 90 minutes Friant had given up trying to halt the landing and was withdrawing, leaving Abercromby free to establish his force ashore. The British casualties totalled just over 700, including 100 sailors, mostly from amongst the boat crews. The French lost half that number because they did not stand to fight it out, but fell back along the isthmus to cover Alexandria.

By the evening of first day, all British troops were ashore, and Abercromby had established a beachhead two miles deep on the sandy, palm dotted isthmus, which was barely two miles wide for most of its 11 miles to Alexandria. High winds prevented the build up of supplies and ammunition ashore for the next two days. 11 March was calmer and some horses were brought ashore. Fortunately the French had no gunboats on Lake Madieh so supplies could be landed by the Navy close behind the troops as they advanced along the isthmus. The water supply problem was eased, on Sidney Smith's advice, by digging wells at the base of palm trees, which proved highly successful.

Reinforcements had meanwhile reached Friant, who decided to hold a delaying position on the higher ground around the ruins of Roman

Canopus or Roman Camp, covering the dyke between Lakes Madieh and Mareotis along which Menou might arrive from Cairo. Abercromby advanced against him on 13 March in three columns with Moore's Reserve on the right, heading for the Roman Camp ruins, the key to the French position. It was a slow and tiring advance with the troops trudging through deep sand and bluejackets hauling 16 of the field guns in place of non-existent horses. The clash, when it came, gave the British troops confidence and was a warning to the French that they were no longer fighting Mamelukes. Moore swept them out of the Roman ruins so precipitately that Friant withdrew in haste to his main defensive position within a mile of Alexandria. The British columns pressed on, but came under increasingly aggressive French artillery fire, which they could not silence with the few guns that could be hauled forward. Abercromby and Hely-Hutchinson, both of whom had poor eyesight, misjudged the strength of Friant's position due to mirage conditions and incurred unnecessary casualties before deciding to withdrew to the Roman Camp to organise a deliberate assault on Alexandria's defences.

Abercromby was in an unenviable position as his men dug in amongst the Roman ruins. Lack of horses meant guns, ammunition and supplies had to be hauled forward through the sand by men; food was scarce, and the only fuel available for cooking was palm tree wood which burnt badly and stank; and sick lists were lengthening alarmingly. He had no hard intelligence of French strengths and movements, and his experience of French artillery during the latter half of the actions on 13 March was not encouraging. Another British failure like Den Helder stared him in the face. Had it not been for the incompetence of Menou and the home-sickness of the French troops, this might well have been the outcome.

Menou reached Alexandria on 19 March with substantial reinforcements, bringing the French strength up to 10,000, including 1,400 cavalry. He decided to attack at once before the Turks under Capitan Pasha could arrive from Rhodes and the Grand Vizier, Yussef, at El Arish started to advance on Cairo again. Menou's plan was to unhinge the British position by storming the Roman ruins, held and fortified by Moore's Reserve in true Napoleonic fashion, with massed infantry columns. As he had to cross the open ground to reach the British positions, Menou decided to attack before dawn on 21 March.

Fortunately for the British, Abercromby was expecting a night attack. He had ordered his troops to sleep fully accoutred in their battle positions, and had ordered a stand-to an hour before dawn. As it happened Moore was duty major-general that night and was on the spot when at about 5 am 'a confused hubbub of drums beating the charge, and hoarse voices shouting "Vive la France! Vive la République!"' broke out below the Roman ruins.[19] Moore's troops were already mustered for the dawn stand-to and ready for what was to be the day during which Napoleon's veterans of his

Italian campaigns realised that they were up against worthy opponents. The British did not run, and they did unto the French what the French had done so often to the Mamelukes. With great steadiness they poured withering volleys into the French columns, decimating them wherever they attacked; and British gunboats joined the fray, battering the French flanks. Moore was wounded in the leg early in the battle, but able to carry on, riding from one threatened point to another always in control of his regiments.

Menou, having failed to storm the Roman ruins or breach the British centre, launched the first of two cavalry charges. It came to grief amongst unseen holes, which had been dug by British troops to make shelters until their tents arrived. In desperation, he launched the rest of his cavalry in a second charge. Moore had to gallop for his life, keeping clear of them, but Abercromby was not so lucky. A sabre thrust from a French dragoon passed between his right arm and chest, bruising him badly. He was only saved by a large Highlander lifting the dragoon out of his saddle with his bayonet. The sabre stayed entangled in the C-in-C's jacket! Shortly afterwards a musket ball hit him in the thigh, but he called the wound 'slight' and refused to leave the field.

Menou's second cavalry charge fared no better than the first, but the British were running out of ammunition. There was a dangerous pause of about an hour, during which they were punished by the French artillery without being able to reply effectively. Then replenishments arrived, and the British gunners scored two lucky hits. Menou, who had been contemplating disengagement, had his mind made up for him as two of his ammunition wagons blew up. He withdrew his shattered force back to Alexandria, leaving Abercromby a few moments to savour his victory before he collapsed from loss of blood and was evacuated to *Foudroyant*. Unfortunately, the surgeons could not extract the ball from his thigh bone. Gangrene set in and he died a few days later on 28 March on his way home. He was buried at Malta.

The second battle of Alexandria was over by nine in the morning. The British lost just over 1,000 men, about a quarter of casualties suffered by the French. At long last, after defeats by the Americans at Saratoga and Yorktown, by the French in Flanders and Holland, and by their own folly in petty operations in the western Mediterranean and futile attempts on Spanish Atlantic ports, the British Army had regained its confidence. In the longer term, Abercromby's victory over Menou outside Alexandria did more than that: it brought the Union flag ashore in the Middle East for the first time, although the British Government was to act in much the same way as the Bush Administration after the Gulf War in 1991. It tried to disengage as quickly as possible so as not to be drawn into the political maelstrom of Ottoman affairs. It needed to concentrate all its resources for the continuing struggle against Napoleon in Europe and had no wish to be saddled with the administration of Egypt: governing India was quite enough.

Hely-Hutchinson succeeded Abercromby as Commander-in-Chief in Egypt. He was an unpleasant looking man with a violent temper and slovenly in dress. His abilities and courage were not in question, but the soldiers did not know him well, and disliked what they saw of him. Unfortunately, Moore had been severely wounded in the last phase of the battle and was evacuated to the frigate *Diadem*, so Hutchinson was deprived of his services for weeks. However, he still had Sidney Smith to help look after the blockade of Alexandria, where he left Major-General Eyre Coote with 6,000 men and most of his heavier guns to contain Menou. Capitan Pasha did arrive four days after the battle, bringing with him some 4,000 men ready to support a British advance on Cairo along the west bank of the Nile. Hearing of Menou's defeat, Yussef also started to bestir himself at El Arish and agreed to co-operate by threatening Cairo from the east. And in the Red Sea, Blankett had arrived off Suez with three companies of infantry embarked in his ships at Aden and had taken possession of the port where they found great difficulty in buying enough camels to give them some mobility. Unhappily, General Sir David Baird, commanding the main body of troops from India, was delayed by a chapter of accidents and was not to reach the Gulf of Suez until the heat of June had begun to make the place almost unbearable.

Menou, who had left General Belliard to oppose any British advance up the Nile and to hold Cairo with 13,000 men, decided to stand siege in Alexandria while awaiting the arrival of a French squadron under Admiral Ganteaume with reinforcements dispatched to him by Napoleon. Menou was not to know it, but Ganteaume could find no way through the British naval blockade and was never to appear off Alexandria.

Hutchinson was extraordinarily slow in making his arrangements for his advance on Cairo. When he did decide that he was ready at the beginning of May, he was immediately faced with near mutinous protests from his senior officers that it was too late in the season. The heat would decimate their troops; plague was prevalent in the Nile valley; there was a lack of supply depots and hospitals; and French numerical superiority in the Cairo area all made an advance too risky until the autumn. Whilst these arguments had some truth in them, they were, in fact, being used in an attempt to oust Hutchinson. The influential Moore, who was still recovering from his wounds at Rosetta at the mouth of the Nile, would have none of it, and the whole disagreeable plot collapsed.

The advance up the Nile went painfully slowly, although well supported by naval gunboats and supply craft on the river itself. Belliard's rear guards made a few ineffectual attempts to stand, many of his troops surrendering in the hope of a quicker passage home. As Yussef approached Cairo from the East, Belliard sallied forth with 5,000 men to check him before turning north to oppose Hutchinson and Capitan Pasha. This time French military magic deserted them. Yussef's Mameluke cavalry outmanoeuvred Belliard and he was forced to fall back precipitately upon Cairo. On 15 June, Hutchinson called upon him to capitulate. He refused at first, but the news of Admiral Ganteaume's failure to relieve Alexandria changed his mind, and on 22 June he agreed to open negotiations with Hutchinson and Yussef.

This time the British Government was so keen to withdraw from Egypt that it had no difficulty in accepting Belliard's request for the repatriation of all French troops and administrators on the lines of Sidney Smith's earlier El Arish Convention. Hutchinson had, in fact, reached Cairo with only 4,000 British troops. He himself fell ill and handed over to John Moore, who was fully recovered by then. Moore was faced with the embarrassing task of escorting some 14,000 fully armed Frenchmen down the Nile for embarkation at Rosetta. The French, however, were too keen to sail home to France to cause any trouble. On the way north, the British and French troops were brought together by the discomfort of Egypt and the thieving propensities and nascent hostility of the local people.

Menou refused to accept the convention signed by Belliard on 27 June, and went on strengthening the defences of Alexandria. Hutchinson recovered sufficiently from his illness to re-assume command and set about preparing to assault the city. Reinforcements were sent to him from elsewhere in the Mediterranean, and Baird at last arrived in the Gulf of Suez with his own force from India and the reinforcements sent from the Cape Town. Blankett advised Baird that it was too late in the season to land at Suez. Instead he recommended landing at Kosseir, marching across the 100 miles of desert to the Nile and then sailing down it to join Hutchinson at Cairo. Neither he nor Baird could have known what they were asking the troops to do in the July heat. Baird's quartermaster-general, Colonel John Murray, had wells dug at 17 mile intervals along the route and managed to requisition enough camels and water skins to make the march just possible for the 6,000 strong force. Baird reached the Nile on 8 July with the loss of only three men, and sailed down it. He was too late to be of any use to Hutchinson at Cairo, and so sailed on to Rosetta, hoping to be of service at Alexandria.

Far more trying was the march of the three companies landed earlier at Suez by Blankett. They had to cover the 70 miles to the first wells on the Cairo road with only a few camels to carry ammunition and other essentials, and with only the water which the men could carry themselves. It took three day in temperatures of 109°, but they did it with the loss of only nine men from heat exhaustion.

Hutchinson and Sidney Smith co-operated well in bringing Menou to his knees. On the evening of 16 August, Eyre Coote's brigade was landed west of Alexandria and started to threaten Menou's rear. Further troops and heavy guns were landed by the Navy a few days later as Coote pushed back the French outposts and captured some of their outer works with the help of Smith's gunboats. By 26 August, Coote had four batteries in position ready to support an assault when Menou asked for terms. His first demands were outrageous, but on 2 September he accepted the same terms as Belliard with one special exception. At Lord Elgin's instigation, he was made to surrender the Rosetta stone, which Napoleon's archaeologists had found, giving the key to ancient Egyptian hieroglyphics. It now graces the British Museum in London instead of the Louvre in Paris.

The British withdrawal from Egypt started as soon as the last Frenchman had been shipped home in October 1801, and should have been completed by the time the Treaty of Amiens was signed in March 1802, but the last British soldiers did not, in fact, leave until March 1803. Hutchinson left the Grand Vizier, Yussef, to clear up the political mess left by the French, and to re-establish Ottoman rule over their Egyptian Province. In gratitude for British help, the Sultan allowed Lord Elgin to ship what the Turks considered useless statuary and friezes from the ruins of the Parthenon in Athens back to the British Museum as well as the Rosetta stone. Few visitors realise that the Elgin Marbles, as well as being some of the most controversial acquisitions in the Museum, are also an untitled memorial to Britain's first major military foray in the Middle East.

Fortescue provides a suitable epitaph for Abercromby:

Ministers come and Ministers go; politicians of Dundas's type are always among us. and from time to time still find their way to the War Office: but Ralph Abercromby stands forth as an example to British Generals that by serving even a Dundas faithfully they may serve their country well.[20]

Sidney Smith continued his restless, argumentative and self-advertising career for the rest of the Napoleonic wars and their aftermath, dying in Paris in 1840, having achieved the rank of full Admiral and made many more enemies on the way. Moore 'was quite unable to understand the real merit hidden beneath so much extravagance and vanity'.[21] Nevertheless, he should be remembered as the man who stopped Napoleon's advance on India.

CHAPTER 2

THE EASTERN QUESTION
AND THE GREAT GAME

*The Dardanelles, Alexandria, the 1st
Afghan War, and the Lebanon 1802–1850*

---

*It seems pretty clear that sooner or later the Cossack and the
Sepoy, the Man from the Baltic and He from the British Isles will
meet in Central Asia. It should be our Business to take Care that
the Meeting should be as far from our Indian Possessions as may
be convenient and advantageous to us.*

Lord Palmerston writing in 1842.[1]

Throughout the 19th Century, British strategic interest in the Middle East
was dominated by 'The Eastern Question' as far as Whitehall was concerned, and by 'The Great Game' in the eyes of the Honourable East
India Company's government in Calcutta. The former was the struggle
between the Great Powers to fill the vacuum created in the Moslem world
by the accelerating decline and disintegration of the Ottoman Empire; and
the latter was the Anglo-Russian rivalry for politico-military dominance of
the northern approaches to India through Persia and Afghanistan.

British governments handled both the Eastern Question and the Great
Game largely by proxy: through support of the Sublime Porte in the former, with the Royal Navy's Mediterranean Fleet as its principal military
agent; and through alliances with Persian and Afghan princes in the latter,
with that extraordinary band of 'politicos', drawn from the Indian Army
and the Indian Political Service, as its front men. Rarely has British foreign policy been so beholden to the political sagacity or otherwise of naval
and army officers as it was in the Middle East and Central Asia in the 19th
Century.

When the last French troops left Egypt in the autumn of 1801, the
Napoleonic Wars still had some 14 years to run. Not surprisingly, in the
light of long-standing Anglo-French colonial rivalry, the French threat to
India via the Middle East did not fade with their defeat in Egypt. French
agents stayed on in Syria and Egypt, hoping to infiltrate the Ottoman and

Persian Empires in anticipation of Napoleon's future domination of
Europe, which could eventually lead to a more auspicious conquest of an
eastern empire once Britain had been brought to her knees. Nelson's triumph at Trafalgar in 1805 made less of an impact on the affairs of the
Middle East than Napoleon's victories at Ulm and Austerlitz in the same
year. British diplomatic influence waned in Constantinople and Cairo. By
the beginning of 1807, the position of the British Ambassador to the
Porte, Charles Arbuthnot, had become so precarious that he fled the
Turkish capital and sought refuge with the British fleet, which was cruis-
ing off the entrance to the Dardanelles.

At that time, the British Government was concentrating all its efforts
upon manipulating the defeat of Napoleon in Europe, and was engaged in
the opening moves of the Peninsular War. Nevertheless, it could not
ignore the French attempts to re-establish themselves on the overland
route to India. Admiral Collingwood, the Commander-in-Chief of the
Mediterranean, was directed to mount a naval demonstration against
Constantinople in conjunction with a Russian fleet; and General Fox, the
commander of the small detachments of British troops scattered around
the Mediterranean, was instructed to re-take Alexandria as a way of coun-
tering the growing French influence in Egypt. Both operations were
ill-thought through, badly conducted and proved minor disasters, which
are rarely mentioned in histories of the period, although they provided
unhappy precedents for Winston Churchill's Gallipoli Campaign in 1915
and Anthony Eden's débâcle at Suez in 1956.

Collingwood sent Admiral Duckworth, with eight ships-of-the-line, to
overawe Constantinople and to demand the surrender of the Turkish fleet
but, like Churchill in 1915, he did not arrange for any troops to accompany him in case a landing proved necessary. Nothing went right from the
start. There were only a limited number of days per month on which conditions of wind and tide were right for sailing ships-of-the-line through the
Dardanelles. Duckworth waited for some days for his Russian allies, who
failed to appear, and was then delayed for several more days by adverse
winds. All hope of achieving even a modicum of surprise was gone; and
these delays gave the French time to organise the Turkish defences of the
city. Duckworth's ships reached Constantinople unscathed on 20
February 1807, and the admiral entered into a pompous and entirely
futile correspondence with the Porte, who, with strong French support
and the absence of any British landing force, could enjoy deliberate pre-
varication without undue risk.

These further delays were fatal: they gave the French time to super-
vise – as the German General Liman von Sanders was to do in 1915 – the
manning and stocking of the Turkish batteries, covering the Dardanelles
narrows, through which Duckworth would have to withdraw once he
realised that the British Government's gunboat diplomacy had failed. A

very frustrated Duckworth destroyed a few minor Turkish warships, which happened to be berthed in the Golden Horn, and then started his withdrawal to the Mediterranean on 3 March. Having no troops with him to storm the Turkish batteries at the narrows, his ships suffered considerable damage and over 160 casualties, fighting their way through to the open sea. Churchill and the Admiralty were to study Duckworth's misfortunes when contemplating overawing Constantinople in 1915 with a similar naval force, but, as we shall see, failed to profit by his experience.

The troops, whom it would have been more sensible to send with Duckworth, were sailed instead for Alexandria. The Government's instructions to the force commander were vague and left almost everything to his imagination. Fortescue paraphrases them:

> We send you with 5000 men to Egypt, where your object will be the capture of Alexandria only. You are not to occupy the country, but you are to make British influence predominant in it.[2]

Such a task required a commander with political finesse. Fox should have sent Sir John Moore, his second-in-command, but was too loath to lose him. He gave the command instead to Major-General Mackenzie Fraser, a frank, straightforward soldier with no political instincts or abilities!

Egypt had been in turmoil since the British left in 1803. The Mamelukes had opposed the re-imposition of direct Turkish rule, but their Beys were hopelessly divided amongst themselves and had a new mercenary force to contend with: the Albanians, who had been sent to Egypt by the Porte to help drive out the French in 1799. The Albanian second-in-command, Mehemet Ali – an outright adventurer of great ability and ambition, and with an eye for the main chance – emerged from the bloody internal struggle for power as the new strong man of Egypt and forced the reluctant Porte to proclaim him Pasha of Egypt in 1805. The French agent in Cairo picked and backed the winner, telling Mehemet Ali that a new French expeditionary force was being assembled to help him establish Egypt's independence from Constantinople.

The British agent in Cairo was the devious Major Missett, who put his money on a comeback by the Mameluke Beys. Missett was a cripple with an over-active imagination, an exaggerated sense of his own importance, and a propensity for misjudging the Egyptian political scene. It was his reporting to London that suggested a British occupation of Alexandria to pre-empt a French landing and to strengthen the pro-British Mameluke Beys.

Misfortune dogged Fraser's force from the start (*see Map 2*). Over half its transports were dispersed by a storm during the approach to Alexandria; heavy surf on 17 March delayed the landings on the same Marabout beaches to the west of the city, which Napoleon had used in

1798; and Missett's contention that the people would welcome the return of British troops was soon proved wrong. The Governor of Alexandria closed the city gates instead of welcoming Fraser, and the small garrison opened fire. Fraser sensibly marched his small force round the city and occupied Abercromby's relatively secure position on the Aboukir isthmus while awaiting his lost transports and to build up a base from which to attack the city.

Fraser's luck seemed to change on 20 March when the missing ships arrived and the Governor of Alexandria capitulated, having decided that there were now sufficient British troops ashore to justify his doing so without loss of face. Two days later, Duckworth's squadron dropped anchor in Aboukir Bay, making the British force look even more formidable. Fraser had accomplished his military objective without loss, but was without any direction from London as to how the political battle against French influence was to be carried forward. Missett, however, had no doubts and persuaded him that Alexandria would starve unless he extended the area of British occupation to the Nile Delta by taking Rosetta some 40 miles to the east of Aboukir. Rosetta's defences, Missett assured Fraser, were contemptible, and the Albanian defenders were a worthless rabble. Fraser had no way of telling whether this was so or not, but decided that he should fall in with the views of his political adviser. At the end of March, he dispatched a small column of 1,600 men with only four guns under command of Major-General Patrick Wauchope to take Rosetta.

Wauchope, a brave but not very intelligent officer, with an utter contempt for the Egyptians, did not reconnoitre Rosetta carefully enough and was ambushed by the Albanians as he led his column into the narrow streets of the town. He was killed with about a third of his force, which hastily withdrew to Aboukir. The affair did little to enhance British prestige, and should have opened Fraser's eyes to the unreliability of Missett's advice.

It was now clear to Fraser that he was opposed by both the Turks and Albanians, and that he was receiving nothing more than encouraging letters from Missett's friends, the Mameluke Beys. Missett still insisted on the importance of the Delta, and Fraser, despite his original instructions to confine himself to taking Alexandria, weakly agreed to send a larger force of 2,500 men with 11 guns under Brigadier William Stewart to try once more to take Rosetta.

The second attempt, made in mid-April, was even more damaging to British prestige. Mehemet Ali had concentrated enough Albanian infantry and Turkish cavalry to defeat Stewart, who made a number of unfortunate tactical errors and lost 800 men, 500 of whom were taken prisoner. This defeat, however, had unexpected sequels in Egypt and Whitehall.

One of the officers wounded and taken prisoner at Rosetta was sent back to Aboukir with a message for Fraser from Mehemet Ali, saying that he had seen a letter from Fraser to the Mameluke Beys, stating that the British had landed at Alexandria not to conquer Egypt but merely to exclude French influence. This modest objective, Mehemet explained, could be easily achieved through a British financial subsidy and support in Mehemet's struggle to win complete Egyptian independence from Constantinople. As far as he was concerned, there was no difference between British and French gold; and, as the Porte had thrown in his lot with the French, the British were his friends. Fraser, at long last, jettisoned Missett's unwise pro-Mameluke stance and began to co-operate with Mehemet, who withdrew his troops from Rosetta and allowed supplies to reach Alexandria. The whole campaign had been a waste of effort due to faulty local political intelligence and direction.

Map 4: The Playing-Field of the Great Game: 1800–81

In Whitehall, Fraser's two defeats at Rosetta led to fears of a debilitating drain of resources in the Eastern Mediterranean for no significant advantage. Napoleon's victories at Elyau and Friedland had forced the Tsar to patch up a peace with him at Tilsit. Britain was once more alone and needed all the troops she could muster nearer home. When Fraser was ordered to evacuate Alexandria in September 1807, Mehemet Ali released all his British prisoners, who had been exceptionally well treated while in his hands. Four years later, Mehemet Ali disposed of Missett's Mameluke friends by massacring most of them after they had foolishly accepted his invitation to feast with him in the confines of Cairo's citadel.

While Whitehall had been dancing these first steps in the minuet of the Eastern Question, the earliest moves in the Great Game had begun. As early as 1800, Napoleon had reached an agreement with the mad Tsar Paul for a combined Franco-Russian march on India; and, indeed, the Tsar did order the Don Cossacks to press south-eastwards towards India, but they had only reached the Volga when he was assassinated in St Petersburg in 1801 and the expedition was recalled.

The East India Company was not unaware of continued French intrigues to open up an overland invasion route through Persia, but the Governor-General was equally concerned about the much more immediate threat posed by the Amir of Afghanistan, Zaman Shah, to the north-western frontiers of India which, at the turn of the century, lay ill-defined and difficult to defend in the wide plains of the Indus valley. The obvious counter to the Afghan threat was a British alliance with Persia to curb Zaman Shah's ambitions. The French were equally keen to establish friendly Franco-Persian relations to open their own route to India.

The British won the first round in Tehran, thanks to the extraordinary politico-military skills of one young and very large Scottish officer, Captain Malcolm (later Sir John Malcolm, Indian administrator, soldier, diplomat and historian), the forerunner of the many men who were to play the Great Game in Central Asia for most of the 19th Century. The first of his three missions to Tehran was in 1800, when he succeeded in persuading the Shah to accept a three point agreement: to curb the ambitions of the Afghans in exchange for British arms; to exclude the French from Persia; and to give the British exclusive trading rights and privileges in the Persian Gulf.

Napoleon's victories in Europe led to renewed French efforts to denigrate British influence in Tehran. Their first exploratory mission in 1802 was rebuffed by the Shah but, after Austerlitz in 1805, Napoleon dispatched a special envoy to Tehran with precise proposals for a Franco-Persian invasion of India, and an agreement to help the Shah to regain Georgia from Russia. The Shah was reluctant to treat with a regicide nation, and asked the French envoy at their first audience a single question: 'What made you kill your King?'.

The French persisted and two years of devious bargaining followed, in which procrastination by Calcutta over how much British support the Shah should be promised undid most of Malcolm's good work and played into the hands of the French. In the end, the Shah, like the Porte, decided to seek the friendship of the conqueror of Europe. His envoy reached Napoleon at Tilsit in June 1807 during the meeting of the two Emperors

on the raft moored in the River Niemen. With typical Napoleonic duplicity, the French Emperor signed the secret Franco-Persian Treaty of
Finkinstein behind the Tsar's back, promising the Persians French support against the Russians in the Caucasus in return for Persian support for
a French invasion of India. Three months later, the French General
Gardanne arrived in Tehran with a military training team to organise the
Persian Army as a French auxiliary force and to set up depots for a combined advance through Afghanistan.

All the moves in the Great Game were influenced by the harsh realities
of the geography of the north-western approaches to India (*See Map 4*).
There were only two practicable invasion routes through the mountains
guarding the rich Indus plain, both of which started from Herat, a city
claimed over the centuries by both Persia and Afghanistan, lying in a rich
fertile valley with enough grain-growing capacity to serve as a logistic
base for an invading army. In the north, there was the Khyber Pass route,
which ran due east from Herat via Kabul, Jalalabad and the Khyber to
Peshawar; and in the south, the Bolan Pass route ran south-eastwards
from Herat via Kandahar, Quetta, the Bolan Pass and down into the valley of the Indus. To reach Herat, the Russians would have to cross the
deserts of Central Asia between the Caspian and Aral Seas, and invade the
Khanates of Khiva and Kokand; or invade Persia from Caucasia, which
they annexed in 1813, and skirt round the northern edge of the Persian
central deserts via Tehran and Meshed.

At the beginning of the 19th Century, Russia's drive towards Central
Asia had only reached the northern shores of the Caspian and Aral Seas,
and the whole of Persia lay between them and Herat, so their threat to
India was, as yet, minimal. The arrival of the Gardanne Mission in Tehran
towards the end of 1807 was far more worrying to the British and East
India Company Governments, who reacted simultaneously and, as so
often used to happen, without consultation. Both sent missions of their
own to re-establish British influence in Tehran. John Malcolm, now a
brigadier, again led India's mission; and Sir Harford Jones, who later
changed his name to Brydges, was sent from London by sea round the
Cape to Basra.

Malcolm's second mission was a total failure. In spite of arriving in the
Gulf in May 1808, escorted by a powerful naval squadron, Gardanne's
influence was so powerful in Tehran that Malcolm was rudely treated by
the Shah's officers and debarred from approaching the capital. Justly
incensed, he returned to Calcutta where he advised Lord Minto, the
Governor General, that a punitive expedition should be sent to the Persian
Gulf to occupy Kharg island off Bushire as an advance British base for
future military operations against Persia, should they prove unavoidable.

Harford Jones was luckier. He arrived later that year when reaction
against French high-handedness had set in amongst the Persians in

Tehran. They had come to realise that Gardanne had promised more than he could perform, and that French influence in restraining Russian annexations in Caucasia was minimal. A gift of a fine diamond from George III, and the promises of a large British subsidy and military training team, were enough to restore Anglo-Persian relations. General Gardanne and his military mission were handed their passports. The occupation of Kharg Island was postponed *sine die*, but, as might be expected, relations between Harford Jones as Whitehall's man and Lord Minto were far from cordial. While accepting the arrangements contracted with the Shah, Minto condemned the arrogant behaviour of Harford Jones, questioned his bills as over-lavish, and insisted that his own representative should execute the resultant Anglo-Persian Treaty.

Minto once again chose John Malcolm to lead his third Mission to Tehran in 1810, which this time was an outstanding success. The Shah and his officials went out of their way to make amends for the discourtesy shown to his second mission. Sir Percy Sykes in his classic, *A History of Persia*, written in the 1920s, records:

> Malcolm was received with extraordinary marks of esteem and friendship, and his fine character, his justice, and his knowledge of the world impressed the Persians so much that all Englishmen in Persia still benefit from the high qualities displayed by their great representative.[3]

Malcolm's mission was supported by a large staff amongst whom were several officers destined to play important parts in the Great Game. The most remarkable was Lieutenant Henry Lindsay of the Madras Artillery (later Major General Sir Henry Lindsay Bethune), a giant of a man, six foot eight inches tall without his boots, and with the strength and weight proportionate to his height. He took over the training of the Persian Army and led it with success in several engagements with the Russians on the Caucasus front. He did not return to England until 1821. Sent back to Persia by the British Government in 1834, he commanded the Persian forces which fought their way from Tabriz to Tehran to restore the legitimate Shah to the throne during the war of succession of that year. Four years later, he was sent back to Persia yet again, this time as Commander-in-Chief (Designate) of the Persian Army, but misunderstandings with the British Government led to his retirement: he died in Tabriz in 1851.

The decisive part played by Russia in Napoleon's final overthrow gave the Tsar a powerful voice in world affairs and the confidence to pursue expansionist policies, which were soon causing concern in Whitehall and Calcutta. Indeed, after Waterloo, France was replaced by Russia in the minds of British policy-makers and in the imagination of the British people as the main threat to world stability and British interests. The Russian bear, hugging some unfortunate smaller neighbour, was a favourite cartoon subject in the British Press. The expression on the bear's face was usually bloodthirsty, and one paw was often shown clawing at the Dardanelles while the other was scooping up one of the Khanates of Central Asia – romantic places like Khiva, Bokhara, Tashkent and Samarkand – which were seen as potential bases for a Russian invasion of India. France became the wild card in the Great Power pack, always trying to redeem herself by playing a leading, if chauvinistic, role in the Eastern Question, but only a small and indirect part in the Great Game.

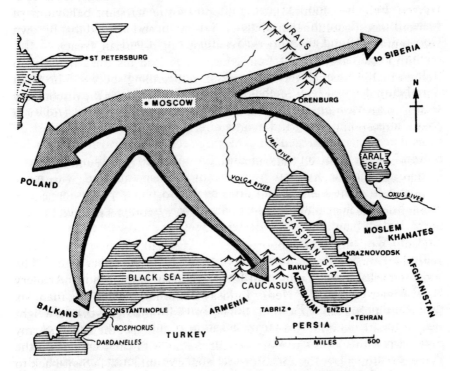

Map 5: The Thrust Lines of Russian Imperial Expansion in the 19th Century

Five potential Russian thrust lines were discernible to British strategists: into Central Europe to create a defensive Slav glacis to the west; through the Balkans towards the Bosphorus and Dardanelles to break out from the Black Sea into the Mediterranean; through the Caucasus into western Persia and Mesopotamia (Iraq today) to gain access to the Persian Gulf; between the Caspian and Aral Seas to dominate the Moslem Khanates of Central Asia; and eastwards through the wastes of Siberia to reach the China Sea. The three central thrusts were closely connected and formed a trident threatening the interests of the Ottoman, Persian and British Empires. The other two – into Europe and across Siberia – were only relevant to the Eastern Question and the Great Game to the extent that they absorbed Moscow's attention and resources, which might otherwise have been employed in their pursuit.

As sail gave way to steam, both London and Calcutta became more aware of the importance of the Middle East to their commercial interests, particularly Egypt and the Persian Gulf. Savings in fuel and time made by pioneering transportation routes from the Mediterranean across the Isthmus of Suez to the Red Sea, and down the Tigris and Euphrates to the Persian Gulf, gradually made the old long haul around the Cape of Good Hope to India less and less economic. And the laying of telegraph cables from India through the Persian Gulf, along the Euphrates to Constantinople and then on across Europe to London, enhanced the region's importance still further.

It was not long before ways of protecting the area from hostile powers were being debated in Whitehall. Maintaining British rule in India was seen as expensive enough without undertaking the additional military commitments of creating and maintaining stability in the Middle East. A general consensus emerged for achieving security of British interests by political rather than military means. Propping up the ailing Ottoman Empire, which the Russians were intent on dismembering with their manoeuvres in the Balkans and drive to the Bosphorus, was seen as the most cost-effective policy. Support of the Porte became a guiding principle in British handling of the Eastern Question, and was to lead to the Crimean War 40 years later.

But it was the Great Game that led to the first major clashes between the British and Russian Empires, although at arms length and by proxy. In the Russo-Persian War of 1827–8, the Persians had been unable to stem the central prong of the Russian trident thrust through the Caucasus, and were forced to accept Russian annexation of all territory north of the Aras river, which flows eastwards into the Caspian Sea just south of Baku. Persia became all but a Tsarist vassal state, with Count Simonich, the Russian Envoy, dominating the Persian court to the disadvantage of the British Envoy, Sir John McNeill. More importantly, from the point of view of the Government of India, the Shah, Fath Ali, turned eastwards to seize territorial compensation at the expense of Afghanistan. Encouraged by Simonich, he laid siege to Herat, raising in British minds the spectre of a Persian advance on Kabul and a Russian foothold being established in Afghanistan.

The first Persian siege of Herat failed in 1833. Fath Ali died in the following year, but his successor, Mohamed Shah, also under Russian influence, continued the war with Afghanistan, laying siege to Herat again in 1837. This time he was thwarted by a young British officer aged 26 of the Bombay Artillery, Eldred Pottinger, who, disguised as a horse dealer, arrived near Herat on a clandestine intelligence gathering mission. Indeed, it was young officers like Pottinger of the Indian Political Service, who dubbed the struggle between Britain and Russia for the control of the approaches to India, 'The Great Game' – it was just that to them.

The 'politicals', as they were called, were young military officers with a flair for oriental languages; with an ambition to play a leading role in India's politico-military affairs; and with a desire to break away from the humdrum routine of regimental soldiering to explore the unknown reaches of the Indian sub-continent and its mountain fringe. In short, they were men who sought adventure and they certainly found it, but their regiments were the losers. The system creamed off some of their most able men, who rarely returned to them and often became brilliant imperial pro-consuls in later life, if they were lucky enough to survive that long.

The Pottinger family were experienced Indian hands, who came from County Down in Ulster. It was Eldred's uncle, Sir Henry Pottinger, who encouraged him to explore Afghanistan in 1837. Sir Henry had been one of the earliest explorers of Baluchistan and eastern Persia, and, by the 1830s was British political agent to the Amirs of Sind. The young Eldred Pottinger reached Herat just as the Persian army was approaching the city, accompanied by Russian advisers under General Perovski. Dropping his disguise, he offered his services at once to the Afghan garrison commander, organising and inspiring the defence. Thanks to his efforts, Herat held out for over a year. Its siege was eventually raised in September 1838 due to a combination of Mohamed Shah's disillusion with Perovski's military competence and continued failure; diplomatic pressure exerted by Sir John McNeill, the British Envoy; and an actual landing, this time by East India Company troops on Kharg Island off Bushire, threatening a British invasion of Persia from the Gulf. Poor Perovski was killed in his final attempt to storm the city, Pottinger playing a decisive personal role in its repulse. Through his extraordinary charisma amongst the Afghans and his military abilities, Pottinger had raised British prestige throughout Persia and Afghanistan, and had checked, for the time being, the rise of Russian influence in the region. Sadly, this was not realised in Calcutta.

The two Persian sieges of Herat had laid a powder trail, which led to the British disaster of the quite unnecessary First Anglo-Afghan War. In the 1830s, the western frontier of British India lay along the Indus and its eastern tributary, the Sutlej. The East India Company was in a period of severe financial retrenchment after its costly wars to extend British rule in Nepal, Central India, Burma and Ceylon in the first two decades of the 19th Century. It had no wish to expand further westwards over the Indus for the time being. The Governor General – the timid, but well-meaning Lord Auckland – believed that the cheapest way to keep the Russian threat through Persia at arms length was by alliances with the three neighbouring groups of states, which lay astride the potential Russian invasion routes: the Sikh empire in the Punjab, blocking the exits from the Herat-Kabul-Khyber

Pass route in the north; the states of the Emirs of Sind and Baluchistan, astride the Herat-Kandahar-Bolan Pass route in the south; and Afghanistan, the starting point and advanced logistic base for both routes.

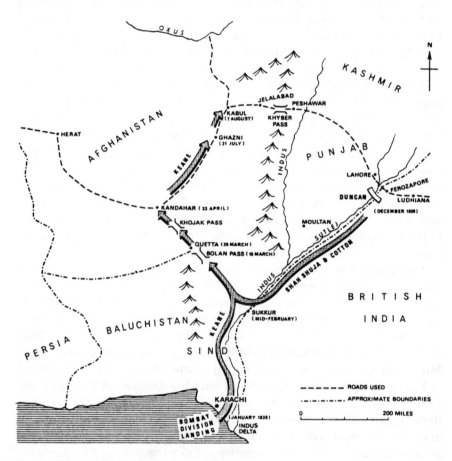

Map 6: The First Anglo-Afghan War: 1839–42

In these early years of the Great Game, the lands beyond the Indus were largely uncharted territory as far as the Government in far off Calcutta was concerned. Little was really known about their peoples, politics or topography, but myths of all kinds abounded. It is hardly surprising, therefore, that Auckland's three principal advisers came to hold grossly erroneous views as to where competence and loyalties lay amongst the rulers of the states, which they hoped could be formed into the defensive western glacis of British India. The three were Sir William Macnaghten, John Colvin and Henry Torrens, all highly intelligent academically, but short on sound practical common sense, which Auckland himself was equally unable to provide when judging their advice.

We need only concern ourselves closely with Macnaghten, who had started his career in the Madras Cavalry, and had risen to be head of the Company's 'Secret and Political Department', responsible for Foreign Affairs, before becoming Chief Secretary of the Government. He had a profound knowledge of the Asiatic languages and customs; was an able administrator; and fancied himself a great military strategist but without the talents to make good his fantasies. Vain and autocratic, he was to become the evil genius of the First Afghan War.

Amongst the rulers of the target states, the best known was Ranjit Singh, the outstandingly able, acquisitive and, above all, cunning, if not treacherous, leader of the Sikhs. By the 1830s, he was on reasonable terms with the British, but was noticeably ageing. The East India Company respected and, indeed, feared him and his well trained army, poised, as it was, at Lahore, not far from its Sutlej frontier. Fortunately, his current ambitions lay westwards at the expense of the Afghans, and south towards Upper Sind. He was certainly no friend of the former because he had taken Moultan and Kashmir from them in 1818 and 1819, and had recently seized Peshawar at the eastern end of the Khyber Pass.

The Amirs of Sind and Baluchistan were nominally Afghan tributaries; lacked a strong leader and were awkwardly xenophobic, always craving independence; but in Calcutta's view they were handleable, as indeed they proved to be, with a judicious mix of diplomatic carrots and threats of force.

The key to the formation of the glacis was Afghanistan. Dost Mohamed, its ruler, was a usurper, who had emerged as the strong man in Kabul after the effete Shah Shuja had been ousted in 1810. By the 1830s, Shah Shuja was languishing in exile at Ludhiana not far from Ranjit Singh's capital at Lahore, enjoying a British pension and scheming to regain his throne with Sikh and British help. None of Auckland's advisers knew much about Dost Mohamed or his policies, and they assumed that the devil they knew, the legitimate Shah Shuja, would be more pliable and hence more useful as a British puppet on the Afghan throne than the reputedly strong-minded usurper, Dost Mohamed, whom they did not, and who might, they believed with some justification, be in contact with the Russians already.

But there were men who did know Dost Mohamed. Another young 'political' aged 31, Alexander Burnes from the 1st Bombay Light Infantry – an officer whose incorrigible womanising was to lead to tragedy – had managed to survey and establish the navigability of the Indus in 1831 by carrying a state coach and five large English dray horses in a flat bottomed vessel from the river's mouth to Lahore as a present from William IV to Rangit Singh. So successful had he been in persuading the various Amirs of the Sind states to allow this exploratory passage of the Indus as a potential trade route for British manufactured goods into Central Asia, that he was allowed to pursue the continuation of the route through the Khyber Pass to Kabul, Bukhara and Khiva with the idea of ultimately using the River Oxus as the principal British trading artery in Central Asia. His journey would also enable him to report on the practicability of the route in reverse for a Russian invasion force. He had set off on this ambitious expedition in March 1832.

As the first Englishman to penetrate the area, he had been well received by Dost Mohamed in Kabul, which he reached at the beginning of May, and struck a cordial personal relationship with him. He reached Bukhara in June 1832, where he established an equally friendly relationship with the Grand Vizier, who warned him not to attempt to reach Khiva. After a month in Bukhara, where he was surprised to see many Russians working as slaves, he set off to return to India through Persia via Mirv, Astrabad and the Persian Gulf, reaching Bombay in January 1833. His ten month journey had been an extraordinary feat of courage and endurance, but it had also required great ingenuity in disguise and negotiating skill to avoid murder in those xenophobic lands. So impressed was the Governor General with Burnes's extraordinary achievement and, indeed, survival that he was sent back to London to brief the Cabinet on the military practicability of the Oxus-Kabul-Khyber Pass invasion route. He was feted as a national hero; received the Gold Medal of the Royal Geographical Society; invited to join the Atheneum; and was received in private audience by King William IV.

Once back in India, Burnes lobbied in Calcutta to be allowed to establish a trade mission in Kabul to start developing an Indus-Kabul-Bukhara trade route. His ideas were initially turned down by officials, but the Governor General, Lord Auckland, accepted his proposals, and he returned to Kabul with a trade mission at the end of 1836. He quickly re-established his rapport with Dost Mohamed, whom he found was by then keen to ally himself with the British because he realised that he could not stay neutral in the Great Game, and he had more faith in the British than in the Russians. In his view the latter were Asiatics, and although more congenial to him than Anglo-Saxons, were 'less thorough, less trustworthy and less stable to lean upon'.[4]

Be that as it may, Burnes recognised Dost Mohamed as a forthright and able man, whose invaluable friendship could be secured, and through whom an effective buffer state might be created in Afghanistan at minimal cost. The price, Burnes reported to Auckland, who was at Simla at the time, would be the Company's recognition of him as Amir of Afghanistan, a modest financial subsidy, and, most crucial of all, favourable British mediation in the Afghan dispute with the Sikhs over Peshawar.

Burnes advised that these terms should be accepted, but he was rebuffed. Auckland's triumvirate of advisers in their impractical way preferred to support Shah Shuja's bid to re-establish himself in Kabul as Amir, plans for which had just been agreed in the tediously negotiated Treaty of Simla between Shah Shuja and Ranjit Singh, and guaranteed by the British. While the Sikhs promised to advance on Kabul via the Khyber, Shah Shuja, with a locally raised force of his own, was to take the southern route via the Bolan and Kandahar. The British were to provide two divisions in support to stiffen the resolve of both princes and to ensure that they met their obligations. In backing Shah Shuja, Auckland and his advisers made the first of four unforgivable misjudgements, which were to lead to the disastrous retreat from Kabul in the winter of 1841/2. What they failed to appreciate was that the turbulent, venal and treacherous Afghan tribes were only likely to resist Russian encroachments under a strong, ruthless man, like Dost Mohamed, who was able to hold their loyalties and crush dissidence. John Fortescue comments on their decision to support Shah Shuja:

> Yet this was the course chosen by Auckland, notwithstanding the military objections of the Commander-in-Chief, at the dictation of three men who abounded in cleverness, but had not found wisdom.[5]

And military objections there were. General Sir Henry Fane, the Commander-in-Chief of the Bengal Presidency Army, on whom fell the responsibility for assembling the British force to support the enterprise, was bitterly opposed to Auckland's policy. It involved an advance of over 1,200 miles through what would almost certainly turn out to be bitterly hostile and barren territory. The logistic problems were horrifying enough, but even if Shah Shuja reached Kabul without much opposition, securing his lines of communication against probable Sikh and Sindi attack would be hazardous and immensely expensive. The triumvirate refused his advice, and he tendered his resignation to the Company's Board in London, only to be told that no suitable replacement could be found for him at that juncture. Fane served on loyally, doing his best to mitigate the operational risks and losing his health in the process.

Ironically, a Russian mission, headed by Captain Vitkevich, arrived in Kabul soon after Burnes. He was cold-shouldered until it became clear to Dost Mohamed that no British support would be forthcoming. Poor Vitkevich offered far better terms than Burnes could do, but his presence in Kabul was soon reported to London. Lord Palmerston, the Foreign Secretary, protested vigorously to St Petersburg about Russian interference in states bordering British India. Such was the Tsar's need in the late 1830s to placate Britain over the Eastern Question that Vitkevich, like Burnes, had his proposals for an alliance with Dost Mohamed repudiated by his own government, but, unlike Burnes, was so distressed by his failure that he shot himself in his hotel room on his return to St Petersburg.

Herat, thanks to Eldred Pottinger's efforts, was still holding out in the autumn of 1838. Realising that something must be done quickly to check further Russian infiltration, Auckland directed the formation of the British force needed to support Shah Shuja's return to Kabul, grandiloquently calling it 'The Army of the Indus'. No sooner had he done so than the siege of Herat collapsed and the Russians withdrew disconsolately, with their Persian allies, removing Auckland's *casus belli*. But the schemes for restoring Shah Shuja to power had gathered too great a momentum for an irresolute man like Auckland to put aside his adviser's plans at so late a stage. Keen to show a degree of resolution that he did not possess, he issued a proclamation that the expedition would go forward:

> . . . with the view to the substitution of a friendly for a hostile power in the Eastern province of Afghanistan, and to the establishment of a permanent barrier against schemes of aggression upon our north-west frontier.[6]

It was stressed that all British troops would be withdrawn as soon as Shah Shuja's legitimate rule had been restored and consolidated.

But there was another reason for going ahead with the campaign. Rumours abounded that the Russians were, as anticipated, developing the eastern prong of their central trident of thrusts towards India. An advance base had been established at Orenburg (*see Map 5*) on the Ural River well to the north of the Aral Sea from which an advance on Khiva and Bukhara was being planned by Count Perovski (not to be confused with General Perovski killed at Herat) to open up the basin of the River Oxus for trade, but also, the British suspected, as an approach to Afghanistan and hence to India. It seemed now or never if Afghanistan was to be turned into a credible buffer state between the British and Russian Empires.

The Army of the Indus was made up of four divisions. Three were concentrated at Ferozapore on the Sutlej just south of Lahore. The first was Shah Shuja's own army of some 6,000 semi-disciplined but British officered troops, who were to lead the way to give the impression that it was Shah Shuja who was the driving force in his own return to power. Behind him would come a division of the Bengal Presidency Army under Major General Sir Willoughby Cotton, a Peninsular War veteran of only moderate military ability, who had served in India too long and whose figure was described as 'unwieldy', and of whom it was said his mind did not carry away much of verbal instructions![7] And the third was a second Bengal division under Major General Duncan, which was to stay at Ferozapore to protect the lines of communication in case of Sikh treachery, and to support Ranjit Singh if he honoured the Simla agreement and did at least threaten to advance on Kabul through the Khyber Pass as he had promised.

The fourth division was to come from the Bombay Presidency Army. It was to be landed at the mouth of the Indus and advance northwards up the west bank of the river to join the Shah Shuja's army and Cotton's division, which were to cross the river at Sukkur, almost 500 miles march south of Ferozapore. The combined force would then head for the Bolan Pass, Kandahar and Kabul, another 700 miles further on through arid inhospitable desert and mountain country. The Bombay force was initially under another Peninsular War veteran, the irascible and unpopular General Sir John Keane, who was to take over as Commander-in-Chief of the Army of the Indus from Sir Henry Fane when the Bengal and Bombay divisions met at Sukkur. Fane, whose health had gone, would continue down the Indus on his journey home. He was never to reach England: he died at sea off the Azores.[8]

One of the weaknesses of the Army of the Indus, which worried Fane, was its unusually low number of British infantry battalions to support the Bengal and Bombay Presidencies' Native Infantry. Cotton, for instance, had only one British to five Indian battalions. However, all the artillery units in the force were European, and three out of the seven Cavalry regiments came from England.

Auckland and the 'politicals' in Calcutta saw the campaign 'as a mere military promenade'. Shah Shuja's force would lead with all the trappings of a peaceful return of a beloved ruler, recalled to his lawful inheritance. The Bengal and Bombay divisions would follow, and were expected to be welcomed 'with general gladness' by the Afghans.[9] Little fighting was envisaged! Herein lay the second of their four crucial misjudgements: the logistic support needed just to move and feed what amounted to a town of 80,000 souls, only a quarter of whom were soldiers, was far beyond the capabilities of the Company's agents and the resources of the country through which the cortège was to pass. Despite all Fane's warnings about the logistic difficulties of the march, nothing was done to pare down the baggage, retinues of servants and camp followers. Some 30,000 camels were requisitioned, which, if marching in single file, would stretch from Charing Cross to Reading. One brigadier commandeered 60 camels to carry what he deemed essential to his comfort! And swelling the locust-like swarm of men, horses and camels were herds of sheep, goats and cattle driven along with the columns as rations 'on the hoof'.

Shah Shuja, with Macnaghten as British Envoy and Commander of Shuja's Army, left Ferozapore at the beginning of December 1838. Cotton's division started ten days later. Sir Alexander Burnes – knighted just before the start of the campaign – was Macnaghten's deputy, with the specific task of acting as Cotton's political agent, negotiating the passage of the Bengal division through upper Sind, while Eldred Pottinger's uncle, Sir Henry, did the same for the Bombay division, which landed at the mouth of the Indus and was immediately hamstrung by lack of camels. The Amirs of Sind were suspicious and disinclined to help Keane; and the Company's local agents had failed to stock the depots along either division's route with enough grain because the harvest had been poor and the local inhabitants obstructive. The only people to come out of the first leg of the advance to the crossing of the Indus at Sukkur with credit were the Bengal Sappers and Miners under Major Thomson, who cleared the routes forward and bridged the river successfully using local boats. Shah Shuja's troops and Cotton's division were across the Indus by mid-February 1839, but Keane was about three weeks behind schedule.

Rumours soon reached Macnaghten that a Russo-Persian force was again advancing on Herat, and that the Baluchi tribes would be blocking the Bolan Pass. He, therefore, pressed Cotton not to wait for Keane and to take the lead with the Bengal Division to speed up the advance. Cotton, not being a man who had much grasp of logistic problems, foolishly agreed without consulting Keane, who had by then taken over from Fane as Commander-in-Chief, was still some way off. Cotton set off across the 170 miles of the Sind desert for the Bolan Pass before adequate supply arrangements could be made, and without ruthlessly reducing his camp followers. Horses, camels and cattle died in profusion from lack of water and forage due to gross logistic mismanagement.

When Cotton did reach the Bolan Pass, which is some 60 miles long, he found it was a boulder-strewn camel track and too narrow in many places to take his artillery and ammunition wagons without prodigious rock shifting work by Major Thomson's Sappers. Burnes had by then won the agreement of the Baluchi Amirs to allow the columns unobstructed passage through the Pass, but this did not stop the local tribesmen attacking isolated detachments and cutting out camels and cattle from the commissariat trains. Practically no local supplies of grain were found during the march from the Indus, and all but the uniformed soldiers had to be placed on half-rations at the Bolan.

Cotton's staff calculated that they had and could carry just enough supplies with them to reach the fertile Kandahar valley, and so he set the Bengal division off on its nightmare ascent of the pass on 15 March. The leading troops debouched from it a week later, and the whole force reached Quetta (then a wretched mud village) on the 26th, having left the pass strewn with the carcases of camels, horses and cattle. Cotton's Commissary reported that a third of his supply camels had been lost, and those that remained were too weak to carry more than half loads. The soldiers had to be reduced to half-rations and the rest to quarter-rations.

Cotton was in an unenviable position: he could not go back, and he would starve if he stayed where he was. Keane, however, reached Quetta on 6 April and belatedly took over command of the advance, which he restarted next day with Major Thomson's Sappers moving ahead to open routes through the Khojak Pass, the last major obstacle before Kandahar. The march began to the dismal sound of some 60 horses being shot: they could march no further.

The passage of the shorter but far steeper Khojak was another nightmare, made all the more so by better organised attacks by the local tribesmen; by rising spring temperatures; and by poor staff work that led to unforgivable jams of units scrambling to get through the pass. The shambles was not helped by men and horses having to drag four large 18-pounder siege guns, which might be needed to deal with Kandahar's defences, up to the top of the pass and to restrain them on the way down on the far side. The Gunners' prodigious efforts proved unnecessary: Macnaghten's 'politicals' managed to sow enough doubts in the minds of the Kandahar chiefs to discourage opposition to Shah Shuja's return.

On 23 April one of the chiefs came out of the city to make his submission to the Shah, and reported that those antagonistic to him had already fled. Macnaghten thereupon held back the British advanced guard and hurried Shah Shuja into the city with a contingent of his own troops. He was received with curiosity, but little enthusiasm. A durbar held a few days later with the Army of the Indus drawn up on parade was boycotted by the inhabitants. Shah Shuja was seen, quite rightly, as a mere puppet in British hands, and the army accompanying him as a scourge, which would strip the valley bare and put up prices in the bazaars.

Reports of the logistic disasters reaching Auckland in Calcutta made him forbid Keane to advance on Kabul until a secure line of supply had been organised from the Indus, and six weeks' rations had been accumulated at Kandahar – both totally impracticable instructions. Keane and Macnaghten agreed between themselves that the only way to solve their logistic difficulties was to establish Shah Shuja on the throne in Kabul as quickly as possible. Alexander Burnes did not anticipate much resistance from Dost Mohamed and reported that the fortress of Ghazni, which blocked the road to Kabul, was weakly held and that its walls could be breached by field guns.

Keane, accompanied by Macnaghten, set off for Kabul on 27 June with the sepoys still on half-rations. They left Major General William Nott, a highly controversial character, who could not abide 'politicals' and whom we will meet again later, to hold the supply line from the Indus through Quetta and Kandahar. To save draught animals, Keane left the four 18-pounder siege guns behind at Kandahar.

When Keane reached Ghazni on 2 July he found most of the intelligence gathered by his 'politicals' was faulty. The fortress was both strongly held, which probably meant it had been stocked with grain to withstand a siege, and its walls would certainly defy field-guns. He had only three days' supplies at half-rations left, but for once luck was with him. A disaffected nephew of Dost Mohamed reported that the north-eastern gate, leading to Kabul, had not been walled up with masonry. Keane turned to his ubiquitous Sapper, Major Thomson, who agreed that it might be practicable to blow in the gate and carry Ghazni by surprise assault, but it would certainly be a hazardous and probably costly operation. Keane had no alternative. It was essential to capture Ghazni's stores of grain before he had to fight Dost Mohamed, who was reported to be advancing with a large army from Kabul and was only five or six days' march away.

Keane moved quickly. During the night of 22/23 July, he had field-guns dragged into position within 300 yards of the Kabul gate; a force was assembled for a feint attack on the southern side of the fortress; a storming party of 240 picked men from the light companies of his four British battalions was formed under Lieutenant Colonel Dennie, ready to rush the Kabul gate if and when the Sappers had managed to blow it in; and the four British battalions themselves – 2nd of Foot (Surreys), 13th Light Infantry (Somersets), 17th of Foot (Leicesters) and the 102nd of Foot (Dublin Fusiliers) – were grouped as the main assault force under Brigadier General 'Fighting Bob' Sale, a veteran of the Burma Wars and a man whose men would follow him anywhere but who did not bear responsibility easily. Fortescue comments 'he seems to have been a man of stupidity so abnormal that he could neither think for himself nor entertain the thoughts of others!'[10] We will be hearing more of him and his wife later.

At the first streak of dawn three Sapper officers, Captain Peat and Lieutenants Durand and Macleod, with a small Sapper carrying party and a bugler, crept stealthily forward towards the gate. They were spotted and fire was opened from the ramparts above them, so they rushed across the bridge over the moat and took temporary cover in a small salley-port on the far side. Durand and his Sappers managed to lay 300 pounds of gunpowder in 12 sacks against the gate and then edged their way back to the salley-port, rolling out the fuse train – a cloth hose filled with powder – behind them.

For some agonising minutes Durand could not get the fuse to light. Captain Peat, thinking that he had been killed, rushed forward and was bowled over by the blast, but got up and ran forward again into the gateway to see if the breach was practicable. Before he could find out how much damage had been done, he was driven out by Afghan swordsmen. Meanwhile Durand, confident that the gate had been blown apart, looked for the bugler to sound the advance, but he had been killed. There was thus some delay in getting Dennie's storming party forward. Nevertheless, they rushed the gate successfully, but needed quick reinforcement to consolidate their foothold. Unfortunately, Captain Peat, who had staggered back towards the main assault column, was overheard by Sale reporting to Major Thomson that he could not see daylight through the gate. Sale jumped to the conclusion that a breach had not been made. His nerves got the better of him, and he ordered the 'retreat' to be sounded. Had Major Thomson not quickly corrected Sale's mistake, Dennie's men would have been lost and the breach in Ghazni's defences re-sealed.

All's well that ends well. Sale suffered an Afghan sabre cut in the rush into the fortress, but clove the skull of his assailant. Afghan resistance soon collapsed, leaving Keane in possession of Ghazni's large stocks of grain and with a reputation for military success, indirectly eroding Dost Mohamed's support amongst the Afghan chiefs, who started to profess new-found loyalty to Shah Shuja. The assault cost only 17 killed and 165 wounded; and it earned Keane his peerage as Baron Keane of Ghazni. The Victoria Cross had not yet been instituted otherwise Peat and Durand would have qualified as recipients, as their Sappers and Miner colleagues were to do for a similar feat of blowing in Delhi's gates a few years later during the Indian Mutiny.

Shah Shuja with Macnaghten at his side entered Kabul in state on 7 August and reassumed the Afghan throne to the half-hearted acclaim of the people of the city. Faced with treachery amongst his perfidious followers, Dost Mohamed fled northwards with a small band of supporters over the Hindu Kush into the valley of the Oxus to await better times; to seek the support of the Khan of Bukhara; and to regain touch with Russian agents. A month later, the shortest route back to India via the Khyber opened by the simple expedient of Shah Shuja paying lavish subsidies to the Khyber chiefs to stop their tribesmen raiding the road.

Auckland and Macnaghten had every intention of fulfilling their promise to withdraw all British troops as soon as Shah Shuja's position was firm enough, but it is never easy to decide when enough is enough. Herein they made the third of their four errors of judgement. They never did find the right moment to go, and were sucked relentlessly into the quagmire of internal Afghan politics.

Macnaghten was largely to blame: he had backed Shah Shuja instead of Dost Mohamed, despite Burnes's advice, and had to prove himself right. In the reports that he sent back to Auckland, he underestimated the xenophobia of the Afghan tribes; overestimated his own abilities as a political strategist and power broker; and was blind to Shah Shuja's ever-growing unpopularity.

Over confidence in the British establishment as a whole was also to blame for the ultimate disaster. Afghanistan was treated as if it were just another part of British India, which would soon settle down once the initial fighting to establish Shah Shuja's rule was over. The obvious differences between the Hindu plainsmen, who were tacitly prepared to accept British political tutelage, and the fanatical Moslem mountain tribesmen, who were not, made little difference to British attitudes. Wives came forward through the Khyber to join their husbands, and the social life of a typical British garrison town was quickly established amongst the people of Kabul – race meetings and all. Shah Shuja did not endear himself to the sirdars of the city by allotting the houses of absentee opponents of his régime to British officers, some of whom alienated the Moslem susceptibilities still further by setting up house with Afghan women. Burnes set the worst of examples by establishing what amounted to a harem in the house allotted to him in the city.

An Amir of Afghanistan could never be more than the head of a proud and turbulent aristocracy, which had to be ruled with a mixture of tact, administrative ability, guile and ruthlessness. If, as Macnaghten believed, Shah Shuja had this rare combination of talents and was as popular as Macnaghten avowed, the sooner he was left to stand on his own feet the better. With adequate British financial and political support, he might become an effective ruler, but if he also needed British bayonets, his supposed popularity would be short-lived. The number of troops required for the effective military occupation of Afghanistan was more than the East India Company could possibly provide or was prepared to pay for; and was to prove beyond Soviet Russia's resources as well in the 1970s and '80s. Moreover, there were the additional risks and expense of maintaining the long lines of communication through potentially hostile Sikh and Sindi territory via the Khyber and Bolan Passes. The success of the Company's Afghan policy would depend upon Macnaghten's ability to make an effective ruler out of Shah Shuja without British bayonets. Unfortunately, he always found reasons for delaying the departure of British troops until their very presence united the normally un-uniteable Afghan tribes in revolt two years later.

At first all seemed to go well. As a token of fulfilment of their avowed intention to withdraw, the Bombay Division was marched back to India via Kandahar, Quetta and the Bolan Pass, meting out retribution as it went upon those tribes who had opposed its original advance. It was decided to leave only two detachments of Cotton's Bengal division in support of Shah Shuja: one at Kabul under Sale, who had been knighted for his services during the advance to Kabul; and the other at Kandahar under the tough and unpopular Nott. Ghazni and all other important strategic points were to be garrisoned by Shah Shuja's own troops. The rest of the Company troops were to be withdrawn before winter. Keane returned to India and Cotton replaced him as Commander-in-Chief, but in name only. Auckland laid down that Macnaghten and his 'politicals' were responsible for directing the Shah's foreign policy and military affairs, leaving the 'military' with only the execution of operations deemed necessary by the 'politicals'.

* * *

1840 was to have been a year of political consolidation in Afghanistan, but it turned out to be one of punitive operations and misplaced financial subsidies. Time and again, Macnaghten's 'politicals' set out with Shah

Shuja's troops to teach some hostile tribe a lesson only to find that they had underestimated its fighting abilities and had to call for British troops to save them from humiliation, thus increasing the British military commitment and making it all the harder to withdraw. Moreover, Macnaghten established a pernicious system of negotiating treaties with recalcitrant tribal chiefs on Shah Shuja's behalf, in which financial subsidies were provided in return for loyalty. The chiefs soon found that by failing to stop their tribesmen looting Government convoys – an almost impossible task anyway – they could blackmail the 'politicals' into offering ever higher subsidies. It seemed to the Afghans that the British rewarded their enemies and neglected their friends. A very sour Nott, in Kandahar, wrote at the beginning of 1841:

> The conduct of the thousand and one politicals has ruined our cause, and bared the throats of every European in this country to the sword and knife of the vengeful Afghan and bloody Baluch, and unless several regiments are quickly sent not a man will be left to note the fall of his comrades. Nothing but force will ever make them submit to the hated Shah Shuja who is the greatest scoundrel as ever lived.[11]

Shah Shuja, indeed, had done little to help Macnaghten in his efforts to make his rule acceptable, and had learned little from his long exile in British India. Arrogant, corrupt, administratively incompetent and politically unforgiving, he was so hated, as Nott says, that he was fast becoming a British liability. The only sensible reason for persevering in Afghanistan was the receipt of hard intelligence of the expected Russian thrust southwards from Orenburg to Khiva and Bukhara in the Oxus valley.

Such intelligence of what was happening in Central Asia came from the extraordinary band of young 'politicals' like James Abbott and Richmond Shakespear, and Charles Stoddard and Arthur Conolly, who journeyed to the Khanates on the secret missions of the Great Game. Abbott and Shakespear followed each other to Khiva in 1840 to try to persuade the Khan to release his Russian slaves, in order to give St Petersburg less reason for attacking his khanate. Abbott managed to obtain an agreement for their release, which he carried to the nearest Russian post some 500 miles to the north. Before the Russians could react, Shakespear had won the slaves' actual release and had escorted them safely to Fort Alexandrovsk (*See Map 4*) on the eastern shore of the Caspian Sea. He went on to St Petersburg where he was fêted for his outstanding achievement; and then to London where he was knighted by the jubilant young Queen Victoria for destroying the Tsar's excuse for trying to annex Khiva! Abbott won fame later back in India where the town of Abbottabad is his memorial.

Stoddard and Conolly were not so lucky. Their target was Bukhara, where they hoped to persuade the Khan that the British invasion of

Afghanistan presented no threat to his khanate. Stoddard arrived first and failed to reach any understanding with its vicious khan and was imprisoned for three years under the most appalling conditions. Conolly went to his rescue and was equally badly treated. Both men were eventually beheaded when British fortunes in Afghanistan were at their nadir at the beginning of 1842, and both were canonised in public opinion as Victorian martyrs.

The situation in Afghanistan changed dramatically and apparently for the better in the autumn of 1840. Dost Mohamed had sought help from the Khan of Bukhara and had been imprisoned for his pains. He escaped and, with dissident northern Afghan tribesmen at his back, advanced on Kabul, hoping to profit by Shah Shuja's unpopularity. Macnaghten dispatched Bob Sale with a battalion of Bengal Native Infantry, two squadrons of the 2nd Bengal Light Cavalry and an artillery battery to capture him. Sir Alexander Burnes went with the force as political agent. They eventually caught up with Dost in the midst of a small force of Afghan horse four days march north of Kabul. The 2nd Cavalry had Dost at their mercy, but for reasons that have never been satisfactorily explained, the troopers turned and fled when the charge was sounded, leaving their five British officers to gallop at the Afghans alone. Two were killed and two severely wounded. By the time Sale came up with his infantry and guns, Dost had escaped, but the action was to have a strange sequel.

At the beginning of November, Macnaghten was out riding near Kabul when he received a letter from Burnes reporting the débâcle and urging an immediate concentration of troops for the defence of the city. Before Macnaghten could return to his quarters, he was approached by a lone horseman. It was Dost Mohamed himself! He dismounted and tendered his sword to the British Envoy as a token of surrender! Macnaghten returned it to him and they rode together into Kabul. It was said at the time that the gallantry of the five British officers led him to despair of ever unseating Shah Shuja as long as he enjoyed British support. A more likely explanation is that he was tired of trying to elude the British, and disgusted with the treachery of his own people.

Whatever the explanation, Auckland and Macnaghten were handed the ideal opportunity for withdrawing British troops from Afghanistan without any loss of prestige. Dost was soon on his way down the Khyber Pass under heavy escort to the same comfortable exile in India on a British pension as Shah Shuja had enjoyed for so long. With his only real rival out of the way and a prisoner in British hands, Shah Shuja was as secure as he was ever likely to be. It was certainly time to get out; and added to the reasons for doing so was the news that Count Perovski's advance on Khiva had come to grief in the snow covered steppes of Turkestan, and he had withdrawn with heavy losses to Orenburg, leaving many of his men to rebuild the collection of Russian slaves in Khiva.

Back in Calcutta there were those who doubted the sanity of Macnaghten in claiming that all was well in Kabul. The wise old General Sir Jasper Nicolls, who had succeeded Fane as Commander-in-Chief of the Bengal Presidency Army, put the position bluntly to Auckland: either increase the strength of the Bengal Army and annex Afghanistan or get out. These alternatives were abhorrent to Auckland and Macnaghten: their political capital was locked in making a success of their Afghan venture.

The first nine months of 1841 saw relatively successful operations against hostile tribes within striking distance of vital communication routes. The semblance of normal Indian garrison life was enhanced by building spacious cantonments for the troops where the usual round of horse-racing, band concerts and other social events took place as if the country was at peace and happy to be under British tutelage. Both Cotton and Sale had pressed for the Kabul garrison to be housed in the Bala Hissar fortress, overlooking the city, but Macnaghten had refused on the grounds that it would give the impression of an army of occupation rather than support for a friendly ruler. Instead the Bala Hissar was used to house Shah Shuja's family, bloated harem and numerous retainers. The British cantonment was laid out in an indefensible but pleasant site on low ground beside the Kabul river a short distance to the north-east of the city. Such was the general over-confidence amongst the British that the Company bureaucrats in Calcutta refused to finance the building of a defensible keep within the cantonment's perimeter, so Commissariat reserves of food and ammunition were stored in a disused fort outside!

Cotton's tour as Commander-in-Chief came to an end in February 1841. He was replaced by Major General William Elphinstone, another Waterloo veteran, who was suffering the agonies of gout and was, indeed, a dying man. He had not wanted the appointment, but Macnaghten would not work with the forthright Nott at Kandahar, who was the obvious choice. Someone senior to Nott had to be found, and the unfortunate Elphinstone happened to be available at the time. Macnaghten saw no need for a fitter and more forceful man in what he saw as the supporting role of his military adviser.

By September Macnaghten was in a state of euphoria. Almost all active opposition to Shah Shuja appeared to have been crushed. He had been told that he would be the next Governor of Bombay and would receive a peerage. Unfortunately, all this was about to change with bewildering rapidity. In England Lord Melbourne's Whig administration had been replaced at the end of August 1841 by Sir Robert Peel's Tories, most of whom were strongly averse to the Afghan adventure. Peel himself had spoken while in opposition of the folly of advancing beyond the Indus, and of its ruinous impact upon East India Company finances. As was to happen so often in the latter half of the 20th Century when Britain was withdrawing from her empire, the Treasury became the dominating influence in the development of Peel's Afghan policy. Auckland had the good sense to resign, and was replaced by Lord Ellenborough, who had been President of the Company's Board of Control in London, and who was determined to liquidate the Afghan commitment for financial rather than strategic reasons.

Macnaghten had little option but to start reducing British expenditure and planning the gradual withdrawal of British troops. The whiff of a British retreat started to permeate the bazaars of Kabul and Kandahar, making political reinsurance a primary concern amongst Afghan leaders. Shah Shuja himself is suspected of secret anti-British intrigues to ingratiate himself with his principal opponents before the British left. Rebellion started to smoulder like a peat fire under the apparent calm of the Afghan political scene. Macnaghten misguidedly expected the Afghans to welcome the British departure and saw no difficulty in agreeing with Shah Shuja a plan for strengthening his indigenous forces and gradually withdrawing the British garrisons. The Afghan mind, however, does not work in that way: any sign of weakness is exploited to the full and loyalties are quickly switched to potential winners. In the autumn of 1841, there was no tribal unity as such, but there was common determination to grab what could be had from the departing British.

Bob Sale's brigade was the first to be ordered back to India. Foolishly one of the economy measures taken by Macnaghten had been to halve the subsidies paid to the tribes along the route through the Khyber Pass to Peshawar. Before Sale started off, it was known that the passes might be blocked by the tribesmen intent on replacing their lost revenues in the way that they enjoyed most. It was expected that he might have to fight his way through ambushes, and so the brigade's families, including the redoubtable Lady Sale – a much more intelligent and forceful character than her husband – were left in Kabul to follow when the route had been re-opened.

He set off on 9 October with the 13th of Foot (Somersets), two battalions of Bengal Native Infantry, a squadron of Native Cavalry and two British artillery batteries. It took him over a month to fight his way through to Jalalabad at the Afghan end of the Khyber, which he reached on 12 November, having suffered considerable losses and without enough draught animals left to continue on down the Khyber to Peshawar. The garrison left behind in Kabul under Colonel John Shelton consisted of some 4,500 fighting men from the 44th of Foot (Essex Regiment), three battalions of Bengal Native Infantry, two squadrons of Bengal Native Cavalry, and 1,400 Shah Shuja's troops. One-armed Shelton – he lost it at the storming of San Sebastian during the Peninsular War – was one of the most unpopular and disagreeable officers in the Bengal Army, but a good and experienced soldier, who could not abide Elphinstone and kept his own counsel.

The Afghan rebellion started in Kabul during the early hours of 2 November 1841 when anti-British elements attacked Alexander Burnes's house in the northern half of the city, close to the Treasury. The idea of killing Burnes and ransacking the Treasury appealed both to the vindictiveness and cupidity of the plotters. Burnes was seen as the man who had first brought foreigners into Afghanistan, and as an abuser of Afghan women. Thinking that he was faced with a petty city riot, probably triggered by cuckolded husbands or irate fathers, he forbade his sepoy guard to open fire and tried to harangue the mob from his balcony to no effect. The house was set on fire, and Burnes, his brother and another British officer with them were hacked down and killed after a desperate struggle.

Under normal circumstances the British would have taken immediate vengeance, but the response was muddled because maintaining order in the city was the Shah's responsibility. His loyalties were divided and his troops incompetent. Burnes's death went unavenged and the rebels gained confidence. Treachery was in the air on the Afghan side and irresolution on the British, who saw themselves as in support of the Afghan Government and not its masters. The rebellion flared and gathered momentum when the British withdrew into and were besieged in their cantonment. Macnaghten summoned help from Nott at Kandahar; ordered Sale to return from Jalalabad; and on 25 November, opened negotiations with the Kabul chiefs to gain time for reinforcements to arrive. The rebel leader turned out to be Dost Mohamed's son, Akbar Khan, whose initial terms for allowing the British withdrawal to go ahead peacefully as planned, were too humiliating to contemplate. Time, however, was on the Afghan side: the first snow of that dire winter fell next day.

Macnaghten, who knew that the chiefs were far from united, tried to negotiate again on 11 December, and this time found them ostensibly more accommodating. He proposed that all the British troops should be withdrawn to India unmolested, the Afghans providing the additional draught animals and supplies needed for them to do so; that Dost Mohamed should be restored, and Shah Shuja should abdicate with the option of staying in Kabul or returning to India; and that no British forces should re-enter Afghan territory without Afghan consent. These terms were accepted and 14 December was set for the start of the march back to India. One of Macnaghten's staff was surrendered as a hostage for British good faith; no equivalent token was given by the Afghans who had other plans in mind. They could not match the British in open combat, but they could weaken them by attrition and double dealing, which they proceeded to do by procrastinating over the provision of the promised transport and food.

The chiefs had, indeed, no intention of honouring the agreement. They were like vultures circling above a wounded lion unwilling to strike until it was nearly dead. But there was more to it than this: Akbar Khan could not count on the support of those chiefs, who were benefiting from the British presence and largesse. To gain their support, he stooped to treachery. A week after the withdrawal had been due to start he sent proposals to Macnaghten that in return for a very large sum he was prepared to join the British and ensure their peaceful withdrawal, provided he was appointed the Shah Shuja's Grand Vizier. If this was agreed, the British garrison could winter in Kabul and withdraw in the spring.

Macnaghten, who had just heard that Nott's troops from Kandahar had been turned back by deep snow and that Sale could not return from Jalalabad, foolishly accepted and signed the agreement put before him by Akbar Khan; and even more foolishly set off without an adequate escort for a conference with the chiefs to finalise arrangements. When he arrived at the meeting place, Akbar Khan accused him of treachery in breaking the original treaty. Showing the chiefs Macnaghten's signature on the new one, he had the British Envoy and the officers with him seized and bundled away. Accounts differ as to how Macnaghten was actually murdered, but his mangled remains were dragged through the streets of Kabul and eventually hung over the main gate of the bazaar.

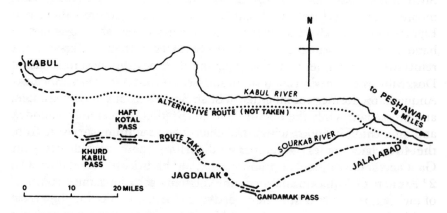

Map 7: The Retreat from Kabul: January 1842

Eldred Pottinger, who took over as Envoy, tried to persuade Elphinstone that he must either stay and defend himself in Kabul until help could arrive from India or he must fight his way out. Elphinstone insisted that further negotiation was the only answer. On 6 January, with the thermometer reading zero fahrenheit and the countryside deep in snow, Elphinstone, having agreed to a further Afghan demand that Sale should evacuate Jalalabad, started his supposedly peaceful and Afghan-escorted march back to India, taking all the women and children and some 15,000 followers along with his 4,500 soldiers, only 700 of whom were British. Shah Shuja, who was implicated in the plot to assassinate Macnaghten and to rid his country of the British, decided to stay in Kabul.

Akbar Khan was only able to control the rapacious tribesmen along the route in so far as they saw profit in obeying him; nor did he have enough men loyal to him to provide an adequate escort. Shelton with the 44th of Foot provided the advance and rear-guards, and with the handful of artillery men and sappers were the only troops to retain any discipline as the intense cold and Afghan attacks killed off thousands as they struggled through the high passes on the 80 mile route from Kabul to Jalalabad. As the column emerged from the Khurd Kabul Pass only 20 miles from Kabul on 9 January, Akbar Khan confessed to Elphinstone that he could not control the local tribesmen and offered to take the women and children under his protection, a promise that he fulfilled to the letter, treating them as honoured guests. The indomitable Lady Sale, who by then had several bullet holes in her garments and a bullet lodged in her midriff, held them all together throughout their ordeal, which was to last eight long months under the most primitive conditions.

By the time the halfway point at Jagdalak was reached on 11 January all Shah Shuja's troops had deserted and not more than 300 fighting men, mostly 44th, were left with the column. Akbar Khan summoned Elphinstone to a conference at which he demanded that Shelton should be handed over as a hostage until Sale evacuated Jalalabad. Elphinstone reluctantly agreed, and then found himself a hostage for the safety of Dost Mohamed. When Elphinstone and Shelton did not return, Brigadier Anquetil, the former commander of Shah Shuja's troops, took command and pressed on. Only the doctor, William Brydon, desperately wounded and on a dying horse, reached Jalalabad. The handful of survivors from the 44th had made their last stand, selling their lives dearly near Gandamak, on 12 January. Elphinstone died of dysentery in captivity on 23 April, but 80 officers and men taken prisoner at various times and most of the women survived in Afghan captivity. The rest of the Kabul garrison perished in that desperate week of Afghan treachery at the beginning of 1842. Shah Shuja did not live long either: he was assassinated in April.

★ ★ ★

Ellenborough arrived in India in February 1842 as the news of the Kabul disaster was seeping through to Calcutta. He was determined to pursue Peel's policy of liquidating Auckland's ill-advised Afghan venture, but only after the prestige of British arms had been restored. The Commander-in-Chief Sir Jasper Nicolls, had already dispatched Major-General George Pollock, a sound and methodical soldier, to Peshawar to prepare a column to relieve Sale at Jalalabad, and to rescue Lady Sale and the other prisoners in Afghan hands by threatening a British vengeful return to Kabul. He had also sent Brigadier Richard England to Quetta with a force to reinforce Nott at Kandahar. The stage was being set for the British, as usual, to win the last battle and the war.

Pollock started his advance up the Khyber Pass at the end of March and enshrined his name in the annals of Indian military history as the first general to adopt the tactics of methodically seizing and picquetting the heights on either side of his line of advance. Much sweat did save blood: the Afghan defenders abandoned the Pass and Pollock joined Sale in Jalalabad with minimal losses on 16 April. England was not so successful and suffered an unnecessary check near Quetta before he eventually broke through with Nott's help to Kandahar.

By the time the news of Pollock's arrival at Jalalabad reached him, Ellenborough had decided to cut the Company's losses by evacuating Afghanistan without a final counter-offensive. Pollock and Nott, however, were men of sterner stuff. Both prevaricated and delayed implementing plans to withdraw: Nott because he could not pull back across the Sind desert until the cooler weather in October and he believed that it would be easier to withdraw via Kabul anyway; and Pollock because he refused to countenance leaving British prisoners in Afghan hands and he too would find it exhausting if not so hazardous to withdraw through the Khyber, 'crowning the heights', in the hot weather.

Ellenborough accepted their excuses, and in effect gave the two generals discretionary powers to liquidate the Afghan commitment as they thought best. He went further: he subordinated all the 'politicals' to the military commanders and put his own very considerable energies into building up enough transport animals to give both forces the mobility that they would need for a combined summer offensive against Kabul. Pollock's force, for instance, needed 50 elephants, 5,000 camels and 4,000 bullocks to support his four brigades, comprising six cavalry regiments and eleven infantry battalions amongst whom the British were the 3rd Dragoons (now Queen's Own Hussars), 13th of Foot (Somersets), 9th of Foot (Norfolks), and 31st of Foot (East Surreys). Once British prestige had been forcibly re-established in Kabul, the premeditated withdrawal back to India would be put in hand as soon as the weather became cooler in the autumn.

Nott set off for Kabul first on 8 August, determined to beat Pollock in their race for the Afghan capital. He had the 40th and 41st of Foot (South Lancashire and Welch), and six Bengal battalions and a regiment of Bombay cavalry with him. By 4 September, he was before Ghazni, positioning the siege guns that Keane had left at Kandahar three years earlier, but the Afghans abandoned the fortress and Nott's sappers levelled it before marching on to Kabul, which he reached on 17 September only to find the Union Flag already flying over the Bala Hissar: Pollock had beaten him by two days.

Pollock had set off to fight his way to Kabul on 20 August with Bob Sale's division in the lead. He was determinedly opposed by Akbar Khan the whole way, but, using his tactics of methodically clearing the high ground, he drove the tribesmen back to a last stand at the almost impregnable Haft Kotal on 13 September. By hard climbing, his three British regiments drove their enemies from crag to crag until they had crowned the summit of the pass. Akbar Khan gave up the struggle and left Pollock's men to advance unopposed through the mangled remains of Elphinstone's force, which still littered the Khurd Kabul Pass, and on into Kabul on 15 September.

Venal to the end, Lady Sale's captors were easily bribed to let the British prisoners go, and she and the other wives were soon reunited with their husbands. With no 'politicals' to hamper their operations, Pollock and Nott stayed less than a month in the city, and started their withdrawal from Afghanistan on 12 October. Before leaving, Macnaghten's remains were recovered from the great Kabul bazaar, which Pollock's Sappers then blew up as a reminder of British power. Their withdrawal was far from unopposed. The tribesmen tried to repeat their successes of the previous year, but could snatch little from the columns directly under Pollock's command. Nott's and Sale's divisions suffered unnecessary losses through not expending the energy to picquet the heights. Fortescue comments:

> From stupid, un-teachable old Sale nothing better, perhaps, was to be expected . . . Nor is it easy to acquit Pollock of blame, for his force was not a large one, and he should have insisted upon proper conduct of the march by his subordinates. But everything in this wretched campaign was of a piece, and from beginning to end it brought little but disgrace.[12]

Dost Mohamed eventually returned to Kabul in 1843 with tacit British agreement after he had made sure that he would be welcomed and command Afghan political support. The wheel had come full circle without the East India Company establishing a reliable buffer state to bar the Russian approach to India. The need for such a buffer was, indeed, to become more pressing as the Tsarist expansion into the Khanates of Central Asia gathered momentum in the 1840s and '50s. One thing the Company was clear about was the need to have secure lines of communication to the Khyber and Bolan Passes. The Amirs of Sind were crushed by General Sir Charles Napier in a lightning campaign and their territory annexed in 1843; and the Sikhs were foolish enough to challenge the Company. In consequence, by 1849 the Punjab had been annexed as well. The routes for a return to Afghanistan, if the Russian threat did develop, were in British hands by the start of the 1850s.

Regrettably, the British were making the fourth of their fundamental mistakes, which they were to continue to make and which would be made a century later by Soviet Russia. No-one appreciated that the Afghans were invincible in their hard, arid and unforgiving mountains, in which they had been bred over the millennia to be as hard as their environment. Internally disunited though they might be, it was they who would always find enough unity to triumph in the end. They were an ideal buffer state against all comers, and needed no help to maintain their independence.

* * *

In the meantime, the Eastern Question had been coming to a fast simmer. By 1839, the five Great Powers – Britain, Austria, Prussia, Russia and France – had become enmeshed in the affairs of the Ottoman Empire. Mehemet Ali, often seen by historians as the Peter the Great of Egypt, had conquered the Moslem Holy Cities of Arabia and all of Syria, whilst maintaining the fiction that he was a still the Porte's loyal Pasha of Egypt. The French-trained Egyptian armies under his son, Ibrahim, defeated every Turkish attempt to bring Mehemet Ali to heel. There were fears in European capitals that the Ottoman Empire was, at long last, about to collapse through its component provinces being torn away from the Porte's governance. While self-interest dominated each of the Great Powers' policies towards Constantinople, they did have one interest in common: a wish to avoid another devastating European war caused by an unseemly scramble for the spoils of partition.

The heat was turned up under the cauldron by the death of Sultan Mahmud II, and the accession of Abdul Medjid, a 16 year old boy, whose Grand Vizier, Husrev Pasha, headed the pro-Russian faction in Constantinople. Political reinsurance began amongst the Ottoman establishment; and the Turkish Fleet deserted the Porte to join Mehemet Ali's Egyptian Fleet at Alexandria. It was clear to the Great Powers that Mehemet Ali must be stopped before he tried to usurp the Caliph's throne and destabilised the Near East.

Thanks to the determined diplomatic efforts of Palmerston in London and of Lord Ponsonby, the dominating and rabidly anti-Egyptian British Ambassador to the Porte, the Great Powers – less France – signed a convention with the Porte on 15 July 1840 'for the pacification of the Levant'. The French, obtuse as ever, preferred to develop their trade with Mehemet's growing Egyptian empire rather than co-operate with the other Great Powers. The convention was, in fact, an ultimatum to Mehemet Ali, demanding his withdrawal from Syria and the return of the Turkish Fleet in exchange for his recognition by the Sultan as hereditary Pasha of Egypt. A reply to these terms was to be given within ten days of their receipt! The only forces immediately available to the Great Powers at such short notice to enforce the Convention was the British Mediterranean Fleet under the command of the elderly and paternalistic

Admiral Sir Robert Stopford. The Austrians agreed to send some ships from the Adriatic as soon as they were ready; the French were opposed to the whole enterprise; the Prussians had no ships or troops available; and Palmerston had no wish to see a Russian fleet in the Mediterranean, hence the short notice given to Mehemet Ali for compliance.

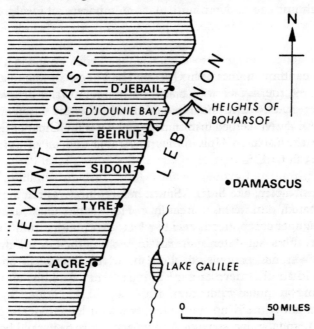

Map 8: The Syrian Campaign, 1840–41

At the time, the Egyptian hold on Syria was being weakened by internal unrest, caused by the harsh rule of Mehemet's son, Ibrahim. The Christian Maronites in the Lebanon were already in open revolt. Ponsonby hoped that the appearance of Stopford's fleet off Beirut, ready to support landings by Turkish troops and with stocks of weapons available for distribution to the rebels, would spread the revolt, encourage the local Amirs to return to their allegiance to the Sultan, and lead to the expulsion of the hated Egyptians. Thus it came about that the Royal Navy intervened for the first time in the Lebanon in an operation that was to be repeated with less success, but under more difficult circumstances, by the United States 6th Fleet a century and a half later.

Another eccentric and flamboyant naval character in the Sidney Smith mode was to stride onto the Levant stage. Admiral Stopford ordered Charles Napier, Captain of the battleship *Powerful*, to hoist the broad pennant of a commodore to command a squadron of six ships-of-the-line, which was to be sent to overawe Beirut. He was to land Turkish troops, and support them with British marines from his ships, to spur on the Maronite rebellion against the Egyptians. The landing force itself was to have been under the command of Brigadier Sir Charles Smith, who had been appointed by the Sultan to command the operations of Turkish troops ashore. Smith, however, went sick and Stopford gave Napier over-all command at sea and on land. A contemporary observer described Napier as:

> about 14 stone, stout and broad built; stoops from a wound in his neck, walks lame from another in his leg and has a most slouching slovenly gait; a large round face with black, bushy eyebrows, a double chin, scraggy, grey, un-curled whiskers and thin hair; wears a superfluity of shirt collar always daubed with snuff, which he takes in immense quantities; usually has trousers far too short, and wears the ugliest pair of old shoes he can find.[13]

But Charles Napier, like Sidney Smith before him, was not a man to be underestimated, despite his appearance. He was not unacquainted with amphibious operations; nor unused to handling politico-military affairs. His two brothers had been generals in Wellington's Army during the Peninsular War, and on a visit to them in 1810 he had taken an amateur part in the battle of Busaco and in the retreat into the lines of the Torres Vedras, being wounded in the leg for his pains. Like Sidney Smith, who took service under the King of Sweden, Napier offered his services to the Queen of Portugal in her struggle to regain her throne in the early 1830s. As Commander-in-Chief of her navy, and a Portuguese Vice-Admiral and Major General to boot, he had defeated her opponents at sea and on land, and been raised to the Portuguese peerage as Viscount Cape St Vincent. In 1840 off Beirut, he considered himself as much a soldier as a sailor and was totally convinced, not without reason, of his own abilities in both environments. Being one of those men who have a contempt for those above them, but are fiercely loyal to their subordinates, Napier's relations with the elderly Stopford were hardly cordial.

Napier anchored off Beirut on 12 August as the ultimatum to Mehemet Ali was expiring, but the Egyptians were far from overawed by his squadron. An intercepted letter showed that they were expecting French support. It was not until 9 September that the Turkish contingent of some 5,000 troops reached him from Cyprus. He landed with them and his marines next day at D'Jounie Bay, some ten miles north of Beirut, to gain touch with the Maronites and to avoid Beirut itself where the Egyptians were at their strongest. With the help of the Austrian General Jochmus, who was in the Sultan's service, he expanded and consolidated his foothold; and for a month lived on and off with the troops ashore, supervising the arming of the Maronites, and leading affrays against

Ibrahim's troops, who occupied positions in the heights of Boharsof, over-looking his base. Playing the part of the Great Powers' military representative in the Lebanon, and using his undoubted political skills and strength of personality, he persuaded the more important of local Amirs to rally to the Sultan's cause and co-operate with him in the task of per-suading Ibrahim to quit Syria.

At sea, Napier dispatched some of his ships to take D'Jebail to the north and Tyre to the south as additional bases for the distribution of arms to anti-Egyptian factions. Both were taken after the ships had demonstrated with a few violent broadsides the uselessness of resisting Anglo-Turkish landings. D'Jebail was occupied on 12 and Tyre on 17 September with trifling losses. Napier had good reason, therefore, to be furious when he heard that the more difficult task of capturing Sidon had been given to one of his captains without consulting him. After a thor-oughly petty exchange of letters in which Napier complained that he had 'all the fag' and none of 'the distinction'[14] Stopford gave way, and Napier sailed with his squadron for Sidon on 25 September, carrying 1,000 Turkish troops and British marines. The Governor of Sidon, who had some 3,000 troops at his disposal, refused to surrender, but after another demonstration of the destructive power of naval broadsides Egyptian resis-tance collapsed as soon as Napier's troops landed on 26 September. Their loss was again trifling: four killed and 30 wounded.

Operations against Beirut came to a climax early in October. Napier had managed to persuade the Amir Bechir Kassim, the leading Maronite chief, to co-operate in an offensive against Ibrahim's army by attacking the rear of his Boharsof position while Napier's Anglo-Turkish force assaulted frontally. Stopford felt the risks were too high and was delighted when Brigadier General Sir Charles Smith arrived fit and well to assume com-mand ashore. He was even more delighted to find that Beirut had been evacuated by the Egyptians on 10 October, its garrison marching off to reinforce Ibrahim at Boharsof. He had every justification for taking coun-sel of his fears that his forces ashore might come to grief by advancing too far inland to be able to regain the safety of their ships if events turned against them. Early on 10 October, he ordered Napier to prepare to with-draw and to hand over operations on shore to Brigadier General Smith. In true Nelsonian style, Napier ignored Stopford's orders on the grounds that operations were too far advanced to pull back without loss of prestige and without abandoning Amir Bechir Kassim, who was already in Ibrahim's rear.

Napier, like Nelson at Copenhagen, won the day by his own very con-siderable exertions and no thanks to the Commander-in-Chief. That evening – 10 October – he heard the sound of heavy firing behind Ibrahim's positions and realised that the Amir, true to his word, was attacking. The call to arms was sounded and Napier opened his own

assault on the heights of Boharsof just two hours before darkness fell that
night, commenting in his memoirs:

> It was rather a new occurrence for a British Commodore to be on top of
> Mount Lebanon commanding a Turkish Army, and preparing to fight a
> battle that would decide the fate of Syria.[15]

And decide the fate of Syria it did. Ibrahim's army collapsed after some
initially sharp fighting during which Napier was seen 'stirring up with his
stick' one of the Turkish battalions that was not advancing as quickly as he
would have liked. As his army fell apart, Ibrahim withdrew its remnants
eastwards through the mountains towards Damascus, leaving the Lebanon
to the Amir Bechir Kassim. Napier had the great satisfaction in handing
over his victorious troops to Brigadier General Smith and returning triumphant to *Powerful* freed from his military responsibilities ashore.

With Mehemet Ali showing few signs of accepting the Great Powers'
terms, Stopford was directed by London to attack Napoleon's old target,
the fortress of Acre. On 3 November, he disproved the old adage that
ships can rarely defeat the guns of a fortress. In two hours of intense
bombardment his ships overwhelmed the Egyptian defenders, and the
explosion of their main magazine brought resistance to an end. Napier,
who commanded the ships detailed to bombard the western defences, was
criticised rather publicly by Stopford for anchoring *Powerful* in the wrong
place. He demanded a courtmartial, but was dissuaded by his colleagues
from letting his vendetta with Stopford mar the Fleet's successes. It was
some relief to everyone concerned when Napier, knighted for his services
during the campaign, was dispatched with a squadron to overawe
Alexandria.

Napier arrived off the city only to find himself in much the same situation as Sidney Smith in 1800, when he negotiated the Convention of El
Arish and had it repudiated by the British Government for exceeding his
powers. Napier received a copy of a letter sent by Palmerston to Ponsonby
at Constantinople, recommending that despite everything which had happened since the July ultimatum, the Porte should still be persuaded to
recognise Mehemet Ali as hereditary Pasha of Egypt if he returned the
Turkish Fleet and evacuated Syria. Napier had in his squadron Captain
Maunsell, who was an old friend of Mehemet Ali's, so he sent him ashore
under a flag of truce on 22 November to see if he could persuade the old
man to accept the Porte's demands without further bloodshed and pointless resistance to the Great Powers.

Maunsell was well received and found that he was pushing on an opening door. Mehemet Ali was obviously looking for a way to end his
confrontation with the Porte and the Great Powers. He felt let down by
the French, who had misled and ill-advised him. Napier realised that the

approach of winter weather might make his station off Alexandria untenable at any moment, so in his impulsive way seized time by the forelock and opened negotiations at once with the Grand Vizier, drawing up a short four article convention for the return of the Turkish Fleet and the whole of Syria to the Porte in exchange for Mehemet Ali's reinstatement as hereditary Pasha of Egypt. Entirely without instructions from Ponsonby, who wished to drive Mehemet Ali out of Egypt as well as Syria, and pointedly without consulting Stopford, his Commander-in-Chief, Napier signed the Convention with the Grand Vizier on 28 November 1840.

Napier was luckier than Sidney Smith in that although his Convention was repudiated locally by Stopford, Ponsonby and the Porte, Palmerston was happy to accept it as an armistice and a basis for detailed negotiations at diplomatic level. The Turkish Fleet was returned to Constantinople in January 1841; and Mehemet Ali was confirmed as hereditary ruler of Egypt in June. The Eastern Question came off fast simmer, but only for the time being.

By the end of the first half of the 19th Century the perceived trident of Russian threats to British interests in the Middle East and India had only partially been contained. The Ottoman Empire's continued existence blocked the western prong; the Persians in the centre were as ambivalent as ever; and Afghanistan was far from secure, although Dost Mohamed was more favourably disposed towards the British in India than to the Russians in Central Asia.

CHAPTER 3

THE END OF THE GREAT GAME

The 1st Gulf War and the
2nd Afghan War 1850-1881

*Abdhur Rahman, the Durani Chief, of him is the story told. His
mercy fills the Khyber hills – his grace is manifold;
He has taken toll of the North and the South – his glory reacheth
far.
And they tell the tale of his charity from Balk to Kandahar.*

Rudyard Kipling: Barrack-Room Ballads[1]

The mid-point of the 19th Century was also half-time in the Eastern
Question and the Great Game, played as far as Britain was concerned to
block Russia's landward approaches to India by propping up the Ottoman
Empire and by checking Russian ambitions in Central Asia. But a third
dimension was soon to be added to Britain's growing involvement in the
Middle East. The construction of the Suez Canal in the 1860s was to rev-
olutionise Indian trade and imperial defence policy, and would give Egypt
greater strategic importance to Britain than the Dardanelles or
Afghanistan.

Ever since 1798, when the French Directory had included digging a
canal across the isthmus of Suez as one of the objectives of Napoleon's
invasion of Egypt, the de Lesseps family had continued to explore the possibilities of such a project. They were helped by the British desire to avoid
further entanglement in Egyptian internal affairs. Westminster, Whitehall
and the City of London doubted the technical feasibility of such a canal
and were mulishly slow to appreciate its potential, preferring instead to
put money into the financially less risky construction of the Alexandria-
Cairo-Suez railway, which was started in 1851 and completed in 1857.
The French, on the other hand, continued to build up their influence in
Cairo and, in 1854, Mehemet Ali's son, Sa'id Pasha, granted Ferdinand
de Lesseps a 99 year concession to build the canal, financed almost
entirely by Paris and opposed steadfastly by the British, who feared that it
would open up a new invasion route rather than an improved line of communication to India.

The strategic problems that would be presented to London and Calcutta by the construction of the Suez Canal still lay in the future when, in 1854, the Eastern Question bubbled up from fast simmer to a tumbling boil with the outbreak of the Crimean War. The war itself was fought outside the Middle East and so its battles do not concern us directly. Its causes and its consequences, however, were all part of the Russian threat, as perceived by the British, to their interests in the region.

While four of the five Great Powers still favoured propping up the Ottoman Empire as a way of preventing a European war over the spoils if it were to collapse, St Petersburg saw the whole ramshackle edifice as already beyond redemption, and was intent upon hastening its demise in a way which would ensure that the richest pickings fell into Russian hands. The Tsarist ploy was as elegant as it was devious. By demanding the right to be the acknowledged protector of Orthodox Christians living in Moslem lands, the Tsar would always have a potential *casus belli*, in which the other Great Powers, as Christian states, would find it difficult not to give their support, if the Porte refused him. On the other hand, with two fifths of the population of the Ottoman lands confessing the Orthodox faith – Romanians, Serbs, Bulgars, Greeks and Armenians – acceptance of such a demand by the Porte would enable St Petersburg to achieve political dominance in Constantinople during the terminal phases of Ottoman decline.

The Tsar misjudged the anti-Russian instincts of the other Great Powers, particularly Britain and France, who came together, despite their chauvinistic competition in the Levant, to oppose what they saw, quite rightly, as another effort by the Tsar to turn the Porte into a Russian satellite and to control the Dardanelles. Misjudgements, misunderstandings, diplomatic blunders, pride, obstinacy and sheer stupidity on all sides led to the Crimean War of 1854-56, which none of the Powers wanted and which took place almost by accident. It was fought in an equally chaotic way. Not surprisingly, the Great Game was re-opened immediately by the Russians as a diversionary effort; and, after their defeat in the Crimea, the more ambitious Russian generals sought to remake their names in Central Asia.

The diversionary ploy was in the hands of the large Russian embassy in Tehran. The Persians were successfully persuaded by the Tsar's Envoy, General Duhamel, to try to undermine British influence in Afghanistan by renewing their claims to Herat. Sadly, British interests in the Persian capital were badly served at that time by the crass and overbearing behaviour of the British Envoy, Charles Murray, who picked a quite unnecessary domestic quarrel with the Shah's court and precipitately struck his flag in November 1855 when he could not have his own way, appealing to London and Calcutta to make the Persian Government 'howl' for their insults.

With Murray out of the way, the Persians advanced with Russian encouragement against Herat, which they occupied in October 1856, seven months after the Peace of Paris had brought the Crimean War to a close. Herat was still as vital as ever to the forward defence of India, but it was generally accepted in London and Calcutta that there could be no question of a British force marching once more through the Bolan Pass to drive the Persians out. Memories of the First Afghan War were too painfully etched on Afghan and British minds to make this a practicable proposition. There were, however, two other possibilities: to help the Amir of Kabul, still Dost Mohamed, to get rid of the Persians by supplying him with arms, cash and British military advisers; or to disrupt the Persian economy by taking and holding one of their principal Persian Gulf ports until the Shah agreed to leave Herat. Both courses were adopted: an agreement was reached with the ageing, but still strongly anglophile, Dost Mohamed, to finance and supply arms for Afghan operations against Herat; and the Indian Government was directed by London to assemble an amphibious force for British operations in the Persian Gulf.

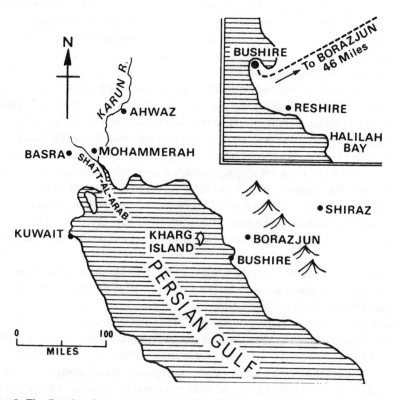

Map 9: The Persian Gulf Campaign of 1856–57

In London, Lord Palmerston's Cabinet took two bites at the cherry. The Governor General, then Lord Canning, was at first instructed to dispatch one division of two infantry brigades with cavalry, artillery and engineer support, totalling about 6,000 fighting men, to the Gulf to retake Kharg Island as an advanced base, and then seize the port of Bushire, the capture of which could damage the trade of Shiraz and the southern Persian provinces. However, doubts were soon cast as to whether the loss of Bushire would be enough to persuade the Shah to give up Herat. Calcutta was subsequently ordered to prepare a second division of similar size for an advance on Shiraz or for extending operations to the head of the Gulf. In the latter case, Mohammerah (now Khorramshahr) on the Shatt-al-Arab was to be taken as the advanced base for a thrust up the Karun River to threaten and, if need be, take the city of Ahwaz.

The 1st Division was drawn from the Bombay Presidency Army and placed under the command of Major General Foster Stalker, a worthy but undistinguished officer of 58 years of age, described by a junior officer as 'a nice old fellow, not valiant in Society, but they say very sturdy and sensible'. He was, however, the best that Bombay could provide, its Governor writing that there was little more than dead wood at the top of his Presidency's army, and agreeing with Lord Canning that Stalker 'might do'! Like many other officers in the Company's Army, Stalker was burdened with debt and hoped to clear some of it with prize money from the campaign – a hope that was to prove his undoing.[2]

The selection of Stalker's naval colleague was even more unfortunate. Command of the supporting fleet of eight war steamers of the Indian Navy, seven hired steamers and thirty sailing ships was initially given to Captain 'Grim Dick' Ethersey, one of the ablest and most respected officers in the Indian Navy with long experience of the Gulf coasts and waters. He was, however, intensely disliked by the Naval Commander-in-Chief India, Sir Henry Leeke, a 70 year old Admiral from the Royal Navy with no experience of the Indian Ocean let alone the Persian Gulf, and with something of a chequered career behind him. He prevailed upon Canning to let him command the naval forces in the Gulf despite Company standing instructions forbidding the Commander-in-Chief who held an entirely administrative appointment – to leave Bombay. Ethersey was demoted to second-in-command with responsibility for the tactical handling of the bombarding ships.

Stalker's 1st Division, embarked in Leeke's motley fleet of steamers and sailing ships, was off Bushire in late November. Its men were dressed for the first time in the Army's history in khaki drill instead of scarlet jackets. The advanced base on Kharg Island was established without opposition, and Ethersey went off to find a suitable landing place for troops near Bushire, which he found at Halilah Bay ten miles south of the port. The landing started early on 7th December after a short naval bombardment

of some inoffensive date groves, which were thought might conceal enemies. None appeared and a chaotic landing went ahead, which was
fortunately un-opposed by the Persians.

There had been a British consulate in Bushire for over a century, and
yet little seems to have been known about the place. Leeke expected to be
able to requisition local craft to supplement his ships' boats, but none
were to be found; and Stalker was depending upon finding local draught
animals for moving supplies forward, but he too was disappointed. The
troops spent two cold nights without cover before Stalker deemed it practicable to start his advance on Bushire along the stony, trackless coastal
plain. Any chance of surprise was gone, but fortunately the Persians were
overawed by the sight of the ships off shore, and by the way in which
Ethersey provided fire support from the sea when the British started to
advance on 9 December.

Little opposition was met until the old Dutch fort of Reshire was
reached half way to Bushire, which was held by some 800 Tangistanis, the
fierce descendants of Arab pirates. Stalker had to deploy three battalions – the 64th of Foot (North Staffords), the 2nd Bombay European
Light Infantry and the 20th Native Infantry – who took the place by
storm. Brigadier General Stopford, who led the assault, was shot dead on
the top of the parapet. Then Colonel Malet of the 3rd Bombay Cavalry
was shot in the back by a Tangistani whose life he had just spared and
there were some 50 other casualties. Many of the garrison escaped over
the rough stony ground, which made rapid cavalry pursuit almost impossible. Stalker's men spent a third cold night in the open.

Next day Ethersey moved his ships close in shore to bombard Bushire's
forts, while Stalker advanced the last few miles northwards. The Persian
garrison had taken up a position across the low-lying isthmus which links
Bushire to the mainland, but as soon as the ships opened fire their courage
failed them and they rushed back into the protection of the town's walls.
Despite the praiseworthy way in which the Persian gunners served their
pieces, Ethersey, in contradiction of Leeke's orders, boldly closed the
range until most of his ships went aground on the mud as the tide ebbed,
but were able to stay in action until the Persians struck their colours
when Stalker's troops came within assaulting distance of the walls at
about midday. That evening, the Union Flag was flying over what
remained of the British Residency in Bushire after the bombardment.
The ships had been ordered not to shell it, but it was found to be the most
heavily damaged building in the town!

The news of the capture of Bushire reached Calcutta on Christmas day
1856. It was known that all was not well behind the scenes in the Gulf.
Admiral Leeke had been quarrelling with everyone; the landings had been
a shambles due to shortages of landing craft, Canning noting 'throughout,
the whole of the Naval arrangements showed great want of method'; and

his incompetence had almost ruined the attack on Bushire. Leeke was recalled, leaving Ethersey to bring order out of logistic chaos.[3]

Stalker's performance had been reasonable until the fall of Bushire, but then he committed the sin of doing little to exploit success and concentrated instead upon fortifying his position and trying to solve his logistic problems which were, indeed, appalling. Lack of local boats, labour and indigenous supplies meant that every day half his men had to be used on fatigues, unloading essential supplies from the ships and landing camp construction materials needed urgently to give his troops some cover before the hot weather. He did not possess the drive to get things done, and was haunted by the fear that he would be pilloried like the generals in the Crimean War for administrative incompetence. Whilst there was no serious loss of morale, a tired boredom engulfed his men.

Meanwhile the 2nd Division, also drawn from the Bombay Presidency Army, was preparing to sail to the Gulf. Its commander was Brigadier General Henry Havelock, who was later to win fame during the Indian Mutiny and become a Victorian folk hero. He was the antithesis of Stalker: small, lightly built and earnest in appearance; dynamic with a character as upright and unyielding as his ramrod like spine; and a committed Christian soldier of the Baptist Church, who later founded the Army Temperance Movement.

Havelock was also the complete opposite of Lieutenant General Sir James Outram, who was appointed by the cabinet in London, against Canning's wishes, to be Commander-in-Chief of the two divisional force in the Gulf. Whereas Havelock was a soldier of pure gold, Outram, who was also to become a household name amongst Victorians during the Mutiny, had a streak of the charlatan in him. A powerful looking, dark bearded man, he was one of the Indian Army's 'politicals', who had made a name for himself both as a soldier and administrator, but was not averse to using the Press to advance his career. When he eventually wrote his book on the war in the Gulf, he entitled it *Sir James Outram's Persian Campaign*, conveniently forgetting Stalker's and Havelock's part in it.

Charlatan or not, Outram transformed the situation at Bushire when he landed at the end of January 1857. Intelligence reports suggested that a Persian army under its Commander-in-Chief, Suja-ul-Mulk, was being built up at Borazjun some 46 miles inland on the road to Shiraz with the intention of retaking Bushire. Outram wasted no time in getting the first brigade of Havelock's division ashore, and within three days was advancing with a force of 4,600 men and 18 guns to disrupt the Persian concentration. They carried no tentage, each man having only his great coat, a blanket and two days cooked rations. Three days dry provisions were carried by the commissariat wagons.

Although it was winter, Outram persisted in the Indian Army custom of marching by night for comfort, but also to achieve surprise. The weather was at its worst with a violent dust storm followed by torrential rain. Nevertheless, his columns reached the Persian entrenched camp in 48 hours and deployed for attack early on 5 February. To the disgust of all ranks, the whole of the Persian force was seen to be retreating towards the mountains, which lay between Bushire and Shiraz. The Persians had abandoned large quantities of ammunition, weapons and food in their camp, suggesting that they had been surprised by the speed of Outram's night marches. Outram intended to pursue them, but was dissuaded from doing so by his staff, who pointed out his lack of supplies and transport for a prolonged campaign in dangerous mountain country where he could easily be ambushed.

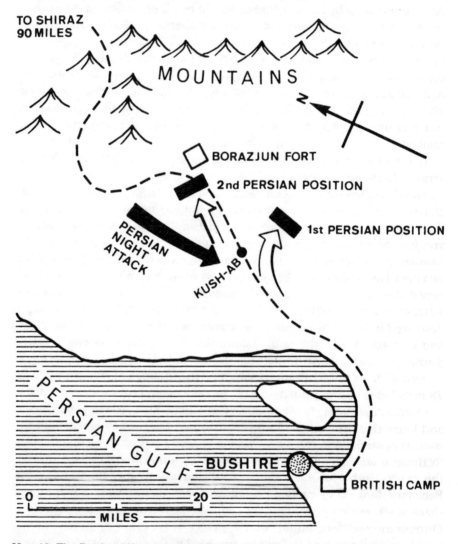

Map 10: The Battle of Kush-ab; 8th February 1857

Outram spent two days at Borazjun, destroying stores and searching for abandoned guns. There was no interference from the Persians, which convinced him, wrongly, that they had sought the safety of the mountains and would not attempt to impede his return to Bushire. During the afternoon of 7 February his Sappers blew up 40,000 pounds of Persian gunpowder, which had to be abandoned for lack of transport to carry it away, and the regiments prepared to march off that night. The explosion was heard many miles away and alerted the Persians to a probable British withdrawal.

This time it was night that enabled the Persians to surprise Outram. After dark, his marching columns were suddenly attacked by milling masses of Persian horsemen blowing trumpets, firing their weapons and yelling like fiends while one or two of their guns opened indiscriminate fire. Confusion reigned for about half an hour while they were being driven off and the regiments were formed into a defensive box to wait for dawn under sporadic sniping and gun fire. Outram himself was unlucky. His horse stumbled in the dark and rolled on him. With the Commander-in-Chief unconscious for several hours, the command devolved again on Stalker.

When dawn did come, the Persian army was seen drawn up in battle-array a short distance away with their right resting on the walled village of Kush-ab and their left on a fortified tower. The British artillery and cavalry came into action at once to give the infantry time to redeploy from their night square into an attacking formation. By the time their manoeuvres had been completed, the battle was almost over. Gunners' fire tore swathes in the Persian ranks and opened the way for the cavalry to make two decisive charges. The Poona Horse captured the colours of its opponents, the 1st Kushkai Regiment, and the 3rd Light Cavalry (later the 17th/21st Lancers) broke the square of the 1st Fars Regiment and destroyed it. By the time the British infantry began to close, the Persians had had enough. They wavered and then broke in headlong retreat, throwing away their arms, which lay strewn over the battlefield, which was littered with some 700 Persian dead. The British lost only six officers and 78 men killed and wounded.

Outram did not have the resources to pursue his opponents to Shiraz, and knew that the British Government wanted him to move his force as soon as possible to the Shatt-al-Arab to threaten Ahwaz. The march back to Bushire was again carried out by night in pouring rain, which turned the tracks into glutinous mud. The troops reached Bushire on 10 February, looking more like a defeated than a victorious army. Nor was there much rejoicing amongst the senior officers, most of whom disliked Outram intensely and had much to criticise in his callous handling of his troops and subordinates, which was to bear bitter fruit ere long.

On the Persian side, Suja-ul-Mulk was replaced as Commander-in-

Chief by the over-powerful and unpopular commander of the Shah's bodyguard, Sirkesheck-chee Bashi, nicknamed 'Cheeky Bashi' by British troops. It was a poisoned chalice: the Shah foresaw little chance of glory for him, fighting Outram in the Gulf.

Havelock and the second brigade of his division did not reach Bushire by sea until 6 March. In the meantime, the troops were employed on strengthening the fortifications of the Bushire base, and preparations were made for the move to the Shatt-al-Arab where the Persians were known to be concentrating 13,000 men for the defence of Mohammerah. Outram decided to leave Stalker to hold Bushire with 3,000 men, and to give Havelock command of the Shatt-al-Arab force. This was too much for Stalker: superseded in command, his finances in ruins, reduced opportunity for prize money and general worry about becoming a scapegoat in Crimean War style, he retired to his tent and blew out his brains. A few days later 'Grim Dick' Ethersey took the same way out: he too shot himself. He was found dead in his cabin with an official reprimand from his Commander-in-Chief, Sir Henry Leeke, lying beside him. Like Stalker, he feared being made a scapegoat for the Indian Navy's inadequacies.

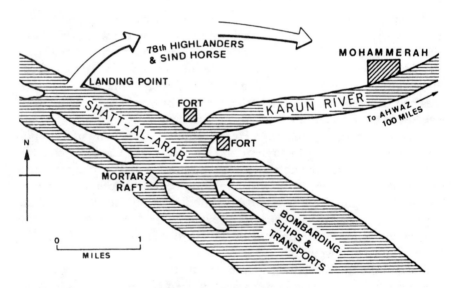

Map 11: The Battle for Mohammerah: 26 March 1857

It was not until 24 March that four armed steamers with transports in tow, now under command of Commodore John Rennie of the Indian Navy and carrying Havelock's force of 5,000 men, moved up the Shatt-al-Arab towards Mohammerah, which stood on the north bank of the Karun River where it joins the Shatt. The entrance to the Karun was defended by two strongly built forts, making it hazardous to attack the town from the

Karun itself. The alternative course was to attempt to run the transports up the wider Shatt-al-Arab, passing the forts at longer range and landing to the north of the town where the defences were weakest. Islands in the Shatt, which might have been practicable as mortar battery sites for neutralising the forts, were found by the Sappers to be too marshy for the construction of platforms, so they built a raft of casks and ship spars to take four mortars instead and managed to position it secretly after dark behind the islands, with a boat full of hay anchored in front of it to give the gunners under Captain John Worgan of the Bombay Artillery some protection. Worgan's men were the equivalent of the 'forlorn hope' in the assault on Mohammerah. Anchored all night on that flimsy raft in a fast flowing stream and right under the guns of the two forts, their chances of survival when dawn came were not deemed very high.

Rennie's and Havelock's battle for Mohammerah started at dawn on 26 March when the mortars lobbed bombs with remarkable accuracy into both forts, surprising and confusing the Persian gunners, who then came under bombardment by the ships' naval 68 pounders. This lasted for three hours while the steamers, carrying the landing force, ran the gauntlet past the forts. The landing, when it was made, was far from easy, but once ashore the 78th Highlanders, (later to become the Seaforths) with a detachment of the Sind Horse, advanced determinedly towards the rear of the town. The Persians did not wait to receive them and fled in panic, leaving all their guns behind them and 300 dead in the fortifications. The British losses in killed and wounded were less than 50.

No pursuit in strength was practicable for logistic reasons, but Outram dispatched a small probing force of 300 men, drawn from the 64th of Foot and the 78th Highlanders, under Captain GH Hunt of the 78th – an accomplished artist, whose etchings record the whole campaign – in three small steamers up the Karun towards Ahwaz, 100 miles away. On l April, they landed near the town and advanced upon it, supported by the steamers' guns. They tried to look like the advanced guard of Outram's main body, and they succeeded, thanks to a lucky shot from one of the steamers, which hit Sirkesheck-chee Bashi's headquarters, killing two of the horses of his green carriage. Once again, Persian courage failed and they withdrew further upstream without a fight.

Hunt's entry of Ahwaz ended the Anglo-Persian War of 1856–57. Unbeknown to Outram, Persia had sued for peace after the battle of Kush-ab. By the terms of a treaty signed in Paris when Outram's force was approaching Mohammerah, the Shah agreed to leave Herat and to recognise the independence of Afghanistan. An apology was tendered to the British Envoy, Charles Murray; Anglo-Persian relations were restored to cordiality and Russian influence in Tehran went into decline. As soon as Herat was evacuated by the Persians, all British troops were withdrawn from the Gulf back to India.

The postscript to the campaign was uttered by one of the Persian commanders:

Oh Allah, if there was no dying in the case, how the Persians would fight![4]

* * *

The Persians could not be compared with the hard men, bred in the harsh environment of the Afghan Mountains, with whom the British were to become entangled once more within 20 years. In that interval, Calcutta was embarrassed by the Indian Mutiny in the Bengal Presidency Army, which had begun in January 1857 during the Persian Gulf Campaign. The India Act of 1858 ended the East India Company's existence and brought India directly under the British Crown with Queen Victoria later declared Empress of India, her Viceroy ruling from Delhi instead of Calcutta.

The Indian Mutiny seemed to the Russian commanders on the unmarked frontiers across the steppes of Central Asia to offer great opportunities for avenging Russia's defeat in the Crimea while Britain's back was turned, and for winning their own glory by raising the Tsarist flag over the Moslem khanates as stepping-stones to an eventual Russian conquest of India. While St Petersburg was intent on maintaining good relations with London as a potential ally in the eventual partition of the Ottoman Empire, the frontier generals, who were Anglophobes to a man, were pressing for a 'forward policy' in Central Asia. These two streams of Russian endeavour converged in the simple philosophy of diverting British attention and resources away from the Eastern Question by pursuing the Great Game in Central Asia. The ambitions of the frontier generals were further helped by the long-standing Russian tradition that, once the Russian ensign with its two headed Imperial Russian eagle had been raised over a territory, it must never be struck. Their *modus operandi* was to raise the flag first and ask permission later, leaving St Petersburg to justify to London yet another annexation in Central Asia.[5]

There were two similarly contradictory schools of strategic thought within the British and Indian Governments, but they did not converge in any way and were starkly alternative policies adopted by Tory and Whig Governments. The Tories tended to pursue the 'forward policy' of taking active steps to secure India's frontiers by annexations. The Whigs adopted the policy of 'masterly inactivity' when they were in power, preferring to put their faith in the physical and political difficulties of invading India from Central Asia. The First Afghan War in the 1840s, fought on the basis of the forward policy, had been such an unmitigated disaster that the philosophy of 'masterly inactivity' reigned supreme in London and Calcutta during the 1850s and '60s, while the Russian generals sought their glory in Central Asia, always able to convince St Petersburg that, if they did not strike first, the British would surely pre-empt them.

Two and a half decades of relentless Russian advance in Central Asia began in 1859, when Russian missions were first established in Khiva and Bukhara. There were three principal reasons for the Russian thrust into this remote and fiercely Moslem part of the world. First, there was the constant fear that the British would get there first and monopolise its supposedly rich and untapped markets. Secondly, there was imperial pride: the desire to follow the other European powers in establishing large colonial empires. And thirdly, there was the more distant vision of paving the way to the eventual invasion of India. There was also a shorter term economic requirement. The American Civil War, 1861–65, had cut off Russia's cotton supplies from the United States. Tashkent and Khokand were known to be excellent cotton growing areas and might be able to provide an alternative source of supply.

One of the men, who provided the dynamic behind the Russian drive towards India and, incidentally, Vladivostok as well, was Count Nikolai Ignatiev, a young ambitious 'political', who had the ear of the Tsar and an unquenchable desire to out-play the British in Asia. He was to prove himself one of the leading exponents of the Great Game, and provided classic demonstrations of the 'domino' system of colonial aggression. The khanates were toppled in succession from the north where the cotton growing areas were the initial attraction. General Mikhail Cherniaev took Tashkent in 1865; and after he was relieved for exceeding his powers too blatantly, General Konstantin Kaufman was appointed Governor General of Turkestan and went on to absorb Samarkand and Bukhara in 1868, Khiva in 1873, Khokand in 1875 and Merv in 1884.

Before each new step was taken, the Russian Ambassador in London would assure Her Majesty's Government that the Tsar-like Hitler – had no further territorial claims in Central Asia. Then one of the frontier generals would march into yet another slice of Moslem territory and raise the Russian flag, leaving St Petersburg to find excuses for his actions. With the 'masterly inactivity' school dominant in the British and Indian Governments, diplomatic protest was the limit of British reaction even to the most flagrant Russian double-dealing. The Indian Government contented itself with maintaining good relations with Persia and Afghanistan, making the first Anglo-Afghan Boundary Agreement with Dost Mohamed in 1859, just four years before his death in 1863, and the second with his successor, Sher Ali, in 1873.

The 'masterly inactivity' school went into steep decline, however, from 1874 onwards when Disraeli, the passionate imperialist, displaced Gladstone as Prime Minister and brought Lord Salisbury into the India Office. By then, Russian duplicity over their advances in Central Asia had become intolerable, and the 'forward school' gained more of a hearing in the corridors of power in Westminster and Whitehall. The shift of opinion had started rather earlier in 1869 when the Russians secretly established a base at Krasnovodsk on the south-eastern shores of the Caspian Sea from which they intended to build a railway eastwards, linking European Russia to Merv, Bukhara, Khokand and Tashkent. There were obviously sound commercial reasons for doing so, but the railway's construction would clearly increase the credibility of the Russian military threat to India by easing their logistic problems. News of the project soon reached British ears.

With the Russians getting too close to India for comfort, and with only the sketchiest reports available of what was really going on in Central Asia from the British 'politicals', playing the Great Game amongst the tribes of the Hindu Kush and Pamirs, Disraeli's cabinet decided that a British mission must be established as a listening post in Kabul, and possibly in Herat and Kandahar as well. Lord Lytton was dispatched to Delhi in 1876 as the new Tory appointed Viceroy of India with a 'forward policy' brief to open negotiations with Amir Sher Ali in Kabul. Lord Northcliffe, Lytton's predecessor, warned London before he left India that the abandonment of the policy of 'masterful inactivity' would lead to another unnecessary and costly war with the xenophobic Afghans. His advice was ignored.

Meanwhile the Eastern Question, which had only been brought off the boil temporarily by the Peace of Paris, was again disconcerting the Great Powers. Russia had recovered from the Crimean War disaster and the 'forward school' in St Petersburg, spurred on by Ignatiev, who had become the Tsar's envoy to the Porte, and by the pan-Slav lobby, started to develop plans for another attempt to partition the Ottoman Empire. In 1875, Russian-inspired rebellions broke out in Bosnia and Herzegovina, where the mainly Orthodox Christian peasantry rose against their Turkish landlords and pashas, giving the Tsar the excuse to intervene. A similar revolt in Bulgaria the following year was put down by the Turks with such appalling brutality that British public opinion was enraged and momentarily sided with the Tsar. Cooler heads saw the whole affair for what it was – a renewed attempt by St Petersburg to reach the Eastern Mediterranean, and, hence, to endanger the Suez Canal, which was, by then, seen in Whitehall to be even more important than the Dardanelles.

British opposition to the construction of the Canal had been reversed well before its triumphal opening by the Empress Eugenie of France in 1869. As soon as it was clear that the project was going to succeed, British shipping companies began preparations to use it to capacity, and by 1875, when Disraeli, with Rothschild's help, bought Khedive Ismail's controlling interest in the Canal Company, four-fifths of the ships transiting the Canal were British. From that moment onwards, the security of the Canal became Britain's primary strategic interest in the Middle East.

At first it was thought that there would be no need to annex Egypt to ensure the safety of the Canal: British sea power would suffice, provided friendly relations were maintained with the Porte and there was a stable government in Egypt. Therein lay the rub: Egypt's stability was coming increasingly into doubt. Mehemet Ali's son, Sa'id Pasha, who had granted de Lesseps his Canal concession, had died in 1863. His successor, Mehemet's grandson, Ismail Pasha, who was later promoted Khedive by the Porte for his great efforts in modernising Egypt, was a complex and controversial character. He was seen either as a man of vision or an incorrigible spendthrift. During his reign, parts of Cairo and Alexandria were rebuilt as replicas of Paris; railways criss-crossed the Nile delta; laws and education were modernised; irrigation was improved; and cotton production was increased a hundredfold to profit by the American Civil War cotton boom. But there were unpaid bills piling up, and Ismail's credit, based upon Egypt's boom-time cotton crops, was seeping away with the ending of the American Civil War.

The trouble was that Ismail carried out his programmes by granting over-generous concessions to European entrepreneurs. By 1865 there were 80,000 Europeans living in Egypt, who would need protection if things went wrong. As long as the cotton boom lasted, Ismail could just about pay his way, thanks to the keenness of European bankers to invest in Egyptian enterprises. But as cotton revenues declined with the recovery of American cotton farming, those bankers were just as keen to call in their loans. By 1876, Ismail reached the end of his financial tether with debts of £90m. Under pressure from the bankers, the British and French Governments imposed an International Commission of Debt under a British and a French Controller General. Within two years, Ismail was forced to accept the Controllers General as members of his cabinet, and the system of government, known as 'Dual Control', was imposed upon him. As the months went by, more and more British and French administrators were drafted into Egyptian ministries in an attempt to improve efficiency and to ensure that Egypt's debts were repaid. France was intent on protecting her financial and commercial stake; Britain had the additional strategic interest of protecting the Suez Canal and so took the lead in 'advising' the Egyptian Government.

1877 was a milestone in the linked affairs of the Eastern Question, the Great Game and the Suez Canal. The expected Russo-Turkish War broke out in May, the Tsar overtly intervening on behalf of the Orthodox Christians, but covertly aiming to create a pan-Slav state from the Danube to the Aegean. As a diversion, Kaufman was given a free hand in Central Asia to develop plans for the ultimate invasion of India. And in Egypt, European interference started to generate a xenophobic nationalist fervour, which could, and eventually did, threaten the security of the Canal.

The Russians crossed the Danube in June, but made slow progress against the Turkish armies, which had recently been re-equipped with the breach-loading rifles and the Krupp's artillery that had enabled Prussia to crush France in 1870. The Russian advance came to a halt in front of the fortress of Plevna in July, where it remained stalled until December when Turkish resistance collapsed and the Tsarist armies were able to advance to within ten miles of Constantinople. A British fleet entered the Dardanelles and anchored in the Sea of Marmara while St Petersburg was warned that any attempt to enter the Turkish capital would mean war with Britain. The Turks, however, accepted the draconian terms offered by the Russians, and signed the Armistice of San Stephano in February 1878.

Under the armistice terms, most of the Balkan states were to be granted their independence, which the British Government welcomed, but it bridled at the Tsar's further proposal to establish a pan-Slav state of Greater Bulgaria, stretching from the Danube to the Aegean. Such a state would provide Russia with a springboard for settling the Eastern question in her favour once and for all in a few years time. Anti-Russian feeling welled up in Britain with a tide of war-mania. Disraeli refused to recognise the terms of San Stephano and ordered the British fleet to anchor off Princes Island at the entrance of the Bosphorus. An expeditionary force was mobilised under General Sir Garnet Wolseley, and the word 'Jingoism' entered English folk-law as the music-halls rang with the ditty:

> We don't want to fight, but by Jingo if we do, we've got the men, we've got the ships, we've got the money too!

But the more sober citizens realised that Britain did not possess a military base in the Levant from which the Royal Navy could be supported by the Army in opposing a further Russian advance towards the Dardanelles and onwards to the Suez Canal. Several suggestions were made for acquiring one: Alexandretta, Crete, Lemnos, Mitylene and Cyprus were all mentioned. In the end the British Envoy in Constantinople, Sir Henry Layard, was directed to negotiate with the Porte for the lease of Cyprus. In June 1878, the Cyprus Convention was signed by which Britain was allowed to occupy the island in case of further Russian aggression, but it would stay under Turkish sovereignty. This it did until the Turks sided with Germany in the First World War, when it was annexed outright by Britain.

For some months the strongest elements in the armed might of the Russian and British Empires stood facing each other on the shores of the Sea of Marmara – the Russian Army at San Stephano with the Royal Navy anchored off-shore. Russia was, however, near bankruptcy and was forced at the Congress of Berlin in the summer of 1878 to accept that the southern Bulgarian frontier was to be pulled back to the mountain range some 200 miles north of Constantinople.

Meanwhile Kaufman, the Governor General of Turkestan and Lytton in Delhi had been squaring up to each other over Central Asia. Before

Lytton left London in 1876, the Russian Ambassador had put proposals to him from Kaufman for a mutually advantageous partition of the Moslem states bordering India to provide a stable frontier between the two empires. Lytton would have none of it, stating bluntly that it was British policy to support rather than annex the border states, and that in any case he did not trust Kaufman's protestations of friendship: intelligence sources reported that Kaufman's staff were actively planning an advance on Afghanistan. While the Russian Army and the Royal Navy glowered at each other in the Sea of Marmara in the summer of 1878, Kaufman was authorised by the Tsar to start a preliminary advance by three columns from Tashkent, Bukhara and Krasnovodsk towards the Upper Oxus. They made extraordinarily slow progress, due to logistic difficulties, but ahead of them rode a Russian military mission under General Count Stolietov, heading for Kabul with a brief to seek the co-operation of Amir Sher Ali in a combined Russo-Afghan invasion of India.

Lytton had been chosen by Disraeli from amongst his personal friends as a man likely to be able to overcome India's reluctance to adopt a forward policy as well as having the 'presence' to announce Queen Victoria's assumption of the title of Empress of India. He was an experienced and able diplomat, and also a poet and writer of repute. He had not dealt with eastern affairs before, nor was he a military strategist, but he took with him a team of military advisers under Colonel George Pomeroy Colley, one of Garnet Wolseley's protégés, who had studied the recent Franco-Prussian War and was convinced that a British battalion armed with modern breach-loading rifles could march the length and breadth of Afghanistan without let or hindrance. Colley had some justification for his other view that the Indian military establishment had to be cut free from the psychological shackles of its experience in the First Afghan War, fought when many of its senior officers had been impressionable subalterns. Lytton referred to the Indian Army commanders as 'the powers of military darkness'.

Lytton opened negotiations with Sher Ali's representatives at Peshawar early in 1877, but failed to overcome their objections to the establishment of a British agent in Kabul. No amount of economic aid would persuade them to change their minds for two valid reasons. If they accepted a British embassy, they would have no excuse for rejecting a Russian delegation; and they could not guarantee that some bigoted tribesman with ever fresh memories of the assassinations of Burnes and Macnaghten would not murder a newcomer and bring down the wrath of the British Raj on their heads – a premonition that came all too true. Lytton broke off negotiations just before the Russians crossed the Danube in June 1877.

There was little love lost between Lytton and the old India hands – civilian and military – on his Council. Whereas Auckland had been weak but well meaning, Lytton was dogmatically determined to energise the torpid Indian Government into implementing his forward policy. He clashed straight away with the able and experienced Commander-in-Chief, General Sir Frederick Haines, over the size of force that would be needed if Sher Ali had to be compelled to accept British agents. Advised by Colley, Lytton accused the military of over-insuring and draining the Indian revenues at a time when every rupee was needed for famine relief after the recent calamitous crop failures in Southern and Western India.

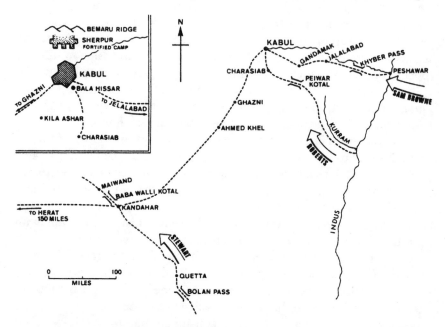

Map 12: The Second Afghan War: 1878–81

Lytton's relations with Disraeli's Cabinet, most of whom felt that his appointment was a grave error of judgement, were no better. They saw him as a forward policy extremist, who could lead India into another costly and quite unnecessary Afghan war unless he was held on a tight rein. For his part, Lytton viewed Whitehall, and particularly the dilatory Lord Cranbourn, Secretary of State for India, as lacking in resolution. He did not endear himself to the Cabinet by acting precipitately on several occasions without allowing time for proper considerations of his proposals.

The one thing that Lytton dreaded most was failure to establish his forward policy before his tenure as Viceroy came to an end. Obtusely, he ignored the import of Disraeli's words, when arriving back in triumph from the Congress of Berlin in July 1878, he declared, as Neville Chamberlain was to do after Munich in 1938, that he had 'secured peace for our time'. The Cabinet could but look askance when Lytton reported that Count Stolietov's mission was approaching Kabul. They feared that he was intent on leading them into war in Central Asia at a time when the Eastern Question had been taken off the boil by the Treaty of Berlin.

The Cabinet's fears were realised: Lytton was soon reporting that Count Stolietov's mission had reached Kabul on 22 July and had been well received by Sher Ali. He insisted that this affront could not be allowed to pass un-challenged and proposed to dispatch a strongly escorted mission to Kabul and to demand the expulsion of the Russians from this area of British interest. The mission, which was only to turn back if opposed by force, was to be led by General Sir Neville Chamberlain, who had become a friend of Sher Ali after being wounded and taken prisoner during the retreat to Jalalabad in 1842. His 'political' was to be Major Pierre Louis Napoleon Cavignari, a direct descendant of the great Napoleon.

Unbeknown to London or Delhi, Stolietov had already been recalled by St Petersburg on the signing of the Treaty of Berlin, and had departed from Kabul for Tashkent on 24 August, leaving some of his staff behind to look after Russian interests. The Tsar had no wish to alienate Britain in the face of the growing power of Bismarck's Germany. Lytton, like Auckland in 1838, had lost his *casus belli*, but unlike Auckland, who had been too weak to stop the momentum of military preparations, Lytton drove on despite strong military opposition to his plans. The Chamberlain Mission was assembled at Peshawar in September 1878.

Cavignari, a man with the self-confidence of his great forebear, rode ahead of the mission, entering the Khyber Pass on 21 September. He was met by the local Afghan commander, Faiz Mohamed, who refused to allow the mission through the pass. When asked by Cavignari the straight question of whether he intended to oppose the mission by force or not, Faiz Mohamed replied in the affirmative, saying that Cavignari was lucky not to have been fired on for crossing the Afghan border without authority.

Disraeli was furious with Lytton when this rebuff was reported to London, because by then it was known that Count Stolietov had been withdrawn in response to British diplomatic pressure. British prestige in Afghanistan had been jeopardised quite needlessly. Lytton was instructed to find out whether Faiz Mohamed had acted under Sher Ali's instructions or on his own initiative. In the meantime, he was authorised to assemble forces ready to cross the frontier if the Amir continued to refuse British demands.

On 19 October, Lytton received what he wanted: an insolent reply from Sher Ali, which enabled him to ask London for a declaration of war. Despite the fury of several members of Disraeli's Cabinet, who saw Lytton's action as an attempt to dictate British foreign policy from Delhi, he was authorised to present an ultimatum to the Amir, demanding an apology and acceptance of the Chamberlain Mission. A reply was required by 21 November. None came; so General Haines was authorised to put his plans for the military coercion of Sher Ali into effect.

There was none of Auckland's and Macnaghten's 'military promenade' nonsense about Haines's entry into Afghanistan at the end of November 1878. Instead of the two divisions, which had been deployed to back up Shah Shuja's motley forces in 1838, Haines had assembled five divisions, armed with the latest rifles and guns, to deal with Sher Ali. All the troops were drawn from the Bengal Army and organised into three separate field forces. Lieutenant General Donald Stewart concentrated two divisions at Quetta and advanced on Kandahar; Lieutenant General Sir Samuel Browne, the inventor of the Sam Browne belt, worn by officers of the British Commonwealth armies to this day, assembled two more at Peshawar for an advance through the Khyber to Jalalabad to threaten Kabul from the east; and in between was Major General Frederick Roberts VC – 'Bobs' to his friends and eventually to the British public at large – with one well trained and hard hitting division, which was to penetrate the Kurram valley, outflanking the Khyber and approaching Kabul from the south-east.

Stewart received a bad press for his logistic arrangements but otherwise met little opposition and entered Kandahar unopposed on 8 January. Sam Browne's operations also came in for criticism, particularly from Lytton who considered that he should have been court-martialled. He followed Pollock's successful 1842 tactic of seizing the high ground, on either side of the Afghans' main blocking position in the pass, which he intended to attack when the out-flanking forces had unsettled its defenders. Unfortunately, the two brigades sent to scale the flanking heights lost their way and did not appear for 48 hours. In the meantime, Sam Browne had badly mishandled the advance up the pass itself and received what is best described as 'a bloody nose' from Faiz Mohamed's 4,000 Afghans holding the pass. Next day, the tables were turned as the flanking brigades reached their intended positions, and Faiz Mohamed beat a hasty retreat before he could be cut off. Sam Browne, like Stewart, entered his objective, Jalalabad, unopposed on 20 December.

Only Roberts, a small, dynamic Gunner officer, who had won his VC during the Indian Mutiny and was a close friend of Lytton's, avoided criticism. His advance up the Kurram drove the Afghan defenders under Karim Khan back to a strong defensive position on the Peiwar Kotal, a saddle between the hills at the head of the valley, barring the route to Kabul. Leaving only a small force to guard his camp and to demonstrate frontally in the valley, Roberts led the rest of his division, not without considerable navigational difficulties, in an out-flanking march up and along pine covered ridges during the bitterly cold night of 1 December with snow on the ground. Progress was slow next day as he methodically cleared the Afghan positions along the ridges flanking their main position.

He camped at dusk for another cold night without cover in the snow at 9,000 feet, unaware that his force in the valley below had managed to reach a point where its gunners could see the Afghan camp behind the Kotal. Two mountain guns were man-handled up the hillside to within range, and the surprise arrival of their shells created such panic in the camp that the Afghan defence of the Kotal collapsed. Roberts was left master of the gateway into central Afghanistan at a cost of less than 100 casualties.

Soon after these British operations began, Sher Ali turned to the Russians. Kaufman could do little to help. With the full extremes of winter approaching, his columns could not reach the Oxus in time to intervene effectively, even if St Petersburg authorised him to do so, which was most unlikely. Accepting defeat, the Amir abdicated in favour of his son, Yakub Khan, and set off for Tashkent with the residue of Stolietov's mission. Broken in body and mind, he died deserted and unlamented in February 1879.

Lytton was uncertain how to exploit the situation. A British force had just been massacred by Zulu warriors at Isandlawana, so it was not a time to take further military risks by advancing on Kabul. Yakub Khan, however, came to his help by offering to negotiate a new Anglo-Afghan treaty. It took Cavignari, who was entrusted with the task, four months to win all that Lytton could reasonably expect. In the Treaty of Gandamak, signed on 22 May 1879, the new Amir accepted British control of his foreign policy with an embassy in Kabul and the right to establish political agents in frontier districts. In return the Government of India would provide money and arms if the Amir faced unprovoked aggression. Jalalabad would be returned to Afghanistan, but the Kurram, the Khyber Pass, and Afghan enclaves around Quetta and the Bolan Pass would be 'assigned' to the Indian Government with local administration left in Afghan hands. Cavignari was knighted and appointed British Envoy Extraordinary and Minister Plenipotentiary to the court of the Amir. He and his staff with a 75 strong escort from the élite Corps of Guides of the Punjab Frontier Force under Lieutenant Walter Hamilton VC reached Kabul in July and set up the British Embassy in the Bala Hissar. Roberts, whose father had commanded Shah Shuja's troops in 1839–40, and knew something of the Afghan view of European envoys, did not rate Cavignari's chances of survival very high.

Yakub Khan's assumption of the Amirate did not go unchallenged. Several regular Afghan regiments from Herat arrived in Kabul, claiming that they had not been defeated by the British and demanding three months arrears of pay owed to them by Sher Ali before his abdication. There were intelligence warnings that anti-British trouble was brewing, but Cavignari, like Burnes and Macnaghten before him, refused to take them seriously, putting his trust in Yakub Khan, whom he reported to

Lytton was proving a reliable ally. He sadly underestimated the Afghan people's rabid hatred of Europeans. His last telegram to Lytton dated 2 September reported all was well, but next day Sher Ali's refusal to accept a British embassy because he could not guarantee its safety was proved to be fully justified.

On 3 September the disaffected regiments marched into the Bala Hissar, demanding to be paid by the Afghan Treasury. Only one month's pay was available in its coffers, and so the troops turned on the nearby British Embassy, shouting that the British should pay them the balance since they now ran the country. Cavignari, like Burnes and Macnaghten, tried to reason with them from the Embassy balcony, but with just as little success. The Afghan Commander-in-Chief arrived to sort out the trouble, but was unhorsed and trampled underfoot by his own troops, who by then had been joined by the city mob. Cannon were hauled into position and the Embassy was stormed. Cavignari was one of the first to fall, shot through the head while firing a rifle from the roof. The rest of the staff and the escort were eventually cut down after an epic, but hopeless, fight for survival. The last man to die was Jemadar Jewand Singh, who cut down eight of his assailants before he was killed.

Lytton and Roberts were at Simla when the news of Cavignari's murder arrived in the early hours of 5 September. The Viceroy's Council met at dawn. Lytton bared his teeth, and acted with a terrible avenging energy. All withdrawals from Afghanistan agreed in the Treaty of Gandamak were stopped. Unfortunately the withdrawal programmes of Sam Browne's and Stewart's field forces from Jalalabad and Kandahar were already in progress, but Robert's force in the Kurram, which was not being given up under the Treaty, was still available. Roberts was quickly appointed to command a punitive force, the Kabul Field Force, drawn from his own Kurram Field Force and reinforced from India to a strength of 7,000, comprising four regiments of cavalry, and three British and four Indian infantry battalions, together with supporting artillery and engineers.

In public proclamations it was announced that Roberts was marching speedily to Kabul in support of the Amir, who had lost control of his mutinous troops; but in private letters to Roberts, Lytton made it quite clear that swift retribution was to be his main task. The people of Kabul were to be disarmed; those implicated in Cavignari's murder were to be executed promptly with minimal judicial procedure; and the Afghans were to be taught to respect the power of the Queen Empress. Speed was to be the essence of Roberts' advance on Kabul and of his vengeance, Lytton's letters containing two oft quoted lines:

Your object should be to strike terror, and strike it swiftly and deeply; but to avoid a 'Reign of Terror' . . .

There are some things which a Viceroy can approve and defend when they have been done, but which a Governor-General in Council cannot order to be done.[6]

Roberts left the Kurram in the last week of September. Afghan opposition was unco-ordinated and sporadic because Yakub Khan's position as Amir was too insecure for him to dominate the Sirdars, and he himself was uncertain whether to throw in his lot with the British or fight them. Much to Roberts' embarrassment, he chose the former and arrived in Roberts' camp with his son, a number of Kabul Sirdars and the Afghan Commander-in-Chief just as the Field Force was approaching the heights of Charasiab, the last strong defensive position before Kabul. Yakub pleaded to be allowed to deal with the Herat mutineers without the British actually occupying Kabul. Roberts, however, already had evidence of Yakub's duplicity and probable connivance in Cavignari's murder. Cavalry reports showed that some 13 Afghan regular regiments were taking up positions on the Charasiab heights from which to oppose the British advance. Holding the Amir in his camp ostensibly as an honoured guest in whose support he was operating, Roberts launched one of his well organised flank attacks on the heights. By that evening, 6 October, the Afghans were in full flight leaving 20 guns and several hundred dead behind them. Roberts had less than 100 casualties. Two days later he entered Kabul unopposed.

When Yakub Khan returned to Kabul in Roberts' train, he found his position intolerable and untenable. He had been accused by the Sirdars of letting the British in originally by signing the Treaty of Gandamak, and now he had returned to Kabul as their puppet. A fickle and devious man, he abdicated on 12 October, the day before the victory parade mounted in his honour, telling Roberts that he detested the Afghan people. Roberts was forced to impose British military government on the city, and Lytton was left with the task of finding a new and reliable Amir, who would be strong enough to hold Afghanistan together and maintain the required treaty relationship with British India.

Roberts' first task was to avenge Cavignari. He imposed punitive penalties for the carriage of arms and hostile acts in and around Kabul, and had gallows erected in front of the blackened ruins of the British Embassy, where the remains of Cavignari's slaughtered entourage and escort were found lying unburied when the Bala Hissar was re-entered. 87 Afghans, rightly or wrongly judged by summary courts martial to have been implicated in their murder, were hanged, including the Mayor of Kabul. By sabotage or accident the Bala Hissar powder magazine exploded, causing a number of British casualties. Roberts ordered the whole fortress complex to be razed to the ground, and set up his base camp in the Sherpur cantonment, which Sher Ali had built on the site of Elphinstone's old camp, north-east of the city, backing onto the steep Bemaru ridge. It was larger than Elphinstone's camp, but, unlike his, it was well fortified on its three open sides, and Roberts saw to its stocking with large reserves of ammunition, food and fodder. He also ordered all the surrendered Afghan artillery to be dragged within its walls – a precaution that was to pay a handsome dividend later. The camp's only weakness was the extent of its walls, which were longer than his 6,000 soldiers could man effectively. Successful defence would depend on the speed with which reserves could be moved to threatened points.

The deterrent effect of Roberts' draconian military rule in Kabul did not last long. The mullahs were soon preaching *jihad* against the infidel invaders. Early in December, three large groups of tribesmen were reported converging on Kabul. Roberts decided to check and defeat each in detail in true Napoleonic style, but he grossly underestimated their strength and speed of movement. Due to a series of misunderstandings, a cavalry force under Brigadier Dunham Massy rode into a vastly superior Afghan force near the village of Kila Ashar, some five miles north-west of Kabul. Roberts managed to extricate it, but was himself attacked by a village headman and only saved by the timely intervention of an unhorsed trooper of the 1st Bengal Lancers.

Although the débâcle at Kila Ashar was a minor reverse in military terms, the news of this Afghan success spread quickly and grew with the telling. The tribal leaders hoped that 1841/42 could be repeated: winter was approaching; a new national uprising was taking place; the British had shown that despite their modern Martini-Henry rifles they were not invincible; and the expectation of loot was all compelling. But Roberts was no Elphinstone, and his troops were far from demoralised. Fighting a series of successful spoiling actions, he withdrew into the Sherpur defences, which his Sappers had been working, night and day, to strengthen. Law and order collapsed in Kabul, and the city was looted by the apparently victorious tribesmen.

If the Afghan tribes had possessed any real unity of purpose other than the common desire for easy loot, Roberts would have been in difficulties. As in December 1841, their leaders offered him outrageous terms for an unopposed withdrawal to India, but such a course of action did not enter Roberts' calculations: on the contrary, he intended to draw the Afghans into attacking him at Sherpur where his firepower and their lack of artillery should be decisive.

One stroke of luck did come Roberts's way. A spy gave him the plan and timing of the Afghan assault, which was delivered just before dawn on 23 December. The British and Indian infantry and gunners were standing-to with weapons ready, and with reserves poised to reinforce the threatened sector, when the sword wielding, yelling tribesmen rushed forward in their masses to fling themselves against the fortifications. Roberts had some anxious moments, but it was, in fact, a massacre. Colonel Colley's dictum about the power of modern European weapons against fanatical tribesmen was amply proven. As the tribal rushes faltered and died away, Roberts' cavalry completed the dispersal of the Afghan survivors. Over a thousand tribesmen lay dead in front of the defences: Roberts had lost only five killed and 27 wounded.

Next day, reinforcements, which Roberts had summoned from Jalalabad reached him, and Kabul was reoccupied on Christmas Day 1879: there was no repeat of 1841–42. The Afghan leaders made their escape and the tribesmen dispersed disconsolately back to their villages, vowing to return in the spring. In the meantime Lytton still had to find a new and amenable Amir so that he could re-start the withdrawal of British and Indian troops from Afghanistan and relieve the strain on the Indian revenues.

The only man likely to be able to rule Afghanistan effectively was Sirdar Abdhur Rahman, a nephew of Sher Ali. Unfortunately, he had been a pensioner of the Russians in Tashkent for the last 12 years, but he had a burning desire to regain the Amirate, which his father had once held for a short time in 1866. With Afghanistan apparently disintegrating, the Russians sent him back with a supply of cash and arms to reclaim his inheritance. By March 1880, he was rallying the northern Afghan tribes to his banner and had made it known that he was willing to negotiate with the British to regain the throne of Kabul for his family.

Lytton took what has been described by his biographer as 'the greatest leap in the dark on record'.[7] He agreed to negotiate, while General Haines took steps to strengthen the British hold on strategically important positions in Afghanistan. He sent up a Bombay division under Lieutenant General Primrose to relieve Stewart at Kandahar so that the latter could march his Bengal division to reinforce Roberts at Kabul. The move was complicated by Stewart being senior to Roberts, who felt slighted, and by gossips suggesting that Roberts was being superseded because of the Liberal press outcry in England about his reported brutality in Kabul when avenging Cavignari. Stewart, like Keane 40 years earlier, had to fight his way from Kandahar to Kabul, which he reached at the end of April 1880, having fought and won the battle of Ahmed Khel south of Ghazni, which was one of those 'close run things'. He took over supreme political and military command from Roberts, but tactfully left 'Bobs' as commander of the Field Force.

Far away in London, Disraeli was ousted from office by Gladstone; Lytton resigned and was replaced as Viceroy by Lord Ripon; the 'forward policy' was stalled, but events in Afghanistan stopped 'masterly inactivity' re-asserting itself. Ripon wanted to break off talks with Abdhur Rahman, but the very fact that the Sirdar was negotiating with the British had increased his standing amongst the tribal leaders; and it was suspected that he was planning to lead another *Jihad*, if he did not win British support. On Stewart's advice, Ripon also took a calculated risk of offering him terms in June 1880. The Treaty of Gandamak was to be re-confirmed, but instead of a British embassy returning to Kabul, the Government of India would be content to be represented in the capital by a Vakil – an Afghan national in British service. On 22 July, Abdhur Rahman was declared Amir at a formal durbar in Kabul and British plans for total withdrawal were announced. No troops would be left to help the new Amir secure his throne as had been done in the days of Shah Shuja with such dire results.

The British proclamation of Abdhur Rahman as Amir was not welcome in Western Afghanistan, where the ruler of Herat, Ayub Khan, was one of his bitterest rivals. It was not long before intelligence reached Primrose in Kandahar that Ayub was massing a force to march on Kabul via Kandahar and Ghazni. Primrose, like Roberts when he first entered Kabul, under-estimated the strength of Ayub's army, which contained several regiments of the former Afghan regular Army. He sent out too weak a brigade under Brigadier General Burrows to check Ayub's advance in case he tried to slip past Kandahar and made straight for Ghazni. He paid a terrible price for his mistake. The 66th of Foot (later the Berkshires) with two Bombay battalions and two Bombay cavalry regiments with six Royal Horse Artillery guns, some 2,000 bayonets and 500 sabres – were overwhelmed by 8,000 Afghan regulars, 3,000 irregular horse and 15,000 tribesmen at Maiwand on 21 July. It was one of those epic Victorian battles in which the attack by the Afghan regulars was successfully repulsed, but sheer weight of numbers told as the tribesmen closed around the flanks. The Afghans lost over 5,000 dead, but half Burrows's force was massacred and the rest struggled back to Kandahar as best they could.

Primrose panicked; abandoned his cantonment and withdrew within the walls of Kandahar, expelling all the inhabitants; and tamely accepted siege by Ayub's triumphant followers. The news of Maiwand caused consternation in Delhi and a national outcry in London, but Haines kept his head. He dispatched reinforcements from Bombay, and to speed Primrose's relief he directed Stewart to revise the Kabul garrison's withdrawal plans in order to march a powerful striking force back to India via Kandahar instead of through the Khyber. This plan would have the added advantage of blocking any attempt by Ayub Khan to thrust for Kabul to unseat Abdhur Rahman.

Stewart generously gave command of the striking force to Roberts, while he himself organised the final stages of the withdrawal of the rest of the Kabul garrison back to India through the Khyber. Roberts picked a veteran force of three British and nine Indian infantry battalions with three Indian cavalry regiments, all of whom had already fought with distinction under his command. Stewart gave him the best pack animals available, but there were only enough horses and mules for three batteries of pack artillery. With whips out, he covered the first 280 miles in 20 days, reaching Ghazni on 15 August. News from Kandahar was re-assuring so he slackened his pace. As he approached the city on 31 August, Ayub abandoned the siege and withdrew to a strong defensive position just to the north on the prominent feature, called the Baba Walli Kotal. Roberts found Primrose and his troops thoroughly demoralised, their only sortie having been a botched and costly affair.

Roberts reconnoitred the Baba Walli Kotal position in force immediately, and when he withdrew to camp that night the Afghans thought they had won another resounding victory. They were soon to regret their jubilation. Next day Roberts again mounted one of his renowned turning movements. Everything went according to plan. Nevertheless, there was severe fighting before Ayub lost control of his army. By dusk he was riding for Herat with the remnants of his cavalry and artillery, leaving the rest of his men to disperse to their villages. Roberts lost 40 killed and 228 wounded; Ayub left over 1,000 dead on the field.

Ripon and Haines wanted to annex Kandahar. It was in a wide healthy plain with abundant food and fodder; it could be supported from Quetta, to which a railway was being built; and it would provide a base from which any further Russian or Persian threats to Herat could be deterred. Gladstone would not hear of it: he had been elected to put an end to imperial adventures. Abdhur Rahman was provided with money and arms to establish his own governor in Kandahar, and Roberts marched back to India, while Stewart carried out the final evacuation of Kabul. Poor Primrose was sent home to England in disgrace. The last British troops left Afghanistan on 4 May 1881.

Lytton's 'great leap in the dark' in opening negotiations with Abdhur Rahman, and Ripon's post-war faith in him, paid off. Ayub Khan tried to re-take Kandahar in September 1881. Abdhur Rahman took the field personally with the main Kabul army to oppose him at Kandahar, while sending a diversionary force towards Herat. He routed Ayub's forces outside Kandahar on 22 September, and when Ayub fled back to Herat again, he found it was already in the hands of Abdhur Rahman's diversionary force. Ayub escaped to Tehran and eventually joined Yakub Khan as a pensioner in British India. Abdhur Rahman went on to rule Afghanistan with a rod of iron. With British political and financial help, he countered every Russian move to annex Afghan territory with one important exception, which almost led to Britain and Russia going to war over continued Russian annexations in Central Asia.

In 1882 the Russians annexed the last Turcoman province of Merv, presenting a renewed threat to Herat, and hence to India. The alarm bells rang again in London and Delhi, and vigorous British diplomatic protests in St Petersburg resulted in an agreement to set up an Anglo-

Russian Boundary Commission to define the northern Afghan frontier. The Commission did not assemble at the oasis of Sarakhs, where the ill-defined frontiers of Afghanistan, Merv and Persia met, until October 1884. By this time the local Russian commanders had, as ever, pursued their personal ambitions by making ground southwards towards Herat at every opportunity and on a variety of excuses, and had reached the oasis and caravan serai of Pandjeh (*See Map 4*). They claimed that it belonged to Merv: the British were equally certain that it was in Afghan territory. The Russians refused to start work with the Commission until their claim to Pandjeh was resolved. This they achieved by goading the Afghan troops in Pandjeh to attack them. Using this minor incident as an excuse, they took the place, slaughtering the garrison and the inhabitants in the process.

The crisis caused by this high-handed piece of local aggression was such that even the American press predicted that Britain and Russia would be at war in a matter of days. Moreover so certain did war seem that the Stationery Office in London printed proclamations ready for a declaration of war; and, as we will see in the next chapter, the crisis halted operations in the Sudan in case reinforcements were needed by the Government of India.

Fortunately, cooler heads in Whitehall and St Petersburg won the day. The Tsar could not afford to lose British support in Europe, and Gladstone was determined to avoid adding to British imperial commitments. Both sides drew back and the Boundary Commission started its work, which dragged on until 1887. Pandjeh was left in Russian hands in exchange for other pieces of territory that the Government of India considered strategically more important to the defence of Afghanistan.

It remained to resolve the line of the north-eastern frontiers of Afghanistan with China and India in the Pamirs. The acceptance of the Pamir Boundary Commission recommendations in 1895 brought the Great Game to its close as the frontiers between the Russian and British Empires were settled and the German threat in Europe became ever more menacing, making collaboration with Britain one of the main planks of Russian foreign policy. Abdhur Rahman, who acted with great statesmanship throughout the last tense years of the Great Game, did not die until 1902. The Amir, whom Lytton had the courage to install, had become a much respected friend of Britain and a ruthless tyrant amongst his own hard people. Rudyard Kipling's poem in *Barrack-Room Ballads*, quoted at the head of this chapter, suggests another kindlier side to his character, but he should be remembered in history as the man who ended the Great Game by giving British India a stable frontier neighbour for the rest of the 19th Century.

CHAPTER 4

SEIZING THE WORLD'S STRATEGIC CROSSROADS

The British Occupation of Egypt and Conquest of the Sudan 1882–1898

Via Suez armies could now sail from Europe to India in a month, altering the whole pattern of imperial defence. The Canal had become, in effect, an extension of India; for the rest of the century the British would think of Suez and India in the same breath . . .

Jan Morris. Heaven's Command.[1]

As the Great Game faded with the successful establishment of the friendly Amir, Abdhur Rahman, on the throne of Afghanistan, the Suez Canal and, *ipso facto*, the defence of Egypt, replaced it as the British and Indian Governments' primary strategic concern in the Moslem world. Three potential threats had to be considered: the possibility – remote though it might be – of a gradual French takeover in the Levant; the ever present danger of a further Russian attempt to take Constantinople and partition the Ottoman Empire; and, most dangerous of all, internal instability in Egypt, which could lead to the Canal's closure.

By the end of the 1870s, it was the last of these threats that alarmed London, Paris and Delhi. Management of the Egyptian national debt through Anglo-French Dual Control pleased the European bankers, but it embittered Khedive Ismail, his pashas, the Islamic religious leaders, the Army and, most dangerous of all, nascent nationalist elements in Egyptian society. Grudging Egyptian co-operation turned into anti-European intrigue, and led to the Porte being compelled by the British and French Governments to replace Ismail with his more pliable son, Tewfik, as Khedive of Egypt in 1879.

Egyptian nationalist sentiment first found effective expression, as it was to do 70 years later, in disaffected middle ranking Army officers under the leadership of Colonel Ahmed Arabi, the forerunner of Colonel Abdul Nasser, Egypt's dictator of the 1950s and 1960s. The two men's backgrounds were very similar. Arabi was the son of a village headman and of fellah stock, who had received a basic education at the al-Azhar University in Cairo before being conscripted into the Egyptian Army. Tall and strongly built, and with a dominating personality, he was commissioned when Sa'id Pasha, Ismail's predecessor, opened up officer recruiting to outstanding fellah boys instead of relying entirely on Turks and Circassians. Sa'id appointed Arabi as one of his ADCs, and he had reached the rank of lieutenant colonel by the time Sa'id died in 1863. Ismail had no time for fellah officers so Arabi languished without further promotion until Tewfik became Khedive and appointed him commander of one of his three Guard regiments quartered in Cairo.

Egypt's finances were improved by retrenchment imposed by the Anglo-French debt commissioners, but at a price. There were savage cuts in the military budget, which Turkish and Circassian officers in the higher command of the Army made sure affected the fellah officers more than themselves. Arabi became the spokesman for his fellah colleagues. On 1 February 1881, he was summoned with the two other Guard colonels to the Army headquarters in the Kasr-el-Nil barracks ostensibly to discuss the ceremonial for the wedding of a royal princess. Suspecting a trap, the three colonels left instructions for their regiments to march on the Army headquarters if they did not return in two hours. As soon as they reached the barracks, they were arrested and taken before a disciplinary tribunal. The tribunal turned into farce when Arabi's men arrived and chased its members out of the court room, throwing their ink-wells after them! The three colonels then marched at the head of their regiments with bands playing to Tewfik's Abdin Palace. With no loyal troops available to protect him, Tewfik was forced to accept Arabi's demands for the dismissal of the War Minister and redress of the fellah officers' grievances. The three colonel's then re-pledged their loyalty to the Khedive. Nevertheless, Tewfik's rule had been seriously weakened and the nationalist challenge to foreign control of the Egyptian Government was correspondingly strengthened. The Anglo-French commissioners obtusely saw the affair as an internal army matter and nothing to do with their administration!

Within seven months Arabi was back at the Abdin Palace at the head of the Guard regiments, demanding the dismissal of the Khedive's cabinet, the convocation of a national assembly and a substantial increase in the military budget. Tewfik again gave way; Arabi became a national hero; the spirit of Egyptian nationalism erupted; and Europeans began to fear for their own safety as unrest was fanned by Moslem zealots. The Commissioners could no longer ignore the threat to European interests.

Gladstone had no wish to intervene, believing that Egyptian internal affairs were the responsibility of the Porte: any military action should be undertaken by Turkish troops. The French Government, with larger investments at stake, pressed for a declaration of the Anglo-French intentions. On 8 January 1882, a joint note was published in Cairo, expressing full Anglo-French support for Tewfik and opposition to any attempt to disrupt the established order. Its immediate effect was to unite all Egyptians against the 90,000 Europeans in their midst. Tewfik was seen as a puppet of the Debt Commission, and Arabi, promoted Minister for War, as the man who would get rid of the hated Dual Control.

Anglo-French diplomatic pressure in Constantinople failed to persuade the Porte to act, and so Gladstone, despite his deep involvement in the Irish problem at the time, was forced to go along with French proposals to send warships to overawe the Egyptian Government, which was under Arabi's control in all but name. On 20 May, British and French naval squadrons, under the overall command of Admiral Sir Beauchamp Seymour, anchored off Alexandria, posing a threat of military intervention if European lives and interests were endangered. The Commissioners demanded the dismissal of Arabi and when the Khedive agreed, the whole of his cabinet resigned. He could then find no one willing to form a new government. Arabi had to be reinstated, and Tewfik took the precaution of moving his court to Alexandria in case he had to ask Seymour for asylum.

On 11 June nationalist inspired riots broke out between Moslems and Christians in Alexandria during which some fifty Europeans were killed. Seymour did not have enough Marines embarked in his ships to intervene effectively. European businesses started to close and their owners to leave Egypt in growing numbers. Lights burned late in the War Office and Admiralty in Whitehall as contingency plans were drawn up for intervention if the situation worsened and the Suez Canal traffic was disrupted.

On 3 July, General Sir Garnet Wolseley, the Adjutant General, who was responsible for operational planning in those days, presented outline plans to Gladstone's cabinet. An advance force of two battalions under Major General Sir Archibald Alison would leave Malta for Cyprus on 8 July to provide Seymour with a landing force if he needed one. An expeditionary force of two divisions and a cavalry brigade from England and the Mediterranean garrisons (24,000 men), and a third division from India (8,000 men), all under his own command, were to secure the Canal by landing at either end, and then advance on Cairo. Reservists would have to be called out to provide medical, transport and logistic support for the force, which was worked out in meticulous detail by Wolseley's highly professional team.

Soon after the Alexandria riots, the Egyptians were observed by Seymour's fleet to be strengthening the city's seaward defences. A young Royal Engineer officer, Horatio Herbert Kitchener, with whom Egypt and Britain were to become all too familiar in the years to come, was landed secretly, disguised as a Levantine trader, to reconnoitre the fortifications. He reported that there were 180 guns in battery positions, which stretched for some four and a half miles on either side of the city.

Seymour, with British and French Government authority, lodged a strongly worded protest with the Egyptian Governor of Alexandria, who agreed to stop work. The searchlights of Seymour's ships, however, soon revealed that work was still going on by night. Faced with this duplicity, Seymour issued, entirely on his own authority, an ultimatum, demanding not only the cessation of work but also the surrender of all the Egyptian batteries, on the grounds that they threatened the Allied fleet. His ultimatum was ill-timed because he issued it before Alison's battalions had arrived from Cyprus to help enforce its terms.

Chauvinistic as ever, the French refused to take any part in Seymour's military action, believing that their interests throughout the Levant would be jeopardised for no sufficiently good reason. Before Seymour's ultimatum expired, the French squadron sailed off, leaving the British to bear the brunt of Egyptian and perhaps international opprobrium.

Seymour was left with eight iron-clad battleships and eleven gunboats to destroy the Egyptian batteries, but with no troops, other than his ships' marines, to occupy them or to quell any trouble in the city that the bombardment might provoke. Fire was opened soon after first light on 11 July. It took until 4.30 pm to silence all the Egyptian guns, many of which were bravely served, but scored few hits on the ships. As was to be expected at a time of rapidly advancing naval technology, there were British equipment failures: the latest fire control equipment proved unworkable in action; some new types of shell were found to be faulty; and there were ship design weaknesses revealed by the bombardment. Thus, quite fortuitously, the Admiralty was warned in time to be able to correct these faults before the Anglo-German naval armaments race began at the turn of the century.

Arabi, who had taken charge of Alexandria's defence at the last moment, ordered the abandonment of the batteries that evening and withdrew his troops to a defensive position some 14 miles south-east of the city, blocking the road and railway to Cairo. Alexandria was left to the mercy of the mob, which was soon looting and burning European property. It was three days before Seymour decided that he must intervene ashore and landed an ad hoc force of seamen and marines to fight the fires and restore some semblance of order. It was another three days before Alison's two battalions – the 1st South Staffords and the 3rd 60th Rifles – arrived to relieve the exhausted naval landing parties and to probe Arabi's defensive position.

Seymour's un-authorised action made a full scale British military invasion of Egypt almost inevitable. With the Fleet committed and Alison's troops ashore, the majority of the Cabinet sided with Wolseley against Gladstone, who sought, as Anthony Eden was to do three-quarters of a century later, to limit operations to securing the Canal. Wolseley insisted that the political objective should be the occupation of Cairo with the aim of toppling Arabi and restoring Ottoman rule.

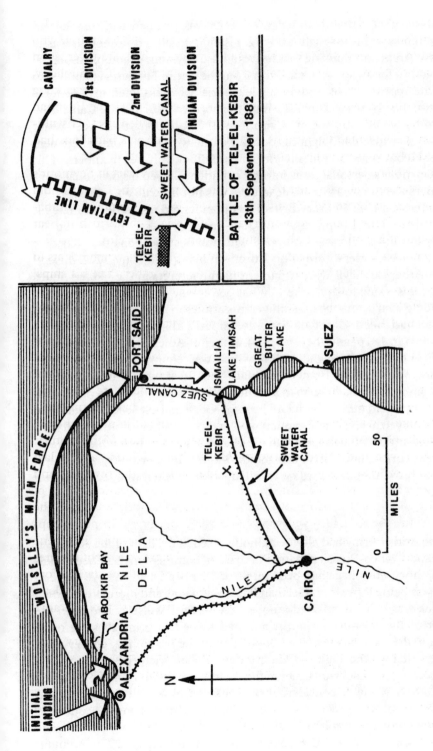

BATTLE OF TEL-EL-KEBIR
13th September 1882

CAVALRY
1st DIVISION
2nd DIVISION
SWEET WATER CANAL
INDIAN DIVISION
EGYPTIAN LINE
TEL-EL-KEBIR

WOLSELEY'S MAIN FORCE
INITIAL LANDING
ALEXANDRIA
ABOUKIR BAY
NILE DELTA
PORT SAID
SUEZ CANAL
ISMAILIA
LAKE TIMSAH
GREAT BITTER LAKE
SUEZ
TEL-EL-KEBIR
×
SWEET WATER CANAL
CAIRO
NILE
NILE
N
MILES
0
50

Map 13: The Occupation of Egypt

Wolseley's Egyptian campaign of 1882 was planned with meticulous care, thanks to his foresight and organisational skill. His intention was to deceive Arabi into thinking that he would use Seymour's foothold ashore at Alexandria for an advance on Cairo from the north. His actual plan was to give the appearance of landing at Alexandria, while his main striking force was switched by sea to Ismailia within the northern reach of the Canal from which he would advance on Cairo from the east along the Sweet Water Canal. He expected to fight his decisive battle with Arabi somewhere near Tel-el-Kebir, some 50 miles from Cairo. He took only key members of his and Seymour's personal staffs into his confidence. Even his divisional commanders were unaware that Alexandria was not his true objective.

For once a 19th Century British commander did not underestimate his opponent. The Egyptian Army had recently been modernised on European lines, and was equipped with the best weapons that Khedive Ismail's lavish expenditure of his European loans could buy. With the end of the American Civil War, armament manufacturers in the United States had been seeking fresh markets. What better way of selling weapons than providing instructors to train indigenous armies in their use? An American officer had been Chief of Staff to Ismail's disastrous campaign in Abyssinia in 1876; and there were a number of American instructors with the Egyptian Army in the 1880s, which was equipped with American Remington rifles. The Franco-Prussian War had also made its impact: the Egyptian artillery had German instructors and was equipped with the latest Krupps field guns, which had become German best sellers around the world. Nevertheless, the Egyptian soldiers were still conscripted fellahin, who had little stomach for a real fight, and who were treated atrociously by their Turkish and Circassian senior officers. In later years, the fellahin were to prove themselves to be excellent soldiers when well led by British officers.

* * *

The British Army had also been modernised in the light of the American Civil and Franco-Prussian wars. Purchase of commissions had been abolished; the Staff College had been set up at Camberley; an embryo General Staff was being formed on German lines; and a new and more professional outlook was being inculcated amongst its officers. Wolseley had been the leader of the pressure group, which had helped to bring these reforms about in the face of determined opposition of the reactionary conservative officers, led by the Duke of Cambridge, Queen Victoria's cousin, who had been Commander-in-Chief of the Army since 1856. Both men loathed each other, Wolseley considering the Duke an obstacle to progress; and Cambridge believing Wolseley to be disloyal, overbearing and bumptious to a degree. Wolseley's military successes, and hence public popularity, were greater than even a royal Commander-in-Chief could ignore. The Adjutant

General had been proved right so often that the expression 'it's all Sir Garnet' entered Victorian phraseology. Given command of the Egyptian Expeditionary Force, Sir Garnet was to live up to his reputation for efficiency and sound military judgement.

The first transports left English ports on 23 July 1882. Seymour was instructed to sail warships into the Canal to secure it from Port Said to Ismailia, ostensibly to prevent Arabi blocking it as Nasser was to do in 1956. Alison at Alexandria, who had been reinforced from Mediterranean garrisons, was to probe Arabi's position south of the city with a series of reconnaissances in force to draw Egyptian reinforcements towards Alexandria. The battleship *Orion* anchored off Ismailia on 27 July and several of Seymour's ships were stationed at Port Said to prepare for the main landing. On 12 August, Wolseley arrived off Alexandria with his 1st Division, which included the 1st Guards Brigade under the Queen's third son, the Duke of Connaught, whose presence Wolseley deemed it politic to accept although he must have had doubts about Connaught's physical stamina and professional abilities.

The 1st Division's disembarkation at Alexandria was given full coverage by the world press. Its officers and men were as confident as Arabi that the decisive battles would be fought around Alexandria, and the subsequent British advance on Cairo would be along the Alexandria–Cairo railway for which engines and rolling stock were being landed. Wolseley stepped ashore on 15 August to the full pomp and ceremony accorded to the arrival of Commander-in-Chief. He directed Lieutenant General Sir Edward Hamley, who had arrived in command of the 2nd Division and was a quick tempered officer with an international reputation as a military writer, to take charge of the planning of the direct assault on Arabi's position. The 1st Division was re-embarked, and the press and Hamley were told in strictest confidence, it was to outflank Arabi with a landing in Aboukir Bay where Nelson had fought the Battle of the Nile in 1798.

Hamley never forgave Wolseley for deceiving him as well as the press and the rest of the Army. The 1st Division did sail on 18 August, escorted by Seymour's warships, into Aboukir Bay where the gunboats bombarded Egyptian positions on shore. When dusk fell the whole armada slipped quietly away again and arrived next morning at the Port Said entrance to the Canal. The Navy had cleared all merchant shipping from the water way and were ready to control the one-way movement of troopships into Lake Timsah for discharge at Ismailia. Meanwhile, Hamley, back in Alexandria, was about to launch his frontal assault on Arabi's position, when he opened a sealed envelope, left by Wolseley and marked not to be opened until 20 August. To his fury, he found a letter from his Commander-in-Chief telling him that he was not landing at Aboukir but at Ismailia instead; the 2nd Division's assault was to be cancelled despite all his careful planning and rehearsals; it was to be replaced by harassing operations to hold Arabi's troops for as long as possible; and Hamley and his troops would be shipped to Ismailia in time to take part in the advance on Cairo.

The landing at Ismailia was a slow business due to the inadequacy of the jetties, which the Sappers did their best to improve. Ferdinand de Lesseps did not help. He was bitterly opposed to the naval takeover of 'his' Canal and withdrew all Suez Canal Company co-operation. It took three days of intensive effort to land the 1st Division, and a further three weeks to bring the Indian Division up from Suez and the 2nd Division round from Alexandria. During the build-up ashore, the Egyptians blocked the Sweet Water Canal reducing Wolseley's supply of fresh water; and they obstructed the Ismailia–Cairo railway which he intended to use for supplying his advance. He cleared both in a series of infantry and cavalry skirmishes during which the Guards Brigade felt frustrated by several hot, but abortive forced marches in the midday sun without actually coming into action. By 12 September, his leading troops were in touch with the Egyptian main defensive positions, which Arabi was hastily preparing at Tel-el-Kebir, as Wolseley predicted, to block the main road to Cairo.

Wolseley used 12 September for careful reconnaissance of Arabi's positions, which consisted of four miles of continuous earthworks dug by the long-suffering fellahin across the flat desert landscape. They ran northwards from the Tel-el-Kebir bridge over the Sweet Water Canal and had some ten redoubts spaced along the line of earthworks with one advanced redoubt, which the desert mirage prevented the British scouts realising was well ahead of the main enemy line. Wolseley's Intelligence Staff estimated that Arabi had managed to concentrate about 30,000 troops and 60 to 70 guns in his defences, to which the only approach was across a flat, gravelly plain, affording easy marching for infantry, cavalry and guns, but absolutely no cover.

Wolseley decided to surprise Arabi by risking a silent night attack, although no night operations had been practised above brigade level and there was no time for rehearsal. His two divisions were to attack side by side each with one brigade up on a 1,000 yard front and the others in support close behind it. The 1st Division was on the right on the desert flank, and the 2nd Division on the left and nearest to the Sweet Water Canal. The artillery would advance between divisions, ready to drop into action as soon as surprise was lost. The Indian Division would attack Egyptian outworks on the south side of the Sweet Water Canal. The Cavalry Division was to ride round the desert flank once the infantry had broken into the main Egyptian position. Naval detachments manning Gatling machineguns and railway mounted 40 pounder guns were to support the assault once the artillery had opened fire.

The night of 12–13 September was pitch black with no moon when the divisions formed up on the start-line, marked out by the Sappers with white posts. Direction-keeping was entrusted to a naval team under Lieutenant Rawson RN, who successfully used astral navigation. All was ready by 11pm when Wolseley rode round his troops, checking with their commanders that they all knew what he expected of them. At 1.30am the long advance *en masse* began. Direction keeping proved difficult and so, after an hour and a half's marching, a halt was called to correct alignment and to rest the troops before the assault. Quite fortuitously, the movement of the stars drew both leading brigades off their intended centrelines. In consequence, 1st Division's leading brigade under Major General Gerald Graham VC veered towards a weaker section of the Egyptian line; and the 2nd Division's Highland Brigade led by Alison missed the Egyptian advanced redoubt, which would have given the alarm if they had run into it.

Almost complete surprise was achieved when the Egyptian earthworks were reached at 5am just before the dawn started to lift the cover of darkness. The Highlanders – the Black Watch, Gordons, Camerons and Highland Light Infantry – were only 200 yards away when an Egyptian sentry gave the alarm and opened fire; Graham's men – the Royal Marine Light Infantry, Royal Irish Fusiliers, York and Lancasters and Royal Irish Regiment – still had some 700 to go; but both brigades successfully stormed their objectives in the growing light, using cold steel in close quarter fighting to clear ways through the Egyptian defences. It was far from a walk-over, although the fighting lasted for barely an hour: the Egyptian infantry, particularly the Sudanese, resisted with unexpected stoicism. At one point both Alison and Hamley had to rally their shaken men before they could press on into the rear of Arabi's army. It was on Graham's front that Egyptian courage first began to fail as the Cavalry Division, led by Major General Drury Lowe, swept round their northern flank. Their complete collapse came as Graham's brigade, closely supported by the Duke of Connaught's Guards, started to thrust southwards behind the main line of earthworks. By 6am the battle was virtually over both north and south of the Sweet Water Canal, where the Indian Division had been equally successful. An hour later, Wolseley was able to ride onto the Tel-el-Kebir bridge, where the Indian and 2nd Divisions met.

Wolseley's victory, brought about by his extraordinary feat of bringing three divisions, deployed in battle formation, across five miles of desert to attack fixed defences, just as dawn was breaking, was complete. Arabi fled back to Cairo with the remnants of his cavalry while the rest of his demoralised troops were rounded up. Around 2,000 Egyptians had been killed: British casualties were 57 killed and 412 wounded. The Highlanders lost most because they had to assault the stronger sector, and the Guards, much to their chagrin, were barely committed before the Egyptian collapse started. Drury Lowe's cavalry were half way to Cairo by nightfall, and entered the city next day, 14 September. That night Arabi and his second-in-command surrendered their swords to Drury Lowe at the Abbassiyeh Barracks. Arabi and seven of his nationalist colleagues were handed over to the Khedive for trial on the charge of rebellion against the Porte. They were condemned to death but, on the advice of the British Commissioner, Sir Edward Malet, who wished to see no martyrs created, the Khedive commuted their sentence to perpetual exile. They were transported to Ceylon.

Gladstone and his Cabinet had no intention of keeping British troops in Egypt any longer than they were needed to re-establish stability in Egypt and hence the security of the Suez Canal. Gladstone's sincere desire to leave Egypt was, however, matched by a determination of the British establishment not to surrender the dominant position that Britain had acquired at what was already seen as the world's most important strategic crossroads. These two aims – withdrawing British troops from Egypt and yet continuing to dominate the Canal – proved incompatible for the next 70 years. The protection of the Suez Canal was to become the tyrant of British foreign and military policy until 1956.

In January 1883, the British Government sent a note to the Great Powers formally claiming the lead in European control of Egyptian affairs. If this were recognised, and if freedom of navigation through the Suez Canal were guaranteed, Britain would withdraw her troops, except for a small garrison in Alexandria to provide a port of entry if fresh intervention were to become necessary. The other powers made no difficulties about freedom of navigation, but neither France nor Turkey would give Britain a free hand in Egypt. The Cabinet concluded that the troops would have to stay until an Egyptian Government could be established that was stable, efficient and pro-British – not an easy thing to achieve. The man they chose for this crucial quest was Sir Evelyn Baring, later to become Lord Cromer.

Baring was in much the same position as Macnaghten in Kabul in the early 1840s. He too had to find the optimum moment to withdraw British troops, and, like Macnaghten, he never did find it but with less dire consequences. The two men were antitheses and the two situations incomparable. Baring had started his career as a Gunner officer, but through an appointment as ADC to the British High Commissioner at Corfu, he had acquired a taste for diplomacy. This was reinforced when he became Private Secretary to the Viceroy of India, his cousin, Francis Baring, Lord Northbrook. When the Egyptian Debt Commission was set up, he was appointed as one of the first British commissioners, having by then acquired the nickname of 'Overbearing' for his strong minded, clear-headed and unemotional approach. He was promoted British Commissioner General in 1880, but fell out with his French colleague through taking the side of the overtaxed fellahin rather than blindly supporting the European bond-holders. As it was British Government policy to co-operate with the French, Baring was sent back to India as finance member of the Viceroy's Council. In Delhi, he proved himself financially conservative but politically liberal with a keen appreciation of the lot of the Indian peasants. His previous experience in Egypt, and his reputation as a hard but fair man, now made him an obvious choice for the task of bringing good government and stability to Egypt, Britain's primary strategic requirement in the Moslem world.

Baring, again like Macnaghten, was faced with governing indirectly an Islamic state in which nationalist and religious fanaticism could break surface in unpredictable ways, and intrigue and venality were ways of life. There the similarities end: the Egyptian did not possess the ruthless fighting spirit of the hard Afghan tribesmen; and the Nile delta was so well equipped with roads and railways that military control was far easier than in the mountains of the Hindu Kush. The same could not be said of the arid Sudan, which was soon to give the British soldiers as much hard campaigning as Afghanistan had done.

The Debt Commission was still in existence when Baring took over from Wolseley in September 1883, a year after Tel-el-Kebir. With the ending of British military government when Wolseley departed, Baring, as Agent of the occupying power, was *de facto* master of Egypt and *de jure* principal political and financial adviser to Khedive Tewfik, who had returned to power in Cairo after Arabi's defeat. Wolseley had been given the task of re-raising and training the Egyptian Army on British lines to Major General Evelyn Wood, who was made its first Sirdar; and Colonel Valentine Baker was made responsible for reorganising the Gendarmerie. Baring was faced almost immediately with a crisis involving both of these forces, which was to do more to anchor British troops in Egypt than anything else. It was not a recurrence of nationalist unrest in Egypt, but the Mahdi's Islamic fundamentalist rebellion in the Sudan, which deflected Baring from running down the British garrison of Egypt as quickly and prudently as possible.

The Sudan had been conquered by Mehemet Ali in 1820. Since then the Egyptian administration of the territory had become more and more corrupt, administratively inefficient and militarily lax. The slave trade still flourished, although the Porte and the Khedive of Egypt were committed to its abolition: the pickings were too tempting and the area too remote for its abolition to be taken seriously. Khedive Ismail, wishing to disarm European criticism, had appointed Colonel Charles Gordon, Royal Engineers, as Governor of the Sudan in 1874 with a brief to stamp out slavery. Gordon, a religious fanatic and the highly successful leader of Chinese irregular troops during the Boxer risings, was a neurotic officer with intuitive impulses and driving energy, who saw himself as an agent of

God's will. He spent five years curbing but never entirely abolishing corruption, injustice and the slave trade in the Sudan.

After Gordon left the Sudan in 1879, all the old evils of lax Egyptian government returned, but a new Moslem religious leader, just as fanatical as Gordon, emerged in the Southern Sudan, dedicated to freeing the land from Egyptian oppression. Mohamed Ahmed proclaimed himself the long awaited Mahdi, the saviour of his people. Egyptian garrisons were brutally slaughtered as the rebellion spread and his Dervish hordes surged northwards towards Khartoum. Soon after the Battle of Tel-el-Kebir, Tewfik gathered a force of 10,000 from the remnants of Arabi's army and sent them off to check the Mahdi. He gave its command to an aged Turkish pasha with a retired British Indian Army colonel, William Hicks, as his chief of staff. Disaster followed: this untrained and reluctant rabble was surrounded in the Kordofan desert, short of water and food, and was massacred. Hicks and his handful of European officers sold their lives dearly in their last stand against the Mahdi's followers.

Baring saw that the cost of recovering the Sudan was beyond Egypt's debt-ridden resources. He recommended to London that he should be instructed to 'advise' the Khedive that the Sudan should be abandoned until Egypt's economy improved. The pride of Cairo's pashas was outraged by this 'advice'; the Prime Minister resigned and Tewfik protested vigorously. Baring was rocklike in his refusal to vary his advice. Nevertheless, evacuation was easier to prescribe than execute. The Mahdi's forces were lapping around Khartoum, and the surviving Egyptian garrisons and administrative posts were widespread, with many being within the Mahdi's area of influence. An outstanding man was needed to carry out the evacuation with any chance of success. Whitehall recommended Charles Gordon, now a major general, but Baring neither liked nor trusted Gordon, and he also hoped to avoid British entanglement in the Sudan by appointing a forceful Turkish or Circassian commander. None could be found to accept such a thankless task. Baring had no option but to appoint Gordon despite the incongruity of sending a Christian zealot to deal with a Moslem fanatic.

Gordon left London on 18 January 1884, doubtful whether evacuation was either the right or the practicable answer, but determined to do his best with the help of Divine Providence. The prayers of the Queen and all her subjects went with him. They saw him as a Christian knight being sent to rid a heathen land of the curse of slavery even though his brief was to evacuate it.

There were two alternative routes by which Gordon could reach Khartoum, and by which the Egyptians could be evacuated: up the Nile for 850 miles from the railhead at Wadi Halfa; or down the Gulf of Suez to Suakin and across 250 miles of waterless desert to Berber on the Nile. Gordon hoped to use the Suakin route, but was stopped from doing so by a Mahdi-ist rebellion led by a wily old slaver, Osman Digna, amongst the Hadendoa and related tribes around Suakin, whom the British soldiers came to know as 'Fuzzy-Wuzzies'. Gordon used the Nile route while the Egyptian Government tried to deal with Osman Digna. The training of Evelyn Wood's new Egyptian Army was not yet complete, so Valentine Baker was despatched at the end of January 1884 with his Gendarmerie to Suakin where their worthlessness as soldiers was quickly demonstrated when they advanced from the port. Baker was lucky to get back to Suakin alive after his force had been ambushed and dispersed by the Hadendoa.

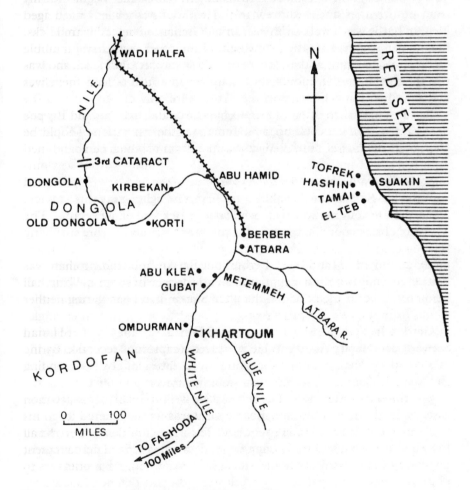

Map 14: The Sudan Campaigns of 1885 and 1898

It was clear to Wolseley, now back in Whitehall, that British troops would have to be used to reopen the Suakin route if the evacuation of the Sudan was to succeed. Baring was drawn down the slippery slope of British intervention by Wolseley's arguments, and agreed to land Marines at Suakin to hold a bridgehead for the arrival of two brigades – one from the garrison of Egypt and the other diverted on its way home to India. Command of the force went to Major General Gerald Graham VC, who had led the 1st Division's assault at Tel-el-Kebir. Graham soon avenged Baker's defeat by inflicting heavy losses on the wild Hadendoa at El Teb on 29 February and at Tamai a fortnight later, but Osman Digna escaped from both battles and withdrew inland without acknowledging defeat. Neither battle was a walk-over. At Tamai, Graham advanced with his two brigades in square formation, one behind the other, with naval manned Gatling machineguns at the corners of each square. A Gatling jammed, as was their wont, in the leading square and let in a rush of fearsome spear and sword wielding Fuzzy-Wuzzies. They were only driven out and the square re-established after desperate hand to hand fighting, and by the timely arrival of the second brigade. Tamai was the inspiration of Kipling's *Barrack-Room Ballad*, 'Fuzzy-Wuzzy', the refrain of which runs:

> So 'ere's to you, Fuzzy-Wuzzy, at your 'ome in the Sudan;
> You're a poor benighted 'eathen but a first class fighting man;
> An 'ere's to you, Fuzzy-Wuzzy, with your 'ayrick 'ead of 'air;
> You big black boundin' beggar – for you broke a British square.[2]

Graham wanted to push on to Berber, but Baring, still trying to limit the British commitment and Egyptian expenditure, insisted on his brigades being returned to Egypt and India after Suakin had been garrisoned by troops from the new Egyptian Army.

Gordon had reached Khartoum on 18 February with Colonel Hamill Stewart, his military Assistant. He was given a rapturous reception by the 50,000 inhabitants, two-thirds of whom were slaves, and by the Egyptian garrison of 6,000 regulars, 3,000 irregular volunteers and the crews of the seven armed river steamers. Those steamers were to be his most precious asset in the defence of the city, moated, as it was, in the junction between the White and Blue Niles. He set about restoring confidence by righting the worst Egyptian abuses: halving taxes; destroying official debt records; improving food distribution and stocking the city with six months' supplies; and setting the garrison to work strengthening defences. He wisely made no attempt to interfere with local slavery. He was, however, too honest for his own survival, making no attempt to disguise the fact that he was in Khartoum to organise the Egyptian evacuation of the Sudan. The wealthier inhabitants – Syrians, Copts, Greeks and Turks – started to re-insure with the Mahdi, whom they saw as the future ruler of the country;

and the Mahdi-ists were given ever greater confidence as they started to invest Khartoum. By mid-March Gordon's Nile link with Egypt was cut by the important town of Berber, 180 miles downstream of Khartoum, joining the Mahdi's cause.

Baring became increasingly anxious about Gordon's safety, but also irritated by the stream of eccentric and contradictory telegrams from Gordon, aimed at blackmailing London into authorising a British relief force, which would lead to the reoccupation of the Sudan and obviate the need to carry on with the evacuation. Baring went as far as recommending the dispatch of a force in the autumn if one could not be provided earlier, but Gladstone was determined not to undertake any more operations from Egypt: the safety of Gordon was the Khedive's responsibility. In his view Gordon had exceeded his brief, and should not have allowed himself to be locked up in Khartoum. Public pressure, the Queen's expression of concern, demands from both sides in the Lords and Commons, and constant nagging by Wolseley, all failed to shift the Prime Minister from his avowed intention not to allow more British blood and treasure to run to waste in the desert sands, fighting a colonial war of conquest against a people struggling for their freedom. By the end of July, the Cabinet split over the issue: Lord Hartington, Secretary of State for War, threatened to resign if a relief force was not dispatched immediately. On 5 August, Parliament voted the money for one – six months had been lost by Gladstone's liberal morality and military myopia.

While final preparations were rushed ahead for Gordon's relief, Gladstone clung to the hope that it would not be needed. He was encouraged by reports that Gordon had inflicted a number of reverses on the Mahdi and even hoped to reopen the river past Berber. Wolseley was given command of the relief force, which he had been preparing on a contingency basis, despite Gladstone's opposition. He chose to use the Nile route, because having commanded the Canadian Red River expedition earlier in his career, he fancied that he knew more about riverine operations than most British officers, which was perhaps true; but also because he considered the severe water problem on the Suakin-Berber route prohibited its use.

Wolseley proposed to organise his force into a river and a desert column. For the former, he had 800 whalers specially built, and he recruited supposedly experienced Canadian boatmen to pilot them. For the latter, he called for volunteers from the Cavalry, Guards and Rifle regiments to form a Camel Corps of four regiments: Heavy (Household Cavalry, Dragoons and Lancers); Light (Hussars); Guards with one company of Royal Marines; and Mounted Infantry (Rifle regiments and others); in all about 2,000 men. While the River column slowly rowed its way up the Nile, the Desert Column would make a quick 200 mile dash across the great bend in the Nile between Korti and Khartoum to rescue Gordon.

The Camel Corps sailed from English ports on 26 September, unkindly referred to as 'London society on camels', there being 15 titled officers in its ranks. The rest of Wolseley's force of 6,000 men was drawn from the Egyptian garrison and given whaler practice with their Canadian pilots, many of whom seemed to know little about river craft, having been recruited with only cursory checks on their declared abilities. His build-up at Wadi Halfa was delayed by the decrepitude of the Egyptian railways; by indifferent staff work by his hastily assembled headquarters; by differences of opinion between his chief of staff, Redvers Buller, and his Naval adviser, the stormy Lord Charles Beresford; and by falling water levels in the Nile, all of which ate up precious time.

The River column, commanded by Major General William Earle, described as an old martinet who kept in touch with his troops and was all for fighting, did not set off until 6 November – three months after Gladstone had authorised the expedition. Gordon was expected to be able to hold out until Christmas, but Wolseley hoped that the arrival of his leading troops, the 1st South Staffords, at Korti would be sufficient to deter the Mahdi from attacking Khartoum. The Desert Column under Major General Sir Herbert Stewart, a dashing cavalry officer of the 3rd Dragoon Guards, who had led the cavalry into Cairo after Tel-el-Kebir and had commanded Graham's mounted troops at Suakin, set off a week later and reached Korti on 14 December, three days ahead of the Staffords. Hearing alarming reports of Gordon's dwindling supplies and continued Mahdi-ist pressure on Khartoum, Wolseley set Stewart off on his dash across the Nile bend, heading for Metemmeh on the Nile 150 miles away and some 80 miles north of Khartoum.

The Camel Corps was an awe-inspiring sight with its men riding in a great square 40 abreast in a cloud of billowing dust. Shortage of wells delayed Stewart because he had first to dump water as far forward as he could safely do so along his route and then advance in two echelons, using the rear echelon camels to ferry forward water before carrying its own fighting men. With him went Lord Charles Beresford with a 57 strong naval detachment to help man Gordon's steamers if they came down river from Khartoum to Metemmeh as Wolseley hoped. The sailors brought with them a five-barrelled Gardner machinegun, capable of 400 rounds per minute, but prone to stoppages like the Gatling.

Stewart was not opposed until he was approaching the wells at Abu Klea, 30 mile from Metemmeh on 16 January. It was too late to attack that night so he decided to do so on foot early next day. For his attack, he formed his force into a large hollow square with his guns, their ammunition camels and Beresford's Gardner gun inside it. As the advancing square approached the wells, some 5,000 Dervishes sprang for the scrub and tried to rush it. A gap developed, which Beresford tried to fill by his sailors manhandling the Gardner into position. It jammed and the naval crew were overrun and slaughtered, Beresford himself having a lucky escape. Desperate hand-to-hand fighting was again necessary to restore the situation and to put the Dervish horde to flight. The whole action lasted barely ten minutes, but over a thousand Dervish dead were left behind, and Stewart had lost 74 killed, including nine officers, and 94 wounded – a heavy loss for a force of 2,000.

One more successful action had to be fought at Gubat before the Nile was reached at Metemmeh on 19 January. Tragically Stewart was badly wounded and the command devolved upon Colonel Sir Charles Wilson, a highly qualified Intelligence officer, but no fighting soldier. There was no sign of Gordon's steamers, and Wilson wasted two days attacking the Mahdi's garrison in Metemmeh instead of riding straight for Khartoum. The steamers did arrive on 21 January and, after a further three days' delay, while Wilson reconnoitred up and downstream for any signs of the Mahdi arriving in force to attack him, the Desert Column set off upriver on the 24th, supported by the steamers. Wilson embarked on one of them, and reached the White and Blue Nile junction on 28 January. There was no Egyptian flag flying over the wreckage of the Governor's palace; the steamer came under fire from both river banks; and flag waving crowds rushed along them proclaiming the Mahdi's victory. Wilson was two days too late. However, Gladstone had wasted five months so it is hardly fair to heap all the blame on the unfortunate Wilson.

Kitchener, who was to avenge Gordon in 1898, was an intelligence officer with the Desert Column and with Wilson on the steamer as it approached Khartoum. He wrote an official report which ended:

> The memorable siege of Khartoum lasted 317 days, and it is not too much to say that such a noble resistance was due to the indomitable resolution and resource of one Englishman. Never was a garrison so nearly rescued, never a commander so sincerely lamented.[3]

Such was the outcry in England that Gladstone was goaded into taking surprisingly robust action. He agreed to the consolidation of the positions reached in the Sudan with three measures: retaking Berber; landing a new force at Suakin; and building a railway from that port to the Nile in anticipation of reconquering the Sudan as soon as it was completed. Wolseley had just begun to implement this directive when all operations were halted abruptly – the Pandjeh incident on the Afghan frontier pointed to imminent war with Russia. Gladstone jumped at the opportunity to end his involvement with the Sudan, which had brought him so much public disfavour and personal anguish. He ordered the total evacuation of the Sudan so that British resources could be concentrated to meet a renewed threat to India – the last spasm of the Great Game.

Negotiation settled the Pandjeh issue and the principal actors in the

Gordon drama left the stage: Gladstone was defeated for the penultimate time in June; the Mahdi died in the same month and was succeeded by an equally charismatic leader, the Khalifa, upon whom the Mahdi imposed his death-bed wish that his movement should be extended to encompass Egypt as well as the Sudan; Wolseley returned to the War Office a disappointed man; and the Khalifa's attempted invasion of Egypt was easily defeated by a small British and Egyptian force at Wadi Halfa in December. Only Baring was at all pleased with the outcome: he could now concentrate on creating a prosperous, contented and well governed Egypt without the financial strain of on-going military operations.

Despite French obstruction in the Debt Commission, Baring brought Egypt's finances into balance, and by 1889 he had achieved a small surplus. He had done much more than that as far as the fellahin were concerned. By spending money on irrigation, he had increased the tillable acreage and hence the revenues to the extent that he was able to reduce the fellah farmers' taxes. Moreover, his partnership with Tewfik and his pashas worked, and his efforts were rewarded in 1892 by his elevation to the peerage as Baron Cromer.

Egyptian politics centred upon three groups: Cromer and his officials; the Khedive and his conservative pashas; and, in between them, a growing body of nationalists and Moslem leaders, bent upon winning independence from the Porte as well as from Britain. The European educated middle class was too small to provide for the needs of commerce and the civil service upon whom Cromer had to depend for the execution of his financial and administrative policies. Against his better judgement, he was forced to allow increasing numbers of British officials to occupy posts in Egyptian ministries. Egypt was fast becoming a British protectorate in all but name.

Cromer's partnership with the Khedive came to an end in 1892 with the death of Tewfik, who was succeeded by his teenage son Abbas. It was not long before nationalist elements were pressing the impressionable young Khedive to get rid of the occupying power, which they could justifiably claim had put their house in order and should be dismissed with genuine thanks. A nationalist delegation, followed by Abbas himself, set off for Constantinople to seek the Porte's help in persuading the British to leave. They were rebuffed: the Sultan had no intention of encouraging nationalist sentiments anywhere within his shaky Ottoman Empire!

Abbas returned to Egypt to vent his spleen on British officials. Cromer temporised, knowing that he might not be supported by British public opinion if he was reported by the liberal press to be bullying the young Khedive. He had to wait until Abbas presented him with a suitable opportunity for a showdown. It came in 1894 when Abbas went to Wadi Halfa to attend a ceremonial parade in his honour, given by his British officered Army. He publicly abused the parade commander, Colonel Kitchener, and his British officers, who had wrought miracles in turning fellahin into reliable soldiers. Cromer's protest was backed by the symbolic diversion of a British battalion, homeward bound from Port Said, to march on Cairo. Abbas ate his bitter words and nationalism went to ground once more.

By this time the British intention to leave Egypt at the earliest possible moment was dying on the vine. Strategic interest in the Dardanelles had been replaced by growing concern for the Suez Canal, which had become vital to British trade with India, the Far East and Australasia. There was also national pride and a sense of Victorian imperial mission fulfilled in Cromer's success in establishing good government in Egypt. But the crucial issue, which swung opinion towards staying indefinitely in Egypt, was the European scramble to partition Africa, which was gathering momentum. The French had established themselves in Tunis, Algeria, Morocco and Senegal, and were making their way across Equatorial Africa to the upper reaches of the Nile; the Italians were established in Eritrea and Libya; and the Germans were seeking their 'place in the sun' in East and West Africa. British strategists did not want to see the French emerging from Equatorial Africa into the Sudan, whence they could threaten the route to India through the Red Sea. British public opinion was equally concerned about reports of the Khalifa's brutality and exploitation of slavery in the Sudan. And young Abbas and his clique were turning covetous eyes on their lost Sudanese province.

These factors would not have been sufficient to persuade Lord Salisbury's Government to direct Cromer to recover the Sudan, using the Egyptian Army, had it not been for the Italian disaster at Adowa in Eritrea (*See Map 1*) in March 1896, where an Italian army had been overrun and slaughtered by the Abyssinians. It was felt in London that this humiliation of a European power would have a knock-on effect and encourage the Khalifa to honour the Mahdi's death-wish by attempting another invasion of Egypt. Neither the Debt Commission nor Cromer wished to finance the reconquest of the Sudan, but nor was Whitehall willing to foot the bill for operations that were for the benefit of Egypt. With great reluctance the Commissioners granted half a million pounds for operations by the Egyptian Army to reoccupy the province of Dongola as a preliminary step to test the Khalifa's powers of resistance and the abilities of the new Egyptian Army.

By this time, Kitchener had been advanced to become head of the Egyptian Army. His appointment as Sirdar was far from popular: his imperious aloofness and cold manner alienated Egyptian society and many of his less gifted military colleagues, but his professionalism, tactical and administrative skill and his dedicated ruthlessness won him the respect of the Egyptian Army. As a fellow Royal Engineer, he had been angered by Gordon's death and had always hoped to be his avenger.

Using the Commissioners' half million pounds to best effect, Kitchener opened his campaign to retake Dongola in September 1896 with his Egyptian and Sudanese battalions, supported by a fleet of vintage 1885 armed steamers and with very little British help. By the 26th his Egyptian troops had confirmed their superiority over the Dervish armies by chasing them out of Dongola and up the Nile as far as Wolseley's old base at Korti. Kitchener wanted to continue upstream to take Berber, but Cromer could not provide the necessary cash from Egyptian revenues, and insisted that Kitchener should seek financial help from Lord Salisbury, who had ordered the reoccupation of the Sudan in the first place. The Sirdar was successful in prising another half million pounds out of the British Government, which he spent on a fleet of more modern gunboats, weapons and, most important of all, railway construction equipment, engines and rolling stock.

The Nile railway had been extended since the Gordon Relief Campaign to within 50 miles of Dongola, but the line did not have the capacity to support the size of force that would be needed to retake Khartoum. Kitchener, therefore, proposed that the Royal Engineers should build a new higher capacity line at minimal cost from Wadi Halfa 250 miles across the desert to Abu Hamid and then a further 100 miles along the Nile to Berber. On New Year's Day 1897, the Sappers started work. Workshops were set up at Wadi Halfa and wells were sunk as far along the proposed alignment as it was safe to do without the protection of a covering force, which was to be provided as the line approached Abu Hamid. Where no water could be found, storage tanks were built to which water was ferried forward on the railway as it was progressed. Once the fellahin labour force had mastered track laying, the railhead advanced about one and a half miles per day.

By 23 July the railhead was half way to Abu Hamid and was becoming vulnerable to Dervish raids. Kitchener dispatched a flying column from Korti, based on the three battalions of Brigadier General Hector Macdonald's Sudanese recruited Brigade and supported by gunboats on the Nile, to surprise the Dervish garrison of Abu Hamid. Macdonald was the son of a highland crofter, who had been commissioned from the ranks during the 2nd Afghan War and had served in the 1st Boer War of 1881 before joining the Egyptian Army. We will be meeting this large, tough highlander again at Omdurman. Marching only by night, he covered the 150 miles in eight days, and then circled round the town to attack it from the rear. Only a few horsemen escaped, and in their flight back to Berber, ran into and panicked Dervish reinforcements on their way to oppose Macdonald. The Khalifa's commander in Berber lost his head and abandoned the town.

The premature evacuation of Berber upset Kitchener's plans because his railhead was not yet far enough forward to support further operations for the time being without undue risk. An advance to occupy Berber straight away could leave him vulnerable to attacks by Osman Digna from the east and by the Khalifa from the south before his build-up in the forward area could be completed. Moreover, he knew that he would need substantial reinforcements from the British Army for his eventual encounter with the Khalifa's main host, thought to number about 50,000 around Khartoum. On the other hand, risky though it might be, rapid action might well demoralise the Dervish commanders and make his subsequent advance on Khartoum all the easier. Much to Kitchener's chagrin, Cromer in Cairo, backed by Salisbury in London, refused to take the risk. He was allowed to occupy Berber, but was then to wait for the completion of the railway.

Kitchener was assailed by two fears, one military and the other personal. He suspected that the Khalifa's commanders would recover their confidence and mass against him before he was reinforced by British troops; but the arrival of those reinforcements could lead to his supersession in command by a more senior general. He might not, in the end, be the man who avenged Gordon.

Cromer understood Kitchener's personal worry and set it to rest by winning War Office agreement to his appointment as Commander-in-Chief of all British and Egyptian troops south of Aswan. The railhead reached Abu Hamid by 1 November and British troops, now all dressed in khaki drill for the first time in the Sudan, were brought forward from Egypt and from other Mediterranean garrisons. They had just been re-equipped with the new Lee-Enfield rifle with its ten round magazine, which doubled their rate of fire; and the unreliable Gatling and Gardner machineguns had been replaced with the Maxim. The Egyptian troops still had to make do with the out-dated Martini-Henry rifles.

In order to cover the concentration of his troops around Berber, Kitchener built an advanced fortified base at Atbara, 20 miles further upriver, at the confluence between the Nile and the Atbara rivers. His flotilla of seven gunboats, commanded by Commander Keppel RN, operated further upstream to give warning of a Dervish approach. In mid-February 1898, the Intelligence staff detected the beginnings of a co-ordinated Dervish plan to envelop and attack Atbara. Osman Digna was to advance eastwards from Suakin, while a 20,000 Dervish force under Mahmud, the Amir of Metemmeh, would come down the Nile from Khartoum. On 14 March, the gunboats began reporting Mahmud's advance, and Kitchener moved 14,000 troops of all arms, including the first British brigade to arrive, forward to Atbara. Mahmud tried to move round the Atbara forts by leaving the Nile some 20 miles to the south of them and cutting across to a ford, called Nakheila, on the Atbara river, where he hoped to be joined by Osman Digna.

Kitchener pre-empted the junction of the two Mahdi-ist forces by marching rapidly up the east bank of the Atbara to the ford. Douglas Haig, the future British Commander-in-Chief in France during the First World War, was commanding one of the Egyptian cavalry squadrons which discovered Mahmud's camp near the ford on 30 March. It was surrounded, as was the practice of both sides by what appeared to be an extensive and dense zariba of thorn branches. There was no sign of Osman Digna, so Kitchener had the opportunity to crush the isolated Mahmud, if he attacked at once. Nevertheless, he hesitated: attacking a well built zariba could result in heavy casualties. Moreover, it was generally considered better tactics to let the Dervishes do the attacking so that the disciplined firepower of the British troops, using their magazine loading rifles and Maxim machineguns, could display their lethality. Kitchener's staff were divided on the issue; and Cromer and Whitehall counselled caution. The health of the newly arrived unacclimatised British brigade, however, settled the issue. It was deteriorating so rapidly in the growing heat of April that an immediate attack was imperative.

Reconnaissances in force on 4 and 7 April enabled Kitchener's commanders to locate the weakest points in the zariba. After dark on 7 April, the Anglo-Egyptian force advanced in four brigade squares, one behind the other, with the British leading. They halted for water and a short rest around midnight, and moved into their assaulting positions with brigade squares in line just before dawn. The British brigade was on the left; Macdonald's Sudanese in the centre; and one of the two Egyptian brigades on the right, the second being held in reserve. The Maxims and artillery were deployed between the squares. The Egyptian cavalry covered the flanks. All told there were 12,000 men, 24 guns, four Maxims and a rocket troop deployed.

The artillery opened the battle with a preliminary bombardment as dawn broke at 6.20am, and then limbered-up to accompany the infantry, who advanced in steady lines, played forward by English fifes and drums, Scottish pipes and Egyptian brass blaring encouragement. Covering fire was provided by section volleys within battalions. When the clash came, the zariba proved less formidable than it looked from a distance and it stopped no one. It was either trampled down or pulled aside by hand. The Dervishes, however, did not give up easily and had to be prised out of their rabbit-warren of entrenchments, most refusing to surrender. The ceasefire was sounded at 8.25am as the troops reached the banks of the Atbara river on the far side of the Dervish camp. Mahmud was a prisoner and 2,000 of his men were dead. Many of his Sudanese, who did surrender, were later enlisted in the Egyptian Army. Only the Dervish horsemen escaped. Kitchener had lost fewer men than he expected: 80 killed and just under 500 wounded. Osman Digna never did reach the battlefield. Instead, he slipped away southwards to join the Khalifa at Khartoum.

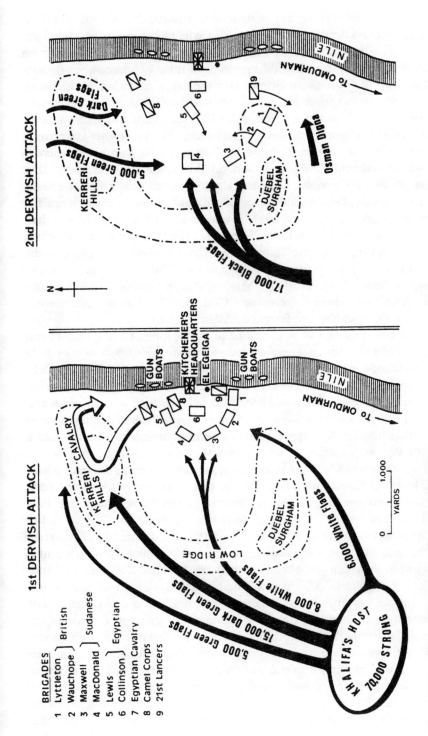

Map 15: The Battle of Omdurman: 2 September 1898

After the Battle of Atbara, Kitchener withdrew his troops into hot-weather quarters on the banks of the Nile while his Sappers extended the railway to Berber. By August, his Nile Expeditionary Force had been built up to a strength of 26,000 men, only a third of whom were British. He had two divisions: one British and the other Egyptian. The British division was stronger in firepower, but had only two brigades to the Egyptians' four. The former was under Major General Gatacre – an irascible, restless officer, nicknamed 'Backacher' by his soldiers, who had commanded the British brigade at Atbara. Now numbered the 1st Brigade, it was under Brigadier General Wauchope and consisted of the desert hardened Warwicks, Lincolns, Camerons and Seaforths. The newly arrived 2nd Brigade, derided for their 'white knees', was under Brigadier General Lyttleton and had been assembled from Mediterranean garrisons – Grenadier Guards from Gibraltar, Rifle Brigade from Malta, and Northumberland and Lancashire Fusiliers from Cairo. The Egyptian division, under Major General Hunter, had two Sudanese brigades under Brigadier Generals Maxwell and Macdonald, and two Egyptian brigades under Brigadier Generals Lewis and Collinson. Collinson's brigade was newly formed and had not fought at Atbara.

Kitchener's mobile troops consisted of the Egyptian Cavalry and Camel Corps, and the 21st Lancers, who were commanded by Colonel R M Martin, whose aggressive manner concealed a slow mind and lack of battle experience. The 21st Lancers were the junior lancer regiment in the Army and had never been in action throughout their 40 year existence. Colonel Martin was determined to perform some remarkable feat to earn them their first battle honour. Riding as one of their troop commanders, was the young, impetuous and abrasive Winston Churchill from the 4th Hussars, who was also a correspondent for the *Morning Post*. And on the Nile, Keppel's flotilla of seven gunboats was increased to ten by the addition of three of the latest screw-driven vessels, each armed with four guns and four Maxims.

The Khalifa was thought by then to have 70,000 men in and around Omdurman, the fortified township on the west bank of the Nile opposite Khartoum, in which the Mahdi's large domed tomb had been built and was thus sacred to all Mahdi-ists. The Khalifa and his amirs were uncertain whether to stand on the defensive, making best use of Omdurman's 14 foot high walls and protecting its hallowed ground, or to take the offensive with his fleet-footed Dervishes in the open desert, where they could out-manoeuvre and surround the slower, though better armed, British and Egyptian troops, who were only a third of his strength. Kitchener, for his part, decided that he must deter the Mahdi-ists from trying to defend Omdurman, which could lead to a costly siege and brutal street fighting in which his infantry would be unable to use their Lee-Metford rifles to best advantage. He achieved this by sending

Keppel's gunboats on 1 September to demonstrate the power of their guns against the mud-brick walls of Omdurman. Some of their shells went through the dome of the Mahdi's tomb, creating an outcry in the English liberal press about wanton desecration of holy places. The Khalifa took the point and opted for an offensive battle in the desert.

Between Omdurman and the open desert there is a half-circle or arc of low hills not more than 260 feet high, forming a natural amphitheatre in which Kitchener was to fight his decisive battle with the Khalifa. On the northern side of the arc, lie the Kerreri hills; and on the south-western side, about two miles from the river, is the prominent Djebel Surgham, the ridges of which run down the Nile some seven miles north of Omdurman. Between the Kerreri hills and Djebel Surgham, there is a long low ridge, which was just high enough to mask any concentrations of Dervishes in the desert behind it from the village of El Egeiga on the Nile's west bank, where Kitchener was to set up his headquarters for the battle.

Kitchener had started his advance from Atbara on 28 August with his army moving in a vast fighting formation ready for a surprise Dervish attack at any time. The two British brigades were on the left nearest the Nile; the two Sudanese brigades in the centre; one Egyptian brigade on the left; and the other in the rear, protecting the logistic units. The gunboat flotilla guarded the river flank; the 21st Lancers screened the British brigades; the Egyptian Cavalry looked after the Sudanese and Egyptian brigades; and the Camel Corps patrolled the outer desert flank.

The 21st Lancers reached the Kerreri hills on 1 September as Keppel's gunboats carried out their noisy demonstration at Omdurman. The Lancers and the Egyptian Cavalry found the hills unoccupied and rode on towards Djebel Surgham, where Winston Churchill recalled seeing, at about midday, a long black line with white flags along it in the desert some four miles away, looking like a zariba. As the cavalry patrols pushed nearer, they saw that it was a Dervish skirmishing line, advancing towards Surgham, with five huge groups of banner waving warriors behind them and with horsemen darting about between them. The whole of the Khalifa's host of 70,000 men seemed to be advancing to do battle. It was an awe-inspiring and frightening sight, which Churchill was sent back to report to Kitchener, who had just reached El Egeiga village with the main body of his army.

Expecting a battle to be fought that afternoon, Kitchener halted and turned his brigades to face the on-coming Dervishes. The infantry collected what scrub there was to form a zariba, and where there was none they scraped out shallow fire-trenches and built up obstacles of stones to provide a rudimentary perimeter defence. Then news arrived that the Dervish masses had halted out of sight behind Surgham. The cavalry stayed watching them until dusk, but they showed no sign of advancing any further for the time being. Kitchener's troops settled down for the night in full battle-order not knowing whether they would be attacked that night or not. Double sentries were posted, officer patrols were sent out, and every man got what sleep he could, lying with his weapons beside him. The gunboat searchlights lit up the desert all night.

Kitchener had drawn up his brigades in a half-circle, some 2,000 yards in diameter, with the river at his back and the gunboats supporting both flanks. From south to north, the brigade deployment was: Lyttleton nearest the Nile; Wauchope facing south-west; Maxwell and Macdonald with their Sudanese facing due west; Lewis's Egyptians facing north; and Collinson's Egyptians in reserve covering Kitchener's headquarters and the rear echelons. His 44 field guns and 20 Maxims were deployed between brigades. During the night, the 21st Lancers bivouacked behind Lyttleton, and the Egyptian Cavalry and Camel Corps behind Lewis.

At dawn, the 21st Lancers rode out to the ridge between Surgham and the Nile; one squadron of the Egyptian Cavalry climbed Surgham; and the rest of the cavalry and Camel Corps set off for the Kerreri hills. The question in everyone's mind was would the Dervishes appear over Surgham, or had they marched off into the desert, abandoning Omdurman and Khartoum, intending to fight the British under more propitious circumstances on another day?

Just after 6am the question was resolved when the cavalry were seen retiring towards the zariba. Gradually the banner waving Dervish hordes came into view, and the cavalry squadrons wheeled to the flanks to clear the fields of fire. Four large groups emerged from behind Surgham: one of about 6,000 with white flags came in against Lyttleton's front; another 8,000 with white flags against Wauchope, Maxwell and Macdonald; and a third much larger group of 15,000 carrying dark green flags veered off into the Kerreri hills, aiming presumably to complete the encirclement of Kitchener's position and to cut off his retreat. This third group was only opposed by Camel Corps and some of the Egyptian cavalry under Colonel Broadwood, who skilfully drew the Dervishes away from the battlefield and then succeeded in withdrawing to the zariba by about 9am with the help of the gunboats' covering fire. The fourth group of 5,000 with green flags, which was not seen at the time, was doing an even wider hook round the north of the Kerreri Hills. The Khalifa seems to have held an élite force of 17,000 carrying black flags which remained in reserve behind Surgham.

The gunners in Kitchener's main position opened fire on the white banner groups at just under 3,000 yards range and caused some confusion in the Dervish ranks, but they came on relentlessly until at 2,000 yards they were hit by the first section volleys fired by the Grenadier Guards in Lyttleton's brigade. Section volleys of aimed fire became general all along the line; the Lee-Metfords became too hot to handle and the Maxims boiled; and still the Dervishes came on very fast and very straight, but few managed to come within 800 yards of the zariba. The British soldiers did the job that they were trained to do, but it did not stop them pitying their brave opponents, whose fanaticism and belief in their heavenly reward for dying in battle, led them to rush on against impossible odds. The first white flag carrying wave of the Khalifa's attack was slaughtered within the hour.

Kitchener then made one of his few tactical mistakes. Not being able to see what still lay behind Surgham, he decided on a general advance to mop up and intercept any remaining Dervish groups before they could withdraw into Omdurman to oppose him there. He also despatched Colonel Martin with his 21st Lancers to reconnoitre the low ridges, running down from Surgham, across his route to Omdurman.

Martin's leading scouts reported a line of blue dressed warriors in a shallow watercourse ahead of him, so he wheeled the regiment left to take them in the flank, but as he did so his Lancers came under heavy rifle fire from the right. Without hesitating to see what was really in front of him, Martin wheeled right again, bringing the regiment into line and ordering the charge. So certain was he that he could overrun the enemy that he did not even bother to draw his own sword as the lances came down and the regiment gathered speed. With only 100 yards left to go, he realised that he had been cunningly ambushed. The wily Osman Digna was waiting for him with 2,000 white-clad Hadendoa spear and swordsmen crouching 12 deep in a nullah. It was too late to turn the regiment: 300 lancers and their mounts crashed into the Fuzzy-Wuzzy hedgehog. Churchill wrote 'the collision was prodigious'. For about two minutes, close quarters thrusting, slashing and stabbing went on with lance and sabre against spear and broadsword in which the horses suffered most. Sixty-five men and 119 horses had been killed by the time the regiment rallied some 200 yards beyond the nullah.

Martin survived and kept his head. He courageously dismounted two squadrons and engaged Osman Digna's horde with carbines. Discomforted, the Hadendoa made off towards Surgham, where the sound of renewed firing announced the beginning of the Khalifa's second attack at about 9.40am. By this time Kitchener's line was unfolding as he wheeled it southward for his resumed march on Omdurman. Lyttleton, Wauchope, and Maxwell were already marching south echeloned back from Lyttleton, who was leading. Kitchener was bringing Lewis's Egyptians into the line between Maxwell and Macdonald so that he would have Macdonald's reliable Sudanese on his exposed flank. There was still a large gap between Maxwell and Macdonald, which Lewis was due to fill, when the Khalifa's 17,000 black flagged reserve appeared over the northern shoulder of Surgham, rushing towards Macdonald's partially isolated brigade.

Kitchener reacted quickly to the new threat. He changed front again to due west ordering Lyttleton and Maxwell to clear Surgham while Wauchope's brigade was doubled across to support Macdonald's left and the Camel Corps was rushed up on his right. Macdonald, as cool as ever, stood his ground. At one critical moment, he called a ceasefire to harangue his Sudanese for being overexcited and for ragged musketry. They then settled down to thinning the ranks of their attackers while the rest of the army poured in supporting fire from the flanks. By about 10am, the black flag effort was spent, but Macdonald then found himself attacked from the north by the green flag group, who were returning from chasing Broadwood through the Kerreri hills. Macdonald's men did not falter, but they were immensely relieved by the arrival, at the double, of the Lincolns from Wauchope's brigade.

By 11.30am, the spirit of the Dervish attacks had been dowsed by the devastating effects of the controlled rifle volleys, Maxim fire and artillery shelling. The survivors of the Khalifa's army faded away into the desert, and this time Kitchener was able to resume his march on Khartoum, which he entered that afternoon. 10,000 Dervish dead were left on the battlefield for the cost of 48 killed and 434 wounded on the Anglo-Egyptian side. Macdonald and his Sudanese were 'the men of the match'. Broadwood deserves recognition for drawing off the large green flag group until it was really too late to affect the issue. But Kitchener, the captain, deserves the lion's share of the credit, although there were plenty of critics, like Douglas Haig, intent on belittling his achievement. It was Kitchener who assembled the Anglo-Egyptian Army, equipped it, built the railway to Berber, had the gunboats constructed, and finally brought about the decisive battle of Omdurman. He deserved his elevation to the peerage as Lord Kitchener of Khartoum; or 'K of K' as he soon became known to the world at large.

On Sunday 4 September Kitchener, his principal commanders and staff, attended a moving memorial service to Charles Gordon in the grounds of his ruined residency. The Union and Egyptian flags were raised. The hard, unemotional Sirdar was seen to weep as Gordon's favourite hymn, *Abide with me*, was sung. Queen Victoria noted in her diary: '*Surely, now he is avenged*'.

The Khalifa made his escape into the Southern Sudan and was never betrayed. He was eventually tracked down by a force led by Major Wingate of Kitchener's Intelligence Staff and was killed together with his potential successors in his last battle, fought with Wingate close to the White Nile 200 miles south of Khartoum, in November 1899. Osman Digna also escaped, but he too was tracked down and captured. He died in an Egyptian prison. By the turn of the century, the Sudan was free from Mahdi-ism.

Kitchener's Sudan campaign had been triggered by evidence of French ambitions in Equatorial Africa and the upper reaches of the Nile. Three days after Gordon's memorial service, news reached Khartoum of the arrival of a small French force at Fashoda on the Nile, 400 miles south of Khartoum. Kitchener set off at once with two companies of Cameron Highlanders and two Sudanese battalions in five of Keppel's gunboats. Ten days later, he found the French tricolour flying over Fashoda and a small force of Senegalese soldiers under Major Le Marchand in occupation. They had been there since July, having trekked 3,000 miles in two years across Africa from Senegal on the Atlantic coast. Kitchener, dressed as a general of the Egyptian Army, informed him that he was infringing Egyptian territory, and asked whether he had the authority of Paris to resist the re-raising of the Egyptian flag. Le Marchand confessed that he did not, so the two flags flew together and it was left to the British and French Governments to settle the issue of sovereignty. Kitchener and Le Marchand remained on the most cordial terms.

Public opinion in London and Paris was far less cordial. The British and French popular press worked their readers up into a nationalistic frenzy. Had it not been for French fear of the Germans and their need for the British as allies in Europe, there might have been war over Fashoda. In March 1899, a tentative dividing line was agreed between the British and French areas of influence in Africa. It was not until 1904, however, that the *Entente Cordiale* brought French recognition of British primacy in Egypt and the Sudan, and British recognition of the French annexations in North-West Africa.

Under Cromer's wise direction, the Sudan was recognised as an Anglo-Egyptian condominium outside the remit of the International Debt Commissioners in Cairo. Since few Egyptians wished to serve south of Wadi Halfa, the Sudanese Civil Service became almost entirely British officered and was soon rivalling the Indian Civil Service in attracting able men and achieving comparable efficiency. Kitchener was appointed Governor General of the Sudan in 1899, as well as being Sirdar of the Egyptian Army.

Cromer went on serving Egypt to the best of his outstanding ability until 1907, always fearing that British liberalism would lead to giving way too soon to Egyptian nationalist pressure before the country had a fully trained and experienced administration to handle autonomy successfully. He felt that he had only just started Egyptian education in good government. He hoped that the nationalists would not try to force Egypt to run before she could walk, but he was to be disappointed: to nationalists, independence always seems preferable in prospect to good but alien government in practice.

By the turn of the century, the Eastern Question and the Great Game had become part of history. The British, though they did not appreciate it at the time, had seized the great strategic crossroads of the world: the bridge between Africa and Asia; the artery of sea-borne trade; and ere

long the source of oil and the junction of world air routes. The Russians
had turned to exploit their expansion in the Far East and had lost interest in an invasion of India and in breaking through the Dardanelles into
the Levant. A new threat to British interests in the Moslem world was
already emerging. Germany had won the contract to build the
Constantinople–Baghdad railway and began work on it in 1899, symbol-
ising the Kaiser's growing interest in the Middle East.

CHAPTER 5

THE NEAR SUCCESS OF THE TURCO-GERMAN *JIHAD*

The Start of the Palestine and Mesopotamian Campaigns 1900 to 1916

Turkey was expected not only to defend the straits and protect her frontiers at immense distances, but conquer Egypt, make Persia independent, prepare the creation of independent states in Trans-Caucasia, threaten India from Afghanistan if possible, and in addition furnish active assistance in European theatres.

General Liman von Sanders' Epilogue.[1]

Napoleon's invasion of Egypt had drawn British military forces into the Middle East in 1798 to protect the shortest route to India; almost exactly a century later, Kaiser Wilhelm II's Germany harboured similar ambitions to threaten Britain's imperial communications and to build a great new German empire in the East. German geopoliticians and military planners nursed the concept of the *Drang nach Osten*, the 'drive to the East'; their industrialists and merchants sought new markets in the Middle East; and their diplomats reflected these ambitions. They all had one thing in common: belief in the use of strategic railway construction to turn distant geopolitical dreams into eventual reality.

The first positive sign of growing German interest in the Middle East came with the arrival in Constantinople in 1883 of Colonel (later Field Marshal) Freiherr Colmar von der Goltz with a large military mission to modernise, re-equip and train the Turkish Army on Prussian lines. From then onwards German interest in the Middle East burgeoned politically and commercially as well as militarily; and, most important of all, German engineering firms won the contract to build the Constantinople–Baghdad railway with a branch line running southwards through Palestine to the holy cities of Mecca and Medina in the Hejaz. The Hejaz branch line was completed from Aleppo to Medina by 1908, but the main line was delayed by the tunnels needed through the Taurus and Amanus mountains, north and north-west of Alexandretta, which were not completed until 1918.

123

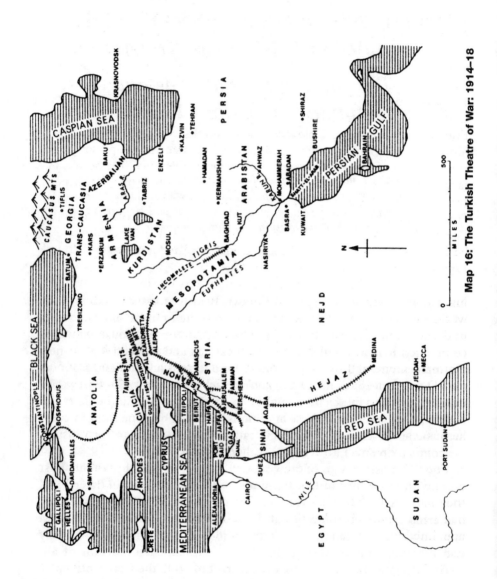

Map 16: The Turkish Theatre of War: 1914–18

The Young Turk revolution in Constantinople in 1908 started to align Turkish and German strategic ambitions. The revolutionary Committee of Union and Progress, which sought to modernise the Ottoman establishment, was not unfavourable to the Entente powers (Britain, France and Russia), which were vying with the Central Powers (Germany and Austro-Hungary) in the pre-1914 struggle for advantage in Europe. Nevertheless, the Turkish leaders sought to free Egypt from British control and to recover the lost Moslem provinces of the Caucasus and the Crimea from Russia. The loss of Libya in the Italo-Turkish war of 1911–12, and the Turkish defeat in the Balkan Wars of 1912–13, led to Enver Pasha's Coup of 1913, which swept away the liberal and pro-Entente members of the Committee, and established hardliners like Enver himself, who were pro-German. Military affairs became the preserve of a ruling triumvirate: Enver, the most powerful personality, had been military attaché in Berlin and was an ardent admirer of all things German; Izzet Pasha, Minister for War, had several years service with a German Hussar regiment at Cassel and on the German General Staff; and only Djemal Pasha, Minister of Marine, still had some feeling for the Entente – he admired the British, who had a strong naval mission under Admiral Limpus with the Turkish fleet.

In June 1913, the triumvirate strengthened its German links by inviting a new German mission not only to put right the Turkish Army's weaknesses revealed during the disastrous Balkan wars, but also to undertake mobilisation and operational planning, and to provide the commanders or chiefs of staff for the more important Turkish army formations. General Liman von Sanders arrived in Constantinople in mid-December 1913 with a mission of 42 hand-picked officers (subsequently raised to 70).

Liman, to put it bluntly, was an unbalanced, awkward cuss: cantankerous, egocentric and quarrelsome. He would not co-operate with the German ambassador, and although he got on well with the Turks, who respected him as a good soldier, he could be abrasive and unreasonable, on one occasion threatening to fight duels with Enver and Djemal over their lack, as he saw it, of any real desire to enter the war before Russia had been defeated in Europe. On his arrival, he demanded and was appointed to command the lst Corps, which garrisoned the Turkish capital and controlled the Bosphorus.

A German general in command of the Straits was more than St Petersburg could tolerate. Relations between the Tsarist and Turkish governments became more strained than usual. Diplomatic face was, however, saved by promoting Liman to full general in the German Army. The original agreement to set up the mission had stipulated that German officers would hold one rank above their German rank while serving in the Turkish Army. Liman, therefore, had to be accorded the rank of field marshal by the Turks, and as such he was too senior to command a mere corps, so he was made Inspector General of the Turkish Army instead. The officers, whom he brought with him, took over key staff appointments within Turkish formations and started the uphill struggle to overcome out-dated Turkish concepts of war.

In the summer of 1914, it was by no means certain that Germany would be able to draw Turkey into the war on the side of the Central Powers. Indeed, Turkey stayed neutral when war broke out in Europe, despite the German and Turkish Governments concluding a secret treaty of alliance on 2 August. Turkish public opinion generally favoured the Entente, but had been shaken by Britain's apparently high-handed action in requisitioning two new Turkish battleships, which were almost com-plete in British shipyards.

British strategic requirements in the Middle East had changed little since the turn of the century. The security of the Suez Canal was of pri-mary concern, but increasing emphasis was being given by the Admiralty to an unimpeded flow of oil from the recently developed Anglo-Persian Oil Company's wells in the hills of Persian Arabistan (Khuzestan today), north-east of Awaz, by pipeline to its tanker terminal on Abadan island at the head of the Persian Gulf. The German backed Turkish hostility posed a far greater threat to British interests in the Levant and Persian Gulf than had ever been experienced in the 19th Century.

Militarily, the Turkish armies, ramshackle though they might be by British standards, were composed of some of the world's toughest fighting men, inured to hardship and able to survive on next to nothing if need be. They were acclimatised to the harsh conditions of the Arabian deserts, the steaming marshes of the Euphrates and Tigris valleys, and the rigours of the Caucasus and Anatolian mountains. 'Johnnie Turk' was to win the admira-tion of the British 'Tommy' for his stoicism and powers of endurance. While not short of manpower, the Turks' Achilles' heel lay in the great length and primitive nature of their lines of communications, which restricted the size of forces they could deploy, and were only partially alle-viated by the incomplete German engineered railways where they existed.

A Turkish entry into the war posed another more worrying threat to British imperial interests worldwide. The Sultan was the titular Caliph of all Islam and could proclaim a universal *Jihad* against the Entente powers. This might not in itself be particularly dangerous, because Moslem co-ordinated action is no easier to achieve than Christian unity, but there were many political and religious leaders amongst the followers of Islam in India and Britain's other dependent territories, who were ready to exploit any British military embarrassment. With the marked improve-ment in world communications, the implications of British political and military action in Moslem lands had to be assessed against the probable reaction in the rest of the Islamic world.

Fortunately, Ottoman rule was seen by many people in the Middle East as more oppressive than British imperial paternalism. In Egypt, however, there had been a period of political malaise after Lord Cromer retired on grounds of ill-health in 1907. His Under-Secretary for Finance, Sir Eldon Gorst, succeeded him, and did the one thing that Cromer feared most: he tried to return administrative responsibility to Egyptian ministers too soon. The Egyptian nationalists, covertly supported by Kitchener's old enemy, Khedive Abbas, were quick to exploit the slackening of the Consul General's reins, and in Cairo lack of confidence became general amongst Europeans and pro-British Egyptians alike. Gorst, however, died in 1911, and, much to the relief of most Egyptians, Kitchener returned to Cairo to take over Cromer's mantle with a firm unerring hand. In his view, Egypt was not ready for Western style party politics: indeed, he viewed them as disorientating for most oriental races. Instead, he concentrated his efforts on improving Egyptian agriculture. When he went back to England on leave in June 1914, the Egyptians looked forward to a British rather than a Turkish victory in the coming war.

Other parts of the Ottoman Empire were equally lukewarm to an anti-British *Jihad*. In Arabia there was neither respect for the Porte's government, nor acceptance of the Sultan as Caliph of all Islam. The Sultan was a Turk and not descended from Mohamed as most of the important princes of Arabia could claim to be. They dreamed of throwing off the Ottoman yoke and recreating the glories of the great 9th and 10th Century Arab Empire of the Abbasids, stretching from the Indian Ocean to the Taurus mountains. Any *Jihad* proclaimed by the Sultan would have less religious compulsion if left unratified by the Grand Sherif of Mecca, Hussein Ibn Ali, the Keeper of the Holy Places of Islam, and he had the incentive of winning future independence to withhold his support.

Turkey maintained a perilously hostile neutrality for the first three months of the First World War. The friendly reception on 10 August of the German cruisers *Breslau* and *Goeben* at Constantinople after evading British and French attempts to intercept them in the Mediterranean, and the Porte's refusal to intern their crews, were hardly the acts of a genuine neutral. This was followed by the dismissal of the British naval mission on 9 September; and by the two German ships hoisting the Ottoman ensign while taking part in the Turkish Fleet's bombardment of Russian Black Sea ports on 29 October. Next day, the British and French Ambassadors demanded their passports, and the formal declaration of war came on 5 November.

The British Government decided to handle war in the Middle East with the time-honoured division of responsibilities between the British and Indian Governments: Whitehall would direct and supply operations based upon Egypt, while Delhi looked after the affairs of the Persian Gulf and provided the troops and resources for operations there. Two separate

British campaigns developed: one to protect the Suez Canal and the other to ensure the continuing flow of oil from the Anglo-Persian oil fields. The unfortunate Turks, with the Germans breathing down their necks, were faced with fighting on five distant fronts, admittedly with the advantage of interior lines, enabling them to switch forces, albeit slowly, between them: in the Balkans against the Greeks, Serbs and Bulgars; in the Caucasus against the Russians; in the Levant and Mesopotamia against the British; and in the close defence of Constantinople itself against a concerted attempt by the Entente powers to seize the Dardanelles.

Most of Britain's major wars are fought in three phases: the initial defensive period during which inadequate peacetime regular forces try to buy time for the country to rearm and commanders struggle to stem disaster; then the attritional second phase, while her expanded forces and her chosen commanders learn their business the hard way; and finally the last battles, which the British have a habit of winning. These phases certainly applied to the Middle East campaigns against the Turks in the First World War, but they were made all the starker by the low priority accorded to them in the Entente's overall strategy. Despite the strategic importance of the Suez Canal and the Persian Gulf oil, they could hardly be anything but secondary to the European fronts upon which the very survival of Britain, France and Russia depended.

British preparations for the defence of Egypt and the Suez Canal started with the arrival in Cairo on 8 September 1914 of Lieutenant-General Sir John Maxwell as Commander-in-Chief. We have already met him as one of Kitchener's two brigade commanders of Sudanese troops at the battles Atbara and Khartoum in 1898. Before that he had taken part in the Battle of Tel-el-Kebir in 1882, and in the abortive Nile campaign to rescue Gordon in 1884–5. During the Boer War, he had been in at the capture of Pretoria and had become its military governor, fulfilling the task with tact and humanity. He was back in Egypt as General Officer Commanding British Troops from 1908 to 1912, incidentally becoming an Egyptologist of repute. He was not, however, a deeply read man, but he possessed a well balanced sense of proportion in practical matters, was a good administrator and was always ready to shoulder responsibility. On his arrival back in Cairo as Commander-in-Chief, he was faced straight away with an untimely demand from the War Office in Whitehall for the replacement of most of the British regular troops in the Egyptian garrison by the 42nd East Lancashire Division of the Territorial Army, who would know little or nothing about internal security operations.

The War Office demand was untimely because there was bound to be trouble in Egypt ere long. Popular conviction throughout the Middle East was of German invincibility, and hence that Turkey, as Germany's ally, would be a winner too. Local ministers in the Egyptian Government were alarmed about the prospect of hostilities against their Sovereign and

Caliph, not through any devotion to the Ottoman cause, but for their own safety if the Central Powers won! Political extremists, ever active in Cairo, scented opportunities for exploiting the German military successes already unfolding in France and in East Prussia. Martial Law was declared in Egypt on 2 November 1914, and a march by the East Lancashire Division through the streets of Cairo did much to steady nerves. At the same time, the British Government gave a solemn pledge that it took full responsibility for the defence of Egypt and would not call on the Egyptian people for help. This was not enough for some of the Egyptian ministers and they resigned; nor did it solve the problem of the rabidly anti-British Khedive Abbas, who was in Constantinople at the time. The further step was taken of formally declaring Egypt to be a British Protectorate and installing Abbas's uncle, Hussein Kemal, as Sultan of Egypt instead of the Khedive. The Consul General's title was changed as well to British High Commissioner, a post that was filled by an acting High Commissioner until Sir Henry McMahon arrived in January 1915 as Kitchener's successor.

Turkey could not give direct military help to the Central Powers in Europe but, at German prompting, accepted the task of drawing Entente strength away from Europe with four diversionary operations: attacking the Russians in Trans-Caucasia, in the hope of winning back Armenia and Azerbaijan; crossing the Suez Canal and restoring Ottoman rule in Egypt; seizing the Anglo-Persian Oil Company's wells and pipeline; and raising the whole of the Moslem world against the British and French by pro-claiming *Jihad*. The Germans themselves dispatched a number of clandestine missions to Persia, Afghanistan, Baluchistan and India to help inflame Moslem opinion, and their official diplomatic missions sought to persuade the Shah in Tehran and the Amir in Kabul to side with the Central Powers.

There were two distinct factions within the Turkish High Command: the pan-Turks and the pan-Islamics. The former, led by Enver Pasha, were only really interested in using the war to reunite and hold what they saw as the heartlands of the Turkish race – Anatolia, Trans-Caucasia, Azerbaijan and Turkestan. They were far less interested in the Syrian and Arabian provinces, which the pan-Islamic clique deemed the most important as the cradle of Islam. Baghdad topped Jerusalem in the pan-Turk strategic priorities because they saw it as the gateway to Azerbaijan and Turkestan. Those who thought in pan-Islamic terms, like Djemal Pasha, were more interested in retaining sovereignty over the holy cities of Mecca, Medina and Jerusalem. The Germans backed both horses: Enver, because his desire to drive due east paralleled their wish to discomfort the British in Persia, Afghanistan and India; and Djemal, because his policy could be used to threaten the Suez Canal and Egypt.

The first Turkish offensive was launched by the Minister for War, Enver

Pasha, in pursuit of pan-Turk ambitions against Russian Armenia. He took personal command of the strong 3rd Turkish Army and advanced from Erzarum on Kars, intending to surprise the Russians with a wide outflanking movement through the mountains. Liman von Sanders and Enver's German chief of staff warned him that such an operation was impracticable in winter, but he obstinately persisted. Only 12,000 out of the 90,000 men sent on this foolhardy operation at the end of November 1914 survived.

While Enver was being thwarted on the Caucasus front, the pan-Islamic Djemal Pasha undertook the offensive towards Egypt with marginally greater success, in that most of his troops did survive to tell the tale. He took over as Governor and Commander-in-Chief Syria and Palestine, a post that he was to hold for the next three years, and ordered the Turkish 8th Corps at Damascus to concentrate at Beersheba in southern Palestine for the offensive against Egypt. He was an ambitious and unscrupulous megalomaniac with little military ability and an intense dislike of his German allies, but an able administrator who overcame many of the acute logistic problems of the Palestine front. The commander of 8th Corps was another Djemal, called Kuchuk or lesser Djemal. He was a good soldier, but the brains and driving force behind 8th Corps' operations was its German chief of staff, the Bavarian Colonel Freiherr Kress von Kressenstein, who got on well with the Turks and understood their psychology better than most of the Germans seconded to the Turkish Army. It was mid-January 1915 before 8th Corps was ready to advance from Beersheba with the 25th (Arab) and 10th (Turkish) Divisions, a cavalry regiment and a force of mounted Bedouins. The whole force was some 20,000 strong, and was supplied with water, food and ammunition by 10,000 camels, but it possessed no reconnaissance aircraft.

Djemal Pasha knew that 20,000 troops would not have much of a chance of success unless the Egyptians rose in revolt behind the British when 8th Corps reached the Canal. One of the many plots detected in Cairo was hatched by the German explorer, Baron Oppenheim, for the murder of all Europeans when the Turks crossed the Canal. The presence of tough Australians and New Zealanders, who were arriving in large numbers for training in camps near Cairo, discouraged any real challenge to British authority.

By January 1915, Maxwell's forces in Egypt had been reinforced with the 10th and 11th Indian Divisions. He gave responsibility for the defence of the Canal to Major General A Wilson, who divided it into three sectors: Port Said to El Ferdan; El Ferdan to Deversoir; Deversoir to Suez. With a hundred miles, front to cover, Wilson decided to hold the west bank and to use the Canal itself as the principal obstacle in front of his main defences. Nevertheless, he established fortified outposts, each held by about two companies of Indian infantry, on the east bank, covering the main ferry and bridge sites, which might be chosen as Turkish crossing places. The gaps between were watched by platoon posts about half a mile apart, and British and French warships were stationed in the Canal ready to steam to any threatened sector to support the army with their guns.

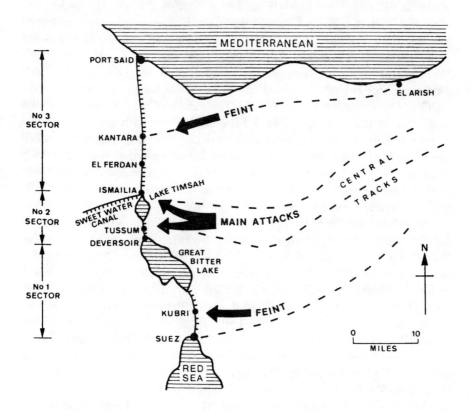

Map 17: The Turkish Advance on the Suez Canal: January 1915

Djemal and Kress had three practicable approach routes from which to choose. In the north, they could advance along the Mediterranean coast to Port Said where there was some fresh water to be had, but it was under the guns of the Royal Navy, and a large area east of Port Said had been deliberately flooded. In the centre, there were good but waterless tracks through the Sinai desert, which led towards Ismailia where the main sluice gates on the Sweet Water Canal were located. If they could take Ismailia, they could cut off all fresh water supplies to Port Said and Suez, and, of course, to the troops manning the defences along the Canal. The southern route to Suez had nothing to commend it. They opted for the central tracks, but used the northern and southern routes as well for diversionary purposes.

Although Liman von Sanders claims in his memoirs that 8th Corps' approach came as a surprise to the British, Wilson was, in fact, tolerably well informed of its march from air reconnaissance reports. These showed all three routes being used, but with the largest columns noted on the central desert tracks. On 26 and 27 January, unconvincing feint attacks were made at Kantara in the north and at Kubri in the south, but neither deceived Wilson, who had located the main Turkish concentrations opposite the stretch of the Canal between Lake Timsah and the Great Bitter Lake just south of Ismailia. British and French warships were moved into the Central Sector to support the 22nd Indian Brigade and the 28th Frontier Force Brigade on whom the Turkish attack was most likely to fall.

The Turks attempted to cross at Tussum, half way between the two lakes during the early hours of 3 February. Their 25th (Arab) Division succeeded in launching pontoons and constructing rafts, but were detected when their first three platoons started to cross. Intense British fire from the west bank put an end to the crossing. The few Arab soldiers, who did get across, were killed or captured and all the pontoons and rafting equipment were destroyed.

Despite the failure of his night attack, Djemal Kuchuk pressed on with further unsuccessful attempts to force a crossing in daylight. Djemal Pasha, who accompanied Kuchuk so as to be on hand to exploit the expected Egyptian uprising, lost heart when no rebellion was reported and ordered withdrawal to Beersheba although the 10th (Turkish) Division was still uncommitted. Wilson had defeated the first Turkish attempt to invade Egypt at the cost of only 150 casualties. Djemal Kuchuk lost around 1,500 men, but he does deserve the credit for managing to cross the parched Sinai desert in the first place, and for dragging his pontoons and heavier guns with teams of oxen over the 200 miles of rock strewn track from Beersheba to the Canal. It was a logistic feat, which showed that large forces could be brought forward to threaten Egypt if the Turks decided to try again.

When the First World War broke out the Indian Government had not expected to have to provide troops for the Persian Gulf. The Indian Expeditionary Force 'A' of three infantry and two cavalry divisions was to be dispatched to the BEF in France; troops to form the 10th and 11th Indian Divisions in Egypt were sent, as we have seen, to defend the Canal; and other troops were earmarked for East Africa as Force 'B'. Only three divisions were left to defend the North West Frontier and to curb any unrest amongst the Moslems that war with Turkey might engender. With the threat to the Persian oilfield and to British interests in Baghdad and Basra growing by the hour as Turkey edged towards war, the British Government accepted the deletion of Lieutenant General Sir Arthur Barrett's 6th (Poona) Division from the Force 'A', destined for France, and authorised its dispatch instead as Force 'D' to the Gulf. Lieutenant-Colonel Sir Percy Cox of the Indian Political Service, who was Foreign

Secretary in the Indian Government, was appointed political adviser to Barrett.

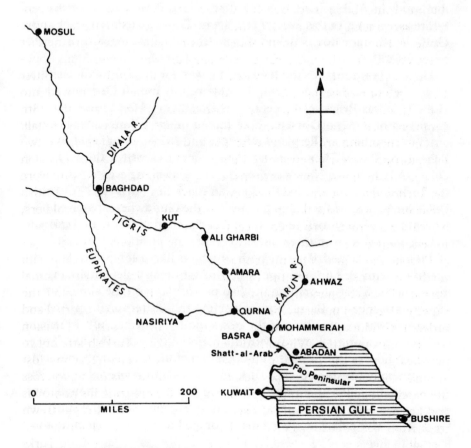

Map 18: Mesopotamia: 1914–15

Lord Hardinge, the Viceroy, commented on Cox's appointment: 'Cox's knowledge of the Chiefs and Gulf politics is unique'.[2] It certainly was. In 1899 he had been appointed political agent to the Sultan of Muscat, whom the French were trying, with some success, to wean away from his alliance with Britain. Cox's fluency in Arabic, his dignity and Wellington-like presence so impressed the Sultan that French influence was neutralised. He went on to dominate the affairs of the Gulf as British political resident for the first decade of the century. He won the friendship and loyalty of the Sheikh of Mohammerah on the Shatt-al-Arab at the head of the Gulf, which Outram had bombarded and taken during the Anglo-Persian War of 1856–7. It was through Cox's influence that the Sheikh leased Abadan island to the Anglo-Persian Oil Company for its Gulf oil terminal. Perhaps even more importantly, he strengthened British ties with the ruling el Sabah family in Kuwait, and, through them, opened friendly relationships with the ambitious and anti-Ottoman Wahabi ruler, ibn Saud, in Arabia. Cox was the first British diplomat to foresee the future ascendancy of this warrior statesman. During Cox's ten years in the Gulf, British trade doubled, and, despite the appalling climate, his health never failed.[3]

General Headquarters in Delhi did not wait for the Turkish declaration of war before sailing the leading brigade of 6th Indian Division for the Gulf. This was Brigadier-General W S Delamain's 16th Indian Brigade, consisting of the 2nd Dorsets, three Indian infantry battalions, two batteries of mountain artillery and a Sapper and Miner company. It was off Bahrain on 23 October in its transports under escort of the battleship *Ocean* and the Indian Navy's cruiser *Dalhousie*, awaiting events. As soon as the Turkish fleet bombarded the Russian Black Sea ports on 29 October, Delamain's force was sailed to the head of the Gulf, where it arrived on 3 November, two days before the formal declaration of war with Turkey.

Delamain was given three tasks: to secure the positions of the Sheikhs of Mohammerah and Kuwait, both of whom had a long history of co-operation with Britain and opposition to Ottoman rule; to land at the mouth of the Shatt-al-Arab on the Fao peninsular with the aim of a subsequent advance on Basra; and to occupy the oil terminal on Abadan island. He was to take Basra if the opportunity occurred, but this might have to await Barrett's arrival with the main body of the division. There were high hopes of securing the co-operation of the local Arab tribes, who were generally considered anti-Turk, but it was also appreciated that the Arabs usually allied themselves with whichever side they thought was going to win. The chances of easy loot, or of obtaining lucrative subsidies for co-operative behaviour, were more compelling in the tribal mind than the call to *Jihad*.

The Mesopotamian Campaign, which started with Delamain's landing at Fao on 6 November, was a river war, waged on the Tigris and Euphrates, and in the floods which engulfed vast areas during the winter and spring of each year. The key lay in the availability of river steamers, shallow draft vessels and local craft. Prevailing water levels in the rivers and canals at particular times of year were critical to most military operations by both sides.

It was also a campaign in which it was difficult to know where to stop. The capture of Basra, for instance, was expected to give adequate security to the oilfields, but then Qurna, at the junction of the Tigris and Euphrates, beckoned as a more effective covering position; soon Amara, further up the Tigris, was deemed essential; then Kut. Finally, Baghdad became the glittering but fatally unattainable objective which the resources of India could provide in 1915. The need to show the Moslem world continuing success in order to give the lie to the Turco-German agents' efforts to spread and ferment *Jihad* throughout Persia and Afghanistan and on into India, and the relative ineptitude and inefficiency of the Turkish forces during the first year of the campaign, were the magnets that drew the British commanders ever forward despite their own misgivings about available resources.

Delamain landed his brigade near Fao without much difficulty and against only sporadic opposition from the ill-equipped Turkish troops of their 38th Division, guarding the entrance to the Shatt-al-Arab with a few antiquated guns, thanks to the close co-operation with the Royal Navy, which was to become a feature of the campaign. The sloops *Odin* and *Espiègle*, together with several armed yachts, tugs and launches, gave invaluable service during the river war. By the time General Barrett arrived with the second brigade of the 6th Division on 13 November, Delamain had secured the Abadan oil terminal and had his brigade firm in a defensive position on the west bank of the Shatt opposite Abadan, awaiting a Turkish counter-offensive which the Sheikh of Mohammerah warned him was being prepared by elements of the 38th Turkish Division, garrisoning Basra. Heavy rain was making movement on land difficult for both sides.

Barrett, who assumed command that day, decided to pre-empt the Turks by attacking a force of some 3,500 men that they were concentrating to oppose his advance up the Shatt towards Mohammerah. In two sharp engagements on 15 and 17 November, Delamain's brigade hustled the Turks out of their positions in the palm groves along the river bank with turning movements round their open desert flank while the *Odin* and *Espiègle* shelled them from the river. The Turks lost nearly half their force, but the British casualties, amounting to just under 500, were not light.

These British successes gave the Dorsets and the Indian battalions of the brigade confidence that they could match the fighting qualities of Johnnie Turk; and they had their first experience of two tactical problems, which were to plague them throughout the campaign. First, artillery targets were difficult to pin-point in the lush palm-strewn strip of cultivated land along the river banks, and Turkish positions in the open desert beyond were equally hard to locate due to the frequent mirages which occurred once the sun was fully up. And secondly, casualty evacuation was and remained a nightmare. With little wheeled transport available, the wounded had to be carried long distances on stretchers to the river bank, and then man-handled into launches or local craft for their journey down river to the nearest field hospital or steamer fitted out as a hospital.

Barrett intended to advance on Basra as soon as his third brigade arrived. On 20 November, the Sheikh of Mohammerah brought him news that the Turks had evacuated the town, which was being looted by the local Arabs, and were withdrawing to Amara 130 miles up the Tigris. Barrett had not realised the extent of the demoralisation of the local

Turkish forces; nor did he, of course, know of the consternation that the British landings in the Shatt-al-Arab had caused in Constantinople. Until that moment, the Turkish General Staff had questioned the idea of Britain taking the offensive anywhere in the Middle East. 'How could England, with its little army,' they asked, 'add aggressive action against the Turks to her contest with the German millions?'[4] The Turkish 12th and 13th Corps, which were the pre-war garrison of Mesopotamia, had been sent to the much more dangerous Trans-Caucasian front to hold off the Russians. Only the under-strength 38th Division had been left in Mesopotamia, largely for internal security purposes, and it had to depend on recruiting local Arabs to help fill its establishment. Enver Pasha at once put in hand the immediate reinforcement of Mesopotamia, vowing to drive the British out, but distance, poor lines of communication, and the Russian threat, limited his initial efforts to do so.

Barrett's 6th Division made its ceremonial entry into Basra on 23 November 1914. The squalor of the place revolted even British troops already hardened to the poverty of India. The maze of tortuous narrow lanes were ankle deep in filth, offal and litter; there was no sanitation whatsoever; and the disease ridden brothels made the place entirely unsuitable for billeting troops. For the first few days, every man was employed on cleaning up the extraordinarily dirty surroundings of their selected camp sites, improving sanitation and improvising the rudimentary necessities of life. Drinking water was only obtainable from the river, but it was so contaminated near the banks that it had to be drawn from the centre of the stream and chlorinated. There were no buildings suitable for a base hospital, but the Sheikh of Mohammerah placed his palace at Barrett's disposal for the purpose. Basra was also a disappointment as a base port. Ships could not come alongside the few jetties that existed, and had to be discharged in mid-stream into local craft. The water-table was only a few inches below the surface of the ground, and most of the roads were un-metalled. The nearest practicable source of road-making stone was India, whence it had to be shipped in vast quantities as the base was developed.

In the first flush of victory, Barrett and Cox recommended an immediate advance on Baghdad before the Turks could recover their balance, and to generate a snowballing of Arab support. Reporting to the Viceroy, Cox wrote:

> After earnest consideration of the arguments for and against I find it difficult to see how we can well avoid taking over Baghdad. We can hardly allow Turkey to retain possession and make difficulties for us at Basra, nor can we allow another power [Russia] to take it; but once in occupation we must remain, for we could not possibly allow the Turks to return after accepting Arab co-operation afforded on the understanding that the Turkish régime had disappeared for good.[5]

The Commander in Chief India, Sir Beauchamp Duff, saw the force of Cox's arguments, but, as the man who had to provide the resources, he advised the Viceroy against going so far so soon. He calculated that, although Barrett might be able to take Baghdad by *coup-de-main* with one brigade group, he would need a complete division to hold the city and a second division to protect the 500 mile river supply route back to Basra. Arab co-operation would be vital to success: the smallest reverse could lead to the defection of important riverine tribes and hence to the isolation of a British garrison in Baghdad. But the deciding factor in Duff's view was India's inability to provide a second division without withdrawing troops from the North-West Frontier. The Amir of Afghanistan had stoutly resisted the Porte's call for *Jihad*, and refused the blandishments of a Turco-German mission, which had arrived in Kabul to seek his co-operation. However, fanatics amongst the frontier tribes, who never respected the rule of Kabul anyway, were delighted to have an excuse for raiding India. Trouble in Waziristan had already necessitated the reinforcement of the frontier garrisons.

Whitehall concurred with Duff's appreciation, but were more concerned about the Russian factor, hinted at by Cox. While not wishing to see the Tsar's forces occupying Baghdad, the War Office saw greater dangers in a Russian defeat or winter snows halting operations in the Caucasus, allowing the Turks to divert troops from the Russian front to Mesopotamia as, indeed, was to happen before long. Both Whitehall and Delhi, however, were agreed on two things: more depth was needed to protect the Basra bridgehead; and Arab co-operation was vital. Barrett was authorised to advance the first 50 of the 500 miles to Baghdad by working his way up river to Qurna, which lies at the junction of the Tigris and Euphrates, and at the divide between the rich cultivated lands of the Shatt-al-Arab and the arid areas of central Mesopotamia. In Islamic legend, it was the site of the Garden of Eden. It also marked the furthest point upstream that the ocean-going sloops like *Odin* and *Espiègle* could reach at all times of year without undue difficulty.

At the beginning of December, Barrett sent a two battalion group of all arms up the Shatt-al-Arab in four river steamers with three sloops and several armed launches to reconnoitre and, if possible, take Qurna. It met with stiff Turkish resistance, and it was not until 6 December when Brigadier General Fry arrived with the rest of his 18th Indian Brigade (2nd Norfolks and three Indian battalions) – the recently arrived third brigade of Barrett's Force 'D' – that any real headway was made. In three days' hard fighting, during which the sloops and launches played a vital part, Fry broke the Turkish defence and compelled the surrender of the garrison of just under 1,000 men on 9 December. The filth and squalor of this legendary paradise disgusted the British soldiers even more than Basra: it would have needed no angel with a flaming sword to keep them out of it! However, the surrender of the Turkish garrison had a salutary effect on Arab assessments of British chances of final victory, but it also drew the British commanders into considering advances to the next two strategically important towns, the capture of which would bring the whole of the Basra province under British control: Nasiriya on the Euphrates and Amara on the Tigris, both a further 100 miles up river.

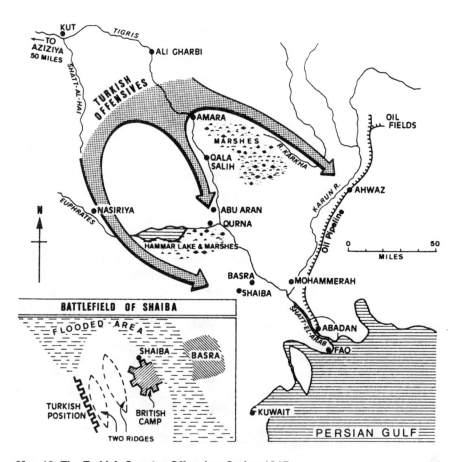

Map 19: The Turkish Counter-Offensive: Spring 1915

Neither Delhi nor Whitehall welcomed this suggestion when it was put forward by Sir Percy Cox, largely on political grounds, but supported by Barrett, who saw an advance to Amara as an essential preliminary to the occupation of Baghdad. Cox was concerned that unless the British showed continuing success the Arabs would lose confidence and start re-insuring with the Turks. In common prudence, such an advance would need more troops, but the *Jihad* was spreading and risks would have to be taken to maintain momentum. The black tented Bakhtiaris, in whose territory the oilfields lay, were showing signs of dissatisfaction and had forced Barrett to detach a small force from Basra to Ahwaz to re-establish confidence; there was more trouble brewing on the North West Frontier of India; and a major plot had just been uncovered in the Punjab for a repeat of the Indian mutiny. Extra troops could not, in all truth, be spared by India for the Gulf. Nevertheless, precautions were taken by GHQ Delhi to prepare a fourth brigade group – Brigadier-General Lean's 12th Infantry Brigade – for service there if the threat to the oilfields increased.

On 26 January Barrett reported that there were clear signs of a three pronged Turkish counter-offensive under Sulaiman Askari Bey – a highly educated and able soldier, who had been severely wounded in fighting north of Qurna a week earlier – to recover Basra and to threaten the Persian oilfields. The easterly prong was a large Arab force under Sheikh Ghazban of the powerful Bani Lam tribe, supported by Turkish cavalry and infantry, who were answering the call to *Jihad* by advancing from Amara towards Ahwaz to cut the oil pipeline. In the centre, a concentration of Turkish troops was being built up on the Tigris just north of Qurna, largely scraped together from the 38th Division. And to the west, another Turkish force from the 35th Division, which had been marched back from Armenia, together with some 15,000 Arabs in support, was advancing across the desert from Nasiriya on the Euphrates towards Shaiba, intent upon attacking Basra from the west. Delhi accepted Barrett's clear case for the immediate dispatch of Lean's 12th Infantry Brigade (2nd West Kents and three Indian battalions) from India to the Gulf.

In the first week of February the inevitable occurred. News of the Turkish advance on Ahwaz excited the local tribesmen in the oilfield area. They rose, looted the oilstores and breached the pipeline. Fortunately, the water levels in the Euphrates and Tigris were rising, swollen by the melting snows in the Caucasus. Large areas of the flood plain sank beneath sheets of water or turned into squelching mud. Qurna became an island; and the approach to Basra from Shaiba was severed by extensive, but not impassable, flooding. Barrett was able to thin out around Qurna in order to dispatch forces to check the Turkish flanking advances on Ahwaz and Shaiba.

Anxiety grew in Delhi and Whitehall, where fears were expressed of a general uprising from the Euphrates to the Indus, if Barrett's Force 'D' suffered a major setback. Necessity proved the mother of invention. Two extra Indian Brigades were found to reinforce him: Major General Gorringe's 33rd Brigade was dispatched in haste from India, consisting of the l/4th Hampshires and three Indian battalions; and Major General Melliss VC's 30th Brigade with three Indian battalions only was shipped from Egypt. Neither could arrive much before the end of March when the main Turkish counter-offensive was expected to develop. Barrett did, however, receive the one thing that he had been screaming for ever since the campaign began: a tiny air component of just two reconnaissance aircraft, manned by Australians and New Zealanders, who did a splendid job for him, keeping a check on the progress of Turkish concentrations.

There was just a chance that the Turkish counter-offensive would evaporate. On 19 February, the British and French fleets had started the preliminary bombardment of the Dardanelles. Colonel Wehrle of Liman von Sanders' mission took charge of the shore batteries and German naval personnel supervised the mining of the narrows. A month later, on 18 March, the Allied fleets tried to break through the narrows into the Sea of Marmara and came within a few heavy artillery rounds of doing so. The Turkish shore batteries were almost out of ammunition, which could only be replenished from Germany, but three battleships had been sunk (two British and one French) by mines or gunfire, and three others had been badly damaged. Admiral de Robeck, who was in command, gave up, not knowing that he could have broken through next day with one more effort. The Turkish Government had left Constantinople for Anatolia, expecting the collapse of the Dardanelles defences at any moment. Had the Allied Navies succeeded, Turkey might have been driven out of the war then and there.

* * *

Like the Crimean War, the Gallipoli Campaign was fought outside the Middle East *per se,* and its story has been told so often that there is no need to do more than sketch its outline here in so far as it affected operations to protect the Suez Canal and the Persian oilfields. Soon after the naval failure to break through the Straits, the Allies decided to try again with a combined naval and military operation to seize the Gallipoli Peninsula; and Enver Pasha gave Liman von Sanders command of the Turkish Fifth Army tasked with its defence. General Sir Ian Hamilton, who had made a name for himself under Kitchener in South Africa, landed with a force of five divisions – one British, two ANZAC, one naval and one French – astride the entrance to the Dardanelles on 25 April, but only managed to secure toeholds on the peninsula against the determined and well organised Turkish defence. As was happening in France, the defence had the upper hand with machine-gun and wire dominating the battlefield on the steep rock-strewn hillsides of Gallipoli. The bitter struggle went on with severe losses on both sides until 6 August, when Hamilton tried to break the stalemate by landing the newly arrived 9th Corps under the ageing and pedestrian General Sir Frederick Stopford at Suvla Bay to get behind the Turkish defences. Stopford was too slow in exploiting his landing and Liman von Sanders was lucky to have Mustapha Kemal, the future dictator of Turkey, in charge of the counter-attacking 19th Turkish Division. Liman succeeded in restoring the stalemate, which lasted until the Allies, on Kitchener's advice, decided to abandon the Gallipoli peninsula at the end of 1915.

★ ★ ★

The Gallipoli landings did not result in any withdrawal of Turkish forces in Mesopotamia. In anticipation of the arrival of the two extra Indian brigades at Basra, the Government of India decided to reorganise Force 'D' into the 2nd Indian Corps of two divisions, each of three brigades, and to place it under the command of General Sir John Nixon. Barrett, whose health was failing, was to return to India and his place as commander of the 6th Division (now the 16th, 17th and 18th Brigades) was to be taken by Major General Charles Townshend. The new division, styled the 12th, was given the 12th, 30th and 33rd Brigades, and placed under command of Major General George Gorringe of the 33rd Brigade when he arrived with it from India. 33rd Brigade would be taken over by Brigadier-General Wapshare.

Nixon and Townshend were to dominate the 1915 campaign in Mesopotamia. Nixon was an Indian cavalryman of 58; an energetic commander and able staff officer; and tough enough to withstand the Gulf climate. As a young officer, he had taken part in the 2nd Afghan War and in many a punitive expedition into the tribal fastnesses on India's mountain fringe during the last years of the Great Game. He had commanded cavalry columns in the Boer War, and had risen steadily to become the commander of India's Northern Army. As a cavalryman, he prized offensive action, but he had two besetting sins: a tendency to underestimate the Turk, and an over-optimism, which flawed his operational judgement.[6]

Townshend had always been a highly controversial character: restlessly ambitious and egocentric. He had started his military career in the Royal Marine Light Infantry. After serving with the Desert Column in the Nile campaign to relieve Gordon in 1885, he decided that the Marines were a dead end and transferred to the Madras Infantry; then to the Sikh Infantry; and a little later to the Central Indian Horse. An inveterate lobbyist, he was never satisfied with any job he was given: other pastures were always greener. He gained operational experience in Chitral and Kashmir in the 1890s; in Kitchener's Omdurman campaign in which he commanded a Sudanese battalion; and in the South African War. In 1900 he transferred yet again, this time to the Royal Fusiliers in England. Despite all his operational experience and undoubted military ability, he had antagonised higher authority, who saw him as unbalanced. His entry in the Dictionary of National Biography pulls no punches when describing the doldrum period of his career after the Boer War:

> Many idiosyncrasies, regarded with amused tolerance in a young officer, proved less becoming in a soldier of standing and distinction. A passion

for theatrical society, gifts as an excellent raconteur and entertainer, a constant flow of quips and quotations in French obscured some merit. A remarkable knowledge of military history was warped by a lack of systematic training and by a self-confidence that often failed to impress. Townshend's abilities were, thus, perhaps not un-justifiably, regarded as unbalanced and he now went through a period of lean years.[7]

Fed up with service in England in the early 1900s, he returned to India and by the outbreak of war was commanding the Rawalpindi Brigade. In the rush of promotions to fill senior posts in the expanding Indian Army, his lobbying for active service brought him the poisoned chalice of command of the 6th Division in the sweltering heat of the Tigris valley.

Nixon arrived in Basra on 9 April with his 2nd Corps staff and took over just as reports were coming in of the beginning of the Turkish offensives on the Shaiba and Ahwaz fronts. Shaiba was at that time cut off from Basra by a flooded area some ten miles wide. All supply had to be by local craft or by pack mules wading up to their bellies through the water. Shaiba itself had been turned into an entrenched camp with a three and a half mile perimeter in which Delamain's 16th Brigade held the northern half and Fry's 18th Brigade the southern. Fry, the senior of the two, was in command. Major General Melliss VC of 30th Brigade was acting commander of 6th Division in Basra until Townshend could arrive from India on 22 April.

Sulaiman Askari Bey, though still suffering the effects of his wounds, advanced on Shaiba with 12,000 Turkish troops and 10,000 Arab irregulars. He launched attack after attack on the Shaiba defences during 12 April and was hurled back with heavy losses by Delamain's and Fry's brigades, which suffered only five killed and 75 wounded. Melliss and the 6th Divisional staff reached Shaiba in local craft that night and took over command.

The whole of 13 April was spent by both brigades and the cavalry in reconnaissance in force to locate the position to which Sulaiman Askari had fallen back during the night and to establish the positions of his flanks. The ground rises slightly west of Shaiba to a couple of low parallel ridges no more than 25 feet above the flood water and about two miles apart. The first ridge was cleared in brisk fighting, but mirages soon made Sulaiman's main position behind the second ridge extraordinarily difficult to locate accurately because most of it was on the reverse slope. His northern flank rested on the floods and his southern was covered by a swarm of Arab irregulars. By the time Melliss was satisfied that he knew enough about Sulaiman's position it was too late to attack before dark.

The battle next day was memorable for the stoicism of the British and Indian infantry. The two brigades once again cleared the first ridge and then advanced on the second in a frontal assault, Melliss having decided not to risk entanglement with the Arabs on the southern flank and not having enough boats to move round through the floods to the north. As the brigades breasted the second ridge, they came under heavy fire from two lines of Turkish trenches, whose occupants had the British line silhouetted against the skyline. An intense fire fight began and went on until mid-afternoon, in which neither side would give way. At 3.30pm, Melliss summoned his brigadiers and asked for a last supreme effort, while at the same time making prudent arrangements for a withdrawal to the Shaiba defences if all else failed.

The troops responded magnificently to Melliss's appeal. Ground was gained piecemeal here and there; the Turkish artillery fire started to fade; and sensing a Turkish collapse, the British line surged forward, over-running the Turkish frontline as the shadows lengthened around five o'clock. The second line had still to be taken, but before an assault could be organised, white flags appeared and a mass of fugitives were seen rushing rearwards. The British artillery was unable to profit by the Turkish disorder because the guns were almost out of ammunition; and the cavalry could not pursue because they were on their way back to take up positions from which to cover the withdrawal if it were to prove necessary.

Pursuit, in fact, was not an option open to Melliss for another reason. The men had been fighting continuously for three days in the intense heat, and on the last day had lain for hours in the exposed firing-line under the midday sun. Dehydration had led to the phenomenon of men falling asleep in their firing positions during the battle. But lack of British pursuit scarcely mattered: the Arab irregulars, fickle and self-seeking as ever, turned on the Turks and reaped a gruesome price for their failure. The Turkish losses in the battle are recorded as 4,000 Turks and 2,000 Arabs killed and wounded, and 1,000 captured, out of a force of 15,000 actually engaged. The British losses were not light: 161 killed and 901 wounded out of a fighting strength of 4,595 rifles and 733 sabres, the infantry losing 20 per cent of their strength.

Melliss's victory at Shaiba was summed up in a pamphlet published by the Turkish General Staff:

> The accursed mirage-ridden battle of Shaiba was a contest between knowledge and ignorance. On one side ignorance and medieval manoeuvres, on the other the skill and experience of 40 years soldiering possessed by Fry, Melliss and Delamain . . . Our troops were not equal in numbers or quality to their task.[8]

The Turks withdrew back to their base at Nasiriya on the Euphrates. Poor Sulaiman Askari did not accompany them. His unhealed wounds had compelled him to command from a litter. When Turkish resistance collapsed, he committed suicide after denouncing the treachery of the Arabs.

Shaiba was very much 6th Division's battle although its 17th Brigade, under Brigadier-General Dobbie, was detached, holding Qurna. Nixon toyed with the idea of ignoring the direct threat to Ahwaz by advancing from Qurna up the Tigris to Amara, thus seizing the base from which the Turkish thrust towards the oilfields was being supplied. Shortage of river craft denied him this option for the time being until more could arrive from India, but the crucial factor, which decided his next move, was a cable from Whitehall expressing the Admiralty's concern for the rapid restoration of oil supplies. Nixon, therefore, gave Gorringe's newly constituted 12th Division the task of restoring the security of the Persian oilfield and the pipeline, which ran down the Karun river to Abadan. Townshend, who took over 6th Division on 22 April, was to prepare for an advance up the Tigris to Amara and the Euphrates to Nasiriya when sufficient steamers and craft had been assembled.

At the end of April, Gorringe moved up the Karun with Melliss's 30th Brigade to join Lean's 12th Brigade, which was already garrisoning Ahwaz. He advanced north-west with these two brigades astride the Karkha River which flows into the marshes just east of Amara. The Turks did not stay to oppose him and withdrew precipitately back down the river. Gorringe pursued, mainly opposed by the local Arabs, who acted treacherously whenever they had the chance to do so. The real enemy, however, was the increasing heat in the sweltering marshes of the region, which had laid low almost a quarter of his force by the time the oilfields and pipeline were secure. The oil started to flow again on 13 June.

Before Nixon could revert to his plan for the advance up the Tigris, a high level *contretemps* began between the India Office in Whitehall, the Indian Government in Delhi, and the men on the ground – Nixon, the theatre commander, and Cox, his political adviser. Delhi's original instructions to Nixon were to plan the occupation of the Basra Province, lying roughly within the triangle of Basra–Kut al Amara–Nasiriya, preparatory to an advance on Baghdad. The India Office belatedly objected to Nixon being given Baghdad as a future objective, the Secretary of State, Lord Crewe, cabling the Viceroy, Lord Hardinge, on 24 April:

> I presume he [Nixon] clearly understands that Government will not sanction at this moment any advance beyond the present theatre of operations. We must confine ourselves during the summer to defence of Basra Vilayet [province] and our oil interests. . . . Strategically our present position is a sound one, and at present we cannot afford to take risks by unduly extending it. We must play a safe game in Mesopotamia.[9]

Nixon and Cox held a diagrammatically opposite point of view.

Unnecessary delay would enable the Turks to reorganise after the series of defeats which they had suffered, and any loss of momentum would discourage the Arab tribes from defecting to the British side. British tactical superiority had been amply demonstrated and should be exploited to the full as soon as five steamers and four armed launches, which had just arrived from India, were ready for operations.

Delhi veered towards the Nixon/Cox stand-point and supported a plan which Nixon submitted for an advance up the Tigris from Qurna, timed for the last week of May, on the clear understanding that he would not need reinforcement. Lord Crewe reluctantly authorised the advance on being assured that Nixon would not go beyond Amara, and that he could hold the place throughout the hot weather despite the probable arrival of Turkish reinforcements at Baghdad.

While these arguments had been going on, Townshend had been preparing to attack the Turkish positions, which blocked the Tigris five miles north of Qurna. The whole area was a vast expanse of flood-water with a series of sandy islands on which the Turks had built defensive positions and emplaced their artillery. Townshend looked for a way round but there was none so it had to be a frontal assault through the floods which were from one to three feet deep, but across which there were deeper irrigation channels, which could not be seen and made wading hazardous. He decided instead to use the small local craft, called bellums, each of which would carry an infantry section. Fitting an armoured shield across the bows would provide some protection; and when lashed together into rafts they could carry machineguns and light artillery pieces. The Sappers were to build larger improvised rafts for the heavier guns, but the greatest reliance of all was to be placed upon the fire support of three sloops, *Odin*, *Espiègle* and *Clio*, and several armed launches, some of which were fitted as minesweepers. The naval flotilla was under command of Captain W Nunn RN, in *Espiègle*, which was to act as the headquarters ship. 17th Brigade, now under Colonel Climo because Brigadier-General Dobbie had been invalided sick, was to lead the assault, using 372 bellums, and Delamain's 16th Brigade was to be embarked in steamers to exploit upriver if the Turkish position collapsed, or to reinforce Climo if it did not.

Townshend prepared the operation, nick-named 'Townshend's Regatta', with meticulous attention to detail and careful rehearsal, which paid off handsomely. He intended to take two bites at the Turkish position, which was over six miles deep. In his first bite, he hoped that 17th Brigade in their bellums would be able to clear the first three miles of island positions. He suspected, however, that the main Turkish position might be just beyond the floods on a three mile long north-south ridge, running parallel to the Tigris and with the village of Abu Aran at its southern end, close to the river bank. In his second bite, 16th Brigade would probably land at Abu Aran to assault this ridge dry-shod, while 17th Brigade turned in from the west still using their bellums.

The operation began in the early hours of 31 May as the sloops moved up river to reach their supporting positions, and a feint assault was made up the east bank while it was still dark. The ships opened fire at 5am, and an hour later 17th Brigade's armada of bellums started its advance towards the first Turkish held island. The men had on occasions to get out and shove their bellums through the shallower places, but the naval gun-fire and artillery support was so effective that little resistance was met, and all the Turkish island positions had been taken by late afternoon. Townshend decided to halt operations and to prepare for the assault on the Abu Aran ridge next day.

On 1 April, 17th Brigade set off again in their bellums through reed filled swamps to turn the Abu Aran ridge from the west, while 16th Brigade landed at the village. It was all a waste of time: one of Nixon's two reconnaissance aircraft dropped a message on the deck of *Espiègle*, report-ing that the ridge had been evacuated by the Turks, who were fleeing upriver in every available craft. Townshend immediately ordered the con-centration of his force at Abu Aran while Captain Nunn probed upriver to see if any steamer could be passed through a line of sunken craft with which the Turks had tried to block the Tigris a couple of miles north of Abu Aran.

Fortunately the block was incomplete. A passage was soon buoyed for the armed mine-sweeping launches *Shaitan* and *Sumana* to start off in pursuit while a wider channel was cleared for the sloops and steamers. By 3pm, the three sloops were through the obstruction with Townshend and Nunn in *Espiègle* and the chase proper was on. Just before 6pm *Shaitan* opened fire with her 12 pounder on the Turkish gunboat *Marmariss*, which was covering the Turkish retreat, and damaged her. The sloops then came into action with their heavier 4-inch guns. Panic seized the Turkish steamers, whose captains started casting off the lighters that they were towing, many full of soldiers and warlike stores, in order to increase their speed. *Odin* was left behind to round them up, and Townshend left one of his staff officers with her to speed the advance of his own steamers. As darkness fell, navigation became too hazardous and Nunn decided to anchor until the moon came up.

The pursuit began again at 2am, the British ships passing the aban-doned *Marmariss* and other Turkish vessels, and collecting more lighters full of troops. By dawn, it was clear that the Turkish retreat had become a demoralised rout. Navigation, however, was becoming difficult for the sloops. *Espiègle* ran aground and *Clio* was too deep to go any further, so Nunn and Townshend, who had been joined by Sir Percy Cox, transferred to the paddle yacht *Comet* and pushed on with the shallower draft craft throughout the rest of 2 June, reaching Qala Salih, where Townshend spread the news of the arrival of a formidable British force by ordering the local sheikh, who was summoned on board, to collect supplies for 15,000 men.

Next day Townshend called a halt 12 miles south of Amara so that the leading brigade could be brought up in relays by the steamers. It seemed unlikely that the Turks would abandon Amara without a fight. Nunn soon persuaded Townshend to change his mind and to take the risk of pushing on with the armed launches. *Shaitan*, commanded by Lieutenant Mark Singleton, led the way and brazenly sailed past the town, using his 12-pounder to discourage opposition from large numbers of Turkish troops on the river bank, who fled without firing a shot. *Comet* arrived shortly afterwards and Townshend accepted the capitulation of Amara and all the Turkish troops in the area, which included some of the force that had been driven away from the oilfields by Gorringe. He had no more than 40 sailors and marines at his back: the Turks were only too willing to surrender to avoid falling into the unmerciful hands of the local Arab tribes, who had turned against them. The leading brigade, the 16th, did not reach Amara for another two days. The whole operation had cost only four killed and 21 wounded!

Nixon had every right to be pleased with Townshend's feat. Not only had the operation been well planned and executed, Townshend had also engendered a great spirit of enthusiasm into his 6th Division. Morale was high; there had been remarkably few heat casualties, despite the June temperatures rising to 110 degrees in the shade; and there was very little sickness. All three prongs of the Turkish counter-offensive had now been broken. It only remained to block the Euphrates route by which the Turks could attack the British lines of communication along the Tigris. This was thought to be best done by taking Nasiriya, the trading centre of the most powerful Euphrates tribes. Nixon gave this task to Gorringe's 12th Division.

As June advanced, so did the heat, which the old European residents recalled as the most oppressive in living memory. Sickness began to rise dramatically. Townshend, himself, fell ill towards the end of the month and was evacuated to India for two months' sick leave. Delamain took over 6th Division, defending Amara, during his absence.

While preparations were being made for Gorringe's operations against Nasiriya, the debate on whether to risk an advance to Baghdad was re-opened. The pressure for the occupation of the city, which was still 370 miles away, came largely from the political authorities, who saw its capture as a way of ending the virulent Turco-German intrigues in Tehran and Kabul, and of showing the Mesopotamian tribes which was the winning side.

There were a number of strategic reasons as well. Turkish forces were currently pinned down in the desperate fighting at Gallipoli, and in the

Lake Van area of Kurdistan, where the Russians had again been victorious and were only 30 marches from Baghdad. The chances of the Turks being able to reinforce their hard pressed troops in Mesopotamia seemed remote – a point admitted by the Turkish General Staff after the war. The only objections were military: cold General Staff calculations showed that Nixon did not, in fact, have the resources – military, naval and logistic – to reach Baghdad and maintain himself there at the extremity of a 500 mile river line of communication, on which low water levels from July to November might stop the larger steamers operating. However, the ease with which he had taken Amara undermined these practical considerations in Whitehall and Delhi, and in his own mind.

There was a halfway house – Kut al Amara on the Tigris – another 150 miles nearer Baghdad. It lay at the entrance of the Shatt-al-Hai, a lateral water-way linking the Tigris to the Euphrates from Kut to Nasiriya, by which Turkish forces were being switched between the two rivers. It was also another politically important centre as far as the Arabs were concerned and an even better position than Amara from which to check a renewed Turkish thrust towards the oilfields. The decision to advance on Kut, however, need not, indeed could not, be taken until the outcome of Gorringe's operations against Nasiriya were known since most of Nunn's naval flotilla, on which an advance upon Kut would depend, was needed to support his advance up the Euphrates.

It took Gorringe a month to master Nasiriya. His 12th and 30th Brigades were embarked in river steamers. He and the ubiquitous Captain Nunn had their headquarters in the steamer *Bloss Lynch*, from which they commanded a mixed flotilla of armed launches and stern-wheelers, some of which had seen service with Kitchener on the Nile and were showing their age. Nunn's sloops drew too much water to pass through the shallows of Hammar Lake and soon had to be left behind. The main problem was finding navigable passages through the swamps of the Euphrates, which breaks up into innumerable marshy channels between Qurna and Nasiriya, the most practicable of which the Turks had blocked with sunken vessels, covered by guns on shore. To make matters more difficult, water-levels were already starting to drop, making navigation even more hazardous.

The Gorringe/Nunn force set off on 26 June and took until 6 July to fight its way, often against determined opposition, through to the far side of the marshes. The infantry frequently had to fight from bellums, dragged knee-deep through muddy reeds to clear Turkish and Arab positions, covering blocks in the few practicable channels. Twenty-five miles from Nasiriya the marshes disappeared and the main stream of the Euphrates ran in a 200 yard wide channel through some of Mesopotamia's richest agricultural land. It was not until Gorringe's advance guard came within nine miles of Nasiriya that any substantial opposition was encountered. A force estimated at 5,000 to 6,000 men under Sulaiman Askari's successor, Ahmed Bey, was entrenched on both banks in a series of strong positions behind a number of unfordable creeks. The whole defensive complex covered a three mile stretch of the river, which was itself blocked with sunken craft and cables at the beginning of the defended stretch.

Gorringe decided that discretion was the better part of valour. Sickness, which was mounting uncontrollably in the dank heat of July, had reduced Melliss's 30th Brigade to less than 2,000 rifles, so he spent almost a week reconnoitring in force while his steamers went back to ferry forward 12th Brigade. His initial attacks on 14 July with a brigade on either bank failed, and convinced him that he would need further reinforcement. With the water in the Hammar Lake dropping fast, it took another week to bring forward 18th Brigade, which belonged to 6th Division, from Qurna to act as general reserve, when he renewed his attack at dawn on 24 July. Fighting was severe on both banks, but by midday the strongest Turkish positions had been taken with the invaluable help of Nunn's naval guns, and both leading brigades were advancing towards what was thought to be the last Turkish line of defence. Shaiba repeated itself: Turkish resistance collapsed quite suddenly, and by dusk Captain Nunn was off Nasiriya in the stern-wheeler *Shushan* (used by Kitchener at Omdurman), accompanied by two other armed steamers.

Although white flags were flying over the town, some Turks or Arabs fired on the ships from the roof-tops, seriously wounding the captain of the *Shushan*, so Nunn decided to anchor for the night. Next morning, the local sheikh surrendered the town, and 12th and 30th Brigades occupied it during the afternoon. Ahmed Bey's losses had been 2,500 killed, wounded or taken prisoner: Gorringe's battle casualties were just over 500, but his sick rate was very much higher, particularly amongst the British battalions, whose health was beginning to cause real concern.

The decision had now to be taken whether to allow Nixon to continue the advance up the Tigris to Kut so as to maintain momentum as he and Cox advocated, or to play safe by going on the defensive at Amara and Nasiriya until the hot weather was over, which was the course preferred by Whitehall and to a lesser extent by Delhi. The Turks themselves reinforced Nixon's case by moving troops down the Tigris from Kut to threaten Amara. Delamain, who was commanding 6th Division in Townshend's absence, advanced to meet them with 16th Brigade and by the end of July was holding Ali Garbi, half way to Kut already.

Two new wild cards appeared amongst the arguments for and against pushing on up the Tigris. Austen Chamberlain, who had taken over from Lord Crewe as Secretary of State for India at the end of May, stressed the need for military success somewhere in the Middle East to offset the failure of the Suvla landings at Gallipoli on 7 August. The capture of

Baghdad would impress the whole Moslem world, but he did not advocate taking the military risks involved unless reserves could be provided from Egypt. A Turkish attempt to take Aden had just been foiled by the rapid dispatch from Egypt of Major General George Younghusband's 28th Indian Brigade (2nd Leicesters and three Indian infantry battalions) and there was a possibility that it could be sent to Nixon, although Kitchener wanted it returned to Egypt. As it happened, however, a debate had begun in Whitehall about withdrawing the Indian infantry divisions from France before the onset of winter weather. Here too Kitchener disliked the idea: he was opposed to any reduction of strength on the Western Front. Nonetheless, opinion in Whitehall and Delhi was moving towards their shipment to Egypt as a general reserve in the war against Turkey. The redeployment of one or two of these divisions to Mesopotamia would make the taking and holding of Baghdad more practicable if they arrived in time, but in August there was no certainty that they would be released from France. These tantalising future possibilities strengthened the case for seizing Kut as a stepping-stone to Baghdad.

By the time Townshend reassumed command of 6th Division at Amara at the end of August, the Viceroy had reluctantly authorised an advance on Kut with the caveat that there was to be no advance on Baghdad without the Government of India's sanction. He was far from sanguine about Nixon's policy of adding another 150 miles to his line of communications in the hot weather when the water levels in the Tigris were too low for fully loaded steamers and before the theatre could be reinforced.

Nixon was delighted with the decision to advance to Kut, and hoped that it would lead inexorably to the early capture of Baghdad. He found Townshend, who had the responsibility of carrying out the advance, much less enthusiastic. There was never any question, as has sometimes been suggested, of it being Townshend who wanted to go for Baghdad regardless of risk; nor who underestimated the problems of doing so. Intelligence reported that a strong defensive position was being built at Ctesiphon on the north bank of the Tigris, some 20 miles south of Baghdad, by a new Turkish commander, Nur-ud-Din, who had been sent by Constantinople to defend the city. Townshend did suggest to Nixon that if he stampeded the Turks at Kut, as had happened at Shaiba, Qurna, Amara and Nasiriya, he would like to pursue them to Baghdad, but only if they were really on the run. Nixon agreed, adding that he would accompany Townshend into the city.

It took until the end of August to move 18th and 30th Brigades round from Nasiriya to Amara: the former to rejoin 6th Division for the advance on Kut, and the latter to garrison Amara as part of Gorringe's 12th Division, which Nixon made responsible for the defence of the lines of communication.

On 1 September, Townshend started to concentrate his three brigades

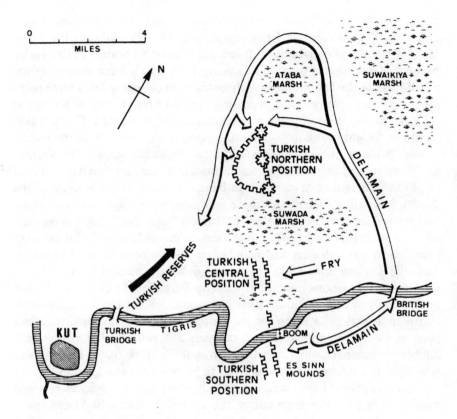

Map 20: The First Battle of Kut: 28 September 1915

(16th, 17th and 18th) at Ali Garbi. Captain Nunn was away in *Espiègle*, which was undergoing repairs in Ceylon, and his place as Senior Naval Officer was taken by Lieutenant Commander Cookson with a much reduced flotilla, due to lack of water in the Tigris. Unlike previous operations, most of the troops marched along the banks of the Tigris, covered by the flotilla's guns and supplied from the shallower draft steamers. Temperatures climbed to 120 degrees in the shade, so marches were carried out in the early morning and evening. Even so numbers of heat casualties were again climbing alarmingly by the time Townshend had managed to concentrate his division a few miles downstream from Nur-ud-Din's defensive position covering Kut.

The Turks had spent several months preparing a line of fortifications, stretching some miles out into the desert on both banks of the Tigris, called the Es Sinn position, and had built a floating bridge behind their front for the movement of reserves. Townshend assumed that Nur-ud-Din would be ready for thrusts up both banks of the Tigris, as had happened in all earlier British attacks. He therefore deployed as if to do the same again, with Delamain commanding the south bank force based upon 16th and 17th Brigades, while Fry commanded 18th Brigade on the north bank. A pontoon bridge was built just out of sight and range of the Turks, by which Townshend intended to bring Delamain's force over onto the north bank at the last moment with instructions to carry out a wide turning movement to envelope and destroy Nur-ud-Din's northern flank. For the first time in the campaign no bellums would be needed! Every action would be fought in the dry scrub of the desert well away from the river.

On 26 September Delamain and Fry advanced against the Turkish fortifications and delivered a series of probing attacks on that day and next to pin the Turkish reserves on both banks. Then during the night of the 27–28 September Delamain's force was passed over the pontoon bridge and started its march round the Turkish left flank. Navigation across the desert was surprisingly good, but the ten mile march took far longer than expected. It was well after daybreak before the two brigades started to outflank the Turkish line, while Fry pinned down the bulk of their troops in the strongest positions near the river. The Turks fought back and did not give in easily as their positions were attacked in succession from the north and rear. It was exhausting for the British and Indian troops, who had been up since 2am and were each carrying 200 rounds of ammunition – double the normal issue – as well as two water-bottles. As the broiling sun rose higher, a strong hot wind started to blow up the sand around them, and mirages played havoc with direction keeping and range finding. It was midday before the northern half of the Turkish defences had been taken and a short halt could be called, during which Turkish harassing fire stampeded many of the water-carrying mules when they were brought up to replenish water bottles.

During the afternoon, all three of Townshend's brigades reopened their attacks, but had to meet and defeat the Turkish reserves, which Nur-ud-Din had belatedly hurried across his boat bridge to reinforce his crumbling north bank positions. Darkness fell before Delamain's brigades could break through to the river. They pulled back slightly and bivouacked under arms almost stupefied with exhaustion, hungry, thirsty and miserably cold with the temperature falling 50 degrees during the night. They had lost 1,233 men of whom 94 had been killed, but when their patrols pushed forward again at dawn next day, they found the Turkish positions empty.

Townshend first learned that Nur-ud-Din was withdrawing upriver from air reconnaissance reports early on 29 September. He was ready to repeat his successful pursuit to Amara, but the river sided with the Turks and stopped him doing so. Soon after dusk, at the end of the battle on the 28th, Commander Cookson's sailors had tried to break through the Turkish boom across the river. Turkish defensive fire, however, was so heavy that Cookson would not risk his men and attempted to cut the

cables himself. He was killed instantly, and the attempt had to be abandoned. (He was later awarded a posthumous VC.) It was not, however, his
gallant failure that caused the delays which hampered Townshend's pursuit: lack of water in the Tigris stopped his steamers as they tried to push
up river. It took two days' hard work to get them past Kut! By then Nur-
ud-Din was withdrawing methodically towards his main position, on
which he intended to defend Baghdad, at Ctesiphon. Townshend halted
his pursuit on 5 October at Aziziya, another 100 miles up river from Kut,
but still about 50 miles from Baghdad. Air and intelligence reports showed
that Nur-ud-Din was firmly in occupation of the Ctesiphon defences and
had no intention of abandoning Baghdad without a fight.

Nixon was in duty bound to seek Delhi's concurrence before directing
Townshend to attack Nur-ud-Din at Ctesiphon. He had already exceeded
his instructions not to go beyond Kut without authority, and it was now
abundantly clear that Baghdad was unlikely to fall to a *coup de main*. The
three-sided debate between Austen Chamberlain in Whitehall, Lord
Hardinge in Delhi, and the Nixon/Cox team in Mesopotamia on what to
do next was reopened, but a fourth party of influence soon emerged:
Townshend decided that he must speak up for his exhausted troops.

There was general agreement that the early capture of Baghdad would
be of immense political and military value. The bone of contention was
whether the city could be held until the Indian divisions from France
could reach Basra and take over the defence of the Tigris supply line so
that both 6th and 12th Divisions could be concentrated at Baghdad.
Chamberlain doubted it and Hardinge was sceptical, but both agreed
that the men on the spot should decide whether Nur-ud-Din could be
defeated at Ctesiphon and hustled away from Baghdad with the forces
already at Nixon's disposal. Nixon was utterly confident that Townshend
could repeat his victories at Qurna, Amara and Kut; Townshend was
equally certain that it was idiocy to try until the Indian divisions from
France were actually on the Tigris. He cabled to Nixon on 3 October,
when he realised that he had failed to stampede the Turks:

> If I may be allowed to express an opinion I should say that our object up
> to the battle of Kut has been the consolidation of the Basra Vilayet and
> the occupation of the strategic position of Kut. . . . If Government does
> not consider the occupation of Baghdad is yet politically advisable . . .
> then we should on all military grounds occupy ourselves with consoli-
> dating our position at Kut. . . . On the other hand, if Government
> desire to occupy Baghdad then I am of the opinion that a methodical
> advance from Kut by road by two divisions or one army corps or one
> division closely supported by another . . . is absolutely necessary unless
> great risk is to be incurred.[10]

Nixon did not agree. His chief of staff replied:

> The Turkish force there [at Ctesiphon] is inferior in numbers and
> morale to the force you successfully defeated at Kut and the position is
> not nearly so strong. It is the Army Commander's intention to open the
> way to Baghdad, as he understands another division will be sent from
> France and he would like to know your plan for effecting this object with
> the force you had at Kut . . .[11]

Nixon was unswayed by Townshend's views, and Townshend felt it was
not for him to protest further, but to get on with whatever his
Commander-in-Chief ordered him to do. In Whitehall, the issue was
deemed so important that the Cabinet set up a special inter-departmen-
tal committee to advise on whether Nixon should be authorised to
advance on Baghdad or not. In reply, dated 8 October, to a personal
cable from Austen Chamberlain, Nixon was categoric in his views:

> I am confident that I can beat Nur-ud-Din and occupy Baghdad with-
> out any addition to my force. But if the Turks should turn their serious
> attention to the recovery of Baghdad and should send to Mesopotamia
> the large organised forces which would be necessary for such an opera-
> tion then I consider that I should require one division (and I would like
> one white cavalry regiment) in addition to my present force to watch
> both the Tigris and Euphrates lines of approach and defeat the enemy
> as he comes in reach.[12]

On 2 October the Cabinet authorised Austen Chamberlain to cable
Hardinge saying:

> Nixon may march on Baghdad if he is satisfied that force he has avail-
> able is sufficient for the operation. Reinforcements will take time owing
> to relief and transport arrangements, but two divisions will be sent as
> soon as possible.[13]

Kitchener seems to have been the only member of the Cabinet to dissent,
because he was loath to part with the two divisions, which, if not kept in
France, he wanted for Egypt, and because he foresaw more clearly than
his colleagues the impact on the affairs of the Middle East of Bulgaria's
entry into the war on the side of the Central Powers. He sent an amplify-
ing cable to Hardinge warning him that the Germans would soon be able
to supply Turkey with guns and ammunition direct. Moreover, the War
Office calculated that the Turks would be able to dispatch 60,000 to
70,000 troops to retake Baghdad if Gallipoli were to be evacuated, which
seemed very probable. He did relent on refusing reinforcements for Nixon

by authorising the dispatch of Younghusband's 28th Brigade to Basra from Egypt to which it had returned after its successful defence of Aden. 28th Brigade could not reach Basra until early December.

No one on the British side realised the impact of Nixon's victories at Amara and Nasiriya in June and July on the Turco-German command in Constantinople. It had two far reaching results. First, Field Marshal von der Goltz, who had trained the Turkish Army on Prussian lines in the 1890s and had more recently been German military governor of the Low Countries, was appointed to command all Turkish forces operating between Lake Van in Kurdistan and the Persian Gulf, grouped together as the new Turkish 6th Army. He was also given the responsibility for directing the Turco-German politico-military *Jihad* in Persia, Afghanistan and India. Secondly, great efforts were made to divert troops from Armenia and Kurdistan to reinforce Nur-ud-Din at Ctesiphon. Two strong and experienced Anatolian divisions, the 45th and 51st, under the 18th Corps, were marched southwards towards Baghdad, commanded by Halil Bey. The arrival of these troops and of German staff officers as chiefs of staff or principal operations officers in Mesopotamia was to tip the balance of advantage decisively in the Turks' favour.

These changes on the Turkish side were reported by British intelligence sources, but were discounted as being impossible for the Turks to implement before the extra Indian divisions arrived on the Tigris from France. There had been so many similar reports of large Turkish reinforcements moving towards Baghdad in the past that Nixon took them all with a pinch of salt and relied on his own local intelligence assessments of what stood in front of him. When Townshend started his advance on Ctesiphon from Aziziya on 15 November, Nixon estimated that Nur-ud-Din had at the most 10,000 to 11,000 demoralised troops of the 35th and 38th Divisions, now grouped under the 13th Corps, to hold the two lines of fortified entrenchments, which stretched six miles north-eastwards from the Tigris into the desert, blocking the road to Baghdad. In fact, the 45th Division was already at Ctesiphon and the 51st Division was being positioned in general reserve behind the front as it arrived. Nur-ud-Din's strength of about 20,000 was double Nixon's estimate!

Townshend still had real qualms about British strategy. Writing up his diary later he said:

> . . . our strategy should have been to have remained on the defensive with minimum forces sufficient for that purpose. All my study [of military history] indicated disaster to me. However.the die was cast. And so, when Sir John Nixon asked me on the eve of the battle: 'Are you confident of winning Townshend? I replied: 'yes, I shall win alright'. And I did . . .[14]

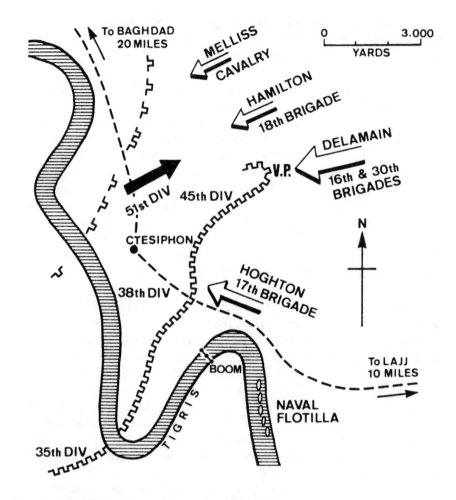

Map 21: The Battle of Ctesiphon: 22 November 1915

Townshend's attack at Ctesiphon on 22 November was a replica of his battle for Kut. Realising that he was up against a numerically superior force, though not how superior, he decided to hustle the Turks out of their positions by shock action in which every man, gun and steamer was to be 'in the shop window' with no general reserve. He organised his brigades into four columns. 17th Brigade, now under Brigadier-General Hoghton, would again open the battle but this time with a holding attack on the southern half of the Turkish line nearest the Tigris. A flying column under Melliss, consisting of the cavalry brigade and an Indian infantry battalion, was to ride right round the Turkish northern flank to threaten their second line and so panic their troops holding the first line. 18th Brigade under Brigadier-General Hamilton would make a shorter hook round the northern flank to attack the rear of the first line. Once all the Turkish reserves had been drawn by these attacks, the ubiquitous Delamain would launch the decisive attack with his trusted 16th Brigade and 30th Brigade under Colonel Climo against a very strong position on some mounds at the northern end of the first line, which Townshend called the 'Vital Point' or 'VP', and which, though he did not know it, was held by the fresh 45th Division. The naval flotilla would as usual try to force the Turkish obstructions in the river and bring fire to bear on the southern end of their line to help Hoghton.

As at Kut, the night march with surprisingly good navigation brought the four columns into their right assembly positions, and this time well before dawn. The early morning haze lay over the flat, almost featureless, plain obscuring the Turkish trenches. Only the great arch in the ruins of Ctesiphon rose out of the mist. Hoghton's brigade had the greatest difficulty in finding the Turkish trenches and drawing fire from 38th Division in the southern sector. The appearance of Melliss's flying column and Hamilton's 18th Brigade in the gap between the two Turkish defence lines seemed to cause a panic in the rear of 45th Division, holding 'VP'. Both Delamain and Townshend saw what they took to be a Turkish withdrawal from 'VP' to face Hamilton's attack, and so Townshend allowed Delamain to launch the main attack on 'VP' without awaiting further developments. What that Turkish movement was has never been discovered, but it certainly was not 45th Division leaving 'VP'. Delamain did take 'VP' but at great cost to himself and the Turks. By early afternoon, most of the Turkish first line was in British hands and their 45th Division was virtually destroyed as a fighting entity, but intense fighting was going on in the two mile gap between the first and second lines as Nur-ud-Din had rushed 51st Division up from reserve to check Melliss's and Hamilton's turning movements.

As the afternoon wore on, Turkish numbers began to tell and the battle started to swing in their favour. 51st Division's counter-attacks were checked, but at a high cost. Townshend saw wounded soldiers coming back escorted by unwounded men: a sure sign that his men were losing confidence. Further efforts to reach the Turkish second line failed and as darkness fell Townshend pulled all his troops back to reorganise and bivouac for the night around and to the south of 'VP'. He knew his losses had been severe and reported to Nixon that he had about 2,000 wounded, who were being collected at 'VP' for evacuation to two hospital steamers on the Tigris, which had a total capacity for 1,500 casualties. Although he did not know it at the time, he had, in fact, lost 4,511 men!

When dawn broke on 23 November, both opposing commanders were in a quandary, not really knowing what had happened to the other side during the battle on the previous day. Townshend hoped to find the Turks were withdrawing up the Tigris as had happened so often in the past. Air reconnaissance reports, indeed, suggested this was so, but he knew his

division was in no condition to pursue. Before he could do anything, he
had to water, feed and rest his troops, and, above all else, evacuate his
wounded to the steamers, using whatever wagons and carts that could be
collected. He decided, therefore, to stand on the defensive in the northern
half of the Turkish first line and to await events.

Nur-ud-Din had been minded to withdraw as Townshend expected,
but, with the tougher Anatolian divisional commanders and German staff
officers at his elbow, he ordered the occupation of the second line and
waited a renewed British attack. It was not until midday that Arab inform-
ers convinced him that Townshend had been seriously weakened and
might withdraw if attacked. It took him even longer to arrange a counter-
offensive. The 13th Corps (35th and 38th Divisions) set off in
mid-afternoon to attack the southern half of the British line, but their
courage failed them when they came under artillery fire and their effort
eventually collapsed. The harder 18th Corps (45th and 51st Divisions) set
off an hour later to attack the 'VP' area and turn the British line. All 45th
Division's attacks, which went on until 2am in the morning, were
repulsed; and the 51st lost its way and was never engaged. Nur-ud-Din
and his staff were, according to the Turkish account, 'in the depths of
despair and despondency', but decided to hold on for another day in the
second line.[15]

The 24th was relatively quiet, but that evening a report came into
Nur's headquarters, saying that Townshend had left a small holding force
at 'VP' and was advancing in a wide turning movement towards the
Turkish rear. Nur did not wait for confirmation and ordered an immediate general withdrawal, which developed into a shambles. By midday on
the 25th, the report was found to be nonsense and a very embarrassed
Nur ordered his troops to counter-march. Townshend had wanted to stay
at Ctesiphon until reinforced, because of the adverse effect that a withdrawal would have on the Arabs. When, however, he received air reports
of Nur's columns advancing eastwards again, he concluded, wrongly, that
he had been reinforced by more troops from the Caucasus. He decided
that he must withdraw certainly to his advanced base at Lajj some ten
miles downriver, if not back to his main base at Kut.

Nixon was as over-optimistic as ever, and tried to make Townshend
change his mind, but the latter replied by cable:

> I consider that with 4,300 casualties – which is the total – and when
> brigades are reduced to little more than a full strength British battalion
> it would have been madness to have remained at Ctesiphon a moment
> longer than I did. At 4pm yesterday [25th] two large columns of Turks
> estimated at 5,000 each by air service were advancing from their
> entrenched line . . . There is no question of my engaging such a force in
> my present state with the men wornout. . . .[16]

Once the withdrawal had begun, the local Arabs became overtly hostile again and did everything they could to impede movement on the Tigris. Turkish numerical superiority was such that Townshend was forced to fall back step by step towards Kut. He had to fight one major rear-guard action to cover the naval flotilla when it was delayed by shoals. The faithful *Comet* and *Firefly* launches were lost during the action. In spite of their heavy losses, particularly amongst the British officers of the Indian battalions, the troops of 6th Division under their stalwart brigade commanders never showed any signs of real loss of morale. In the last stages of the withdrawal, they out-marched the Turks, covering 44 miles in 36 hours without proper food or rest. The British official historians, who do not award accolades lightly, comment most favourably on this extraordinary feat of discipline.

On the Tigris, southward from Kut, a less happy struggle was taking place as the Medical Services strove to save the flood of wounded from Ctesiphon. Their resources were totally inadequate. Massive improvisation, in which towed barges had to be used to supplement the few steamers available for casualty evacuation, was inevitable and only mitigated by the dedicated service of the Indian Medical Corps, who did much to help the wounded, many of whom did not survive the ordeal. A doctor described how he saw one of the hospital steamers arrive at Basra:

> As the ship, with two barges, came up to us I saw that she was absolutely packed, and the barges too, with men . . . When she was about 300 to 400 yards off it looked as if she was festooned with ropes. The stench when she was close was quite definite, and what I mistook for ropes were dried stalactites of human faeces. The patients were so crowded and huddled together that they could not perform the offices of nature clear of the ship's edge . . .[17]

Townshend reached Kut on 3 December with a rifle and sabre strength of about 7,500. The siege of Kut was about to begin as Nur-ud-Din's army, reinforced by two more divisions from the Caucasus, surrounded the remnants of the 6th division in the loop of the Tigris where Kut stands. Two weeks later the Suvla and ANZAC beachheads on the Gallipoli Peninsula were evacuated. Many observers doubted the ability of the British Empire to survive these setbacks in the Moslem world. The Turco-German *Jihad* was verging on success.

CHAPTER 6

THE LOSS OF KUT AND THE ARAB REVOLT

Townshend, Murray and TE Lawrence 1916

Hussein was informed [by Sir Henry McMahon] that, subject to certain exceptions, such as the districts of Mersina, of Alexandretta, and of that portion of Syria lying west of the districts of Damascus, Homs, Hama and Aleppo, which were not purely Arab, Great Britain pledged herself to recognise and support the independence of the Arabs within the territories enclosed by the boundaries which he had proposed.

The British Official History of the
Egyptian and Palestine Campaigns.[1]

1915 had ended with British fortunes in the Middle East at a low ebb. Townshend's pyrrhic victory at Ctesiphon, followed by his withdrawal to Kut, and the evacuation of the Gallipoli Peninsula, should have spelt victory for the Turco-German *Jihad*. The fact that it did not do so, says more about Moslem disunity than the British political and military misjudgements, which caused these misfortunes.

Amongst the Persians and Afghans, the Sultan's call to *Jihad* was neutralised by the long-standing fears in Tehran and Kabul of both the Russians and the British, who, allied together as they were in 1915, were seen as doubly dangerous. Neither Shah nor Amir could see enough certainty in a Turco-German victory to warrant abandoning neutrality; nor did they trust each other sufficiently to co-operate amongst themselves. The Shah was already having to contend with the presence of 11,000 Russian troops under General Baratoff in the north-west of Persia, who had landed at Enzeli (*See Map 16*) on the Caspian coast to the west of Tehran and had advanced south towards Kermanshah to outflank the Turks in Kurdistan and to co-operate with the British advance on Baghdad. Moreover, the British were operating along his Gulf coast, protecting their oil interests, stamping out German inspired local anti-British unrest in important places like Bushire, and generally behaving as if they ruled Persia.

In Arabia, the chance of winning freedom from Ottoman rule with the help of the British was far more compelling than raising *Jihad* against them. Kitchener, while still Consul General in Egypt in the spring of 1914, had been made aware, through a secret visit to Cairo of Amir Abdullah, second son of the Grand Sherif of Mecca, that his father's ambition was to secure the autonomy of the Hejaz. Britain had an indirect interest in events there because of the large number of Indian Moslems, who went on pilgrimage to Mecca each year. When war was declared on Turkey, Kitchener wrote to the Sherif assuring him of British support for Arab independence. In his reply, the Sherif said that he would not adopt a policy hostile to Britain, but that his position in Islam made an immediate breach with the Porte unwise.

Sir Henry McMahon, on arrival in Cairo in January 1915 as British High Commissioner, continued to foster good relations with Mecca to the extent that, by mid-1915, the Sherif had opened negotiations with a specific request for a British guarantee of independence for all Arab lands lying south of the 37th Parallel between the Mediterranean and Red Sea coasts in the west, and the Persian frontier and Persian Gulf in the east. McMahon, mindful of France's long-standing ambitions in Syria, replied guardedly, expressing gratification that the aims of the Sherif and Britain were identical, but that discussion of future boundaries might be premature as many Arab rulers, particularly in Mesopotamia, were siding with the Turks.

While the Sherif took the British reply as being lukewarm, McMahon's and Maxwell's intelligence staffs reported growing anti-Turkish feeling amongst the Arabs. Evidence had come into their hands of a secret society formed amongst Arab officers in the Turkish Army, which was closely linked with a civilian society with the common aim of uniting Arabia, Syria and Mesopotamia under an Arab Caliphate. They persuaded their masters to press Whitehall to adopt a more positive stance towards Arab independence and won the argument. McMahon was authorised to assure the Sherif of wholehearted British support for Arab independence, subject to three reservations: the Lebanon coastal strip, which was not purely Arab, was to be excluded from Arab rule; the British could not act to the detriment of French interests; and the Turkish provinces of Basra and Baghdad would probably be retained under some form of British control.

Towards the end of October 1915, the McMahon Agreement was finalised, enshrining British support for the Arab cause, but leaving many details for future fine tuning. In the meantime, the study and development of policy in Arab affairs were to be handled in Cairo by a new staff, the 'Arab Bureau', under McMahon's direction. Captain, later Colonel, T E Lawrence – Lawrence of Arabia – an archaeologist and Arabist, was one of its members.

The provisos about the Lebanon and French interests were politically prudent, if militarily irrelevant in 1915. Since the 16th Century, France had deemed herself the protector of the Latin Church within the Ottoman Empire. She still held the affection of the Syrian Christians, and expected to have her way in Syria if the Entente powers won the war. The British and French Governments, therefore, decided to delineate their respective spheres of influence. By May 1916, the secret Sykes-Picot Agreement had been thrashed out between Sir Mark Sykes on behalf of Britain and Georges Picot for France. It placed modern Syria in the French sphere, leaving Britain to deal with the rest of the Arab world in any post-war settlement. The Sherif was left in ignorance of this agreement until 1918!

Anglo-Arab relations were further complicated in 1917 by the Balfour Declaration, promising the Jews a 'National Home' in Palestine. The inconsistencies in these three separate agreements – McMahon's, Sykes-Picot and Balfour – sowed the dragon's teeth of the future Arab-Israeli conflict, which was to tear the Middle East apart in the second half of the 20th Century. At the time of the McMahon Agreement, however, the Sherif judged open rebellion as premature – and who can blame him, in view of the British disasters at Gallipoli and on the Tigris?

In Egypt, it was Sir Henry McMahon's and General Sir John Maxwell's policy not to allow the war to affect the lives of the Egyptians more than security demanded: it was not their war. Any local inclination to enter into the spirit of the Sultan's call to *Jihad* was muted by the presence of the large numbers of British troops in the Nile Delta or on their way to Gallipoli, and by the money being made as Egypt was turned, first, into a modest military base for the Gallipoli Campaign, and then into the vast base complex from which British military operations in the Mediterranean and Middle East were to be conducted over the next 40 years. The Levant Base was officially established in June 1915. On the medical side alone, hospital bed capacity rose from 3,500 to 36,000, and the Atlantic liners *Britannia* and *Mauritania* were sailing as hospital ships between Egypt and England, evacuating Gallipoli and Middle East casualties.

Since Djemal Pasha's failure to cross the Suez Canal and raise Egypt in revolt in February 1915, the eastern frontiers of Egypt had been reasonably secure, although Kress von Kressenstein kept the Canal's defenders alert with frequent minor and often ingenious raids. Maxwell, however, was forced to look west towards Cyrenaica where the Grand Senussi, Sayed Amed, was threatening to invade the Nile Delta. He was the politico-religious leader of the Western Desert Bedouin tribes and one of the few Islamic leaders who were attempting to raise a genuine spirit of *Jihad* amongst their people. He was amply supplied with Turco-German weapons and advice handled by Nuri Bey, a half-brother of Enver Pasha, and Jaafar Pasha, an able Baghdadi Arab.

The campaign, which Maxwell fought to stop the Senussi invading the Nile Delta from the west was a minor affair, but it did introduce British soldiers to the Western Desert, which they were to come to know so well in the Second World War. They made their first acquaintance with places like Mersa Matruh, Daaba, Sidi Barrani, Sollum and the Siwa Oasis – names that were to litter the columns of world press from the beginning of 1940 until the end of 1942.

By November 1915, the Senussi's hostile activities around Sollum on the Egyptian frontier had become intolerable, and Maxwell assembled the first Western Desert Force at Mersa Matruh under Major General A Wallace – the second Western Desert Force, of far greater fame, was to assemble at the same place under General Sir Richard O'Connor 25 years later. Wallace's force consisted of a Yeomanry brigade, a Royal Horse Artillery battery, and a Territorial Army infantry brigade, to which Australian, New Zealand and South African units were attached from time to time.

Unwisely, the Senussi, poorly advised by the Turks, tried to challenge Wallace in battle instead of using tribal mobility and knowledge of the desert to wage a guerrilla war. Wallace defeated, but did not manage to destroy, the Bedouin army in engagements at Wadi Senab and Wadi Majld on 13 and 25 December 1915, and at Halazin on 23 January 1916, all of which are in the desert south-west of Matruh. The problems of water supply for men and horses limited the size of the Western Desert Force and its operations. However, on 20 February, Major General W E Peyton, who took over when Wallace went sick, advanced westwards to retake Sollum and was challenged by the Senussi on 26 February at Agagiya half-way to the Egyptian frontier. In the engagement, the Senussi were at last decisively defeated. The Dorsetshire Yeomanry won fame with their spirited charge, which broke up the bedouin retreat after their main position had been taken by the 1st and 3rd South African Battalions. Nuri Bey escaped, but Jaafar Pasha was captured and imprisoned in the Cairo Citadel. He tried to escape down a rope of knotted sheets, which broke under his considerable weight. Later, he became the commander of the Arab regular forces under Amir Feisal during the Arab revolt, and ended the war with a CMG from the grateful British Government!

The Senussi did not give up immediately. He tried the alternative approach to the Nile valley via the oasis of Siwa, deep in the desert 150 miles from the Mediterranean coast. A new mobile desert force was cobbled together to oppose him, but he was not finally driven out of Siwa until February 1917.

In the meantime, at the beginning of 1916, the authorities in London, Delhi, Cairo and Basra had been debating what should be done to repair the political damage done to the Allied cause by the withdrawals from Gallipoli and Ctesiphon. One thing was certain: Turkey, supplied from Germany via Bulgaria and with large numbers of troops released from

Gallipoli, would soon be in a position to threaten the Suez Canal and the Persian oilfields once more.

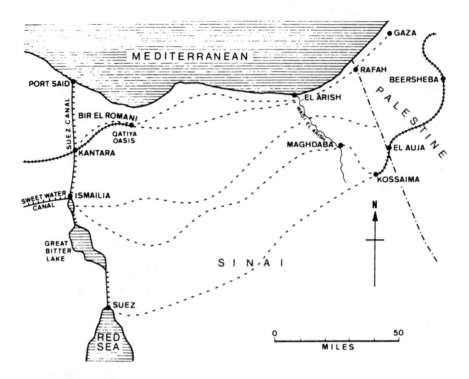

Map 22: The Sinai Front: 1916

Estimates of how many troops Enver Pasha could deploy against Egypt and how soon varied widely. Maxwell thought that he might have to face 250,000 by the spring and suggested that he would need 12 divisions to defend the Suez Canal. The War Office pruned his figures down to eight divisions, but only ordered the dispatch of six, which were shipped to the Middle East at the expense of the build up for the 1916 offensive in France, which became the Battle of the Somme.

Maxwell was loath to consider defending Egypt on the Canal itself, and sought to give his defence greater depth. He put forward an elegant solution for the combined defence of the Canal and the Persian oilfields: an Allied landing in force in the Gulf of Iskanderun, north of Alexandretta (*see Map 16*), which would strangle the Turkish lines of communication to both Egypt and Mesopotamia at the point where the incomplete railway tunnels through the nearby Taurus and Amanus Mountains were already seriously hampering Turkish operations.

Kitchener favoured Maxwell's idea, but the General and Naval Staffs in London opposed it strongly: the Turks would be able to concentrate vastly superior forces against the Allied beachhead; 160,000 men would be needed; and taken together with the 150,000 men destined for the recent landing at Salonika to help the Serbs, this amounted to a gross dispersion of effort, which would not weaken the Germans in any way on the decisive Western Front. Nor did the psychological effects of the Gallipoli failure on Whitehall policy-makers help Maxwell's case. It was, however, the French who killed his plan by refusing to take part in any operation that might endanger their relations with the Syrian Christians. The French Military Attaché in London presented a stiff letter of protest to the Chief of the Imperial General Staff:

> French public opinion could not be indifferent to any operations attempted in a country which it considers as destined to form part of a future Syrian state; and it would require of the French Government not only that no military operations should be undertaken in this particular country without previous agreement between the Allies, but also that, should such action be taken, the greater part of the task should be entrusted to French troops and the French generals commanding them.[2]

As the French were not prepared to find any troops for Maxwell's plan, the less imaginative course of action had to be adopted of reinforcing both fronts in the Middle East with troops from Europe. The Indian divisions were already on their way to Basra, and the six New Army divisions allocated by the War Office to Maxwell were being shipped to Egypt. With the addition of the tired divisions withdrawn from Gallipoli, which needed rest, re-equipment and retraining, Maxwell would have some 14 divisions with which to meet the expected Turkish offensive on the Suez Canal front.

Maxwell was not to stay in Egypt long enough to enjoy this short-lived Whitehall largesse. In the quasi politico-military coup engineered by Lloyd George behind Kitchener's back in December 1915, Sir Douglas Haig replaced Sir John French in command of the BEF in France; Sir William ('Wully') Robertson replaced Sir Archibald Murray as Chief of the Imperial General Staff; and Murray was side-stepped to command the forces being assembled to defend the Canal. The original intention was for Maxwell to look after the internal security of Egypt and the Western Desert front, while Murray prepared to meet the Turkish offensive. This meant dual control in Egypt, which could not, and did not, work. Both Maxwell and Murray volunteered to go so that unity of command could be established. The Cabinet decided that new blood was needed and recalled Maxwell.

Murray, like Maxwell, decided to give up the idea of using the Canal as Egypt's front line. Instead he moved the defences five to ten miles eastwards to protect the Canal shipping from Turkish long-range artillery fire. In the north, however, he went much further – some 30 miles east of Kantara – to deny the Turks the use of the wells in the Qatiya Oasis and at Bir er Romani, and to threaten the flank of any Turkish advance on the central desert tracks, which Djemal had used in his first attempt to reach the Canal.

Murray's plan required a prodigious logistic and engineering effort to make it practicable. Construction materials were shipped in from a variety of sources to build a railway forward to Romani, and for water pipelines to be passed from the Sweet Water Canal by syphon under the Suez Canal to the forward positions. Three lines of defence east of the canal were dug by the voluntarily recruited Egyptian Labour Force, working under Royal Engineer supervision. Extra floating bridges were constructed over the Canal, and the road network was improved with stone shipped up the Canal in barges. The work was never ending.

The Turks were doing much the same thing in Palestine. On Djemal Pasha's initiative, a spur was built off the Hejaz railway down through Palestine to Beersheba, which it reached in October 1915 and was being pushed on south-west to el Auja, Kress von Kressenstein's advanced base. New roads were constructed and depots established, and it became a race between the two sides as to which would be ready first for the next round in the Sinai desert. Kress was determined to attack again as soon as possible: Djemal was less optimistic that he could overcome the logistic difficulties posed by poor communications. In any case, Kress would not be ready until a large German detachment, some 2,000 strong, code named 'Pasha I', could reach him with heavy artillery, mortars, machine-guns and wireless equipments. 'Pasha I' was not expected to arrive in Palestine before the summer of 1916.

Murray had based his plans originally upon Maxwell's estimate of the Turks being able to invade Egypt with 250,000 troops, which 'Wully' Robertson in Whitehall scaled down to a more realistic figure of 100,000 – the largest forces that he believed the Turks would be able to supply. As the early months of 1916 rolled by, it became clear to Whitehall, if not in Cairo, that the Turks were becoming less and less likely to have the resources to advance on Egypt in any strength for the time being. Turkish divisions, released from Gallipoli, were being diverted to the Caucasus where the Russian Grand Duke Nicholas had mounted a surprise winter offensive in Armenia, taking the great Turkish fortress town of Erzarum in February, the important Black Sea port of Trebizond in April, and threatening to thrust deep into the Turkish heartland of Anatolia. Estimates of the scale of Djemal Pasha's expected Turkish offensive against Egypt were reduced step by step, and its predicted date was postponed from month to month. The War Office – always pressed for troops – was soon whittling away the 14 divisions, which had been massed in Egypt in January. Four divisions and the whole of the ANZAC Corps of five divisions were withdrawn to France, and Major General Stanley Maude's 13th Division left for Basra. By June, Murray was left with only four divisions to hold the Canal and maintain the internal security of Egypt.

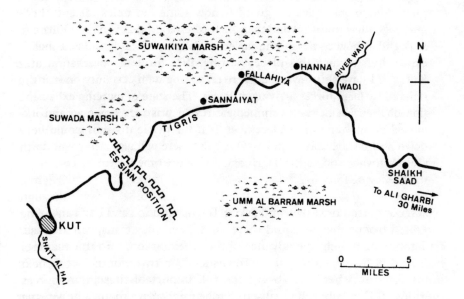

Map 23: Operations for the Relief of Kut: 1916

McMahon's and Murray's problems in Cairo were nothing compared to those of Nixon and Cox in Basra. Townshend had reached Kut on 2 December, convinced that he would only have to stand siege for about a month before the arrival of Younghusband's 28th Brigade from Egypt and the two Indian divisions from France would make his relief possible. After a couple of days rest, he could have continued his withdrawal to Amara, extending the Turkish supply lines and linking up with Younghusband, but due to a chapter of accidents and misunderstandings he chose not to do so. He believed that his men could go no further, although Delamain considered this to be nonsense. It would also have meant abandoning large stocks of supplies and ammunition accumulated there for his advance on Baghdad; and it would have caused further damage to British prestige. Nixon had sent a message to the garrison commander at Kut saying:

> Please tell Townshend that the Army Commander must leave situation to him as to how far he falls back, but the Army Commander's intention is to concentrate as far forward as possible.[3]

Through the oversight of a staff officer, Townshend was not shown this message until he had taken his decision to stay in Kut. In his cable to Nixon on 4 December, he said:

> I am making Kut into as strong an entrenched camp as possible in the time. The enemy advance guard is now some ten miles off and the main body five miles beyond that. As it is reported that von der Goltz is at Baghdad now commanding the enemy's army of six divisions, I shall expect him to turn this place, putting off a force of observation at Kut. . . . I have shut myself up here reckoning with certainty on being relieved by large forces arriving at Basra. The state of extreme exhaustion of the men demands immediate rest. I was very anxious, and it looked at one time on 2 December as if the whole division would lie down and not be able to move. Our being here will also delay von der Goltz's advance down the Tigris and give more time for you to concentrate relieving force. . . .[4]

Nixon concurred next day, and asked Townshend to send back any of his mounted troops that he could spare, and all surplus transport, steamers and gunboats to help the advance of the relieving force. In this message, he said that he hoped to relieve Townshend 'in two months'. It took 24 hours for Townshend to absorb the full import of these words. Next morning, 6 December, he realised that he might have made a grave error of judgement by staying in Kut. He cabled Nixon:

> . . . I have carefully considered your statement of relief within two months and am convinced that would mean the loss of this division, for the whole Turkish force of six divisions would develop long before then; it would be best I think that I should preserve force by retiring to Ali Garbi [half way to Amara] and form covering force to concentration at Amara.[5]

The Turks were still ten miles from Kut when this exchange took place, so Townshend could have withdrawn without much difficulty, but Nixon, optimistic as ever, responded with a veto: two months was an outside figure, which he hoped to reduce – or so he thought at the time. Retirement from Kut was only to be considered *in extremis*. Nixon cabled:

> As long as you remain in Kut the enemy is in ignorance of your plan, and you are fulfilling the duties of a detachment by holding superior numbers.[6]

What Nixon did not know was that, although Younghusband's 28th Brigade had arrived on schedule from Egypt, the 3rd (Lahore) and 7th

(Meerut) Divisions from France were being delayed at Marseilles by German submarine activity in the Mediterranean. They were not only far behind schedule, but were also being loaded on a 'catch as catch can' basis into ships as they became available. The resulting organisational shambles would have to be sorted out when they reached Basra, causing more delay.

There was another hidden factor, which led to some of the misjudgements that resulted in the coming disaster at Kut. Nixon's health had been deteriorating for some time, although this was not known in Delhi. The anxieties heaped on him by the consequences of Ctesiphon proved too great. He was clearly ill when he reached Basra at the beginning of December, and by early January he was so ill that he had to ask Commander-in-Chief India to relieve him of his command. Recalled to England, he became the tragic scapegoat of the Mesopotamia commission of inquiry, set up in August 1916. Poor Nixon was placed first on its list of culprits, the commissioners reporting:

> The weightiest share of responsibility lies with Sir John Nixon whose confident optimism was the main cause of the decision to advance [on Baghdad].[7]

But no one at the time appreciated why things were to go so wrong in the next three months. The warnings were there at Ctesiphon, where the heavy British losses were only partially caused by Turkish numerical superiority. The campaign had been conducted up to that point against Turkish troops raised largely from Mesopotamian Arabs. The arrival of first rate Turkish divisions, manned by European or Anatolian Turks, changed the campaign from colonial into regular European style warfare, in which the lethal combination of rifle, machinegun, entrenching tool and barbed wire in the hands of good soldiers, gave the defence the upper hand, as it had already done on the Western Front and at Gallipoli. Such warfare was as yet outside the ken of the Indian Army officers handling affairs in Mesopotamia.

And there was another factor, which is common to the early phases of any major British war. With a very small army in peacetime, its commanders and staffs have no experience in handling forces much above divisional size. They have no opportunity to develop the corporate intuitive judgement of what can and cannot be done on large scale battlefields with corps and army size formations engaged in life and death struggles. It takes time and unhappy experiences to develop the successful command teams, which usually emerge to bring victory in the end. It was this painful process, which was wracking the British armies on all fronts in 1915–16.

Nixon was replaced by General Sir Percy Lake, the Chief of General Staff, India, who had been in close touch with the Mesopotamian

Campaign since its inception. It was his task to bring order out of the chaos that Nixon's premature advance on Baghdad had caused, particularly at the Basra base which was totally inadequate to handle the arrival of the reinforcing divisions, while, at the same time, supplying the needs of the existing force. He was not in robust health, but was an able logistician, which was what was needed, provided there was a first rate commander and staff to conduct operations to relieve Townshend at Kut.

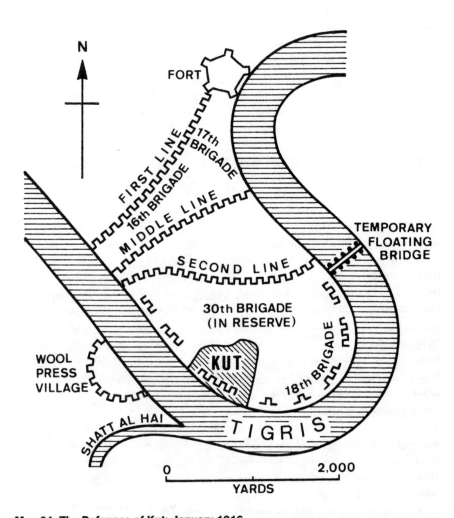

Map 24: The Defences of Kut: January 1916

The choice of commander for the Kut relief force, to be known as the Tigris Corps, was Major General Fenton John Aylmer VC, who had been sent originally from India to take over the command of the 7th Division when it arrived at Basra. Promoted lieutenant-general, he established his new and improvised Tigris Corps headquarters at Amara. His place as 7th Division's commander was taken by Younghusband, whose 28th Brigade was concentrating forward at Ali Garbi, 50 miles downriver from Kut, as the spearhead of the relief force, which would eventually consist of the 3rd and 7th Divisions, 28th Brigade and three other recently formed brigades hastily dispatched from India without a divisional headquarters to command them. At the turn of the year only 28th Brigade was lucky enough to have its own experienced headquarters staff. 7th Division's staff had not yet reached Basra from France and so an ad hoc divisional staff had to be improvised for Younghusband; and Major General Keary's 3rd Division staff had only just embarked at Marseilles for its journey through the Suez Canal to Basra. To add to Aylmer's command problems, he knew few of the brigade and regimental commanders, and they knew little of him or of each other.

But the limiting factor in all operations in Mesopotamia was the acute shortage of shallow draught steamers, which had still not been overcome, despite Nixon's constant demands for more throughout 1915. India was scoured for suitable craft and new construction was put in hand, but it all took time, a commodity in ever shorter supply with Townshend besieged in Kut.

Kut lay on a peninsula formed by an acute bend in the Tigris, which flowed round it on three sides, leaving only the north side open to attack by land. The squalor of Kut itself made Qurna seem, indeed, like the Garden of Eden. It consisted mostly of mud huts with a few more substantial mudbrick buildings amongst them, which, in default of anything better, had to be used as hospital accommodation. There was no sanitation of any kind and disease was rife amongst the 6,000 inhabitants. When Townshend's forward base had been set up there to support his advance on Baghdad, it had been fortified in a rudimentary way with three lines of trenches and redoubts across the neck of the peninsula. As Townshend's division arrived, he set about strengthening the defences as soon as his men were fit enough to start digging. He divided the vital northern defences between Delamain's 16th Brigade on the north-west and Hoghton's 17th Brigade on the north-east. Hamilton's 18th Brigade watched the river and Melliss's 30th Brigade was in general reserve. After absorbing the small existing garrison of Kut, he had 11,600 troops available for defence (3,000 British and 8,600 Indians), of whom only 7,000 were infantry. He was well provided with guns and ammunition, and his logistic staff estimated that they had two months' supply of food. Morale was surprisingly good because the troops, like Townshend, expected early relief and were glad of a rest from constant marching.

Nur-ud-Din had Kut invested by 9 December and began to bombard the town and assault the northern defences that day. His attacks, carried out by his 45th Division, were easily repulsed, but during the night his troops must have dug like moles because by dawn next morning they were all below ground in a line of trenches only 600 yards from the British defences. Nur-ud-Din persisted in a series of attacks for the next three days, and suffered such heavy losses that von der Goltz, who reached Kut on 12 December, directed him to blockade Kut and concentrate on opposing the British relief columns. He told Nur to renovate his old defensive position at Es Sinn, some ten miles downriver from Kut, from which he had been ejected by Townshend in September.

Von der Goltz soon left for Baghdad where he was needed to organise Turkish resistance to Baratoff's Russians advancing on Kermanshah. Nur-ud-Din blatantly disregarded his German Commander-in-Chief's instructions and attacked Kut again on Christmas eve. His troops managed to break in, but were ejected in severe fighting in which the Oxfordshire Light Infantry in Hoghton's brigade distinguished themselves. Next day the mass of Turkish dead in no-man's land bore witness to the costly Turkish failure. Nur was never to attack Kut again, but Townshend was not to know this and began to worry about his reserves of ammunition rather than food when intelligence reached him of the arrival of a fifth Turkish division, the 52nd, at Kut and the possible approach of a sixth – probably the hardened 2nd Division from Gallipoli.

Three attempts were made to relieve Kut, each hurried forward over-precipitately by different causes for alarm. The first effort at the beginning of January was rushed because Townshend feared that his defences would not withstand assault by two fresh Turkish divisions; in the second, at the end of February, it was a combination of fear of ammunition shortage and anxiety about food supplies; and in the third desperate effort in April, it was the spectre of the Kut garrison's starvation that was the goad. For each attempt a further British division arrived upriver, but the winter weather steadily deteriorated: rain during the first attempt; bitter cold and local flooding during the second; and the annual spring flooding of the Tigris plain, caused by snow melting in the Caucasus, during the last abortive attempt.

Despite von der Goltz's instructions to concentrate on defending the Es Sinn position, close to Kut, Nur-ud-Din decided to block the British approach up the Tigris with a series of defensive positions in depth, starting with entrenchments at Shaikh Saad some 40 river miles downstream from Kut and another 30 miles from Ali Gharbi where Younghusband was concentrating his 7th Division. He gave the task of holding Shaikh Saad to the Mesopotamian 35th and 38th Divisions, which he stiffened with some Anatolian units. Their task was to cover the construction by 51st and 52nd Divisions of a major delaying position, designed to block the most probable British approach along the north bank of the Tigris, where it ran through a twelve mile long defile between the river and the Suwaikiya marshes from Hanna to Sannaiyat (*See Map 26*). On the south bank, which the British were less likely to use because Kut lay north of the river, he established a series of supporting positions to stop his entrenchments being enfiladed from the south. The main Es Sinn position, another five miles upstream of Sannaiyat, would be organised by the élite 2nd Division when it reached the front from Gallipoli in February; and the 45th continued to watch and harass Kut.

It was just a month after Townshend shut himself up in Kut that Aylmer's Tigris Corps started to concentrate at El Gharbi. His two divisions would not be fully established there much before the end of January due to the shortage of steamers, but such was the urgency of Townshend's plea for relief before Turkish reinforcements could arrive that Aylmer decided to push upriver with whatever troops were available on 4 January. Younghusband set off with Kemball's 28th Brigade on the south bank acting almost as an independent force, and with 19th Brigade (belonging to 7th Division from France) and 35th Brigade (direct from India) on the north bank under his own hand. He had an ad hoc divisional staff and just enough sappers with local boats, called *danaks*, to build one bridge across the Tigris when he needed to transfer troops from one bank to the other. His medical units were woefully inadequate, and, to make matters more difficult, the winter rains had already begun. Aylmer intended to follow him two or three days later with the 21st Brigade of 7th Division and any other units that had reached El Gharbi by then.

When 7th Division deployed to attack Shaikh Saad on 6 January, Younghusband and Kemball soon realised that they were up against more than the mere covering force, which they thought was in front of them. Their attacks on the Turkish trenches on both banks failed with considerable loss. They and their troops spent a miserable night in battle outpost positions under pouring rain. Aylmer arrived with 21st Brigade and took charge of the battle on 7 January, but it took two more days of hard fighting before the Turks decided to fall back on their main position at Hanna during the night of 9–10 January. Turkish losses had been so high that the remnants of 38th Division had to be absorbed by 35th Division, and the 38th disappeared from the Turkish order of battle. But Aylmer had also suffered 4,007 casualties. His men were too exhausted by their three days' struggle in drenching rain to pursue. He was also hampered by difficulties in evacuating his wounded. He had not made a very propitious start: the battle for Shaikh Saad set the pattern of future events – high casualties on both sides with the British usually prevailing in the end.

Nur-ud-Din, in von der Goltz's opinion, had been insubordinate as well as incompetent. He sacked him and replaced him with the much younger Halil Bey, who proved no more amenable to German direction than Nur.

Instead of falling back to the Hanna-Sannaiyat defile, as von der Goltz directed, Halil decided, as Nur would probably have done, to fight for more time by taking up another covering position behind the easily fordable Wadi river, which meets the Tigris five miles downstream from Hanna. The weakness of the position, which Aylmer recognised, was that its northern flank was not covered by the Suwaikiya marshes and so it could be turned. Aylmer's plan was to give the impression that he was awaiting further reinforcements at Shaikh Saad, while, in fact, he was moving Kemball's 28th Brigade across the Tigris to attack the Wadi position frontally while Younghusband, with the rest of 7th Division, encircled the Turkish inland flank during the night of 12–13 January.

The night was clear and cold, and Younghusband's navigation was good. 7th Division was in position well before dawn, but a thick mist over the Wadi stopped him crossing it until 7.30am on 13 January. There was little opposition at first but Turkish reinforcements were rushed up to hold the line of an irrigation canal running at right angles to the Wadi, thus protecting their open flank. The advance slowed as Younghusband's three brigades came into line and attacked this hastily occupied Turkish position. They came tantalisingly close to reaching the Tigris and cutting the Turks off from their Hanna position. Unfortunately, Kemball's holding operations had not prevented Halil Bey thinning out his front and sending enough of his reserves to hold Younghusband's advance until nightfall. When Kemball did attack in strength in the late afternoon to help Younghusband, there were still enough Turks holding the main Wadi position to defeat 28th Brigade, which suffered the heaviest losses of the whole force engaged that day. By dusk Aylmer had lost another 1,600 casualties.

That night it was battle outposts again in pouring rain. Aylmer hoped to complete the encirclement of the Turkish force when dawn came, but next morning British patrols found the Turkish positions empty. Von der Goltz, who had reached Halil Bey's headquarters during the 13th, realised that the Turks had little chance of defeating the British attacks next day and ordered Halil to disengage. After dark, the Turks slipped away undetected into the Hanna defences, thus avoiding the decisive defeat which Aylmer planned for them. He was bitterly disappointed, and to make matters worse his men were deluged with rain and buffeted by high winds for the next few days.

Aylmer ordered Younghusband to push on during the 14th to turn what he thought was only a Turkish rear-guard out of the Hanna defile. Younghusband was soon disillusioning him. The defile was less than a mile wide and was blocked by several lines of entrenchments facing east and protected by further trenches along the river bank and on the edge of the marshes to check any attempts to outflank the position via river or marsh. In Younghusband's view, a frontal attack was out of the question unless the main Turkish trenches could be enfiladed by artillery deployed on the south bank. In any case, his men could not attack over such sodden ground: there would have to be a pause for the weather to improve.

Aylmer accepted Younghusband's advice but it was easier said than done. The *danaks* had to be towed upstream from Shaikh Saad and brought into bridge again near the Tigris Corps' camp at Wadi so that troops and guns could be deployed on the south bank to enfilade the Hanna trenches. Everything conspired against the Sappers. They had almost completed the new bridge on 16 January when a steamer drifted into it. It was again almost ready for traffic on the 17th when high winds sank some of the *danaks*. The same thing happened in a bigger way during an even more violent storm next day. Half the bridge was torn away and was washed downstream, fouling shipping and many of the *danaks* sinking. The attempt to bridge the Tigris had to be abandoned until the craft could be salvaged and new decking collected. Rafts had to be used instead to ferry troops and artillery over to the south bank – a slow and tedious business over a river a quarter of a mile wide.

The urgency of achieving a breakthrough to Kut was heightened by fresh intelligence of the approach of a new Turkish corps released from Gallipoli and by Townshend reporting that he had only enough food to last until the end of the first week of February. The weather, however, improved on the 19th and Aylmer decided to attack the Hanna lines on the 21st after as heavy a 24 hour artillery bombardment as the limited ammunition supply for his meagre 46 guns would allow. Younghusband was to make a frontal assault using 19th and 35th Brigades, closely supported by 9th Brigade and with 28th Brigade in reserve. Major General Keary, the commander of the 3rd (Lahore) Division, who had just arrived at the front with the leading elements of his division, was given the task of providing enfilade fire from the south bank with the few guns and machineguns that could be ferried across the Tigris in time.

Aylmer was about to attempt a feat that had baffled the BEF in France throughout 1915: breaking through an entrenched and wired defensive position, which could not be turned, and which was held by determined men armed with quick firing rifles and machineguns. No amount of artillery support could ensure success, and Aylmer had only a fraction of the gun density used in France. No one could fault the steadiness and bravery of Younghusband's assaulting brigades on 21 January, but the result was no different from the failures at Neuve Chapelle, Festubert and Loos – heavy casualties for minimal gains.

Despite the virtually uncut Turkish wire, a few men of 35th and 19th Brigades managed to enter sections of the first Turkish line but were bombed out of it. Both 9th and 28th Brigades were committed but could make little ground. The weather broke again before midday, soaking the men and chilling them with a bitterly cold wind. By mid-afternoon Younghusband took the only course open to him. He gave orders for withdrawal back to his original trenches. Aylmer, not knowing how heavy the casualties had been, tried to cancel Younghusband's order because there were still two battalions uncommitted. His order arrived too late to stop the withdrawal; and when he wanted to make preparations for a renewed assault next day, Younghusband, with the full backing of the brigade commanders, had to object. Their men, drenched and tired out, had spent another miserable night in their waterlogged trenches under continuous rain and cold, which was so intense that the marshes froze when the wind dropped. Many of the men's rifles were so clogged with mud that they were temporarily useless, and the psychological shadow of a costly failure hung over the whole of the Tigris Corps. There had been 2,741 casualties, including 78 British officers. The leading battalions had lost between 50 and 90 per cent of their bayonet strength, reflecting the gallantry of the British and Indian troops who took part in the assault, and the determination of the Turks who repulsed it.

Aylmer's defeat at Hanna concentrated minds in Whitehall, Delhi, Kut, Wadi camp and Basra. In Whitehall, 'Wully' Robertson concluded from intelligence at his disposal that the Turks were targeting Mesopotamia rather than Egypt, and that the division of operational responsibility for the Tigris Corps between Whitehall and Delhi was no longer tenable. The Mesopotamian Campaign must be treated as an integral part of the overall war effort and brought under War Office control. His proposal was entirely acceptable to GHQ India, and the first fruits of the change were the dispatch of Maude's 13th Division from Egypt to Basra and three more brigades from India as soon as they could be accepted through the overcrowded port of Basra. At best it was unlikely that 13th Division could arrive up-river until mid-March.

In Kut, Townshend realised that he was not going to be relieved before his military rations ran out, and so he set about uncovering reserves of food held by the town's merchants. Kut was an important grain-trading centre and considerable stocks were found in their stores, which he could requisition without bringing starvation to the 6,000 local inhabitants. With this grain and using his 3,000 horses and mules as food, he reported that he could hold out for another 84 days, i.e. to 17th April. Moreover, the annual spring floods in March should give him added protection from Turkish assault. Aylmer was less than pleased: telegraphing Lake and Townshend, he complained quite justifiably:

> ... this new information, had it been communicated before, would have certainly modified much of what I have unsuccessfully tried to do . . .[8]

Lake reached Wadi camp to review the situation with Aylmer on 28th

January. He had already realised that Aylmer needed a stronger and more experienced staff to handle the acute problems of the Tigris Corps, caused by inadequate river craft, foul weather, heavy casualties and piecemeal arrival of reinforcing formations, all of which could only be overcome by constant improvisation. The very experienced and able George Gorringe was moved from commanding 12th Division on the Euphrates to become Aylmer's chief of staff. The keys to Aylmer's ability to resume his advance on Kut were the arrival of the rest of Keary's 3rd Division and the provision of a proper bridging train with military pontoons rather than the un-decked local *danaks*, which sank too easily in bad weather. In Lake's view, Aylmer was unlikely to be ready to try again before mid-February, and even then he would only have a slender numerical superiority over Halil Bey's forces south of Baghdad, which might well be reinforced by then.

Lake and Aylmer were faced with two problems calling for diametrically opposite solutions. With Townshend reasonably confident that Kut would not be reduced by starvation until mid-April, there was good reason to delay the next attempt to relieve him until the 13th Division had arrived from Egypt and the three brigades from India. On the other hand, the annual Tigris floods were due in mid-March, which could bar attempts to reach Kut in time to save Townshend. Striking a mean between these two time factors, they decided to try again in the first week of March. The whole of Keary's 3rd Division and one of the three brigades from India would have arrived up-river, but Maude's 13th Division would only just be arriving at Basra.

Aylmer's plan was to hold the Turks in the Hanna defences on the north bank with Younghusband's 7th Division, and to turn the main Turkish Es Sinn position on the south bank with a surprise night march between the Tigris and the Umm al Barram marshes by Keary's 3rd Division and an ad hoc division of three independent brigades under Kemball, who was to use his 28th Brigade headquarters' staff to command it. A number of minor operations were mounted to deceive the Turks into thinking that the Tigris Corps was still intent on breaking through on the north bank. In one of these Gorringe was wounded while on reconnaissance, but managed to carry on as Aylmer's chief of staff although he could not mount his horse.

After two postponements, the night march started in the evening of 7 March. Kemball's force was in the lead with orders to attack the Dujaila redoubt, which was thought to be the southern flank of the Es Sinn Line. Keary's 3rd Division followed as the main striking force with which Aylmer hoped to roll up the Turkish defences from the south once Kemball had broken into them. If he was successful, he hoped that Townshend would use all available local craft at Kut to cross the Tigris and link up with him. The elegant simplicity of his concept was, however,

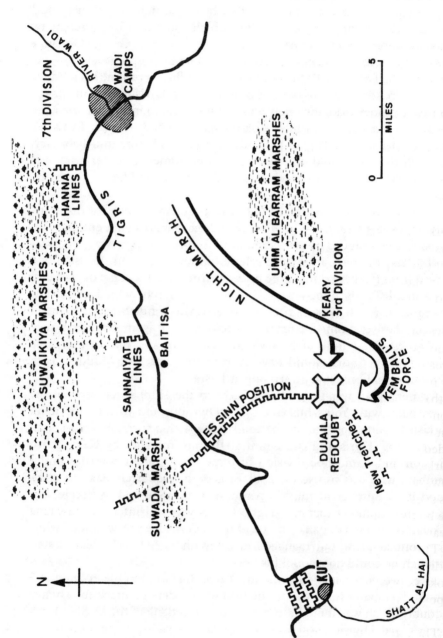

Map 25: The Battle of Es Sinn: 7–8 March 1916

marred by the complexities of his plan and doubts about its practicability amongst his own commanders.

Kemball did not reach his assembly area three miles south of Dujaila redoubt until daylight, so he could not deploy, as had been intended, in darkness. No movement of any kind was seen in the Turkish lines. According to the Turks, the redoubt's garrison was, in fact, fast asleep and could have been overrun if Kemball had attacked off his line of march. He did not do so because he had been caught out so often before in assuming that Turkish trenches were empty; and he believed that his brigade and battalion commanders must be given time to orientate themselves before attacking. Aylmer also mistakenly thought that the Turks must have seen the British troops approaching and that tactical surprise had been lost by Kemball's delay. He ordered his corps artillery to open fire at 7am, and in doing so alerted the Turks to what was afoot before Kemball's brigades could start their advance. What neither he nor Kemball knew was that the Turkish line had been extended south-westwards from the redoubt and was manned by recently arrived units of the experienced 2nd Division from Gallipoli.

In the fighting that followed, Kemball's brigades fought all morning and much of the afternoon suffering severe casualties from well directed rifle and machinegun fire as they tried to clear two regiments of the 2nd Division out of the new trenches, which blocked the way towards the redoubt. Throughout the day Turkish reinforcements arrived in a steady stream both by ferry from the north bank and marching from around Kut. By mid-afternoon, Aylmer realised that Kemball was not going to succeed with his flanking attacks, and so he ordered Keary to attack the redoubt frontally. His 8th Brigade did so just before dusk and managed to break in, but were soon bombed out again in true trench-warfare style. As daylight faded, Aylmer knew that he had failed, but there was still a chance that the Turks might abandon their positions during the night. When dawn came, however, they were still there and Aylmer withdrew all his troops back to his starting point on the south bank of the Tigris opposite his Wadi camp. He had lost another 3,474 casualties: the Turks only lost 1,300 and were clearly the victors.

The disappointment in Kut was acute, particularly amongst the Indians, whose desertion rate increased. The local Arabs in the town looked upon the British cause as lost and acted accordingly. Townshend reported to Lake:

> The conduct of my British troops here is splendid, their discipline and physique un-impaired, cheery and quite patient. I cannot say the same of all the Indian troops i.e., the Mohammedans, and some Hindus also.[9]

The morale of Aylmer's officers and men also remained remarkably high despite their repulse and heavy losses. As was to happen 26 years later after the disastrous battles of Gazala and the retreat to El Alamein, the troops were bewildered by their lack of success, but were in no way discouraged. Lake stood by Aylmer, although Aylmer's health was causing some concern, but the CIGS in London decided that he must pay the price of failure. Townshend for one, thought Aylmer was unfairly treated:

> I deeply sympathised with Aylmer. I knew what a gallant soldier he was, for I had been on service with him in the frontier expedition of Hunza Naga [in the Himalayas] in 1891, when he blew in the gate of Nilt Fort and won a VC. I doubt if the authorities at home grasped the difficulties he had to contend with in the way of floods, rain, want of transport, and last, but not least, want of experience and training in a large proportion of his troops. Of the Indian troops that formed the bulk of his force, large numbers were raw, un-trained recruits.[10]

There was no time to send out a new commander from England or India, so Aylmer was replaced on 11 March by Gorringe, who, though no Montgomery, was a trusted and experienced soldier. Meanwhile Halil Bey wrote to Townshend, telling him of Aylmer's defeat, and suggesting his surrender. He ended his letter:

> For your part, you have heroically fulfilled your military duty. From hence forth I see no likelihood that you will be relieved. According to your deserters I believe that you are without food and that diseases are prevalent among your troops. You are free to continue your resistance at Kut, or to surrender to my forces, which are growing larger and larger.[11]

Townshend rejected this call to surrender, but, being aware of the Turkish defeats in Armenia, assumed that Halil might be under pressure to release troops for the Russian front. If this was so, he might be ready to allow Townshend to withdraw with the honours of war in exchange for the immediate surrender of Kut. Halil, however, was never given the opportunity to consider Townshend's proposals: they were turned down flat by London and Delhi, where every effort was being made to mount the third and last attempt to reach him before the deadline of 11 April.

When Gorringe took over, Maude's 13th Division was beginning to concentrate at Ali Gharbi, prior to moving up to Wadi camp. His first idea was to make an even wider turning movement round the Es Sinn position, marching south of the Umm al Barram marshes to attack Halil's base camps in the Shumran bend of the Tigris, ten miles west of Kut. Reconnaissance, however, showed that much of the desert south of the river fringe could be inundated when the Tigris rose in the spring floods. Gorringe saw that the only practicable way of reaching Kut under the threat of the spring floods was by forcing a passage up the river itself, using 13th Division with the heavier artillery, which was arriving with it, to blast a way through the Hanna defences and defile leading to Sannaiyat on the north bank, while 3rd Division advanced methodically along the south bank. The arrival of new pontoon bridging equipment from India and of extra *danaks* collected locally would give him a marked advantage over the Turks. They would enable him to establish two bridges across the Tigris, over which he could switch 7th Division from bank to bank in about four hours. The Turks' nearest bridge was near Shumran, west of Kut. They were dependent on ferrying in the battle area.

Gorringe's programme for the first phase of his operations was: *1st to 3rd Day*, the breach of Hanna defences by 13th Division, supported by 7th Division and helped by fire from 3rd Division on the south bank; *4th and 5th Days*, 3rd Division, supported by 7th Division, clearing the south bank to opposite Sannaiyat; *6th or 7th Day* to breach the Sannaiyat position with 13th Division. Plans for the second phase would depend on whether the Turks were able to man the Es Sinn position after defeat in the Hanna-Sannaiyat defile. As Townshend could not last out beyond 17 April, the first phase should be completed by the 8th, which meant opening the offensive by 1 April. Unfortunately, delays in bringing up heavy 60 pounder guns, with which to batter the Hanna defences, forced Gorringe to delay the start of his offensive until 4 April. His margins, already too fine, were then squeezed by the weather. On 2 April it poured, delaying Maude's 13th Division take over from Younghusband's 7th in the Hanna trenches. D Day had to be put back to the 5th.

Gorringe's efforts were to be frustrated at almost every stage by the spring floods, which had started in 1916 on 14 March, and by the weather. Sheets of water spread across the desert countryside, helped by the Turks breaching the river's banks in important areas at critical times. Practicable approaches to Turkish positions were reduced; many of the trenches – Turkish as well as British – were flooded; and all movement by men, horses and mules was a struggle through glutinous mud. Day temperatures were rising, bringing back the frustrating and deceptive mirages, but the nights were still icily cold.

Despite these adverse circumstances, Gorringe's offensive opened well. 13th Division attacked the five lines of trenches at Hanna at dawn on 5 April and had overrun all five by 7am. The Turks had, in fact, withdrawn during the night, leaving only rear-guards to delay the British attack. It is not certain whether this was a deliberate ploy by Halil Bey, or whether it was forced on the Turks by encroaching flood water. Maude pushed on through the Hanna-Sannaiyat defile and was stopped for 24 hours by a strong rear-guard position half way to Sannaiyat, which he breached with a night attack.

Air reconnaissance had suggested that it might be possible to turn the northern flank of the main Sannaiyat position by skirting close to the marshes. Younghusband's 7th Division was already poised to attempt this manoeuvre by night, but they lost their way and the wind veered to the north, driving the flood waters of the Suwaikiya marshes southwards and narrowing the approach that they were to use. After a difficult and confused night, he did manage to attack at dawn on 7 April, but the Turks were alert and his attack failed. Gorringe decided that he should try again the following night, but the Tigris rose further that day, stopping all operations, while the troops on both sides struggled to control the flooding of their positions. Worst hit was Keary's 3rd Division on the south bank, which had reached a position opposite Sannaiyat, and was stopped by the Turks breaching the flood banks.

The floods made Gorringe give up his plan to outflank the Sannaiyat position. He decided that his only hope of breaking through was with a frontal night attack by Maude's 13th Division, which he mounted in the early hours of 9 April. Forming up went well, but the men had several hours to wait in the numbing cold, which did their morale little good. At the pre-dawn Zero Hour, the leading lines of infantry went forward at a sharp pace. First a red flare went up and then a green one, which were the known Turkish signals for manning firing positions. In the immediate outburst of rifle and machinegun fire, the leading infantry rushed the Turkish front line, but the supporting lines panicked and could not be rallied. Cold may have contributed, but the memories of Gallipoli still haunted Maude's men. The Sannaiyat position remained intact to block any chance Gorringe might have had of reaching Kut via the north bank by 17 April.

Lake telegraphed Townshend that further delay in his relief was inevitable. The latter reduced his scanty ration scale still further, which would enable him, he said, to hold out until 21 April. He could perhaps last until 29 April if he could be supplied by air drops. These were instituted, but failed due to the small payload of the few available aircraft. Preparations were also made to try running supplies through to Kut in the steamer *Julnar*, which was specially armoured for the purpose and manned by an all volunteer naval crew.

With Lake's concurrence, Gorringe switched his effort back to the south bank where Keary's 3rd Division had reached the Turkish covering position in front of their main Es Sinn Line at Bait Isa on 16 April. Maude's 13th Division crossed the Tigris and came up on his southern flank, and on 17 April Keary's men took Bait Isa. That evening signs of a major Turkish counter-attack were detected and both divisions made ready to meet it. It was launched after dark, striking the junction between the two divisions. Some 12 battalions, including eight from the formidable 2nd Division, attacked in dense, closely-packed columns. They were to find attacking dug-in riflemen and machinegunners no easier than their British opponents had done at Hanna and Sannaiyat. When dawn came it was the British who found Turkish dead heaped around their positions. Several German officers were found amongst the dead. Gorringe estimated that the Turks lost over 4,000 men in this quite unexpected effort to disrupt his advance along the south bank.

Throughout the week's operations on the south bank, the Turks were seen to be ferrying troops across the Tigris from the Sannaiyat position. Assuming that Sannaiyat must have been seriously weakened, Gorringe decided to switch quickly back to the north bank again and to attack the Sannaiyat trenches on 20 April with Younghusband's 7th Division, reinforced with two extra brigades, while Keary and Maude kept up their pressure on the south bank. The Tigris intervened again. There were only five hundred yards separating the British and Turkish trenches at Sannaiyat. On the 18th, the river rose higher than ever, and those 500 yards became a continuous sheet of water from the Suwaikiya marshes to the Tigris. British patrols found an area, some 600 yards wide, where the water was only a few inches deep and quite fordable. Younghusband decided that he must risk using it for a two brigade assault as there was no other way forward and he could not wait for the water level to drop. On the 19th a strong north wind drove more water out of the marshes and flooded 7th Division's trenches. The attack had to be postponed until 22 April, giving the Turks time to move troops back from south of the river.

Away in Baghdad, von der Goltz died on 19 April of typhus, contracted on the Tigris front. Halil Bey, promoted Pasha, took over command of the Turkish Sixth Army, but stayed on near Kut for the finale, which was clearly very close. Townshend was already playing on in extra time, and Gorringe still had unbroken Turkish positions between his troops and Kut.

If it had not been for the need to relieve Townshend quickly, Younghusband would never have attacked under the conditions prevailing at the time. Though Gorringe did not know it, he had no numerical superiority over the Turks in the Sannaiyat position. Just before the attack was about to start, it was found that the water had risen again and there was only enough shallow water for a one instead of a two brigade assault. 19th Brigade, in the lead, would have to punch a narrow hole in the Turkish front through which Younghusband would have to pass his four other brigades – not an inviting prospect.

The inevitable happened. 19th Brigade attacked at 7am as the artillery bombardment lifted. The Turkish front line was found flooded and unoccupied, but their machineguns on drier ground on the flanks raked the British advance, which reached the third out of five lines of trenches. The further 19th Brigade penetrated, the deeper the mud became, men sinking up to their armpits and being unable to work their mud clogged rifles.

The Turks launched a number of counter-attacks from their drier fourth and fifth lines, which were broken up by British artillery fire, but a spontaneous British retirement occurred as the men reached the end of their reserves of courage. By 8.20am 19th Brigade was back in its original trenches without Younghusband having been able to commit his other brigades. The Highland Battalion (the temporary amalgamation of the 2nd Black Watch and 1st Seaforths), which had been outstanding in its gallantry and had hesitated before following the general retirement, perceived that Kut could not be reached through the waterlogged defences of Sannaiyat unless the Turks gave way and this they showed no sign of doing. 19th Brigade lost just under a thousand men in its self-sacrificing effort. Gorringe wanted to renew the attack, but Younghusband persuaded him that it was impracticable to do so.

One last attempt was made to prolong Townshend's resistance. Lieutenant HOB Firman RN with Lieutenant Commander CH Cowley RNVR as his second-in-command and Sub-Lieutenant WL Reed RNR as his engineer, with twelve unmarried volunteer naval ratings as crew, set off in the *Julnar* as darkness fell on 24 April, carrying 270 tons of supplies for Kut. They were engaged by Turkish guns as soon as they were level with Sannaiyat and ran the gauntlet successfully until they reached the Turkish ferry site. One of the ferry cables fouled *Julnar*'s screws and she was swung into the bank under heavy fire. Firman was killed and Cowley and five ratings were wounded. Firman and Cowley were awarded posthumous VCs, Cowley having been shot later by the Turks.

After several days of tense telegraphing between London, Delhi and Lake's headquarters on the Tigris, Townshend was authorised to open negotiations with Halil Pasha for the surrender of Kut with authority to spend up to a million pounds if need be to gain favourable terms. The only other bargaining counter available to Townshend was the hand-over rather than destruction of his artillery. The two men met on launches a couple of miles upstream from Kut. Halil was tempted by both the money and the guns to accept the release of the Kut garrison for return to India on parole, but Enver Pasha in Constantinople refused, under German pressure, to accept anything other than unconditional surrender. Townshend had no option but to surrender, which he did on 29 April after destroying his guns and wireless equipment, throwing the men's rifle bolts into the Tigris and cutting up all harness and saddlery. He handed his sword and pistol to Halil, who returned them to him in recognition of his gallant five month defence of Kut.

Townshend and his senior officers were well treated in captivity; the more junior officers less well; and the other ranks appallingly, according to normal Turkish practice. Of the 10,000 combatants and 2,000 non-combatants taken at Kut, 4,000 died in Turkish captivity through maladministration, negligence, indifference and inertia. Most of the brutality came from Arab guard units, but the Turks made little attempt to restrain them. Three men were outstanding in their efforts to alleviate the suffering of the British and Indian prisoners: successive American Ambassadors, Morgenthau and Elkus; and the Netherlands Ambassador, de Willebois.

Townshend's capitulation at Kut was described in the American press as the greatest British military débâcle since Yorktown. Maybe, but its implications were far less serious. No bands played *The World Turned Upside Down* as they had done in 1781. Indeed, this costly but temporary British reverse, for that is all that it amounted to, was overshadowed by the continuing disasters being suffered by the Turks in Armenia, where they lost in men and equipment more than the total strength of the British forces deployed in Mesopotamia.

Both sides on the Tigris were exhausted and only too willing to go onto the defensive during the intense heat of the summer months. Halil Pasha left for Baghdad soon after Townshend's surrender to take charge of the Turkish forces that von der Goltz had sent north to check Baratoff's advance on Baghdad from Kermanshah. He took with him the 2nd Division, and he disbanded the remnants of the 35th Division, leaving only the 45th, 51st and 52nd on the Tigris to contain the British.

Few of the senior commanders on the British side survived the purge instituted in the summer of 1916 by the War Committee in London to bring younger men into command in all theatres of war. In July, Gorringe was replaced by Maude from 13th Division, but only for a short time, because Lake too was removed; and, at Robertson's prompting, the War Office chose Maude to replace him as Commander-in-Chief. The Tigris Corps was taken over by Major General AS Cobbe. And there we must temporarily leave the Mesopotamian theatre with Cobbe's men dug in close to the Turkish Es Sinn and Sannaiyat fortifications. Events in Arabia and Palestine were beginning to overshadow the summer stalemate on the Tigris.

★ ★ ★

Turkish losses in Armenia influenced Arab nationalist thinking far more than the British defeat at Kut, and suggested that time was ripening for rebellion against Ottoman rule. In the event, it was the brutal actions of Djemal Pasha in his capacity as Governor of Syria that precipitated the Arab Revolt. Evidence of growing Arab dissidence had come into his hands in early 1916. In traditional Turkish style, he had instituted a brutally repressive régime with widespread executions and such savage vengeance on the Arab families implicated that any thoughts of rebellion in Syria were cauterised. Nevertheless, Djemal did not, as yet, have the power or enough troops in Arabia to deal with the Grand Sherif in Mecca, Hussein ibn Ali, although he was highly suspicious of him and his four sons.

Hussein's third son, Feisal, was in Constantinople in the spring of 1916. On his way home, he became aware of Turkish preparations for the dispatch of fresh troops down the Hejaz railway to help Djemal to deal with dissidence in Arabia. It was his observation of these troop movements that made him advise his father that the time had come to throw off Ottoman rule. The troops concerned, 3,500 of them with artillery and machineguns under Khairi Bey, were to act as an escort for a German Mission under Freiherr von Stotzingen, who was to set up a wireless station in the Yemen to communicate with German East Africa and to beam Turco-German propaganda to Moslem lands south of Suez on both sides of the Red Sea and to the Horn of Africa.

Hussein had been gathering his tribal forces together for the revolt for some months under the pretext of raising a Bedouin force to assist von Kressenstein's next attempt on the Suez Canal. Enver and Djemal paid a special visit to Medina to review Hussein's troops and were taken in by their feigned loyalty to the Sultan. Some of the hotter heads amongst the Sherif's followers wanted to murder the two Turks then and there as a trigger for the revolt, but Feisal managed to dissuade them from breaching the desert code of hospitality. They were escorted back to their train safely, but the Arabs could not be certain that they had not noted telltale signs of Arab disloyalty. With no time to lose before Khairi Bey's force arrived, Hussein's sons, Ali and Feisal, raised the standard of revolt near the Moslem holy city of Medina, the terminus of the Hejaz railway, on 5 June 1916.

Sir Henry McMahon was well aware that the revolt was coming, but had hoped it could be delayed long enough for him to supply enough arms and ammunition to help the Bedouin tribesmen to overpower the relatively small Turkish garrisons in the principal towns of the Hejaz. The dispatch of Khairi Bey's reinforcements for the Hejaz garrison brooked no delay. Three ships sailed from Port Sudan loaded with rifles, ammunition and food together with two mountain batteries of Egyptian artillery and a machinegun company under the Moslem officers. There were obvious risks in employing Egyptian troops to drive the Turks out of Arabia, but, in agreeing to accept them, the Sherif specified that only Moslem troops under Moslem officers were to be sent.

Initially the revolt showed few obvious signs of success. Captain TE Lawrence, who was to win world fame as 'Lawrence of Arabia', was appointed from the Arab Bureau in Cairo to be a British liaison officer with the Arabs. The illegitimate son of an Anglo-Irish baronet, he had been a brilliant scholar of modern history at Oxford. He had gone on to acquire fluency in colloquial Arabic and fascination for the Arabs and their way of life during archaeological work in the Middle East before the war. Lawrence's extraordinary grasp of Arabic idiom and Arab ways of thought won him their trust. In his *Seven Pillars of Wisdom*, he describes

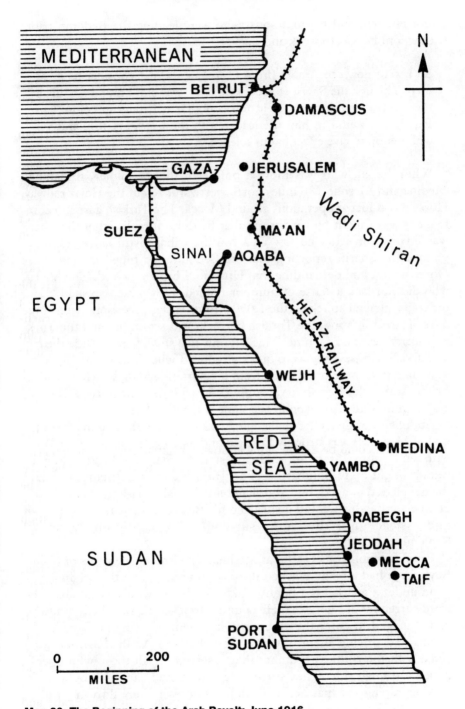

Map 26: The Beginning of the Arab Revolt: June 1916

Sherif Hussein and his four sons, who were leading the Bedouin tribes with whom he was to work and inspire:

> So I went down to Arabia [from Cairo] to see and consider its great men. The first the Sherif of Mecca we knew was old. I found Abdullah too clever, Ali too clean, Zeid too cool. Then I rode up country to Feisal, and found in him the leader with the necessary fire, and yet with reason to give effect to our science.[12]

While Feisal, who was more a politician than a soldier, threatened Medina and Ali rode 180 miles north westwards to cut the Hejaz railway, Hussein conducted operations around Mecca. The Turkish garrison commander was caught by surprise in that he did not realise that the Sherif was involved in what he saw as a routine tribal disturbance. He telephoned the Sherif, reporting that the Bedouin had rebelled against the Government, and demanding that Hussein 'Find a way out'. The Sherif, who did not lack a sense of humour replied 'Of course, we shall!', and ordered a general attack on the 1,000 strong Turkish garrison. After three days of street fighting, the Turkish barracks was set on fire and the Turks in it surrendered on 12 June. This left only two small forts outside the city in Turkish hands. They were quickly reduced when two of the Egyptian mountain guns were brought up from the port of Jeddah, which was taken by the Arabs with British naval support on 16 June. The ports of Rabegh and Yambo were also taken in the same way by 27 June.

Abdullah was given the challenging task of taking Taif, 70 miles southeast of Mecca. It was strongly fortified and had a garrison of 3,000 Turks with ten Krupps 75mm guns. He invested the place until Egyptian guns were brought up to bombard it. The Turkish guns were neutralised and the defences damaged, but Abdullah had no wish to risk the heavy losses of an assault, which could dishearten his Bedouin. Instead, he kept Taif under siege until the Turks surrendered unconditionally on 22 September.

Feisal was not so successful at Medina. The leading elements of Khairi Bey's force had already reached the city and had joined the original garrison under a gnarled old tyrant, Fakhri Pasha, in whose vocabulary the word surrender did not exist. He counter-attacked Feisal's Bedouin, who had managed to enter the city, terrifying them by using artillery in the streets and driving them out into the suburb of Awali. His men then acted with the ruthless brutality they reserved for all those who openly defied Ottoman rule. They surrounded Awali and carried it by assault, sacking, raping and massacring the inhabitants who were thrown, dead or alive, into the flames of their burning houses.[13] This naked terrorism broke every tenet of the Arab code of conduct, and sent a shudder of revulsion throughout Arabia. But, as was intended, it also discouraged many tribes, who were convinced by the Awali atrocity that the Turks would win in the end, as they had always done in the past. Feisal and Ali's chances of holding the tribes together looked frail indeed.

Ali withdrew from the railway and joined Feisal in the hills south of Medina to block any Turkish attempt to recapture Mecca. There were two routes by which the Turks could advance: via Rabegh on the coast or by an inland route, which seemed unlikely because it was devoid of water. McMahon wanted to dispatch a British brigade to Rabegh to insure the safety of Mecca, but the Commander-in-Chief, Sir Archibald Murray, resisted the High Commissioner, first, on the grounds that he could not spare the troops from the defence of Egypt and the Canal, but more importantly because the appearance of Christian troops so near the Holy Places might alienate the Arabs. In this he was supported by Lawrence, who reported that what the Arabs needed was British military advisers, guns, ammunition and explosives, but no troops. Nevertheless, a brigade was stood by at Suez for shipment to Rabegh in case the Sherif changed his mind.

The request never came because Lawrence persuaded Hussein in Mecca and the Arab Bureau in Cairo that the best way to protect Mecca was not by defending Rabegh, but by attacking the Turks' Achilles' heel – the vulnerable Hejaz railway west of Medina along which all their reinforcements and supplies had to come. To do this, a forward base would have to be established at the small port of Wejh, 180 miles north of Yambo, from which raids on the railway could be launched, using hit and run tactics more suited to tribal capabilities than orthodox warfare. Reaching the necessary agreements and making preparations for this bold move could not be achieved overnight, and it was not until early January 1917 that it became a practicable proposition.

The Arab Revolt had an immediate effect on the Suez Canal front. Djemal Pasha was far more interested in crushing the Arab Revolt in the Hejaz than in supporting von Kressenstein's ambition to block the Suez Canal. Many of the troops originally allotted to Kress were syphoned off to the Hejaz. It was only continued reports of British divisions being withdrawn from Egypt for service in France that caused Berlin to demand that Constantinople do something to rekindle British anxiety about the safety of the Canal. Kress was authorised by Djemal to advance on the Canal once more, this time with the limited aim of positioning German artillery permanently within range to harass shipping using it. He was given the 3rd Anatolian Division, an experienced formation, which would be supported by the 2,300 strong German/Austrian 'Pasha I' detachment of artillery, machineguns, aircraft and logistic units.

Kress started his advance on 9 July, using the coastal route soon after the 'Pasha I' detachment reached him. It was a painfully slow business moving forward his heavier guns through the stretches of soft sand that could not be avoided. He was forced to halt for ten days on 24 July within ten miles of the British positions at Romani.

On the British side, General Murray was in something of a quandary. He found it difficult to decide whether Kress was building up an advanced base from which to attack, or was establishing a defensive block on the coastal route to check a British advance into Palestine. He planned to meet both contingencies. If Kress had not attacked by 13 August, Murray would attack him instead.

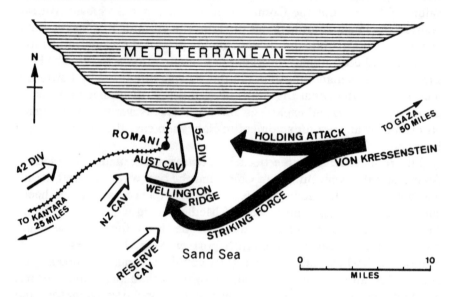

Map 27: The Battle of Romani: 4 August 1916

Kress was a prototype Rommel. He was always up with his leading troops, and he had the Rommelesque flair for quick battlefield decisions, but he was to suffer Rommel's fate of never reaching the Suez Canal. Murray's deployment of his troops and the tactics he used were very similar to Montgomery's at Alam Halfa 25 years later. Montgomery, a true professional, would have studied the Battle of Romani, but he never confessed to being influenced by it!

Murray deployed the infantry that he had allocated to the northern sector of the Suez Canal defences in the shape of a reversed 'L', covering the wells and railhead at Romani. The top of the 'L' rested on the Mediterranean coast and the longer leg ran due south along high dunes for about five miles to a prominent dune running east–west, code-named 'Wellington Ridge', where the front was bent back westwards, or 'refused' in military jargon, to form the shorter leg of the 'L'. To the south of Wellington Ridge lay a jumble of difficult sand dunes, which would impede the Turks if Kress, like Rommel, tried to turn the British line, as

Murray confidently expected that he would. Major General the Hon HA Lawrence's 52nd (Lowland) Division, reinforced with a fourth brigade, was well dug in on the 'L' shaped line. Lawrence (not to be confused with TE Lawrence) was also commander of the Northern Sector of the Canal defences and so was responsible for the tactical handling of the coming battle from his headquarters at Kantara, 25 miles behind the front where he had the best communications. In reserve, behind the front line and echeloned back down the newly built railway, was Major General Sir William Douglas's 42nd (East Lancashire) Division, which had been maintaining internal security in Egypt since the outbreak of war, and was being deployed in battle for the first time.

The key to the battle of Romani, however, lay in the deployment of the large force of mounted troops, which Murray made available to Lawrence: the ANZAC Mounted Division under the Australian Major General Chauvel, consisting of the 1st, 2nd, and 3rd Brigades of Australian Light Horse and the New Zealand Mounted Brigade; the 5th Yeomanry Brigade; and a mobile column of the Imperial Camel Corps. The 1st and 2nd Australian Light Horse were given the task of watching the Turks and delaying their advance if and when it started. They were to fall back into positions prolonging the shorter leg of the reversed 'L', 'the refused flank', which they were to defend dismounted. The rest of the mounted troops were held back in the desert to the south ready to strike the Turkish flank once Kress was irrevocably committed to a turning movement.

Few battles have run so close to their predicted course. Kress did decide to try to outflank the British line while mounting a holding attack on the main position. The Australian Light Horse carried out their task almost to perfection and drew the Turks into the sand-sea south of the refused flank, and then threw back attack after attack on their dismounted positions on Wellington Ridge. Try as they might, the hard men of the 3rd Anatolian Division could not break round the end of the position, which had been extended westwards by the arrival of the New Zealand Mounted Brigade. The New Zealanders not only checked the Turkish attacks lapping round the Australian flank but drove them back into the sand-sea.

By the late afternoon, all Kress's holding attacks on 52nd Division's main position had been repulsed; the mounted troops, against whom most of the Turkish attacks had been directed, were still capable of further effort; 42nd Division was moving up from reserve; and the 3rd Australian Light Horse and the mobile Camel Corps column were probing the Turkish southern flank. It looked as if the 3rd Anatolian Division might be annihilated, but Kress, who was well forward, had realised that the battle was lost quicker than Lawrence had back at Kantara. As darkness fell, he disengaged, and, despite great efforts by all British units in the blazing heat next day, he made good his escape, fighting skilful rear-guard actions against Chauvel's mounted troops for the next five days and reaching his

base at El Arish on 9 August. His Turks simply out-marched their opponents, but Kress had lost almost half of his 16,000 men: 4,000 left as
prisoners in British hands and over 3,000 were killed and wounded. The
British lost only 1,100 men, the bulk from Chauvel's ANZAC Mounted
Division, who had earned and deserved a high reputation as mounted
fighting men. Endowed with a natural aptitude for hard work under
extreme conditions and a fine physique, they became seasoned warriors,
and from Romani onwards were the rapier of the Egyptian Expeditionary
Force.

As on the Tigris, there was little inclination on either side to mount further offensive operations in the scorching summer heat. Djemal had long
accepted that Egypt was irrevocably lost to the Ottoman Empire, but he
was determined not to lose the Arabian provinces as well. He decided to
bequeath the problems of supplying troops across the waterless Sinai
desert to the British, instructing Kress to fall right back when attacked to
the more fertile areas of southern Palestine on a line running from Gaza
to Beersheba. In Whitehall and at Murray's GHQ at Ismailia, the victory
at Romani was seen to have secured the Suez Canal. All that was now
needed was greater depth in front of the Canal, which could best be provided by an advance to El Arish some 70 miles east of Romani and 50
miles from Gaza. Maintaining an advanced position there would be a
logistic nightmare unless the railway, which had reached Romani, was
extended to El Arish – together with a 12 inch water pipeline from the
Sweet Water Canal to supply not only the forward troops but also the railway engines, which could not use the brackish water of the coastal wells.

While Murray settled down to building his lines of communication to
El Arish, the ANZAC Mounted Division made the Sinai desert their
own, dominating it with deep reconnaissance and battle patrols. They
were primarily responsible for screening the advance of the railway and
pipeline, built by the Royal Engineers and the volunteer Egyptian Labour
Corps with material shipped direct from the United States. Field Marshal
Lord Wavell in his history of the Palestine campaign comments:

> The lines of communication organised for the advance across Sinai
> were a typically British piece of work – slow, very expensive and
> immensely solid. The famous epigram of Tacitus on the Romans – 'they
> make a desert and call it peace' – might aptly be inverted for this British
> advance – 'they turn the desert into a workshop and call it war'.[14]

Much the same was happening on the Tigris. Maude was developing Basra
as a base; more river steamers were arriving – slowly; and light railways
were being constructed along the Euphrates to Nasiriya, along the Tigris
from Qurna to Amara, and from Shaikh Saad to the forward troops. Sir
William Robertson argued strongly for a withdrawal back to Amara to

save troops and resources in this secondary theatre of war, but accepted that the effect of such a withdrawal on the tribes in the oilfield area could be disastrous. It was generally agreed that every effort should be made to place the Tigris Corps on a sound logistic footing in its present forward positions in front of the Es Sinn and Sannaiyat Lines. Maude's mission was to continue to protect the oilfields and to control the Basra *Vilayet*. No fresh advance to Baghdad could be contemplated for the time being.

In Europe, the battles of the Somme and Passchendaele had shown how far the Allies were from a decisive breakthrough. To the Westerners amongst the British policy-makers, every man, gun and shell was needed on the Western Front, which, in their view, was the only place where final victory could be achieved. The Suez Canal and the Persian oilfields were now secure, and the raison d'être for offensive action in the Middle East had disappeared. The War Committee in London decided that Murray and Maude should go no further; consolidate defensive positions; and be prepared to release troops for return to the BEF in France. This might have happened had Kitchener not been lost in June 1916 when the *Hampshire* was mined off the west coast of Scotland, while taking him on his mission to Russia. His death enabled the great Easterner, Lloyd George, to usurp his position as Secretary of State for War in June 1916, and then the Premiership in December.

Lloyd George had always advocated 'knocking the props out' from under Germany by attacking her weaker allies – Turkey, Bulgaria and Italy – rather than assaulting where she was strongest – on the Western Front. However, even he could not overturn the closely argued British war strategy overnight. Nevertheless, he did change its emphasis: Murray and Maude were still to consolidate their defensive positions, but with a view to resuming offensive operations as soon as their logistics would allow. Robertson, the convinced and stubborn Westerner and bitter opponent of Lloyd George, curbed any tendency to grandiose ideas by telling both commanders that they could not have any more divisions; but nor would they lose any. Lloyd George, in contrary manner, made it equally clear to them that what he wanted was resounding victory in the Middle East with Baghdad and Jerusalem as worthy political objectives.

Lloyd George overrode Robertson's objections: over the next few months, the Middle Eastern campaigns ceased to be about the defence of the Suez Canal and the Persian oilfields. Their primary objective became the dismantlement of the Ottoman Empire through the defeat of the Turkish Army, and the dissolution of the Turco-German alliance. As the natural heirs to the Ottoman provinces south of the Taurus mountains, the Arabs would have a leading role to play if the Grand Sherif Hussein could maintain the momentum of their revolt and a reasonable measure of Arab unity – no easy task.

CHAPTER 7

LLOYD GEORGE'S POLITICO-MILITARY TARGETS

Baghdad, Jerusalem and Damascus 1917

The Prime Minister, Mr Lloyd George, who was always seeking a strategical 'soft spot' and a way of escape from the slaughter of the Western Front, demanded that these campaigns [Palestine and Mesopotamia] should be set going again with fresh troops and new leaders.

Field Marshal Lord Wavell.[1]

Lloyd George's dreams of offensive action in the Middle East, with the glittering political prizes of Baghdad and Jerusalem as its objectives, depended upon the readiness and dynamic leadership of three separate forces: Maude's Indian Expeditionary Force 'D' in Mesopotamia; Murray's Egyptian Expeditionary Force in Sinai; and, in between, the irregular Bedouin forces of the Arab Revolt under the Emir Feisal in the Hejaz and Transjordan. Maude was ready first and was to prove himself a winner; and Feisal was not far behind him in timing and success; but Murray languished and was a loser!

Sir William Robertson had made no mistake when he nudged the Army Council into promoting Maude so rapidly to Commander-in-Chief in Mesopotamia. Maude had been commissioned into the Coldstream Guards in 1884, and had learnt his soldiering in the Sudan campaigns and the Boer War as a young officer. Besides being a very experienced fighting soldier, he had two great strengths and one marked failing, which emerged early in his career.

First, he had been Brigade Major, Brigade of Guards, at the time of Queen Victoria's Diamond Jubilee and had been responsible for the staff work behind it, showing the flair for the organisation and administration, which he was later to display on the Tigris. His second asset was his ability to win the trust and confidence of his officers and men, which he had demonstrated when commanding a brigade on the Western Front in 1914, and a division at Gallipoli in 1915. He was sent to the latter to pull

194

together the shattered remnants of the 13th Division after its devastating losses in the early fighting. So successful was he, that his division was chosen to provide the rear-guard during the evacuation of Helles in January 1916. He was the last general officer to leave the Gallipoli beaches. Like Montgomery 30 years later, he would never undertake any operation unless it was soundly based logistically and everything was ready. He had great faith in offensive action, but, unlike many other generals in the First World War, he did know when a fight should be broken off before losses mounted needlessly. This understanding, and his unimpeachable judgement of what was practicable with the resources available, lay at the root of the trust, which he inspired. He was, indeed, the very antithesis of the over-optimistic Nixon, who had been prepared to take unjustifiable risks to reach Baghdad in 1915.

His failing, which was magnified by the appalling Mesopotamian climate, lay in a tendency to overwork and a reluctance to decentralise. Everything had to be right and he would only trust himself to ensure that this was so. A meticulous 'workaholic', he preferred to hold the reins firmly in his own hands. He treated his chief of staff, Major General AW Money, more like a chief clerk than his principal staff officer. In one of his letters home he remarked that 'I do most of the General Staff work myself'.[2] He made one exception: he trusted implicitly, and justifiably, his senior logistician, Major General Sir George MacMunn, the Inspector General of Communications, and was never let down. In the end, even his physical stamina could not stand the strain of his punishing, over-conscientious routine, which was to lead indirectly to his untimely death in Baghdad in November 1917.

Maude had every confidence that he could capture Baghdad as soon as MacMunn was satisfied that the port of Basra, the Tigris steamers and the newly laid railways could supply his force's needs for the 250 mile advance up the Tigris from Kut. But he knew that if he made any mention of Baghdad as his immediate military objective, he would certainly lose Robertson's confidence. His declared aim was to retake Kut to give greater security to the oilfields by defeating the Turkish forces ensconced in its defence. He proposed to do this deliberately, step by step, with careful reviews of the situation at each stage. His plan was to hold the Turks on the north bank of the Tigris in their Sannaiyat defences while he developed his operations along the south bank, aiming to attack their advanced base area and communications in the Shumran Bend some seven river miles upstream from Kut, thereby making all their laboriously dug defences downstream of the town redundant. Sir William Robertson accepted his proposals subject to one crucially subjective rider: no operations were to be undertaken that risked heavy losses without adequate return. After the bloody battles of the Somme and Passchendaele, Britain could not tolerate, nor could she afford, a similar scale of loss in the Middle East.

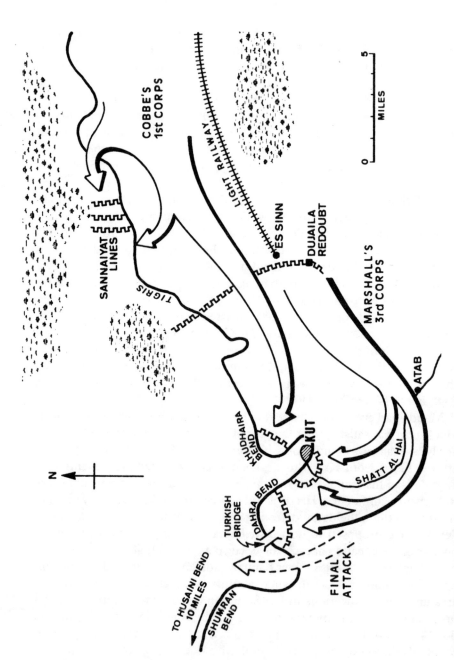

Map 28: The Recapture of Kut: December 1916–February 1917

After Townshend's surrender at the end of April, Enver Pasha had visited Halil Pasha's 6th Turkish Army Headquarters in Baghdad, and had insisted that the 13th Corps should be withdrawn from Kut and sent north to help check Baratoff's Russians advancing on the city from Kermanshah. Halil Pasha had reluctantly done so, leaving the 18th Corps under Kara Bekr Bey with only the 45th, 51st and 52nd Divisions at Kut to hold Maude. To save troops, Kara Bekr Bey had abandoned the Es Sinn lines on the south bank of the Tigris and had withdrawn to the Shatt al Hai, which joins the Tigris opposite Kut and forms a strong defensive obstacle, blocking Maude's approach to Shumran. He took the precaution of fortifying the whole of the north bank from Sannaiyat to Kut to stop any British attempt to cross the river behind his main defences. And around Kut itself he dug strong defensive positions on the south bank to stop Maude pinching out the town with assault crossings aimed at the neck of the Kut peninsula. These south bank defended localities formed three prominent salients: in the Khudhaira Bend; at the mouth of the Hai; and in the Dahra Bend. He had some lesser fortifications covering his floating bridge over the eastern reach of the Shumran Bend.

During his short period in command of the Tigris Corps, Maude had found it too unwieldy. As soon as he took over as Commander-in-Chief, he reorganised it into two self-contained corps and a cavalry division. Cobbe's Tigris Corps became the 1st Indian Corps with the 3rd and 7th Indian Divisions; and a new 3rd Indian Corps was formed under Major General WR Marshall with the 13th British and 14th Indian Divisions. The 15th Indian Division under Major General HT Brooking held the quiescent Euphrates front around Nasiriya, and the original 12th Division was broken up into small forces with specific tasks of securing the lines of communication, the oilfields and Bushire. A second Indian Cavalry Brigade, the 7th, had been sent from France to join the 6th, enabling Maude to form the cavalry division under Brigadier-General SF Crocker. In the air, 30th Squadron Royal Flying Corps, had been reinforced with more modern aircraft and had re-established British air-superiority, which had been lost earlier in the year. The Squadron's air reconnaissance capability was improved and its bombing operations were to become a significant factor in the land battle.

Maude's supply difficulties on the south bank of the Tigris were greatly eased by the advance of the railway across the desert from Shaikh Saad, which had reached Es Sinn in September and was expected to be close up behind the forward troops by the time he opened his offensive. Maude also assembled three bridging trains equipped with British manufactured military pontoons instead of local *danaks*: Nos 1 and 3 were river borne, and No 2 under Captain FVP Witts, another ubiquitous Sapper, was equipped with special wagons drawn by oxen for overland movement. Each train had enough equipment to provide two bridges over the Tigris.

Maude issued his orders for the first phase of his offensive on 10 December. Cobbe's 1st Corps would be responsible for holding operations along both banks of the Tigris, simulating preparations for a frontal assault on the Sannaiyat fortifications, coupled with threatened crossings of the Tigris behind them. Marshall's 3rd Corps would be the striking force and execute the wide turning movement, the first phase of which was to form a bridgehead over the Shatt al Hai at Atab, five miles south of the Turkish Hai salient. Crocker's Cavalry would go even wider and would head for the Turkish floating bridge at the Shumran bend, which the RFC were to bomb at first light on D Day.

Marshall's and Crocker's advances to the Hai in the early hours of 14 December were virtually unopposed. The Hai was found fordable in numerous places. Nevertheless No 2 Bridging Train soon had two bridges over it at Atab in case the Hai rose in flood. The Atab bridgehead was quickly consolidated by the 14th Division. The cavalry made even more rapid progress, coming within a mile of the Turkish bridge at Shumran, which the RFC had 'failed to hit, before being checked by entrenched Turkish infantry. With the chance of rushing the bridge gone, Crocker withdrew to the Atab bridgehead for the night.

In keeping with his step by step policy, Maude spent the next six days consolidating, bringing forward supplies and reconnoitring the Turkish entrenchments for the next phase of operations. While still threatening Sannaiyat, Cobbe took up positions containing the Turks in the Khudhaira bend; Marshall probed the Hai salient; and Crocker did the same in the Shumran area. During the night of 15–16 December, the RFC spotted the Turks dismantling their bridge at Shumran and managed to panic their steamers into slipping the rafts they were towing. Most of them went aground and the Turks were without a bridge over the Tigris for several days.

Reconnaissance reports from both corps showed that none of the Turkish entrenched positions around Kut could be stormed without risking heavy losses, so Maude decided to continue his turning movement with a surprise crossing of the Tigris in the Husaini Bend another ten river miles upstream from Shumran. Crocker's cavalry with infantry and artillery support set out with No 2 Bridging Train on 20 December to make the attempt. They reached the proposed crossing site unopposed, but not unseen. Turkish fire from the north bank soon brought pontoon launching to a halt. Realising that he had not achieved surprise, Maude rightly ordered Crocker to withdraw. The Turks had not been frightened into making any withdrawals from Sannaiyat to defend their communications, but the continuous bombardment of their main positions was reported to be having some effect on their morale.

Robertson in Whitehall was delighted with Maude's progress, which had only cost 720 casualties during the week's operations. Two new strategic factors were coming into play, which suggested that Maude should be ordered to speed up his deliberately cautious operations. Plans for decisive 1917 offensives on the Western Front were being debated, and Robertson wanted the return of the 13th British Division, which was, in theory, only on loan to the Indian Expeditionary Force. Furthermore, intelligence sources were warning that two fresh Turkish divisions, the 4th and 14th, were on their way to Baghdad. Winter was beginning to grip the Armenian and Kurdistan fronts, enabling the Turks to release troops for the Tigris front as they had done in 1916, when they thwarted Townshend's relief. With Lloyd George clamouring for a quick victory outside Europe, and appreciating that the Turks could not easily be manoeuvred out of their positions around Kut without a fight, Robertson authorised Maude to risk up to 25 per cent casualties in storming Sannaiyat, Kut or both. Maude chose Kut, and gave Cobbe the task of clearing the Turkish entrenchments in the Khudhaira salient, while Marshall prepared to do the same in the Hai salient. Every effort was to be made to stretch the Turkish defence by simulated activity at Sannaiyat and along the Tigris east of Kut while the cavalry raided the river west of the town.

In Cobbe's operations, it took the 3rd Division ten days relentless trench warfare from 9 to 19 January to force the Turks to abandon the Khudhaira salient. Marshall started his operations against the Hai salient on 25 January as soon as Cobbe could release the Army artillery, which had been supporting his attacks. By then, the Turkish 4th Division had reached the front and had been fed into the Hai defences. It took until 4 February for 13th and 14th Divisions to drive the Turks out of their entrenchments in a series of deliberate attacks, in which artillery, grenades and bayonets played the principal part. Instead of falling back across the Tigris into Kut, the Turks withdrew into the Dahra bend, hoping that the 14th Turkish Division would arrive in time to let them re-establish themselves on the Hai. Maude's operations had cost 8,500 casualties, including 2,000 killed since 14 December, a figure well within Robertson's limit of 25 per cent casualties amongst his total sabre and bayonet strength of 48,500. The Turks lost well over 10,000. Of these the British buried 2,000 and took 600 prisoners.

On 3 February, Maude received a cable from Robertson which gave him the first intimation that his objective might be Baghdad if he could master Kut. Robertson told him of Russian plans to open in March not only a renewed offensive in Armenia, but also thrusts through Kurdistan on Mosul and Baghdad. He wanted Maude's estimate of the size of force that the Tigris line of communication could support at Baghdad. His cable stressed the hypothetical nature of the question. There was to be no change in current policy of confining operations to the destruction of Turkish forces around Kut. Indeed, no sooner had Maude received the cable than the Russians reported their need to delay their offensives until April, due to unusually late heavy snow in the mountains, and Baratoff was reported to be refusing to advance on Baghdad because he understood that an epidemic, resembling bubonic plague, had broken out amongst the Turkish troops opposing him!

Offsetting these Russian disappointments, Robertson received intelligence from a reliable source that the Turkish troops opposing Maude were being stretched to the limit: Halil Pasha was demanding reinforcements and ammunition from Djemal Pasha in Syria to stave off the abandonment of Kut, which he was beginning to see as inevitable. This intelligence encouraged Maude to go on with his methodical clearing of the remaining Turkish positions from the south bank of the Tigris, hoping to weaken them enough to make an assault crossing practicable, although he had not yet decided where to make it. He gave Captain Witts of No 2 Bridging Train secret instructions to reconnoitre the river, taking soundings under the noses of the Turks, to find the best sites. He did not take his chief of staff or corps commanders into his confidence, in order to ensure complete surprise.

Marshall's 13th and 14th Divisions continued what the Americans in the Second World War called 'meat grinder' tactics to clear the Turks out of the Dahra Bend salient. Turkish resistance was seen to be crumbling, but the piecemeal arrival of their 14th Division helped to prolong resistance until 16 February when Kara Bekr Bey abandoned the south bank. Maude had his personal and highly secret plans ready for a *coup de grâce*.

Captain Witts had reported that it was impracticable to cross the Tigris near Sannaiyat or Kut, but that there was a good bridge site on the southern tip of the Shumran Bend with suitable places for ferries around the former Turkish bridge site on its eastern reach, where a covering force could be rowed across to protect the Sappers building the main bridge. Maude decided, therefore, to draw the Turkish reserves and to pin them down at the eastern end of the front by attacking Sannaiyat before attempting a surprise crossing at Shumran at the western end, where his assault, if successful, would threaten Kara Bekr Bey's line of retreat towards Baghdad.

Maude held his cards close to his chest and was not entirely frank with his corps commanders for good reasons. For his plan to work, the attacks at Sannaiyat had to be convincing and the threat to Shumran disguised for as long as possible. He told Cobbe that, as Turkish strength had been drawn westwards by Marshall's operations, 1st Corps was to mount the decisive attack to drive the Turks out of Kut by breaching the Sannaiyat defences. Nothing was to be spared to achieve success, because Maude doubted the practicability of an assault crossing of the Tigris. He told Marshall that 3rd Corps should make tentative plans for a surprise crossing at Shumran which Witts recommended in case Cobbe failed. The reverse was, in fact, his real intention: Marshall's Shumran crossing was to be the decisive blow, but for success Kara Bekr must be convinced that breaching the Sannaiyat fortifications was Maude's primary aim, and this would only be so if Cobbe's attacks were genuine attempts to break through and not just the usual feints, which 1st Corps had been mounting throughout the British offensive.

Cobbe's first assault at Sannaiyat on 17 February was carried out by his 7th Division, which had been sapping and mining there since its abortive attacks in April 1916 during the Townshend relief operations. Its assault was initially successful in that the first two Turkish lines were breached, but by the end of the day vicious Turkish counter-attacks had regained all their lost trenches. Cobbe had, indeed, convinced Kara Bekr Bey that his Sannaiyat fortifications were in danger and must be reinforced. Turkish reserves were rushed eastwards as Maude hoped. Next day, Maude gave Marshall definitive orders to be ready to cross at Shumran. All preparations were to be made by night, and the troops of the 14th Division, earmarked for the operation, were to be given pontoon launching and rowing practice on the Shatt al Hai well away from prying eyes. In the meanwhile, Cobbe was to make obvious preparations for renewing his assaults on Sannaiyat.

Heavy rain, which brought the Tigris up in local flooding, delayed preparations, but all was ready for Cobbe to attack again at Sannaiyat and to launch two minor feint crossings just east of Kut on 22 February; and Marshall was poised to launch 3rd Corps' crossing at Shumran whenever Maude gave the order. This time, the 7th Division achieved and held a breach in the Sannaiyat defences against determined Turkish counter-attacks. For the next two days, he gnawed his way through with a series of successful crumbling attacks against failing Turkish resistance.

Maude ordered Marshall to start crossing at Shumran just before dawn on the 23rd. Two out of three ferry sites failed, with pontoons being shot to pieces, but the third succeeded and by 8.30am, Captain Witts' Sappers had sufficient cover to start building the bridge. The flood-water current was so strong that two motor tugs, moved overland to the river by teams of oxen, had to be used to lay out the bridge anchors. Turkish shelling inflicted some casualties amongst the Sappers, but did little material damage, and the bridge, almost 300 yards long, was ready for traffic by 4.30pm – a fine feat of which No 2 Bridging Train could be justly proud. By nightfall, most of the 14th Division's infantry were across and Marshall had a secure bridgehead.

Next day, 24 February, the 13th Division and the Cavalry joined the 14th Division in the bridgehead, and the 3rd Corps fought its way northwards up the Shumran peninsula. By dusk they were threatening Kara Bekr's escape route. Halil Pasha authorised the abandonment of Kut that day, and as dawn broke on the 25th, the 1st and 3rd Indian Corps found themselves facing only rear-guards, but these were determined to give the Turkish main body as much time as possible to withdraw in reasonably good order. That order would have been maintained had it not been for the Royal Navy. As usual, the hardy Turks out-marched their British opponents on land, but Captain Nunn, still commanding the Tigris Flotilla of six gunboats mounting 4-inch guns, caught up with them and turned their retreat into a panic-stricken rout. He recaptured some of his own vessels, which had been lost during Townshend's withdrawal from Ctesiphon, and caused, in conjunction with the ever-marauding Arabs, the disintegration of the Turkish army, which had resisted the British on the Tigris for over a year. Maude cabled Robertson in Whitehall:

> In view of the change brought about in situation by recent successes on Tigris front, I shall be glad to learn whether HM Government in any way desire to modify their instructions. . . .
>
> Until I get your reply I do not propose to delay, but intend to follow up retreating enemy closely; being careful, however, to do nothing which will prevent me from adjusting my position readily according to your further orders.[3]

But it was neither Whitehall nor the Turks who made him break off the pursuit near Aziziya, 60 land miles up-river from Kut on 26 February. His Chief of Staff and Quartermaster General both warned him that he must pause to allow the supply system to be reorganised for an advance on Baghdad. MacMunn, the Inspector General of Communications, rushed up from Amara to reinforce their warning. He sweetened this sour logistic pill by promising that Maude's troops would lack for nothing, if he would delay the start of his advance for a week, i.e. until 5 March, to allow reserve stocks to be moved up-river and steamer schedules to be adjusted. Maude accepted MacMunn's demand, and Kara Bekr Bey continued his withdrawal molested only by the increasingly hostile Arabs.

Halil Pasha realised that he had little chance of defending Baghdad, for which he had made no proper preparations. Nevertheless, he ordered Kara Bekr Bey to occupy the old Ctesiphon fortifications to buy time for the Turkish divisions opposing Baratoff to disengage and join him in or near Baghdad. The German staffs and specialists in Baghdad panicked and left in haste. And in Whitehall, the War Cabinet accepted Robertson's advice that Maude should be authorised to advance on Baghdad as soon as he was ready. Memories of Townshend's withdrawal from Ctesiphon instilled a measure of caution into their directive. The second paragraph of Robertson's instructions to Maude read:

> You are required by this decision to press enemy in the direction of Baghdad and so exploit your recent success to full extent which you

judge to be useful and feasible, having regard to your communications, to enemy reinforcements and to importance of your main body not being compelled to fall back for any reason.[4]

Robertson was still goading the Russian High Command into opening their offensives towards Mosul and Baghdad, but he told Maude that it would be some five weeks at the earliest before the thaw would allow them to do so. He suggested delaying any attempt to occupy Baghdad until the Russian offensive started and until Maude's own supply system could support four infantry divisions and a cavalry division in the city. He left the decision on timing to Maude's discretion, but he added one nugget of encouragement: the withdrawal of 13th Division was to be postponed.

Map 29: Maude's Capture of Baghdad: 5–11 March 1917

MacMunn assured Maude that he could supply four divisions and the cavalry in Baghdad straight away, so Maude stuck to the planned date of 5 March for his lunge up-river towards the city. Crocker's cavalry led off ahead of Marshall's 3rd Corps on the north bank of the Tigris, while Cobbe's 1st Corps was moved up more slowly behind them. The first cavalry clash with the Turks occurred at Lajj, seven miles from Ctesiphon, where the 13th Hussars earned fame with their epic Balaclava style charge, which did much to persuade Kara Bekr Bey that the old Ctesiphon defences were too large and dilapidated for his skeletal divisions to hold. He fell back that night without a fight to the Diyala, a 300 feet wide tributary of the Tigris, which provided the last real obstacle in front of Baghdad on the north bank.

In Baghdad itself, the Turkish command was in hopeless disarray. Enver Pasha had entered the fray by insisting that the city, which had been an Ottoman provincial capital with religious and sentimental associations for the Turkish nation since its capture in 1534, must not be abandoned without a fight. Halil knew that his 18th Corps from the Persian front could not reach him in time to save the city. Kara Bekr was pressing him to allow his 13th Corps to march through it to join the 18th Corps to mount a combined counter-offensive once Halil's 6th Army had been concentrated and reinforced. Halil, although he favoured withdrawal to save his Army, decided that he had no option but to obey Enver and do his best to defend Baghdad. Most of his subordinate commanders had doubts about the wisdom of doing so, but were prepared to try.

Marshall's 3rd Corps reached the Diyala on 7 March. The 13th Division attempted to bounce a crossing that night, but failed. Maude left Marshall to prepare a deliberate crossing, while No 1 Bridging Train built a pontoon bridge over the Tigris a few miles south of the Diyala. In the early afternoon of 8 March, Crocker's cavalry led Cobbe's 1st Corps across the bridge for an advance on Baghdad via the south bank. Halil had anticipated this move and had reinforced a series of blocking positions on the south bank in which his troops fought with their usual uncomplaining stoicism against the numerically superior British columns, whose commanders, needless to say, were trying to avoid unnecessary casualties with Baghdad so nearly in their grasp.

The 13th Division tried to cross the Diyala again that night, 8–9 March, gaining only a toe-hold on the far bank, which about 60 men of the North Lancashire Regiment managed to hang onto throughout 9 March, despite determined Turkish counter-attacks. That night, the 13th Division expanded its small bridgehead, and next morning a pontoon bridge was in position, enabling Marshall to develop his attack on the last Turkish positions blocking his way into the city on the north bank.

Cobbe's attacks on the Turkish south bank positions during the 9th were made in swirling dust storms, which made direction keeping extraordinarily difficult. His progress, however, was rapid enough to persuade Halil that he had to choose between standing siege for which Baghdad was not prepared, or extracting his troops to fight again another day: he chose the latter. During the night 9–10 March, his troops withdrew behind strong rear-guards, leaving the British patrols to find out next day that Baghdad was theirs.

Maude landed from his headquarters steamer and entered the city early on 10 March without any formal ceremony. The Union Flag was initially raised over the Citadel, but was then moved to the more prominent clock tower in the Turkish Headquarters Barracks. It now hangs in Canterbury Cathedral. As the British troops marched through the streets to start their pursuit of the beaten Turks up the Tigris and Euphrates, they were received with undisguised enthusiasm by the Baghdadis, but were themselves disgusted by the squalid state of the city. Kara Bekr's demoralised troops trudged northwards, and Halil's staff took the last train to Samarra, the terminal of the short Baghdad section of the German Baghdad Railway.

Lloyd George gained his victory in the East far quicker than he or anyone else expected. Within six months poor Maude was dead. He contracted cholera, it is suspected, from contaminated milk poured inadvertently into his coffee at a Jewish schoolchildren's party given in his honour. He died on 18 November 1917 with central Mesopotamia firmly under British control; with the Persian oilfields secure; and with the Turco-German *Jihad* totally discredited. Long before his death, however, the spotlight of events had fallen on the Egyptian Expeditionary Force in Palestine and on the Arab Revolt.

* * *

Maude had satisfied one of Lloyd George's political objectives by taking Baghdad for him. Murray in Egypt got off to a less auspicious start in meeting the Prime Minister's wish to see Jerusalem in British hands. Having been directed after his victory at Romani to go onto the defensive, he moved his General Headquarters back from Ismailia to Cairo to be in closer touch with the High Commissioner and to be in a central position to oversee operations: against the Senussi in the Western Desert around Siwa, the Arab Revolt in the Hejaz and the defence of Aden, as well as the Sinai front, where he had been directed to the capture of El Arish as a means of giving greater depth to the Suez Canal defences. The move back to Cairo in October 1916 has been rightly castigated by the Official Historians as cutting the Commander-in-Chief off from the main body of his troops. The move would have been acceptable had a clear defensive policy been maintained, but it was not. By December, Robertson was asking Murray what troops he would need to invade Palestine. Murray asked for two extra divisions, making six in all – one for the close defence of the canal, one to guard the lines of communication through Sinai, and four as his striking force. As usual the two extra divisions could only be found at the expense of the Western Front, so Murray was directed to do his best with what he had: take El Arish and, when the railway and pipeline caught up, invade Palestine.

Murray was hardly the man for the job. In 1914, he had been invalided home from France where he had been Chief of Staff to Sir John French and had not stood the strain. He had been side stepped to Egypt after failing again as Chief of the Imperial General Staff to Kitchener at the War Office in 1915. Lawrence in his Seven Pillars of Wisdom describes him as having 'a very nervous mind, fanciful and essentially competitive', and later as 'all brains and claws, nervous, elastic and changeable'.[5] He was devious, and did not have the fixity of purpose to provide the dynamic leadership needed by the Egyptian Expeditionary Force, if it was to accomplish Lloyd George's secret ambition of taking Jerusalem. He certainly could not lead it from Cairo. On the credit side, however, he was a far seeing administrator, who solved the supply problems of operating across the Sinai deserts. He would have made a far better commander of the lines of communication than Commander-in-Chief.

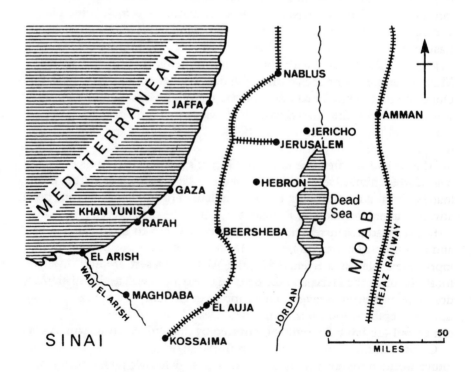

Map 30: Southern Palestine: 1916–17

After Romani, all troops east of the Canal were organised as a corps, called the Eastern Frontier Force, under Lieutenant-General Sir Charles Dobell, who had fought successful campaigns in the Cameroons and Western Desert of Egypt. Although not an outstanding commander, he was less frightened of his own shadow than Murray.

The Eastern Force, to use its shortened title, had a unique component: the Desert Column, consisting of eight mounted brigades under Lieutenant-General Sir Philip Chetwode, a colourful Light Infantry soldier turned Cavalryman with originality, quick grasp of essentials and tactical flair for mounted action, whose frank and downright manner appealed to its many Australian and New Zealand Troopers. The eight brigades were grouped in two divisions: Anzac Mounted Division, which was still commanded by the wise, cautious but highly competent Chauvel, and consisted of two Australian Light Horse brigades, the New Zealand Mounted Rifle Brigade and an English yeomanry brigade; and the newly constituted Imperial Mounted Division under Brigadier-General HW Hodgson, consisting of another two Australian Light Horse brigades, and two English yeomanry brigades. In addition, Chetwode usually had the Imperial Camel Brigade under his command as well. The Desert Column formed the advance-guard and screen for the 42nd (East Lancashire) and 52nd (Lowland) Divisions, which made up the main body of the Eastern Force.

It was not until 20 December 1916, four months after Romani, that Murray felt confident enough about his elaborate logistic system to order Dobell to advance as far as El Arish. That very day, an air reconnaissance sortie reported seeing no Turks in the town or manning its defences. The Desert Column had surrounded the town by nightfall and did, indeed, find it empty next day. It took the Navy two days to clear the minefields off the coast, which were obstructing the landing of supplies on the beaches, and on 23 December the first supply ship from Port Said was off-loading into lighters, easing but not solving the logistic problems of an advance into Palestine.

Kress von Kressenstein had been watching the British build-up closely and had tried to persuade Djemal Pasha to allow him to pull back to the more defensible Gaza–Beersheba line, but Djemal was reluctant to lose his foothold across the Egyptian frontier and would only sanction the abandonment of El Arish provided Kress held onto Rafah, the frontier town on the coast road, and onto the railhead at Kossaima, which lay at the eastern end of the Wadi El Arish some 50 miles inland.

Chetwode set about trying to find out where the Turks had retired to: either northwards up the coast to Rafah, or south-eastwards along the Wadi El Arish towards Kossaima, or perhaps both. He ordered Hodgson on Rafah and Chauvel on Kossaima, but the air reported a largish concentration of Turkish troops at Maghdaba on the Wadi El Arish, halfway to Kossaima, so he cancelled the advance on Rafah and ordered Chauvel to take both mounted divisions to attack the seemingly isolated Turkish detachment at Maghdaba.

On 23 December Chauvel fought the first of two remarkable cavalry 'cutting-out' actions – to use a naval term – in which the troopers, fighting dismounted and with great enthusiasm, won both battles for their commanders after they had decided to disengage. The Turks were holding a circle of redoubts around Maghdaba, which Chauvel had all but surrounded by midday, cutting them off from outside help. His dismounted attacks on the redoubts, however, failed in the mirages created by the noon-day heat. No water could be found locally by his Sappers, so in the early afternoon he ordered a withdrawal in order to water his horses back at El Arish. Before the order could reach the troopers, however, the 3rd Australian Light Horse had rushed one of the redoubts in which a hundred Turks surrendered. This success started the total collapse of Turkish resistance, and by dusk all the surviving Turks – 1,282 of them – had surrendered. Chauvel had lost only 22 killed and 124 wounded. His men and horses arrived back exhausted at El Arish in the small hours of Christmas Eve.

The railway reached El Arish at the turn of the year, enabling Chetwode to set out on 9 January with the Desert Column to raid and, if possible, 'cut-out' a strong Turkish detachment covering Rafah in a good defensive position at El Magruntein, a few miles to the south-west. After a skilfully conducted night march, he had the position surrounded, but as at Maghdaba, all his dismounted attacks failed, and, moreover, his ammunition was running low. Like Chauvel, Chetwode decided in the early afternoon that he must give up, not for lack of water for his horses, but because air reports warned him of approaching Turkish reinforcements. This time it was the New Zealanders who swung the battle in Chetwode's favour before his order to retire could reach them. Their brilliant bayonet charge cleared a key redoubt and triggered another Turkish collapse. 1,580 Turks and 10 Germans surrendered before help could reach them. Chetwode's losses were 71 killed and 415 wounded. The raid completed, he returned to El Arish.

Kress made no attempt to re-occupy Rafah or Maghdaba. He had not wanted to hold them in the first place, and he had lost both garrisons by obeying Djemal's instructions to do so. Instead, he deployed his troops north of the Gaza–Beersheba line within easy supply distance of his railways, and with only a couple of battalions in Gaza itself. He positioned himself with his main reserves behind the centre of his front on the Beersheba railway. Djemal insisted on holding Kress's 53rd Turkish Division back at Jaffa, in case the British tried to land there. When the 16th Turkish Infantry and 3rd Cavalry Divisions did join Kress in February, many of their Arab soldiers deserted, not to the British, but into the local towns and villages, hoping to join in the Arab Revolt, which was by then the talk of the bazaars.

The speed of advance of the British rail and pipe heads towards Rafah dictated the timing of Murray's operations, but he was also sticking out obdurately for the two extra divisions that he had estimated he would need to reach Jerusalem. Not being able to provide them, Robertson advised the War Cabinet not only to postpone the hoped for offensive in Palestine until the autumn, but to withdraw one or two of Murray's divisions for redeployment on the Western Front. Murray was told to use the summer preparing for a major campaign in Palestine in the autumn, but he was also to maintain pressure on von Kressenstein to conform with the overall Allied strategic policy of pinning down the Central Powers on all fronts. The 42nd (East Lancashire) Division, which had been in Egypt since the outbreak of war, was ordered back to England early in February and its place at El Arish was taken by the 53rd (Welsh) Division. A new division, the 74th (Yeomanry) Division, was to be formed from dismounted yeomanry regiments, which had been employed on internal security duties in Egypt since their withdrawal from Gallipoli a year earlier.

Both Dobell and Chetwode, who were in close touch with their troops, realised that morale, particularly of their Australian and New Zealand troops, would slump unless they pursued an offensive policy. They were certain that they were opposed only by about 12,000 Turks. There was, perhaps, a danger that the Russian Revolution, which started in March 1917, might enable the Turks to reinforce von Kressenstein for a counter-offensive. Nevertheless, it would be easier to meet it if Gaza could be taken. There was more water to be had for the Desert Force's horses and camels, and more fresh food would be obtainable. Dobell proposed to repeat the 'cutting-out' operation, which had been so successful at Maghdaba and Rafah, but on a much larger scale, using most of his Eastern Force. Murray agreed, but cautioned him not to get too far ahead of his rail and pipe heads because of the lack of adequate transport columns to supply the forward troops. Maude, in Mesopotamia, had his river steamers: Murray had to depend on the progress of his railway and pipeline construction.

At the beginning of March, both railway and pipeline were within 30 miles of Gaza, which Dobell thought was garrisoned by 2,000 Turks. In fact, von Kressenstein had noticed the British interest in Gaza and had doubled the garrison, which he further strengthened with Austrian and German artillery. He had, moreover, appointed Major Tiller from his staff as commandant of Gaza.

Dobell's plan was for Chetwode to make a wide turning movement with his mounted troops five miles east of the town to isolate it and cut its garrison's escape route to the north, while the 53rd (Welsh) Division, under

Chetwode's direction, attacked it from the south, aiming for the Ali Muntar ridge, the key to the Turkish defence of Gaza, and the place to which Samson is reputed to have carried the pillars of the Gaza temple in biblical times. He kept the 52nd (Lowland) and 54th (East Anglian) Divisions, under his own command: the former in general reserve and the latter to provide a firm base at the crossing of the Wadi Ghuzza, just south-east of Gaza, for Chetwode's mounted troop and to be ready to fend off any attempt by Kress to bring pressure to bear on the rear of Chetwode's containing line.

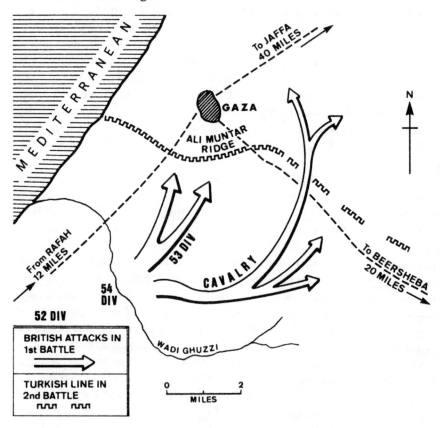

Map 31: The 1st and 2nd Battles of Gaza: 26 March and 17 April 1917

The operation started in the early hours of 26 March, but was hampered straight away by unseasonably thick fog which rolled in from the sea before dawn. Chetwode's cavalry were undeterred and carried out their task almost to perfection, establishing their designated blocking positions east of Gaza, cutting the coast road to the north of the town, and, as a bonus, capturing the commander of the 53rd Turkish Division and his personal staff as they hurried along the coast road to take command of

Gaza's defence. Kress had persuaded Djemal to move the division south from Jaffa when he had clear evidence of the British threat to Gaza.

The fog, however, did seriously delay the advance of 53rd (Welsh) Division because its commanders could not reconnoitre the approaches, which they were to use for their attacks, until it lifted. The actual assaults on Gaza's southern defences did not start until the afternoon. Although they were carried out with great élan, the leading battalions were short of the Ali Muntar ridge when the light began to fade.

Dobell was faced with an awkward dilemma. The mounted troops had found less water than they expected. Fearing that something had gone wrong with the infantry attack, Chetwode had ordered the cavalry to attack the town from the north-east and, indeed, they had managed to penetrate its northern outskirts when Turkish reinforcements started to attack their rear. It was clear that the mounted troops would have to be withdrawn to water unless Gaza could be taken by nightfall, which did not seem likely. As at Maghdaba and Rafah, Dobell decided that he must disengage, but this time the troops could not save the day for him although they came near to doing so. Unbeknown to Dobell when he ordered Chetwode to withdraw the cavalry back to the Wadi Ghuzza, the 53rd Division had taken the Ali Muntar feature as darkness fell, but there could be no question of fighting a way into the town in the dark through the thick belts of cactus hedges, which abounded on its southern outskirts.

The tragedy of Dobell's decision to disengage was that the British intelligence staffs had broken the Turkish cypher and had intercepted desperate messages from Major Tiller to Kress, reporting the Turkish intention to surrender. Had these reached Dobell before he ordered the disengagement, the operations might have ended differently. Turkish reinforcements, including their 53rd Division, arrived in sufficient strength next day to secure Gaza for the time being. The British had lost just under 4,000 casualties and the Turks half that number.

Murray was disingenuous in reporting Dobell's defeat to Robertson, dressing it in the clothing of victory:

> On the 26th and 27th we were heavily engaged east of the Ghuzza with a force of about 20,000 of the enemy. We inflicted heavy losses on him; I estimate his casualties at between 6,000 and 7,000 men, we have taken 900 prisoners including General Commanding and whole of Divisional Staff of 53rd Turkish Division. This figure includes 4 Austrian officers and 32 Austrian and 5 German other ranks . . .[6]

Murray was quite unjustifiably showered with congratulatory letters and telegrams from England. Robertson seems to have been temporarily taken in by Murray's reports, which omitted saying anything about the failure to 'cut-out' Gaza, because he replied on 30th March:

As a result of your recent success and our progress in Mesopotamia the situation has materially altered . . . At present, indications point to fact that Turks are anxious about situation on Tigris and on Persian frontier and are diverting forces to that theatre. In these circumstances, and as you are assured of reinforcements during the summer, your immediate objective should be the defeat of the Turkish forces south of Jerusalem and the occupation of that town.[7]

Murray covered himself quickly with a reply next day cautioning that rapid progress could not be expected and reiterating his original estimate of needing six instead of four divisions for success. Railway construction would limit him to 20 miles per month. This was scarcely what the War Cabinet wanted to hear. Robertson was instructed to tell him:

. . . Everyone is now feeling the strain of the war, and this strain will certainly increase; therefore, the moral effect of success is of great importance, both in strengthening the hands of the Government and in making the public more ready to bear their burdens. For a variety of obvious reasons, success in Palestine will have a very inspiring effect in Christendom. War Cabinet are anxious therefore that your operations should be pushed with all energy . . .[8]

It was an unhappy Murray, who tasked Dobell to prepare a plan to force the Turks to withdraw from their Gaza-Beersheba line, which was beginning to congeal into a tenable defensive position as Djemal fed reinforcements southwards to von Kressenstein, and as German defensive skills, coupled with industrious Turkish digging and wiring, created a continuous line of mutually supporting redoubts around the southern outskirts of Gaza and along the general line of the Gaza–Beersheba road. Every day that passed strengthened the Turkish line east of Gaza. The obvious military answer to Dobell's problem was to use his marked superiority in mounted troops in a wide turning movement to the east of Beersheba, but lack of water and shortage of transport for use beyond the pipe and railheads made such ideas impracticable. Moreover, the developments of the line of Turkish redoubts stretching eastwards from Gaza to Beersheba precluded another 'cutting-out' style operation. The cavalry might get through a gap, but it would soon be closed behind them. Dobell decided, therefore, that his only real option was to mount a set piece frontal attack in the style of a Western Front offensive. He chose the Gaza sector so that he could take advantage of naval gunfire support from the sea.

Dobell's plan was to assault the Gaza defences in the coastal sector, stretching from the sea to just east of Ali Muntar, with his three fully established infantry divisions side by side and the new 74th (Yeomanry)

Division, which was short of artillery, in reserve. Chetwode's mounted troops would pin down the Turkish troops in the redoubts to the east of the main infantry assault. There was nothing intrinsically wrong with his plan, but there were two hidden snags: few of his commanders and their staffs had any real experience of mounting such operations, and by Western Front standards he was woefully under-gunned. The Turkish soldier was even more formidable in defence than German troops when properly dug in, as they were at Gaza.

The 2nd Battle of Gaza needs only the briefest of descriptions because it was a replica of all the failures on the Western Front in 1915 and 1916. It was fought in two phases. On 17 April, Dobell's divisions successfully closed up to within assaulting distance of the Turkish defences. At 7.30am two days later, the assault was delivered after two hours of the heaviest bombardment that Dobell's artillery, the French battleship *Requin* and the British monitors *M 21* and *M 31* could provide within the limits of the ammunition available. It was not enough to suppress the Turkish artillery let alone their machine-guns. By nightfall, the Eastern Force had lost 6,444 men with nothing to show for its gallant but fruitless efforts. Such gains as were made were soon lost to Turkish counter-attacks. The Turks had only 2,000 casualties. Murray wanted to resume the battle next day but Dobell and Chetwode persuaded him that it was pointless to do so.

Dobell had lost Murray's confidence and was relieved by Chetwode, and Chauvel took over the Desert Column. Murray, himself, had lost both Robertson's and the War Cabinet's confidence by his over-sanguine reporting. He received a letter of recall on 11 June. His job was first offered to the South African General Jan Smuts – future Field Marshal and Prime Minister of South Africa – who had just driven Germany's enterprising colonialist, von Lettow-Vorbeck, out of their East African territories. He turned the appointment down because he considered fighting the Turks was just another side-show. The final choice was General Sir Edmund Allenby, the difficult but successful commander of the Third Army in France – a giant of a man with a violent temper, who had justifiably earned the nickname of 'the Bull'. From the moment Allenby arrived, the Egyptian Expeditionary Force knew it had a commander. Nevertheless, he paid a generous tribute to Murray at the end of the war:

> I desire to express my indebtedness to my predecessor, Lieutenant-General Sir AJ Murray, who, by his bridging of the desert [with railway and pipe lines] between Egypt and Palestine, laid the foundations for the subsequent advances . . .[9]

Dobell's second defeat at Gaza brought the Arab Revolt in the Hejaz into the strategic limelight. If the coastal gateway into Palestine was barred, then a way round the eastern flank must be developed. Here Arab ambitions and British strategic requirement coincided nicely. The Arab dream was the capture of Damascus as their future capital, and their means was raising rebellion like a grass fire through the Bedouin tribes along the route of the Hejaz railway east of the Jordan, which would help the British to outflank the Turkish defences of Palestine and draw Turkish resources away from the main front.

By mid-January 1917, Feisal was ready to advance on Wejh as Lawrence and he had planned. By then a team of British military advisers under Lieutenant Colonel SF Newcombe RE had arrived to help the Sherif's forces to use the modern weapons and equipment, which was being sent to them from Egypt, and, more importantly to teach them how to use explosives in raids on the Hejaz railway. The French, ever conscious of the need to protect their own interests wherever the British were operating, sent a small representative mission under Colonel E. Bremond and a detachment of Moslem troops with mountain artillery and machine-guns. Lawrence and Bremond were rarely to see eye to eye, and had good reason to distrust each others' motives in supporting the Arab cause.

Feisal set off along the coast to Wejh (*See Map 26*) on 18 January with an imposing array of 10,000 Bedouin. Shortly before they reached the port, a *coup de main* party of 500 tribesmen was landed from British war-ships and captured most of the small Turkish garrison without much difficulty. In reality, Feisal's capture of Wejh was a very slight threat to Medina, but it had the effect that Lawrence had predicted. Thereafter, the Turks made no further attempt to advance on Mecca, and concentrated upon the futile defence of the railway, which was constantly cut by Newcombe's and Bremond's Bedouin raiding teams led by British and French officers. The 13,000 Turkish troops in the Hejaz became an invested force around Medina and before long began to slaughter its transport animals for food; and Djemal Pasha wasted another 12,000, manning blockhouses along the railway between Ma'an and Medina.

After Murray's second failure at Gaza, the significance of the Arab Revolt belatedly became apparent to the GHQ staff in Cairo. Wejh was clearly too far south to affect events in Trans-Jordan. The obvious next step was to spread the rebellion northwards by taking and establishing a new base at Aqaba, from which to encourage and support tribal rebellions along and to the east of the Jordan valley towards Damascus. Aqaba was, however, not an easy port to attack from the sea, so Lawrence was tasked to persuade Feisal to work his way north to take it from the landward side.

Lawrence had clear ideas of his own about the part that the Arabs could and should play in dismantling the Ottoman Empire. He saw that the Turks would be in an impossible position if faced with a co-ordinated Bedouin rising. In reality the Turks controlled only about a tenth of the Bedouin inhabited lands; the other nine-tenths were possessed by the desert tribes. In his *Seven Pillars of Wisdom*, he rehearses his ideas:

And how would the Turks defend all that? No doubt by a trench line across the bottom, if we came like an army with banners; but suppose we were (as we might be) an influence, an idea, a thing intangible, invulnerable, without front or back, drifting about like gas? Armies were like plants, immobile, firm-rooted, nourished through long stems to the head. We might be a vapour, blowing where we listed. Our kingdoms lay in each man's mind . . .[10]

In his view 'preaching was victory and fighting a delusion'[11] – no Arab lives should ever be squandered in set piece battles; the Turks' Achilles' heel was material and not manpower; and so 'the death of a Turkish bridge, rail, machine or gun was more profitable than the death of a Turk'.[12] One thing, however, worried him: preaching the holy grail of future Arab independence by which he could focus Bedouin ambitions to be free of Ottoman imperialism was, in his view, based on false pretences and dishonest. He knew enough about British and French post-war political intentions to realise that the Colonial Powers were unlikely to fulfil their obligations to grant complete independence to the Arabs, whom they saw as backward peoples in need of the benefits of European tutelage. He saw too that the only way to win the independence that he was preaching to them was to make the Arab contribution to the Allied war effort so outstanding that complete independence could not be denied to them:

. . . I vowed to make the Arab Revolt the engine of its own success, as well as the handmaid to our Egyptian campaign: and vowed to lead it so madly in the final victory that expediency should counsel to the Powers a fair settlement of the Arabs' moral claim.[13]

Lawrence's plan, agreed by Feisal, was to ride north accompanied by Feisal's second-in-command, the Sherif Nasir, and by Auda Abu Tayi, the chief of the eastern Howeitat, who inhabited the deserts east of Aqaba, to gather and organise them for an attack on the port. Auda was one of the best fighting leaders to join the Arab Revolt, but reaching his desert fastnesses in the Wadi Sirhan 150 miles east of the Dead Sea required an epic march across some of the most inhospitable desert country in the world in searing May temperatures. They set off on 9 May, three weeks after the 2nd Battle of Gaza, carrying a potent politico-military mix of gold coin to recruit the Howeitat and neighbouring tribes, and gelignite and gun cotton for use against the Hejaz railway whenever they crossed.

Lawrence reached the Wadi Sirhan on 27 May, and while Nasir and Auda recruited their forces for the attack on Aqaba, he rode on northwards with a small party as far as Baalbek, 30 miles north of Damascus and 500 miles from his starting point at Wejh. He had many interviews with the tribal chiefs, who promised to rise when the time was ripe and not before. There was some pressure on him for an immediate Arab attack on Damascus, but he successfully stalled the hotheads, pointing out that the British were still too far away to help repel the inevitable Turkish come-back. As a measure of deception, he allowed rumours to circulate that Damascus and not Aqaba was the Arab objective.

Back in the Wadi Sirhan on 19 June, Lawrence raided the Hejaz railway north of Amman to draw Turkish attention away from Aqaba, and then crossed the line south of Ma'an with Auda's and Nasir's force of about 500 Bedouin fighting men on camels and horses. They were initially unlucky in that when they attacked and took the Turkish guard post at the head of the pass leading down to Aqaba, a Turkish reinforcement battalion was just arriving in Ma'an and was rushed out to retake the post. The battalion was composed largely of young recruits and was trapped in the valley by Lawrence's Arabs at Abu el Lissal. At sunset on 2 July, Auda charged them with 50 picked horsemen. The Turks broke in panic, and the camel mounted Bedouin with Lawrence at their head hurtled down the hill-side to complete the destruction of the Turkish force. Lawrence's camel was shot dead, hurling him out of his saddle. It was not until later he had to confess that it was a shot from his own pistol, fired in excitement, that killed his mount!

The destruction of a Turkish battalion by a Bedouin force at a cost of only two killed and a few wounded demoralised the local Turkish troops and gave the Arabs new confidence in their own abilities. Aqaba fell to them on 6 July without much resistance from the Turkish garrisons of posts around the port. Six hundred Turkish prisoners were shipped off to Egypt when the Royal Navy arrived some days later. Feisal now had a base from which he could support the Egyptian Expeditionary Force in outflanking the Gaza-Beersheba line, and at the same time acquire the right, in due course, to claim the Arabs' inheritance when victory was won.

Lawrence went back to Cairo to drum up support for the development of the Aqaba base only to find Allenby instead of Murray sitting in the Commander-in-Chief's chair. Allenby quickly grasped the strategic importance of the tribes east of the Jordan with their ability to threaten Turkish communications of Jerusalem. Lawrence gives a light-hearted description of his meeting with the new Commander-in-Chief:

> It was a comic interview, for Allenby was physically large and confident, and morally so great that comprehension of our littleness came slow to him. He sat in his chair looking at me – not straight, as his custom was, but sideways puzzled. . . . He was full of Western ideas of gun power and weight – the worst training for our war – but, as a cavalryman, was already half persuaded to throw up the new school [Western Front style warfare], in this different world of Asia, and accompany Dawnay and Chetwode along the worn road of manoeuvre and movement; yet he was

hardly prepared for anything so odd as myself – a little bare-footed silk-skirted man offering to hobble the enemy by his preaching if given stores and arms and a fund of two hundred thousand sovereigns to convince and control his converts . . . At the end he put up his chin and said quite directly. 'Well, I will do for you what I can', and ended at that.[14]

Brigadier-General Guy Dawnay was Chetwode's Chief of Staff at Eastern Force Headquarters, and, like Chetwode, was an advocate of mobility and manoeuvre. It was Chetwode's and Dawnay's advice that turned Allenby's mind away from the attritional warfare of the Western Front as Lawrence suggests. He arrived at the front by train from Cairo a few days after taking over from Murray at the end of June. He carried instructions from the War Cabinet to pursue a campaign of *strong and unceasing aggression*[15], the aims of which were to be the destruction of the Turkish army in front of him, the capture of Jerusalem, and the expulsion of the Turks from Palestine. His first task, however, was to submit his outline plan and estimate of the additional resources that he would need to carry it out, and these Chetwode and Dawnay were ready to provide.

In a ten day whirlwind tour of the front, Allenby visited all the key sectors and most of the units holding them, impressing his powerful personality on their officers and men. The effect was electrifying. Rumours fly fast in an Army, especially when it is facing stalemate and does not quite know why success is eluding it. Word spread from trench to trench, and camp to camp that Allenby had arrived with a new plan and a promise of extra resources to take the offensive again at the end of the hot weather. Spirits rose, and over the next four months there can have been few soldiers who did not see their new Commander-in-Chief as he toured units. An officer of a Yeomanry regiment wrote at the time:

> Seldom in the course of Military history has the personality of a new commander had such a marked effect on his troops.[16]

Chetwode presented Allenby with what Field Marshal Wavell has described as 'one of the shrewdest appreciations made during the war, the details of which were worked out by his staff officer, Guy Dawnay'[17]. The obvious line of approach was along the coast, taking advantage of the Royal Navy's command of the sea and the relatively abundant fresh water supplies on the coastal plain, but this route was barred by Gaza, which German ingenuity and Turkish picks and shovels had turned into a formidable fortress. The centre of the Turkish line was almost as strong, totally devoid of water and an uninviting prospect. The eastern flank looked more promising. It rested upon the western slopes of the Judean hills, which run north–south between the Mediterranean coast and the

Jordan Valley. It was less well fortified because von Kressenstein thought the problems of water supply would make a major turning movement round his open inland flank impracticable. His main defensive position ended at Hareira, four miles north-west of Beersheba – the town of seven wells – which he had fortified and garrisoned separately to give greater depth to his eastern flank. Although he had wanted to abandon it, destroy its wells and use its garrison to extend his main line into the Judean hills, Djemal had vetoed the proposal as it meant the loss of valuable corn-lands. Beersheba became a hostage to fortune, which Chetwode saw was the key to success since its swift capture would ease the water supply problems of the turning movement he had in mind.

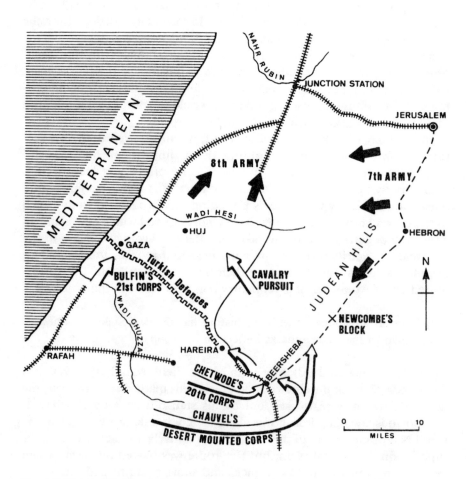

Map 32: The 3rd Battle of Gaza and Beersheba: 27 October–7 November 1917

Chetwode's plan, like all good plans, was elegant in its simplicity. Von Kressenstein was to be induced to expect Allenby's main effort would be against Gaza, whereas it was Beersheba that was to be overwhelmed. His line would then be rolled up from the east, and the mass of the British cavalry would complete his defeat by cutting across his line of retreat along the coast. By attacking westwards from the Judean hills, the British would have the additional advantage of always doing so from the higher ground. Chetwode recommended that Allenby should ask for two more infantry divisions, making seven in all, and considerable artillery and air reinforcements. Robertson managed to meet his demands mostly at the expense of Lloyd George's pet Salonika campaign, which had proved itself to be a dead end. Supplying these additional troops at the front, however, also entailed doubling the railway and pipelines across the Sinai desert during the summer months to be ready for the offensive, which Allenby hoped to mount in October.

Robertson now took the unusual step of sending Lieutenant Colonel AP Wavell out to Allenby as his personal liaison officer, charged with keeping him in touch with Allenby's thoughts and needs. He had the highest regard for Wavell, whom he had known and watched over since he was a student under him at the Staff College. It was a brilliant decision, for Allenby quickly recognised Wavell's true worth and the value of this close link with the man in Whitehall best placed to help him. Despite Wavell's youth (he was only 34), the two men became constant companions and friends for life. Wavell always claimed that no one had had a greater influence upon his own development as a commander than Allenby. His biography of Allenby has done much to secure his place in our history as a leading exponent of the art of mobile warfare.

Allenby had no intention of staying in Cairo as Murray had done. He decided to command his offensive in person. He split his General Headquarters into forward and rear echelons, establishing the former as his operational headquarters at Khan Yunis near the coast only 15 miles south of Gaza, and leaving the latter in Cairo to look after the affairs of Egypt, the Canal and the Middle East Base. Like Maude, when he took over on the Tigris, he decided that the Eastern Force had become too unwieldy. He reorganised it into three corps: the Desert Mounted Corps, still under the now very experienced Chauvel with the ANZAC, Australian and Yeomanry Divisions and the Imperial Camel Brigade; 20th Corps, of four infantry divisions under Chetwode; and 21st Corps, with three divisions under Lieutenant-General Sir Edward Bulfin, a stout-hearted warrior with abundant energy, upon whom Allenby knew he could rely for set-piece infantry battles. There was no wholesale purge of commanders and senior staff. Murray's former chief of staff was replaced by Major General Louis Bols; one divisional commander was sent home and a few elderly cavalry commanders were replaced by younger men; but, in general, Allenby preferred to make best use of existing talent.

★ ★ ★

On the Turco-German side, the schism within the High Command between the pan-Turks and the pan-Islamic cliques began to make itself felt once more. Enver Pasha, the leading pan-Turk, placed the recovery of Baghdad at the top of his strategic priorities: Djemal with his pan-Islamic leanings saw the defence of Jerusalem and Medina, and the recovery of Mecca as the high-points on his agenda. The Germans, at first, favoured Enver's determination to recover Baghdad, and were persuaded to put some muscle into Enver's proposed counter-offensive in Mesopotamia. With Enver's agreement, Field Marshal von Falkenhayn, Ludendorff's predecessor as Chief of the German General Staff, was sent to master-mind the enterprise, for which Mustapha Kemal's 7th Army, the Turkish General Reserve, was to assemble at Aleppo. Kemal, however, resigned his command after a bitter dispute with Enver over the chaotic internal state of the country, caused, as Kemal saw it, by the corruption of the civil administration, which could lead to Turkey's internal collapse if the war continued much longer.

Militarily, Kemal also had grave doubts about the wisdom of concentrating on Mesopotamia instead of Palestine, and he disliked the growing power of the German staff – Turkey should be careful to guard her independence. He was replaced by Fevzi Pasha, who was directed to prepare an advance down the Euphrates to co-operate with Halil's rebuilt 6th Army on the Tigris in driving the British back to Basra.

Von Falkenhayn's headquarters was officially called 'Turkish' Army Group F, but it had a higher than usual content of German staff officers, which led to it and its operations being code-named *Yilderim* (Thunderbolt or Lightning) by the cynical Turks. A specially trained German task force – *Pasha II* – was assembled in Silesia as the 'Asia Corps' to provide some under-pinning for *Yilderim*, consisting of three hand-picked infantry battalions with strong artillery, machine-gun, mortar and aircraft support plus a transport column of some 400 lorries suitable for Middle Eastern conditions, which would make it independent of the crude Turkish railway and supply systems. It was under the command of Colonel von Oppen, a skilled and wary soldier of sterling quality.

Djemal, like Kemal, refused to accept the decision to direct *Yilderim* against Baghdad, and fought back, arguing in favour of reinforcing the Palestine-Hejaz front. In the end, he won the debate, thanks to von Falkenhayn, who supported Djemal's view of the strategic danger of the British breaking through at Gaza and advancing on Aleppo, probably in conjunction with an amphibious landing in the Gulf of Iskanderun (*See Map 16*) – as Sir John Maxwell had proposed in 1915 – which would cut the Turkish lines of communication to Baghdad as well as to Jerusalem and Medina. Djemal, however, did not want *Yilderim*, let alone von Falkenhayn, taking over command in his Syrian theatre, where *his* rule was absolute. He had confidence in von Kressenstein and wanted Fevzi Pasha's 7th Army without a new German *Supremo* and his bloated staff.

Djemal could not have it all his own way. He lost the command battle and was forced to accept the transfer of all operations in Palestine to *Yilderim*. He was left with the political control of Syria and operations against the Arabs east of the Jordan with his 4th Army. Kress's forces in the Gaza Line became the 8th Army, and Fevzi's 7th Army was ordered to protect Kress's inland flank in the Judean hills and to guard Jerusalem. Von Falkenhayn proposed to move his GHQ to Jerusalem as soon as possible, but by the time these Turco-German arrangements were finalised, it was too late. Allenby struck while von Falkenhayn was still at Aleppo, and only one *Yilderim* division had been moved south.

* * *

In most of Britain's major wars a sea change comes over her armies in the field about two thirds of the way towards victory. The harsh realities of war have selected her commanders; staffs have learnt their business the hard way; the officers and men in the fighting units have become battle-inoculated and experienced; and logisticians have mastered their art and have the resources that they need. This was certainly so in Palestine in the autumn of 1917. Allenby, Chetwode, Chauvel and Bulfin were a well balanced command team with experienced staffs and logisticians to serve them. They had as large a force of battle-hardened divisions as the Sinai line of communications could supply, and all their men had been rested and trained for the tasks ahead of them during the six months pause since their defeat in the 2nd Battle of Gaza. The only operation of war that they had not, as yet, mastered was pursuit of a beaten enemy; and the only resource that seriously limited their action was water for their horses away from the coastal pipelines.

Deception planning was one of the crucial elements in Allenby's victory in the 3rd Battle of Gaza, which opened on 27 October 1917. Von Kressenstein did become convinced, as Allenby intended, that the British planned to breakthrough at Gaza, having first drawn the Turkish reserves eastwards with a preliminary attack at Beersheba. One ruse that confirmed this in Kress's mind, was the dropping of a blood-stained haversack and binoculars by a British officer supposedly on reconnaissance, who feigned being wounded but was able to ride off when chased by a Turkish cavalry patrol. The haversack contained a mock agenda for a GHQ conference, indicating the main attack would be on Gaza, coupled with a landing from the sea and a subsidiary attack by mounted troops on Beersheba. After the fall of Gaza, a Turkish order was found rewarding the

NCO who picked up the haversack. Kress apparently believed in the authenticity of the papers, which corroborated other evidence deliberately generated by Allenby's deception staff.

Allenby's offensive should really be called the 3rd Battle of Gaza and Beersheba. It was a four act drama with an overture, which began on 27 October with a heavy three day preliminary bombardment of the Gaza sector from land and sea, while the 40,000 troops of Chetwode's and Chauvel's corps moved eastwards, marching only by night to take up their positions in the wings south-west and south-east of Beersheba, held by only 5,000 men of the Turkish 24th Division, many of whom were Arabs. The British staff work and march discipline were impeccable, and achieved complete surprise when the curtain rose for the first act at dawn on 31 October. By midday, Chetwode's infantry divisions had mastered Beersheba's southern defences, which were four miles from the town, more easily than expected. They were halted in their objectives to allow time for Chauvel's mounted troops to sweep round and into Beersheba from the north-east, cutting off the garrison's escape route and stopping the demolition of the vital seven wells. Turkish resistance to Chauvel's advance, unlike Chetwode's, proved far stiffer than expected. It was not until evening that an inspired charge by the 4th and 12th Australian Light Horse smashed through the last Turkish line and Beersheba fell into Chauvel's hands with its wells intact, although there was much less water in them than had been hoped. Meanwhile, the road and telegraph lines, running north from Beersheba to Hebron and Jerusalem, had also been cut 20 miles to the north by a small camel-mounted force led by Colonel Newcombe, whom we last met blowing up the Hejaz railway with Feisal.

The second act began on the western half of the stage and almost immediately Bulfin's 21st Corps opened its holding attack on Gaza on the night 1–2 November, striking through the sand dunes between the western outskirts of the town and the sea. It had to be a full scale assault by his three divisions to keep Kress convinced that it was the real thing. Practically all its objectives were taken and Turkish counter-attacks were driven off, but at a cost of 2,700 British casualties – double the price of Beersheba.

While Bulfin held Kress's attention at Gaza, Chetwode was probing north-westwards to square up to the strong Turkish defences at the eastern end of their main line around Hareira. Chauvel found his corps strongly opposed as he tried to work round the Turkish flank, and was caught up in heavy fighting in the rock-strewn Judean hills west of the Hebron road. Kress had mistaken the advance of Chauvel's mounted troops as the start of a diversionary raid on Jerusalem and had moved troops from the Hareira sector to counter it, easing Chetwode's future task at Chauvel's expense. The first *Yilderim* units had also just reached Jerusalem and were rushed south to clear Newcombe's block on the Hebron road and to retake Beersheba. Newcombe was forced, in the end, to surrender and the road was cleared for a Turkish build-up for a counter-offensive towards Beersheba. There could be no question of raising the curtain for the third act – the rolling up of the Turkish line from the east – until the British inland flank was itself secure.

Allenby had hoped that 20th Corps' attack on Hareira could be launched at the latest by 4 November, but Chetwode and his experienced staff persuaded him that 6 November was the earliest date for the third act to begin, and that it would have to be performed by fewer actors than planned because one of his infantry divisions and part of Chauvel's Desert Mounted Corps would have to stay blocking the Turks in the Judean hills to guard his flank.

Von Kressenstein still had his eyes fixed on Gaza, where continuous heavy bombardment seemed to presage the opening of a decisive attempt by the British to break through, but he now had doubts about his ability to hold the coastal sector and the town much longer. He realised that he must get his heavy artillery away before it was too late. Von Falkenhayn reached Damascus on 4 November and authorised him to ride Allenby's expected punch by abandoning Gaza. He was to re-establish his 8th Army front on the Wadi Hesi, seven miles to the north, while Fevzi's 7th Army took up positions in the Judean hills to protect Jerusalem and to counter-attack the British flank if they tried to advance northwards up the coastal plain towards Jaffa. The withdrawal was executed on the night of 5–6 November with such finesse that for 36 hours Bulfin's Corps failed to detect it.

Chetwode opened the third act of the drama early on 6 November, launching Allenby's long premeditated *coup de grâce* with a three divisional attack on the Hareira position, which had been weakened by the dispatch of units to help block the Hebron road. The attack was made with great dash and the Turkish line collapsed, forcing the whole of Kress's 8th Army into precipitate retreat to the Nahr Rubin stream–Junction Station– Bethlehem line, covering Jaffa on the coast and Jerusalem in the Judean hills.

Allenby's pursuit of his beaten enemy – the fourth act and finale – fell regrettably short of his expectations. His supply columns could only support one infantry corps of two divisions and the mounted corps once he had to leave his railheads behind him. He gave Bulfin's 21st Corps the task of thrusting up the coast, where he could be supplied to a limited extent by the Royal Navy, while Chauvel's Desert Mounted Corps tried to intercept the retreating Turkish columns with attacks on their inland flank. Chetwode's 20th Corps was grounded at Hareira and his supply columns were used to support the pursuit.

Bulfin had the energy and drive of a steam-driven battering-ram to force the Turks back along the coast, but Chauvel's attempts to cut them off were limited by the difficulties of finding water for his horses, and by the tiredness of his men, who had been in action continuously since the offensive began. Initially, he was only able to free four of his ten brigades from the fighting in the Judean hills, though two more joined him later. During the 8th and 9th – the two critical days of the pursuit – progress was disappointingly slow. The Turkish rear-guards fought with their usual stoicism, and despite the most gallant charge by the Worcestershire and Warwickshire Yeomanry at Huj, Chauvel never managed to break through their screen to reach their retreating columns.

Von Falkenhayn, who had set up his *Yilderim* General Headquarters in Jerusalem on 6 November and had no real feel for Turkish capabilities and susceptibilities, ordered the obvious counter-stroke to be mounted against Allenby's inland flank from the Judean hills. The Turkish commanders grudgingly accepted his direction, but knew that their troops were too tired to respond. Allenby was warned by a wireless intercept of von Falkenhayn's intention, but refused to check his pursuit. When the Turks did attack on 11 November, they were driven back relatively easily by Chauvel's mounted troops, who reported that many of the Turks seemed to be sleep-walking as they advanced to the attack, and those who were captured were almost dead on their feet from exhaustion! Allenby had judged the state of Turkish morale more accurately than their German overlord.

As Bulfin's leading units pushed their opponents back over the Nahr Rubin, took Junction Station on 14 November after another successful Yeomanry charge at El Mughar, and entered Jaffa on the 16th, Whitehall suffered a fit of nerves about Allenby over-extending himself and repeating the Nixon/Townshend folly, which had led to the disaster at Kut. A weaker man might have used the War Cabinet's caution as an excuse to rest on his laurels, but he judged that the Turks were in such a demoralised state that it would be wrong not to attempt to hustle them out of Jerusalem without waiting for his supply situation to enable him to bring forward Chetwode's 20th Corps. Leaving Chauvel's Corps to watch the Turks north of Jaffa, he gave Bulfin the task of pushing into the roadless Judean hills to cut the Jerusalem-Nablus road well north of the Holy City, which he was determined should not be engulfed in the fighting.

Even Bulfin's drive and his troops' enthusiasm to become the conquerors of Jerusalem could not overcome the difficulties of fighting through those stony hills; of the thinning of their ranks over three weeks' continuous fighting; and of dogged Turkish resistance in such ideal defensive country. They were also unlucky in the weather breaking, just as they entered the hills on 19 November. Nevertheless, they almost cut the Nablus road before Allenby decided that they were just not strong enough to frighten von Falkenhayn into abandoning Jerusalem. On 24 November, he called a halt while Chetwode's rested 20th Corps was brought up to continue the thrust through the hills to cut off Jerusalem.

Chetwode's offensive opened on 8 December with one of his divisions advancing up the road from Hebron, due south of Jerusalem, while the other three attacked from the west. The brunt of the fighting fell on the Londoners of the 60th Division. After a cold night march in pouring rain, they carried the main Turkish defences to the west of Jerusalem soon after dawn, but fog and rain delayed the other divisions and the day seemed to end disappointingly. Unbeknown to the British, the Turks had panicked when the 60th Division overran their works. After failing to rally his troops, the local Turkish commander abandoned Jerusalem during the night. Next day, the Holy City, which had so often succumbed to bloody storm and pillage, greeted its newest conquerors with relief tinged with comedy. The mayor came out to surrender the keys, first trying to do so to two Cockney cooks, who had lost their way; then to a sergeant on outpost duty; and a finally to a gunner officer, bringing his battery into action against the Turkish rear-guard. None of these felt equal to such an historic occasion. In the end the keys were accepted on Allenby's behalf by Major General Shea, the commander of the 60th Division.

Allenby made a simple ceremonial entry into the city through the Jaffa Gate on 11 December, walking at the head of his staff with Chetwode in attendance. The British people had received a most appropriate Christmas present; and Lloyd George could add Jerusalem to Baghdad as scalps won by his 'Easterner' policies in his strategic blood feud with the 'Westerner' Robertson, which was to reach its climax with the latter's resignation in February 1918.

★ ★ ★

The Arab armies at Aqaba and in the Hejaz played an indirect part in the capture of Jerusalem. They held about a third of Djemal's available troops pinned down in Medina and trying to defend their railway life-line against constant British-led Bedouin raiding and demolition. Aqaba was steadily built up as a forward operating base for Feisal, whose small force of trained regular troops – mostly deserters or ex-prisoners of war from the Turkish Army – was under the command of Jaafar Pasha, whom we met earlier trying to escape from Cairo's citadel down a rope of sheets after he had been captured serving the Senussi in the Western Desert of Egypt. The intention was for Feisal to operate northwards to the east of the Jordan valley as soon as Allenby was near enough to support him from across the Jordan. That time had not yet come and it would have been dangerous to raise the local Bedouin tribes unless they could be supported: once called upon, they would not respond again if they experienced defeat.

Lawrence did make one direct attempt to influence the 3rd Battle of Gaza. Allenby agreed that he should try to blow one of the railway viaducts in the Yarmuk gorge, just east of Lake Galilee, carrying the main Turkish rail link from Damascus to the Palestine front. It failed by one dropped rifle, which alerted the bridge guards! In the ensuing mêlée, the tribesmen carrying the gelignite panicked and jettisoned it into the gorge. Lawrence and his raiding party escaped, having shown what might be done when Allenby was ready to resume the offensive, if he could maintain Bedouin loyalty and enthusiasm for long enough. Lawrence was not unaware that some of the tribal leaders, including Auda, were reinsuring with the Turks in clandestine negotiations.

1917 had seen the captures of the Ottoman provincial capitals of Baghdad and Jerusalem. Damascus, the remaining Ottoman city in Arab lands, still lay beyond Feisal's reach.

CHAPTER 8

DESTROYING THE OTTOMAN EMPIRE

Allenby's Megiddo 1918

It was a daring plan, even against an enemy so inferior in numbers and morale. It would involve a continuous ride of over 50 miles for the majority of horsemen, and over 60 for some, in the course of which they would have to cross a range of hills in the enemy's possession, passable by only two difficult tracks. There is no parallel in military history to so deep an adventure by such a mass of cavalry against a yet unbroken enemy.

Field Marshal Lord Wavell on Allenby's plan for the decisive battle of Megiddo.[1]

By the time Sir Stanley Maude died in Baghdad in November 1917, he had established as great a depth to his defences around the city as his logistic system would allow. During the heat of the summer of 1917, he had pushed his front line out some 70 miles from the city: in the west to Ramadi on the Euphrates; to the north to Samara on the Tigris; and in the north-east to Shahraban on the main route into Western Persia along the Diyala River (*See Map 33*). Halil's 6th Turkish Army was too weak and disorganised to do more than present a show of resistance: the limits of Maude's advances were almost entirely dictated by supply difficulties. He was not unaware of the probability that the Turco-German *Yilderim* forces, assembling at Aleppo, might be launched against him to recover Baghdad in the autumn. His main concern was to be well balanced, soundly based logistically and in positions of his own choosing, ready to defeat them. The speed with which he could extend the railways from Baghdad up the Euphrates, Tigris and Diyala valleys dictated the timing and extent of any future operations, which he might be asked to mount in support of Allenby's critical operations in Palestine. All three lines were advancing at an average rate of half a mile per day.

There had been hopes that Maude would be well placed to support a planned Russian offensive towards Mosul. As the summer months wore on, it became clear that Kerensky's Russian Provisional Government was failing and could not pursue the war with the vigour it had originally intended. Then ten days before Maude died and was succeeded by General Sir William Marshall, the commander of the 3rd Indian Corps, the Bolshevik *coup d'état* took place in Moscow, bringing with it the disintegration of the Russian armies on the Caucasus front, and the probable release of large bodies of Turkish troops for use in Mesopotamia and Palestine.

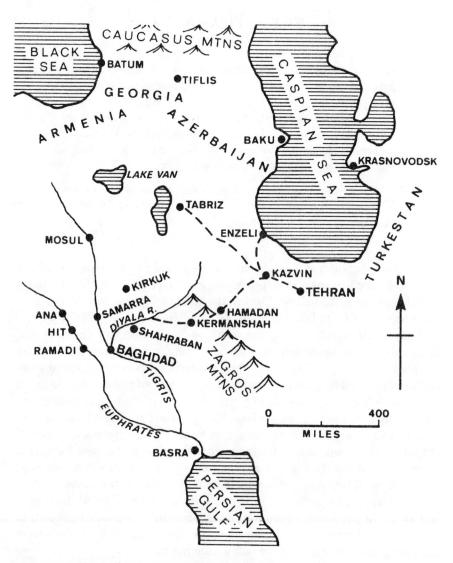

Map 33: British Operations in North-West Persia: 1918

In the event, few Turkish troops left the Caucasus. Enver and his Pan-Turk colleagues saw the opportunity for recovering the Turkish heart-lands for which they craved: Georgia, Armenia and Azerbaijan, annexed by Tsarist Russia in the early 1800s. Their ambitions did not stop there: they wanted to take the ports of Baku and Enzeli on the Caspian Sea in order to cross it to recover Turkestan as well. These ambitions were supported by the German High Command, who wished to exploit the manganese of Georgia and the oil of Baku. Baku became more important than Baghdad in Turco-German strategic planning, and thwarting their advance to the Caspian and into north-west Persia became Marshall's primary concern for most of 1918.

Logistics presented almost insurmountable problems in helping the Russian Armenians and Azerbaijanis to oppose Turkish annexation of their territories. There was only one practicable route for motor vehicles from Baghdad to the Caspian Sea at Enzeli. It ran up the Diyala valley to the Persian frontier and then through the Zagros mountains via Kermanshah, Hamadan and Kazvin in its 635 mile journey to Enzeli. The Zagros passes were from 5,000 to 8,000 feet high and closed for much of the winter by snow. Moreover, the country around Kermanshah and Hamadan had been stripped bare by the Turks fighting Baratoff's Russians. The largest force that it was thought could be maintained over the route after the spring thaw was about a brigade group. If a lot of hard work was done to make it fit for motor vehicles, it might be possible to supply a second brigade group. The War Office and General headquarters in India were not to be deterred. They decided to adopt the traditional British method of dealing with such situations: sending a mission to help and encourage the Georgians, Armenians and Persians to resist the Turks.

The officer chosen to lead the mission was Major-General LC Dunsterville, a 'politico' of some skill and persuasive powers, who reached Baghdad from India on 18 January 1918 with instructions to make his way to Tiflis, the capital of Georgia. He was to be British representative with the newly declared Federal Republic of Trans-Caucasian Peoples. It was planned that his mission, called 'Dunsterforce', should be built up gradually to 150 specially selected officers and 300 NCOs to help raise and train local forces. He left Baghdad with a small advance party on 27 January, and reached Enzeli three weeks later, only to be stopped by the local Bolshevik Committee who refused to allow him to proceed to Tiflis. The whole of the Trans-Caucasus had disintegrated into warring factions, each determined on achieving its own ends in its own way even to the extent of allying themselves from time to time with the hated Turks. There was no obvious anti-Turkish coalition with which Dunsterville could work, but one thing was certain: he must secure the road to Enzeli before anything useful could be done to oppose the pan-Turkish advance to the Caspian. He asked for an infantry brigade, a cavalry regiment, a battery of mountain guns, a number of armoured cars and a detachment of aircraft for reconnaissance to join him at Hamadan when the snows left the passes. War Office acceptance of this demand committed Marshall to a long and wearisome sideshow, which was to go on fitfully, but with some success, in that it thwarted pan-Turk ambitions, until the end of the war.

* * *

In the meantime, British strategic policy for 1918 was being thrashed out by the Supreme War Council at Versailles, where Lloyd George won his final joust with Robertson. Despite the latter's demand that every available man and gun should be concentrated to resist the expected German onslaught on the Western Front by forces released by Russia's collapse, Lloyd George insisted that there should be no relaxation in the war against Turkey. It was agreed after a visit to the Middle East by General Jan Smuts – at that time Lloyd George's military confidant – that Allenby should make the main effort with a thrust through Palestine and the Lebanon to cut the Turkish jugular – the railway bottle-neck north of Aleppo, through which all their fronts were supplied. Marshall was to stand on the defensive at Baghdad and send three divisions and a cavalry brigade to support Allenby's offensive. The only concession made to Robertson's point of view was the withdrawal to France of as many British battalions from the Middle East as GHQ India could replace with Indian units.

Allenby's plan, accepted by Smuts and Whitehall, was to extend his eastern flank across the Jordan to link up with Feisal's Arabs, and to liquidate the Turkish forces still struggling to hold the Hejaz by cutting their railway and other escape routes at Amman. He would then attack with his main body northwards up the Levant coast, bypassing Damascus, which would be the objective of the Arabs and a small British mobile column. He did not promise a rapid advance. His progress would depend on the speed with which his railheads could be pushed forward. He would have liked to have put more weight behind the Arab advance on Damascus, but his engineers advised him that building a rail link across the Jordan Valley would take too long.

Almost as soon as Smuts departed, Allenby sent the 60th (London) Division down the road to Jericho into the weird moonscape of the Dead Sea valley. The Turks evacuated Jericho without a fight, but before an advance across the Jordan could begin, more elbow-room was needed, and so Chetwode's 20th Corps attacked northwards through the Judean hills. They took their objectives, but their advance was slower and more costly than expected, confirming Allenby in his view that his main thrust should be made in the plain where he could use his cavalry superiority to better effect.

Allenby's subsequent operations across the Jordan in the mountains of

Moab were equally disappointing. Opposition was slight at first, but 60th Division's advance was halted well short of Amman by deluging rain at the end of March. A second attempt made a month later was equally unsuccessful and much more costly, not because of weather this time, but because the Turks had reinforced Amman and were blocking all approaches to the railway in strength. By then, the German breakthrough on the Western Front in March and April 1918 had made operations across the Jordan irrelevant in the rush to send as many troops as possible home to help shore up the Western Front. But Allenby had been more successful than he realised at the time in drawing Turkish forces away from the Palestine front. Henceforth, the Turks deployed no less than a third of their *Yilderim* forces beyond the Jordan to protect their eastern flank and communications with the Hejaz.

The crisis on the Western Front was so serious that two of Allenby's best divisions were shipped back to France at once, and no less than 24 infantry battalions and nine Yeomanry regiments went with them as well as a number of heavy artillery batteries and machinegun companies. All told, some 60,000 troops left Palestine, and were gradually replaced by divisions from Mesopotamia, Indian cavalry from France and new infantry battalions from India. The reorganisation was a staff officer's nightmare and took most of the hot summer months to complete, while the front north of Jaffa and Jerusalem had to be securely held. Fortunately, the Turks and their German advisers had major reorganisations on their hands also.

Von Kressenstein was dismissed from command of the 8th Army. Senior Turkish officers held him to blame for their defeats at Beersheba and Gaza. He was sent off to the Caucasus front, and was replaced by Jevad Pasha. Djemal Pasha gave up the governorship of Syria and returned disgruntled to Constantinople after failing to stop von Falkenhayn from taking over command in Palestine. But the biggest change of all was the recall of von Falkenhayn himself on 1 March at Enver's request. *Yilderim* had failed, and the Field Marshal and his inflated, overweening German staff had alienated their Turkish colleagues. This was hardly surprising: they knew next to nothing of Turkish psychology; they had to communicate in French or use interpreters; all written orders had to be translated into Turkish, which could not be checked for accuracy; and the atmosphere was poisoned by recriminations caused by failure.

Von Falkenhayn was replaced by the obtuse Liman von Sanders, who knew the Turks well and could still bask in the inestimable prestige of his successful defence of Gallipoli. He wisely brought with him a Turkish chief of staff and very few German officers. Liman lacked the strategic abilities of his predecessor, but he was a determined, ruthless man. A Prussian officer of the old school – *a good trench fighter*[2] – his tactical aim was always to keep a front closed up. With the scanty resources available to him in Palestine, this meant putting everything into the shop window and holding what few reserves he could muster close behind the front. This policy was to pay dividends for six months while Allenby was reorganising and Turkish attention was focused upon their opportunities in the Caucasus, but was to prove too brittle to withstand a British offensive in which mobility was to play a key role.

There was little fighting in either Palestine or Mesopotamia during the summer. Some generally successful raids were carried out on the Palestine front, primarily to blood new units on the British side, and Liman launched one probing attack in the Jordan Valley, using von Oppen's three German storm battalions of the Asian Corps. The Turks failed to support von Oppen's attack, which was repulsed by the Australians, who took 400 prisoners. The whole episode showed Allenby how sensitive Liman must be to his eastern flank to have used his best troops in the operation. Meanwhile, in Mesopotamia, Marshall probed forward up both the Euphrates and Tigris until the summer heat and the dispatch of divisions to Palestine brought his operations to a halt in mid-May. By then he had reached Ana on the Euphrates and had temporarily occupied Kirkuk in his Tigris operations.

By July 1918, the German bid to wrest victory on the Western Front had clearly failed, but the war was still expected to go on well into 1919. Lloyd George wanted to revert to his policy of knocking out Germany's allies as soon as winter stopped operations in France. He proposed to send Allenby four divisions in the autumn to complete the destruction of the Turkish armies in Palestine. They were all to be returned to France in time for the Allies' planned 1919 offensive. His scheme was totally unrealistic: shortage of shipping caused by the German U-boat campaign, and by the movement of American troops across the Atlantic, as well as the obvious time factor, made it impracticable. The CIGS, Sir Henry Wilson, directed Allenby to do his best with the troops he had, and advised a policy of active defence. Allenby had other ideas: he would attack as soon as the Mesopotamian divisions had arrived and his divisions had absorbed their new Indian battalions. His target date for completion of his reorganisation and retraining programmes was mid-September, which would coincide with the start of the cooler weather and his railheads opening close behind the front.

The ever watchful French were not to be left out if there was any chance of the British grabbing Syria. Their token force, known as the *Détachement Français de Palestine et Syrie* (DFPS for short), was reinforced to a strength of six battalions, half of which were recruited from Armenian refugees, whose indiscipline equalled their burning desire for vengeance on the Turks. In addition they had four squadrons of cavalry, three artillery batteries and their own ancillary services. The Italians also provided a small contingent. The most noteworthy addition of all was the Jewish Legion of three battalions, all recruited in the cities of Britain as the 38th, 39th and 40th Battalions of the Royal Fusiliers (The City of London Regiment) after the signing of the Balfour Agreement in November 1917.

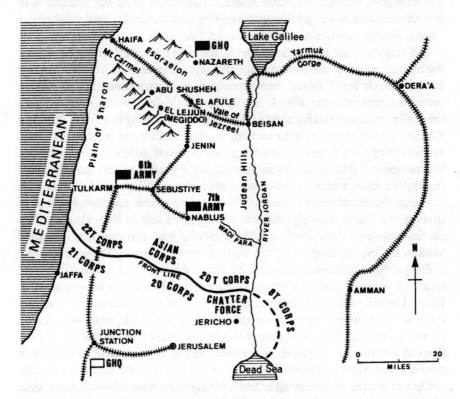

Map 34: Northern Palestine before the Battle of Megiddo in September 1918

The planning for and execution of the decisive battle of Megiddo in September 1918 was carried out entirely on Allenby's personal initiative. He and his three now very experienced corps commanders, Chetwode with 20th Corps in the Judean hills north of Jerusalem, Bulfin with 21st Corps in the coastal plain north of Jaffa, and Chauvel with the Desert Mounted Corps in the Jordan Valley north of Jericho, were convinced that Turkish morale was crumbling, and there was a very real opportunity to sweep them out of Palestine for good. A steady stream of Turkish deserters, and frequent raiding of the Turkish lines, provided ample evidence of Turkish demoralisation.

The concept of operations was also entirely Allenby's and had been developing in his mind throughout the summer. It was a mirror image of his plan for Gaza/Beersheba with the roles of his two infantry corps reversed and the mobile corps hooking round the western instead of the eastern flank. This time Chetwode would do the holding with only two divisions in the Judean hills south of Nablus, and with a specially constituted mobile force based upon the ANZAC Mounted Division, called 'Chaytor Force' after its New Zealand commander, which would take over the defence of the Jordan valley to release Chauvel's Desert Mounted Corps. Bulfin, with a concentration of five divisions plus the French, would carry out the main attack on the western flank in the coastal plain – the biblical plain of Sharon. Chauvel's cavalry could not ride round the flank to reach the Turkish rear as he had done at Beersheba because it rested securely on the sea. Instead, he would have to pass through a breach in the Turkish line made for him by Bulfin near the coast. Passing mobile troops through a breach made by infantry is never easy, but Allenby had no alternative as long as he stuck to his conviction that Chetwode's high casualties in the earlier fighting in the Judean hills showed he must attack in the coastal plain.

Allenby's initial plan presented to his corps commanders in August envisaged a comparatively shallow left hook by Chauvel's cavalry. After passing through the breach made by Bulfin near the coast, the Desert Mounted Corps with the 4th, 5th and Australian Cavalry Divisions would make for the Messudieh Junction halfway between Tulkarm and Nablus about 15 miles behind the front, cutting the railway, which supplied the 7th and 8th Turkish Armies, and intercepting their withdrawal routes. As a bonus they might be able to ride through Jevad Pasha's 8th Army Headquarters at Tulkarm and threaten Mustapha Kemal's 7th Army Headquarters at Nablus (Fevzi Pasha had gone sick and Kemal had returned to his former command).

One morning, not long after his meeting with his corps commanders, Allenby returned from his early morning ride and strode into his office to inform his operations staff that he had decided on a much more ambitious plan. Chauvel's cavalry would make a 50 instead of 15 mile left hook, aiming for the railway junction of El Afule in the plain of Esdraelon (the Vale of Megiddo), and riding on down the narrower Valley of Jezreel to Beisan near the Jordan, thus encircling the 7th and 8th Turkish Armies. This time the bonus would be the discomfiture of Liman von Sanders's General Headquarters at Nazareth. But there was also a snag. The coastal plain of Sharon was divided from the Plain of Esdraelon by a ridge of hills stretching south-eastwards from Mount Carmel, through which there were only two practicable tracks for cavalry divisions. They were really little more than bridle paths and could easily be blocked if the Turks had any inkling of Allenby's plan. The northern track emerged from the hills at Abu Shusheh, and the southern at El Lejjun (the biblical fortress town of Megiddo). It was a daring plan that could only succeed against a surprised and demoralised enemy.

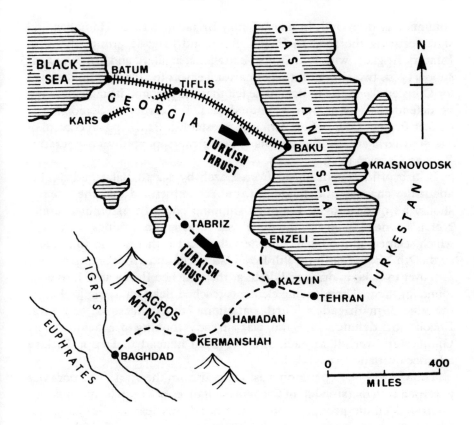

Map 35: British Operations on the Caspian Sea: June–October 1918

Allenby had good reason to believe that the Turkish armies in Palestine were ripe for the picking. Such was the pan-Turk desire to regain the cradle of their race, that Liman was starved of reinforcements to enable Nuri Pasha, brother of Enver, to pursue their ambitions in the Caucasus with German backing. The Turks had seized Batum and Kars from the Russians in April; the Germans had occupied most of the Ukraine and the Crimea in May, and had entered Tiflis in June; and by August Turkish troops were approaching Baku on the Caspian Sea and Tabriz in northwest Persia. The Turkish threat concentrated the minds of the local anti-Turkish factions, and Dunsterville was now asked by the Bolshevik Committee at Enzeli to go to their help. The War Office instructed Marshall to support him with as many troops as his slender improvised line of communication would allow so that he could influence events around the Caspian. A strong British lead might be enough to check the Turks, who were meeting political and logistic difficulties in their drive towards Turkestan.

By June the Zagros passes had been open long enough for a motorised column, based on 36th Indian Infantry Brigade, to reach Hamadan and start securing the road to Enzeli. A second brigade group, the 39th Infantry Brigade, with four British battalions, artillery and armoured car support plus two aircraft for reconnaissance, was fed forward up the road for Dunsterville to use in Baku if he felt that the port and its oilfields could be defended. With it went Commodore DT Norris, the Senior Naval Officer Persian Gulf, whose aim was to establish British naval control of the southern end of the Caspian, using the reportedly co-operative Russian Caspian fleet.

British officers sent ahead from Enzeli by sea to Baku had doubts about the chances of defending it, but recommended that the attempt should be made provided enough shipping could be assembled under Norris's control to ensure the force's safe evacuation if things went sour, which seemed all too likely. Dunsterville decided that he had to try, and so the 7th North Staffords, 9th Royal Warwicks and 9th Worcesters were sent over to Baku in dribs and drabs as they reached Enzeli and ships were found for them. Their leading elements reached Baku on 5 August, but by the time 39th Brigade's fourth battalion, 7th Gloucesters, arrived at Enzeli, the defence of Baku was already looking precarious. The Gloucesters were held back and deployed instead to face a Turkish advance overland from Tabriz.

The whole Baku operation was doomed from the start. The port was governed by a dictatorship of five representatives of quarrelsome and self-interested ethnic groups, whose only bond was fear of the Turk, but whose men were far from keen on fighting them. Serious Turkish attacks on Baku started on 26th August. The first was gallantly repulsed by the North Staffords, who were forced to fall back to a position closer to the port by failure of the local troops on either side of them. Over the next few days, the same thing happened to the other British battalions, who continually bore the brunt of the fighting. By 1 September, Dunsterville had had enough, and advised the dictators that he was withdrawing all British troops and that they should ask the Turks for terms. The British Official History describes their reaction:

> In conclusion, he urged them to take immediate action and not to waste time in making speeches and passing resolutions. He then left them for an hour to come to a decision. His speech caused considerable anger and consternation. But it failed to achieve the desired effect; for when he returned in an hour's time, the assembly was still engaged in useless talking. He begged them to act and again left them for an hour, only to find on his return that they were still passing resolutions . . .[3]

British Intelligence reported the arrival of a German division in Tiflis. The War Office decided that there was no point in staying any longer and authorised Dunsterville to evacuate his troops. This was easier said than done: the dictators refused him permission to leave and continued co-operation of the Russian Caspian fleet could no longer be relied upon. Fortunately, co-operation amongst the dictators was so poor that Dunsterville and Norris managed to complete the evacuation under their noses during the Turks' final and successful assault on the port. Even the guard ships at the harbour entrance failed to intercept the ships com-mandeered by Norris and crammed with British troops as they slipped out of the harbour after dark on 14 September.

Dunsterville and Norris were then charged with the tasks of preventing a further Turkish advance on Turkestan either by sea across the Caspian to Krasnovodsk, or overland from Tabriz through northern Persia. The Indian Government had sent a small column to hold Krasnovodsk on 27 August; Norris established British naval control of the Caspian with ships which he armed and crewed at Enzeli; and the two brigades of Dunsterforce checked the half-hearted attempts by the Turks to advance south-eastwards from Tabriz. By October, the pan-Turk effort in the Caucasus was spent.

★ ★ ★

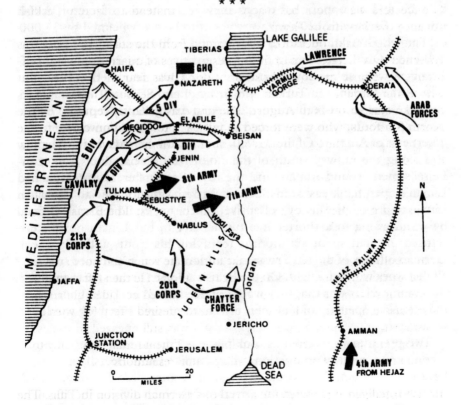

Map 36: The Battle of Megiddo: 17–22 September 1918

Allenby's preparations for his September offensive were completed by 17 September, when the final deployment into battle positions began. As at Gaza–Beersheba, he took elaborate deception measures to make Liman von Sanders believe that his open eastern flank on the far side of the Jordan was to be turned. Rumours were circulated that large quantities of fodder would be needed in the Jericho area; buildings were requisitioned in Jerusalem for GHQ; new bridges were built over the Jordan; extra camps were pitched in the Jordan valley; and those camps, which were to be vacated at the last moment by Chauvel's cavalry, were to be kept alive with tents still standing, dummy animals filling the horse lines, and sleighs drawn by mules raising dust at watering times. The opposite was done in the coastal area where the concentrations of Bulfin's and Chauvel's troops were concealed in the numerous orange groves. All movement westwards was by night; and selected units were marched eastwards by day and returned by lorry after dark to provide the illusion of surreptitious movement eastwards. It all worked: Liman's situation map of British dispositions, captured during the battle, still showed Chauvel's Desert Mounted Corps in the Jericho area.

The balance of advantage was heavily weighted in Allenby's favour, and both his and his opponent's troops knew it. In the coastal sector, 8,000 unhappy Turks with 120 guns were about to be overwhelmed by 35,000 exhilarated British and Indian infantry and 9,000 cavalry, supported by 400 guns. On the remaining 50 miles of the front, as far as the Jordan, strengths were about equal with around 20,000 troops on either side. East of the Jordan, the Turkish 4th Army of about 25,000 was opposed only by Feisal's semi-regular Northern Arab Army and Lawrence's will-o'-the-wisp Bedouin raiders, operating against the Hejaz railway from the desert east of Amman. Of the 25,000, about half were stranded in Medina and along the railway south of the extensive breaches blown in it by Feisal's men around Ma'an, and the rest were to the north, extending Liman's open flank eastwards. Senior Turkish officers tried to persuade Liman to pre-empt Allenby's offensive, which they could see was coming, by withdrawing to a shorter line further north, but Liman obstinately refused: he had spent six months fortifying his front, and, like most German officers of the old Prussian tradition, he was disinclined to waste all that work without a fight. On the British side, the greatest fear amongst the commanders was that they would, indeed, find the Turks gone when the offensive opened, and all their own hard preparatory work would be wasted too.

Two preliminary operations took place as curtain raisers to Allenby's second great military production, which, unlike Gaza–Beersheba, was to have only one act. Chetwode attacked and, after hard fighting, seized some tactically important ground overlooking Nablus in the Judean hills, which drew Liman's attention to the eastern sectors of the front. It was drawn even more firmly in that direction by Lawrence's Arabs, who, after assembling in the desert 30 miles east of Amman, descended upon the Turkish railway, cutting its spurs north, south and west of Dera'a junction. They were not strong enough to take Dera'a itself, but their attacks and bombing by British aircraft, drew some of Liman's scanty reserves, including German troops.

In the battle about to begin, the RAF (formed from the Royal Flying Corps in April 1918) came into its own as a battle-winner rather than as a useful adjunct for reconnaissance and minor harassing raids. Major General Geoffrey Salmond (a future Chief of the Air Staff in the 1930s) had six squadrons with which he first cleared the skies of German and Turkish aircraft and then made ready to attack the principal enemy head-quarters, disrupt their communications and destroy their retreating columns if and when Allenby broke through.

The five divisions of Bulfin's 21st Corps opened Allenby's offensive by attacking Jevad Pasha's over-extended 8th Army at 4.30am on 19 September. There was no preliminary bombardment, the infantry going forward as the 400 British guns opened fire. By dawn, the two Turkish divisions nearest the coast had collapsed and Bulfin had opened the breach needed for Chauvel's horsemen. Arrangements for passing the cavalry through the infantry, for once, worked perfectly. By 10am, both the 4th and 5th Cavalry Divisions – their brigades each consisting of one English and two Indian cavalry regiments followed by the Australian Mounted Division, were through into the open and were riding for the tracks across the Mount Carmel ridge, screened by armoured cars. They reached the defiles as darkness fell and were in the Plain of Esdraelon well before dawn next day, 20 September.

In the meanwhile, Bulfin's divisions had swung north-eastwards, pivoting on his right flank like an opening door. By dusk, Tulkarm and Sebustiye Junction, 15 miles behind the front, had been taken, and the 8th Turkish Army was breaking up in a disorganised rout. The RAF added to the chaos by strafing and bombing their columns, several of which were caught in narrow defiles in the hills, inflicting further demoralisation on the Turks. Liman in his General Headquarters back at Nazareth was unaware of the disaster which had overtaken Jevad's 8th Army. The artillery bombardment and RAF attacks had destroyed its telegraph communications as soon as the offensive began. Kemal's 7th Army communications were also disrupted but not so completely. He might have warned Liman of Jevad's collapse, had he known about it, but he did not. He seemed to be holding his own against Chetwode, and gave Liman no inkling of the disaster in the making.

Liman only realised that something had gone badly wrong when he was woken at 5.30am on the 20th to be told that British cavalry were entering Nazareth. The 5th Cavalry Division, which had passed through the northern defile, had sent its 13th Brigade to round up the *Yilderim* GHQ, but intelligence of its location was sketchy. By the time it was found, Liman had managed to escape and was on his way to Tiberias on the Sea of Galilee, but his papers and over 1,000 prisoners were taken before the brigade rode off to join the rest of its division, which had taken its objective, the El Afule junction.

The 4th Cavalry Division emerged from the southern defile just in time to catch a Turkish column of six companies still in bivouac, which had been sent belatedly to defend Megiddo. Their commander had seen no need to hurry until the Indian 2nd Lancers rode through them, spearing 46 and capturing the rest. The 4th Cavalry Division then rode past the 5th at El Afule and on down the Valley of Jezreel, capturing the garrison of Beisan in the late afternoon. 4th Division had ridden over 70 miles in thirty-four hours, thrusting aside all attempts to impede its passage across the Turkish rear areas. It says much for 4th Division's horse management that only 29 out of its 2,000 horses were lost, mainly from exhaustion. One regiment, the 19th Lancers, rode on through the night and seized the bridge over the Jordan, ten miles north of Beisan.

During the day, Chauvel established his Corps Headquarters at Megiddo and brought up the Australian Mounted Division to Jenin, thus closing the gap between his 4th and 5th Divisions at El Afule and Beisan, and establishing a cavalry net from the coast to the Jordan into which the Turks were being driven by Bulfin and Chetwode. The only escape route for the remnants of Jevad's 8th Army and Kemal's, as yet, undefeated 7th Army, was eastwards along narrow hill tracks into the Jordan valley to the south of 4th Cavalry Division's block at Beisan, and this gap was being narrowed by the advance of Chaytor Force up the Jordan Valley.

Meanwhile Bulfin's and Chetwode's corps were meeting stiffer resistance from Kemal's rear-guards, and particularly from von Oppen's Asia Corps. Chetwode did not take Nablus until midday on the 21st. By then Kemal's 7th Army was also disintegrating, thanks to the work of the RAF, whose bombing and strafing created such chaos that even a resolute man of Kemal's calibre could not save the day as he had done at Gallipoli. Kemal and only about a third of his troops escaped across the Jordan. Many were killed when the RAF trapped his main body in the narrow, precipitous gorge of Wadi Fara. Over the next three days, the remnants of the two Turkish armies, trapped west of the Jordan, were gathered in as prisoners of war – some 50,000 of them. Only von Oppen's small German Asia Corps, reduced by casualties to about 700 men, retained its discipline and fighting spirit as it fought its way out of the trap to join Djemal Kuchuk's 4th Army, retreating up the Hejaz railway to Dera'a. The stalwart von Oppen died of cholera a few weeks later.

Allenby's pursuit after Gaza/Beersheba had disappointed him. This time he was determined that there would be no escape for the Turks, who were to be chased relentlessly out of Syria. He had originally intended to bypass Damascus by advancing up the coast, supplied by the Navy, but his victory west of the Jordan was so complete that the coastal drive became secondary to the destruction of what remained of Liman von Sanders' armies east of the Jordan. He made two preliminary moves at the extremities of the front well before the main battle was over. In the west, 5th Cavalry Division rode off to seize the port of Haifa as an essential supply base. Thanks to a spirited charge by the Jodhpur Lancers, the port was in Allenby's hands by the evening of the 23rd.

In the east, Chaytor's ANZAC Mounted Division was doing its best to pin Djemal Kuchuk's 4th Army around Amman, but was not strong enough to advance to the Hejaz railway until there were definite signs of a Turkish withdrawal. The news of the disaster to west of the Jordan filtered through to Djemal Kuchuk very slowly, and it was not until the 22nd that he decided to withdraw northwards. Even then he hoped to hang on long enough in Amman for the troops holding Ma'an and stations further south to join him. He delayed just too long: Chaytor hustled his rearguards out of the town before the Ma'an troops could arrive. Chaytor left the pursuit of the Turkish main body to the mercies of Feisal's Arabs while he set off southwards to intercept the Turks withdrawing from Ma'an. His leading regiment found them some 20 miles to the south and very willing to surrender, provided the British would protect them from the large numbers of rapacious Bedouin, who were circling around them like vultures waiting for the kill. Chaytor agreed that, as he would not have enough troops forward by dark, the Turks could remain under arms for the night, provided their commander presented himself as a hostage. Next day the inhabitants of Amman were astonished to see some 4,600 fully armed Turkish troops entering the city under British protection from the Arabs.

The worries of the Ma'an force about their ability to fend off the Bedouin were a sign of the times. News of the Turkish disaster at Megiddo travelled fast. There was no need for Lawrence to raise the tribes between Amman and Damascus: they could not have been stopped joining in to harass 4th Army's withdrawal with uncontrollable brutality. But the brutality was not one sided. Some Turkish units took savage reprisals as they fell back. Lawrence records in his *Seven Pillars of Wisdom* the horrifying scenes left by one of Djemal's Lancer regiments in the village of Tafas, the home of Tallal, one of the tribal chiefs who were riding with him:

> We rode past the other bodies of men, women and four more dead babies. . . . By the outskirts were low mud walls, sheep folds, and on one something red and white. I looked close and saw the body of a woman folded across it, bottom upwards, nailed there by a saw bayonet whose haft stuck hideously into the air from between her naked legs. She had

been pregnant, and about her lay others, perhaps twenty in all, variously killed but set out in accord with an obscene taste.[4]

Tallal was so sickened that he charged the Turkish rear-guard single-handed and was killed in a fusillade of fire as he reached the points of their lances. Lawrence adds tersely: 'By my order we took no prisoners, for the only time in our war'[5] His no prisoner edict seems, in practice, to have lasted until Damascus was reached. At Dera'a, which Lawrence's Bedouin force entered ahead of the 4th Cavalry Division on 28th September, the scenes of Arab avenging brutality revolted even the hardened Indian cavalrymen. Few of the 4th Army units, retreating up the railway from Amman, survived the savagery of the local tribes, who had risen spontaneously with the vision of loot rather than freedom from Turkish rule.

* * *

On 26 September, Allenby met his corps commanders at Jenin to confirm orders for the pursuit that he had already been giving to them individually as the battle developed. He estimated that there were still some 40,000 Turks in and to the south of Damascus, and these might be reinforced by the 2nd Turkish Army from around Aleppo. Bulfin was to advance up the coast with Beirut as his objective, using only one of his five infantry divisions with a second in reserve for use only if it proved unavoidable. All available supply columns from his and Chetwode's corps were to be used to support Chauvel's Desert Mounted Corps for an advance inland on Damascus. The Australian and 5th Cavalry Divisions were to pass north of Lake Galilee, while the 4th Cavalry Division rode to Dera'a and then turned north up the ancient Pilgrims' Way, which runs west of and almost parallel to the Hejaz railway. Chetwode's corps was to be grounded as it had been after Beersheba.

The one thing that Allenby impressed on his commanders and staff was the need for speed, not just to hustle the Turks out of Syria, but because the strength of his army was shrinking rapidly – not from enemy action but from sickness, which even the exhilaration of victory could not assuage. Malaria and influenza were decimating its ranks. The former had, so far, been kept under control by oiling all stagnant water within the British lines, but once the troops entered the Turkish held areas where no such precautions had been taken, the malaria rate trebled. No such precautions could stop the latter. An epidemic, caused by a particularly virulent strain of influenza, was sweeping the world, and was at its peak in Palestine in the autumn of 1918.

There was another and perhaps more important strategic reason for speed. Germany's 'props', as Lloyd George called Germany's allies, were indeed showing signs of collapse, as he had always hoped they would. On 27 September, the day Chauvel's cavalry divisions set off for Damascus,

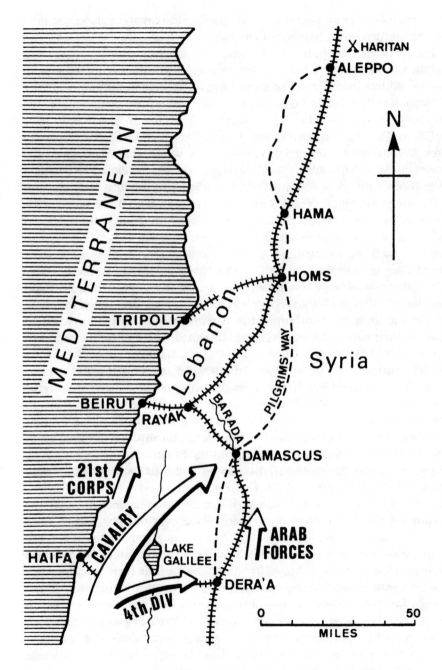

Map 37: The Advance on Damascus, Beirut and Aleppo: October 1918

Bulgaria asked for an armistice, endangering Liman von Sander's supply and reinforcement route from Germany. The Turkish position was also being weakened by political discontent in Constantinople, where the Sultan was manoeuvring to oust Enver and his pro-German clique from power. Allied Intelligence sources suggested that the collapse of the Turkish 'prop' could not be far off. One more rapier-like thrust might topple the shaky Ottoman façade.

Chauvel's divisions, accompanied by the cavalry regiment of the small French contingent, converged on Damascus within a few hours of each other late on 30 September. The Australians reached the cliffs above Barada river gorge, through which most of the Turkish garrison was withdrawing, and caused havoc in their closely packed columns until darkness brought the slaughter to an end. Inside the historic city, Turkish rule had collapsed. Even before Liman von Sanders left that afternoon, Bedouin were riding through the streets, firing their rifles indiscriminately. Some bold spirit ran the Sherif's flag up over the City Hall. Turkish troops trudged past on their way out of the city without trying to pull it down. They were friendless and humiliated. After the Barada gorge was blocked, some units tried to escape up the waterless road to Homs, but the majority phlegmatically settled down in their barracks for the night and awaited their fate on the morrow.

Next day, 1 October, Australian Light Horse units, accompanied by the French, entered the city to a tumultuous welcome. Over 10,000 demoralised Turks surrendered in the barracks without any show of resistance. To the Australians, New Zealanders, Indians and Britons of Chauvel's Desert Mounted Corps, the fall of Damascus was but a phase in their relentless pursuit of Liman von Sanders' Army Group, but to Feisal's regular Arab forces under Jaafar Pasha, and his Bedouin tribal forces led by Lawrence, it was the goal of all their hopes and dreams of re-establishing the great Arab Empire, which had once stretched from India to the Atlantic with its capital at Damascus. But across their ambitions lay the shadow of the Sykes-Picot Agreement, which threatened to turn their dreams to nightmares.

The Sykes-Picot Agreement (*see page 162*), signed by the British and French Governments in May 1916, had not been revealed to the Arab leaders at the time, but its terms were leaked by the Russians after the Revolution. The Turks communicated them to Feisal, hoping to detach the Arabs from their perfidious British ally. They did not succeed: with Lawrence's encouragement, the Arab leaders became more determined than ever to pre-empt the French and be able to claim Damascus and Syria at the Peace Conference by right of conquest.

In all the turmoil of the initial British occupation of Damascus, Lawrence, by sheer strength of personality and reputation damped out tribal rivalries and managed to establish an Arab government in the city loyal to Feisal. Allenby visited Damascus on 3 October, soon after Feisal had reached the city. The two leaders met for the first time in Lawrence's presence. The contrast could not have been more striking: the bull-like British general, accustomed to dominate, meeting the slight, ascetic Arab prince, whose strength lay in political finesse. Yet a bond of friendship and trust encircled these two great leaders almost immediately. Allenby explained in all frankness that the French were to administer the Lebanon, and be the protecting power for the rest of northern Syria. Feisal, as the representative of the Grand Sherif, could set up an Arab military government east of the Jordan from Aqaba to Damascus. A French representative would be attached to his staff. Feisal protested strongly, but accepted Allenby's orders – he had no alternative.

After Feisal left, Lawrence told Allenby that he was not prepared to work with the French, indicating that he believed Britain would be breaking faith with the Arabs if the Sykes-Picot Agreement was put into practice. The extraordinary success of the Arab Revolt and their invaluable military operations east of the Jordan had never been seen as remotely possible in 1916 when the agreement was negotiated. The Arabs deserved their promised independence. Diplomatic steps should be taken to repudiate the Sykes-Picot Agreement, which had been out-dated by events ever since it was signed. He asked for leave, which Allenby granted, realising that Lawrence had crowded more effort, both mental and physical, into his two years with the Arabs than most men expend in a lifetime. He was over-strained in body and mind. The war ended before he had a chance to return. Later, he was to renew his personal commitment to the Arab cause by fighting bitterly in support of Arab independence at the Peace Conference.

On the coast, the 7th Indian Division, which had fought so long and hard on the Tigris, led Bulfin's advance on Beirut, which they reached on 8 October, but were forestalled by naval landing parties from French warships, and by a Bedouin force sent by Feisal, against Lawrence's advice, to support the Arab claim to the Lebanon. The latter were eventually persuaded to withdraw and allow a French administration to take over. The 7th Indian Division pushed on up the coast towards Tripoli, while the 5th Cavalry Division and Feisal's Arabs advanced on Aleppo. The 4th Cavalry Division was to have followed the 5th, but was immobilised by the 'flu epidemic and malaria. There was still a possibility of a Turkish counter-offensive as Turkey's two best army commanders were still in the field: Kemal and Djemal Kuchuk were rallying troops for the defence of Anatolia. Aleppo, however, fell to the Arabs on 25 October and was entered by the 5th Cavalry Division next day.

The last action of the Palestine Campaign was fought on 26 October at Haritan, eight miles north of Aleppo, when two weak regiments of the 5th Cavalry Division, the Mysore Lancers and the Jodhpur Lancers, charged and were repulsed by a column of 3,000 Turks. The Turks, however, withdrew thoroughly shaken by the boldness of the attack. Five days later, Turkey accepted armistice terms.

Allenby's latest achievement can be summed up in the statistics. Since the opening of the Battle of Megiddo on 19 September, he had taken 75,000 prisoners, including 3,700 Germans and Austrians; and he had suffered only 5,700 battle casualties, of whom 850 were killed.[6] Turkish casualties on the Palestine front have never been accurately assessed.

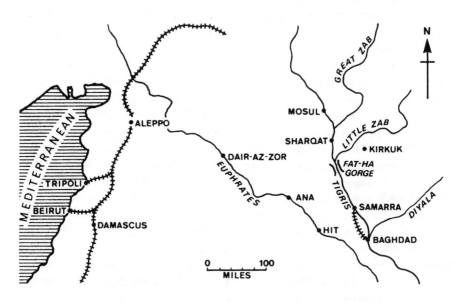

Map 38: The Upper Tigris: October 1918

Allenby's occupation of Damascus and continuing political turbulence in Constantinople impacted on Mesopotamian and the Caspian fronts almost immediately. With Turkish power on the point of collapse, it was clearly time to stake out claims to the spoils of the Ottoman Empire. The War Office asked Marshall at Baghdad whether he could grab Mosul without retarding work on Dunsterville's line of communication to the Caspian, and whether he could mount a cavalry raid up the Euphrates to help Allenby's advance on Aleppo. Marshall quickly explained that supply would limit his operations. He could certainly not undertake the Euphrates raid, but by grounding a large part of his force, he could scrape together enough land transport and river steamers for Cobbe's 1st Corps to advance up the Tigris and occupy the Mosul *vilayet*. Cobbe would need 12 days to assemble his Tigris force.

Since the fall of Baghdad in March 1917, the Turks had been preparing a strong defensive position, blocking the Tigris at the Fat-Ha gorge, 150 miles north of Baghdad and 100 miles south of Mosul, with an equally strong supporting position near Sharqat 30 miles upriver from Fat-Ha. Their Tigris force was commanded by Ismail Hakki Bey and had four weak divisions. Cobbe's 1st Corps had two Indian infantry divisions, the 17th and 18th, which had been rebuilt after the dispatch of so many troops to reinforce Allenby in Palestine during the summer; and only two Indian cavalry brigades, the 7th and 11th, the latter commanded by Brigadier-General Cassels, a future Commander-in-Chief India and father of Sir James Cassels, the last Chief of the Imperial General Staff before the title was abolished in 1964.

Cobbe's plan was to advance astride the Tigris with a division on either bank. After careful reconnaissance of the west bank, he concluded that lack of water prohibited cavalry turning movements there, and so both cavalry brigades were to operate on the east bank. The 7th would mount a short range hook to get behind the Fat-Ha defences, while Cassels' 11th would ride secretly for the Sharqat position, hoping to turn it before it could be fully occupied. Much to Cobbe's surprise the Turks abandoned the Fat-Ha line when he attacked it during the night of 23 October. The subsequent advance by the infantry divisions was impeded more by the broken nature of the country and supply difficulties than by the Turkish rear-guards. Cassels' cavalry made better progress, reaching and crossing the Tigris by a ford north of Sharqat on 26 October. He had only a day's rations left and was very short of field gun ammunition, but he took up a strong defensive position across the Turks' withdrawal route, determined to hold this blocking position against attacks which would probably be mounted against him from the south by the Turkish main body and from the north by reinforcements rushed south from Mosul.

With the help of the 7th Cavalry Brigade, which arrived to reinforce him next day, bringing with it extra gun ammunition and rations, Cassels held his own for three days, although he had several anxious moments, while Cobbe's infantry divisions pressed the Turks north towards his blocking position. British probing attacks throughout the 29th on what appeared to be the main Turkish position, four miles south of Cassels' block, were all repulsed. Cobbe made preparations for a set-piece attack next day, but, when dawn came on 30 October, white flags were seen flying over the Turkish line. Ismail Hakki Bey had given up hope of help reaching him from Mosul. He realised that there was no escape across the desert to the west due to lack of water, and the British were holding the Tigris, barring escape to the east. Surrender was his only option.

It took most of the 31st for Cobbe to re-assemble the two cavalry brigades for an advance on Mosul, which began under Cassels' command that evening. As he approached the city next day, 1 November, he was met by a flag of truce, informing him that an armistice had come into force at noon on 31 October. The Mesopotamian campaign ended with British troops bivouacking around Mosul, having captured over 11,000

Turks since they started their last offensive on 18 October. Arguments over differing interpretations of the armistice terms prevented Cobbe from entering Mosul itself until 9 November when the Turks evacuated the whole of Mosul *vilayet*.

* * *

Away to the north, on the Caspian front, the Turks withdrew from all Persian territory, but tried to hold onto Russian Azerbaijan and Baku by transferring their troops to a puppet Azerbaijani government and raising Turkish officered local levies throughout the Trans-Caucasus. London would have none of it. The Royal Navy had two naval bases operational at Enzeli and Krasnovodsk from which five armed ships, commanded by British officers, manned by Russian sailors, and flying the Tsarist ensign, established naval control of the Caspian. Marshall was instructed to re-occupy Baku, which he did with a mixed British and non-Bolshevik Russian force on 17 November. The subsequent British operations in the area became engulfed in the abortive efforts of the Western Powers to support the counter-revolutionary forces in southern Russia.

The Turkish capitulation was far from unexpected. The collapse of Bulgaria was the trigger, but sheer exhaustion had played an even more important part in the Sultan's eventual success in forcing the resignation of Enver Pasha's Government on the 8 October. Turkey had mobilised three million men since 1914. She had just half a million left, of whom only 100,000 were fighting men. No less than one and a half million had deserted; 325,000 had been killed; and 240,000 had died of disease.[7]

The much respected Izzet Pasha became Grand Vizier, and gave substance to Turkish peace-feelers by sending General Townshend to the entrance of the Dardanelles to inform the British naval Commander-in-Chief, Vice-Admiral Gough-Calthorpe, that Turkey was ready to negotiate a separate peace. Townshend had been well treated since surrendering Kut and allowed an extraordinary measure of freedom to make friends amongst the Turkish establishment in Constantinople, which made him a very suitable emissary. Whitehall gave Admiral Calthorpe plenary powers in the subsequent four days of intense negotiations before the armistice was signed in his flagship *Agamemnon* during the evening of 30 October off Mudros.

One immediate effect of the armistice was the rapid departure of Liman von Sanders, who handed over as Turkish Commander-in-Chief to Mustapha Kemal. Some 10,000 Germans, scattered about the Middle East, were eventually gathered in and sent home via the Mediterranean. Admiral Calthorpe's fleet had the satisfaction of sailing past the Gallipoli battlefields on his way to Constantinople on 12 November after the Dardanelles minefields had, at last, been cleared. And on the landward side, General Milne's (later Field Marshal, the Lord Milne) British

Salonika Army entered the Turkish capital as the principal component of the Allied occupation force with the new and grandiloquent title of the British Army of the Black Sea.

The First World War campaigns in the Middle East were considered side-shows compared with the titanic struggles on the Eastern and Western Fronts. But neither the Palestine nor the Mesopotamian campaigns were minor affairs operationally or logistically. The British Official Histories give the ration strength in Mesopotamia alone as over 400,000, half being fighting troops and the other half 'followers' such as the 42,000 working the Tigris and Euphrates shipping and the 71,000 labour corps. British losses in Mesopotamia were 92,500. Of these 15,000 were killed or died of wounds, 13,000 died of disease and 13,500 were prisoners or missing.[8]

But more significant was the introduction of larger numbers of British men and women to the Middle East than ever before. Over two and a half million had served there during the war. Despite the heat and physical dis-comforts of the deserts, marshes and mountains, they were delighted to have served there and not on the Western Front. The majority of the troops loathed but tolerated the poverty of the towns and villages, and devious selfishness of the people; many of the officers wished to return after the war as administrators to bring a better way of life to the Arab world in the paternalistic style of British imperialism; and others became zealous Arabists, looking to Lawrence as their model. With British troops ending the war in occupation of almost every corner of the Middle East, the British people inevitably became entangled in its complex affairs and have remained so ever since.

By the end of 1918, the British Army was administering almost the whole of the former Ottoman Empire south of the Taurus mountains. It was now the task of the Entente's politicians to determine what should take that empire's place. Unfortunately, it was to prove harder and took longer to put its pieces together into an internationally acceptable pattern than defeating the Turkish armies had done in the first place! And it could not have been accomplished without the repeated interventions by British forces to reimpose the stability once afforded by Ottoman power – but that is anticipating the story told in the sequel to this book.

'THE COCKPIT OF THE MOSLEM WORLD'

By the end of the First World War, Allenby's decisive victory at Megiddo had destroyed the Ottoman Empire, which Britain had tried for so long to uphold as a bastion in the defence of India; and he had nailed down the coffin of Imperial Germany's challenge to British interests in the Middle East, leaving Britain the unchallenged paramount power in the region. India and the Suez Canal were secure: Tsarist Russia was prostrate in revolution; Germany had collapsed; and no other European power could gainsay her. The United States might have done so, but the US Congress was still too isolationist at heart to wish to use America's growing resources in an attempt to put the Old World to rights, although Woodrow Wilson tried his utmost to persuade it to do so. Thus Britain was left in a position to influence, in a decisive way, the post-war reshaping of the former Ottoman provinces, and she had troops for that purpose on the ground.

Although psychologically and materially drained by her titanic struggle on the Western Front, Britain was at the peak of her imperial power, and, unlike the United States, still had the imperial will and colonial enthusiasm to attempt to guide the people of the Middle East into a more stable and prosperous post-Ottoman future.

There were, however, four causes for future concern: Arab nationalism and Moslem extremism lay curled up like genii in many different bottles throughout the Middle East, waiting for favourable conditions to emerge; it would not be long before Germany and Italy would again be claiming their place in the colonial sun along side Britain and France; and the growing involvement of the United States in oil exploration and production in the Middle East would slowly but surely draw Washington's attention to the economic and hence political importance of the region. But the most potent cause for anxiety lay in the dragon's teeth of the contradictory promises made to the Arabs and Jews by Britain during the First World War; the McMahon Agreement promising post-war independence to the

250

Arabs, the Sykes-Picot Agreement partitioning the region into areas of influence between Britain and France, and the Balfour Declaration accepting the establishment of a Jewish national home in Palestine.

In the sequel to this book, covering the second century of the British military presence in the Middle East, the story will be told of how Britain successfully drew the post-Ottoman political boundaries of the Middle East, which are still virtually intact today, and established stable governments in most of the new states through the judicious use of British troops, ships and aircraft when these were needed. Then during the Second World War, she defeated Hitler's efforts to seize the Suez Canal and the oil of Iraq and the Persian Gulf, and negated Mussolini's misguided efforts to expand the Italian African Empire.

When the Second World War ended, Britain was once again triumphant and at the final peak of her imperial power, but her colonial sense of purpose was in decline. Moreover, the balance of world power had swung against her, as the United States and Soviet Union emerged as the two new superpowers; Arab nationalism had burst out of many of its bottles in an unco-ordinated way; and the dragon's teeth were developing into the endless Arab/Israeli struggle and the devastating Iran/Iraq war. The Balkans used to be called 'The Cockpit of Europe': the post-1945 Middle East deserves the title of 'The Cockpit of the Moslem World'.

From 1945 onwards, Britain was to struggle to maintain her leading role in the Middle East in an uneasy alliance with the United States until 1956 when she was let down by Washington during the Suez *débâcle*. Thereafter, she was to concede paramountcy to the Americans, and leave them to try to bring peace to the warring races and religious factions in the 'Cockpit'. Britain and America were to come together again in the Gulf War in a friendly but grossly unequal partnership. Britain's 'Pomp of Yesterday' had, indeed, become 'one with Nineveh and Tyre'.

The sequel to this book will be aptly titled:

'*With Nineveh and Tyre: Britain's Triumph and Decline in the Middle East: 1919–1992.*'

REFERENCES

Chapter 1: The Fore-Runners.

1. Johnston, RM; *The Corsican; a diary of Napoleon's life in his own words*; p 85.
2. Lockhart, JG; *The History of Napoleon Bonaparte*; p 78–83.
3. National Biography; Sir Sidney Smith; p 572.
4. de Bourrienne; *Memoirs of Napoleon Bonaparte*; Vol I; p 120.
5. Packe, SWC; *Sea Power in the Mediterranean*; p 90.
6. Lloyd, C; *The Nile Campaign*; p 29, quoting Spencer Papers, II; p 437.
7. de Bourrienne; p 130–1.
8. Johnston; p 79.
9. *Ibid*; p 90.
10. *Ibid*; p 95–6.
11. *Ibid*; p 98.
12. Lockhart; p 164.
13. Fortescue; the Hon JW; *A History of the British Army*; Vol IV, Part II; p 798.
14. *Ibid*; p 796.
15. National Biography; Sir John Moore; p 815.
16. Fortescue; p 808.
17. *Ibid*; p 820.
18. *Ibid*; p 821.
19. *Ibid*; p 834.
20. *Ibid*; p 847.
21. National Biography; Sir Sidney Smith; p 574.

Chapter 2: The Eastern Question and the Great Game.

1. Palmerston; quoted by TA Heathcote in *The Afghan Wars, 1839–1919*; p 46.
2. Fortescue; Vol VI; p 6.
3. Sykes: *A History of Persia*; p 308.
4. Fortescue; Vol XII; p 22.
5. *Ibid*; p 31.
6. *Ibid*; p 30.

7. National Biography; General Sir William Cotton, p 41.
8. National Biography; General Sir Henry Fane, p 1039.
9. Fortescue; Vol XII; p 32.
10. *Ibid*; p 262.
11. *Ibid*; p 153.
12. *Ibid*; p 277.
13. National Biography; Admiral Sir Charles Napier; p 44.
14. *Ibid*; p 42, and Napier; *The War in Syria*; Vol I; p 71.
15. Napier; Vol I; p 139.

Chapter 3: The End of the Great Game.

1. Kipling, Rudyard; *Barrack-Room Ballads*; p 90.
2. English, Barbara; *John Company's Last War*; p 74.
3. *Ibid*; p 92.
4. Murphy, CCR; *The Persian Campaign of 1856–57*; p 239.
5. Hopkirk, Peter; *The Great Game*; p 295.
6. Robson, Brian; *The Road to Kabul*; p 140, quoting Lytton to Roberts, 9th Sep 1879, LP 518/4; pp 732–5.
7. National Biography; Lord Lytton; p 389.

Chapter 4: Seizing the World's Strategic Crossroads.

1. Morris, Jan; *Heaven's Command*; p 418.
2. Kipling, Rudyard; *Barrack-Room Ballads*; p 12.
3. Barthorp, Michael; *War on the Nile 1882–98;* p 111.

Chapter 5: The Near Success of the Turco-German *Jihad*.

1. Liman von Sanders; *Five Years in Turkey*; p 326.
2. British Official History; *Mesopotamian Campaign*, Vol I; fn p 94.
3. National Biography; Sir Percy Cox; pp 196–98.
4. British Official History, Vol I, p 352, Appx VI, third para.
5. *Ibid*; p 135.
6. National Biography; Sir John Nixon; pp 408–9.
7. National Biography; Sir Charles Townshend; pp 848–9.
8. British Official History, Vol I, Appx V; p 354.
9. *Ibid*; p 235.
10. Sherson; *Townshend of Chitral and Kut*; p 262.
11. British Official History, Vol II; p 7.
12. *Ibid*; p 15.
13. *Ibid*; p 28.
14. Sherson; p 284.
15. British Official History, Vol II; p 98.
16. *Ibid*; p 107.
17. Sherson; p 290.

Chapter 6: The Loss of Kut and the Arab Revolt.

1. British Official History; *Egypt and Palestine*, Vol I; p 217.
2. *Ibid*; p 82.
3. British Official History; *Mesopotamia*, Vol II; p 134.
4. *Ibid*; p 134.
5. *Ibid*; p 136.
6. *Ibid*; p 138.
7. National Biography; Sir John Nixon; p 411, quoting Mesopotamian Commission Report; p 111.
8. British Official History; *Mesopotamia*, Vol II; p 283.
9. Townshend; *My Campaign in Mesopotamia*; p 298.
10. *Ibid*; p 299.
11. *Ibid*; p 310.
12. Lawrence; *Seven Pillars of Wisdom*; p 8.
13. *Ibid*; p 93.
14. Wavell; *The Palestine Campaigns*; p 59.

Chapter 7: Lloyd George's Politic-Military Targets.

1. Wavell, *Allenby*; p 153.
2. Callwell, *Sir Stanley Maude*; p 292.
3. British Official History; *Mesopotamian Campaign*, Vol III; p 185.
4. *Ibid*; p 205.
5. Lawrence; p 61 and p 320.
6. British Official History; *Egypt and Palestine*, Vol I; p 322.
7. *Ibid*; p 322.
8. *Ibid*; pp 324–5.
9. Wavell; *The Palestine Campaigns*; p 92.
10. Lawrence; p 192.
11. *Ibid*; p 173.
12. *Ibid*; p 194.
13. *Ibid*; p 276.
14. *Ibid*; p 322.
15. British Official History; *Egypt and Palestine*, Vol II; p 1.
16. Wavell; *Allenby*; p 158.
17. *Ibid*; p 158.

Chapter 8: Destroying the Ottoman Empire.

1. Wavell; *Allenby*; p 224–5.
2. British Official History; *Egypt and Palestine*, Vol II, Pt 1; p 311.
3. British Official History; *Mesopotamia*, Vol IV; p 158.
4   Lawrence; p 631.
5. *Ibid*; p 632.
6. British Official History; *Egypt and Palestine*. Vol II, Pt 2; p 618.
7. *Ibid*; p 619.
8. British Official History; *Mesopotamia*, Vol IV; p 328–9.

BIBLIOGRAPHY

Anderson, MS; *The Eastern Question*; (Macmillan, New York, 1966).

Barthorp, Michael; *War on the Nile, 1882–98*; (Blandford Press; London, 1984).

Bourrienne, Louis de; *Memoirs of Napoleon Bonaparte*; Vol l; (Richard Bentley, London, 1885).

Braeman, John; *Wilson*; (Prentice Hall, New Jersey, 1922).

Callwell. Sir CE; *The Life of Sir Stanley Maude*; (Constable, London, 1920).

Churchill, Winston; *A History of the English Speaking Peoples*; (Cassell, London, 1958).

Dupuy, TN & GP Hayes; *The Campaigns on the Turkish Fronts*; (Franklin Watts, New York, 1967).

Edwards, Michael; *Playing the Great Game*; (Hamish Hamilton, London, 1975).

English, Barbara; *John Company's Last War*; (Collins, London, 1971).

Fortescue, JW; *A History of the British Army*; Vols IV, VI and XI, (Macmillan, London, 1906).

Fregosi, Paul; *Dreams of Empire*; (Hutchinson, London, 1989).

Gilbert, Martin; *Winston Churchill*; Vol IV (1917–22); (Heinemann, London, 1975).

Goldschmidt, Arthur, Jr; *A Concise History of the Middle East*; 3rd Edn; (Westview Press, Boulder, USA).

Haldane. Lt-General Sir Aylmer; *The Insurrection in Mesopotamia, 1920*; (William Blackwood, London 1922).

Hannah, WH; *Bobs, Kipling's General*; (Leo Cooper, 1972).

Heathcote, TA; *The Afghan Wars 1839–1919*; (Osprey, London, 1980).

Hopkirk, Peter; *The Great Game*; (John Murray, London, 1990).

Howard, John Eldred; *Letters and Documents of Napoleon*; Vol l; (The Cresset Press, London, 1961).

Ingram, Edward; *The Beginning of the Great Game in Asia 1828–34*; (Clarendon Press, Oxford, 1979).

Johnston, RM; *The Corsican*; (Macmillan, London, 1911).

Kearsey, A; *A Study of the Strategy and Tactics of the Mesopotamian Campaign*; (Gale & Polden, Aldershot, 1934).

Keown-Boyd, Henry; *A Good Dusting; Sudan Campaigns 1883–99*; (Leo Cooper, 1986).

Kumar, Ravender; *India and the Persian Gulf*, 1858–1907; (D'Souza, Delhi, 1965).

Lawrence, TE; *Seven Pillars of Wisdom*; (Jonathan Cape, London, 1935).

Liman von Sanders; *Five Years in Turkey*; (Williams & Wilkins, Baltimore, USA, 1928).

Lockhart, John Gibson; *The History of Napoleon Bonaparte*; Everyman's Library, Vol 3, (Dent & Dutton, London 1930).

Lloyd, Christopher; *The Nile Campaign*; (David & Charles, Newton Abbot, 1973).

Miller, Ronald; *Kut: the Death of an Army*; (Secker & Warburg, 1969).

Morgan, Gerald; *Anglo-Russian Rivalry in Central Asia 1810–85*; (Frank Cass, London, 1981).

Morris, James (Jan); *Pax Britannica*; (Penguin, London, 1968).

Morris, James (Jan); *Heaven's Command*; (Penguin, London, 1971).

Morris, James (Jan); *Farewell the Trumpets*; (Penguin, London, 1978).

Murphy, Col CCR; The Persian Campaign of 1856–57, *RUSI Journal*, April 1932.

Napier, Commodore Sir Charles; *The War in Syria*; (John W Parker, London, 1842).

Packe, SWC; *Sea Power in the Mediterranean*; (Barker, London 1971).

Robson, Brian; *The Road to Kabul; the Second Afghan War, 1878–81*; (Arms & Armour Press, London, 1986).

Sachar, Howard M; *The Emergence of the Middle East: 1914–1924*; (Allen Lane, The Penguin Press, London, 1969).

Searight, Sarah; *The British in the Middle East*; (Weidenfeld & Nicolson, London, 1969).

Sherson, Erroll: *Townshend of Chitral and Kut*; (William Heinemann, London, 1928).

Stewart, Desmond; *The Middle East; Temple of Janus*; (Hamish Hamilton, London, 1972).

Sykes, Sir Percy; *A History of Persia*; Vol II; (Macmillan, London, 1930).

Townshend, Sir Charles, VF; *My Campaign in Mesopotamia*; (Thornton Butterworth, London, 1920).

Trumpner, Ulrich; 'Liman von Sanders and the German-Ottoman Alliance'; *Journal of Contemporary History*, Oct 1966.

Yapp, ME; *The Making of the Middle East, 1792–1923*; (Longman, London, 1987).

Volodarsky, Mikail; 'Persia and the Great Powers'; *Middle Eastern Studies*; (Ministry of Defence Library; 1983).

Warner, Oliver; *Nelson's Battles*; (BT Batsford, London, 1965).

Wavell, FM Viscount; *The Palestine Campaign's*; (Constable; London, 1931).

Wavell, FM Viscount; *Allenby, Soldier and Statesman*; (Harrap, London, 1944).

Zetland, Marquess of; *Lord Cromer*; (Hodder & Stoughton; London, 1932).

British Official Histories:

First World War:

Egypt & Palestine: Vols I & II.

Mesopotamian Campaign: Vols I, II, III, IV.

INDEX

Abdul Medjid 60
Abercromby, Gen. Sir Ralph 19–26, 28, 32
Afghanistan 34–5, 38–60, 65, 67–8, 76–7, 81–92
  Afghan rebellion 55–6
  First Anglo-Afghan War 39–41, 68, 76, 81
  and Russia 35, 43–4, 46, 91–2
  Second Afghan War 1878–81 82–92
  sieges of Herat 39, 44
Africa, European scramble to partition 111
Agreements concerning Arabs and Jews, conflicting promises contained in 162, 250–1
Ahmed Bey 149
Air-power 197, 219, 239–40
Akbar Khan 55–7, 59
Alison, Maj. Gen. Sir Archibald 95–6, 99, 101
Allenby, Gen. Sir Edmund 213, 216–17, 219–27, 230–5, 238–42, 244–7
American Civil War 77, 79, 98
ANZACs 140, 167, 191–2, 207–9, 219, 234, 241
Arab Bureau 161, 186, 189
Arab Revolt 161, 163, 185–9, 194, 205, 209, 213–15, 245
Arabs
  see under Ottoman Empire
Arabi, Col. Ahmed 93–6, 98–104
Armenia 129–30, 166, 180, 185, 199, 228–9
Auckland, Lord 39–45, 49–50, 52–4, 57, 81, 83–4
Auda Abu Tayi 215–16, 226
Aylmer, Maj. Gen. Fenton 171, 173–7, 179–80
Ayub Khan 90–1
Azerbaijan 228–9, 235–6, 248

Baird, Gen. Sir David 26–7
Baker, Col. Valentine 103, 105
Balfour, Arthur 162
Balfour Declaration/Agreement 162, 233, 251

Balkan Wars, 1912–13 125, 128
Baluchistan 41, 46
Baratoff, Gen. 160, 172, 185, 197, 200, 202, 229
Baring, Sir Evelyn (later Lord Cromer) 102–4, 106–7, 110–14, 121, 127
Baring, Francis (Lord Northbrook) 102
Barrett, Lt. Gen. Sir Arthur 132–41
Belliard, Gen. 26–8
Beresford, Lord Charles 108–9
Blankett, Commodore John 13, 15, 21, 26–7
Bols, Maj. Gen. Louis 219
Bremond, Col. E 214
British Army, modernisation of 98
Broadwood, Col. 118, 120
Brooking, Maj. Gen. HT 197
Browne, Lt. Gen. Sir Samuel 84, 86
Brueys, Adm. F-P 6, 11–13
Bulfin, Lt. Gen. Sir Edward 218, 221–4, 233–4, 238–40, 242, 245
Bulgaria 242, 248
Buller, Redvers 108
Burnes, Sir Alexander 41–2, 45, 47, 49–50, 52, 55, 81, 85–6
Burrows, Brig. Gen. 90

Cambridge, Duke of 98
Canning, George 69–70
Capitan Pasha 24, 26–7
Cassels, Brig. Gen. 247
Caucasus 35–6, 38, 128–30, 166, 180, 185, 199, 228–31, 235–7, 248
  disintegration of Russian armies on Caucasus front 228
  Fed. Republic of Trans-Caucasian Peoples 229
Cavignari, Maj . PLN 83, 85–7
Chamberlain, Austen 149, 153–4
Chamberlain, Gen. Sir Neville 83
Chauvel, Maj. Gen. 191–2, 207–8, 213, 218–19, 221–4, 233–4, 238–40, 242, 244
Cherniaev, Gen. Mikhail 77
Chetwode, Lt. Gen. Sir Philip 207–10, 213, 216–19, 221–5, 230, 233–4, 238–40, 242

Churchill, Winston 116–17, 119
Climo, Col. 145, 157
Cobbe, Maj. Gen. AS 185, 196–201, 204, 246–7
Colley, Col. George Pomeroy 81–2, 89
Collingwood, Adm. 30
Collinson, Brig. 115–16, 118
Connaught, Duke of 99, 101
Conolly, Arthur 51–2
Cookson, Lt. Commander 151–2
Coote, Maj. Gen. Eyre 26–8
Cornwallis, Lord 19
Cotton, Maj . Gen. Sir Willoughby 44–6, 50, 53
Cowley, Lt. Comm. CH 184
Cox, Lt. Gen. Sir Percy 132–4, 136–8, 144–6, 149, 153, 167
  important achievements of 133–4
Cranbourn, Lord 82
Crewe, Lord 144–5
Crimean War 67–8, 78
Crocker, Brig. Gen. SF 197–8, 204
Cromer, Lord
  see Baring, Sir Evelyn
Cyprus 62, 80

Dawnay, Brig. Gen. Guy 217
de Lesseps, Ferdinand 66, 79, 100
de Robeck, Adm. 140
Delamain, Brig. Gen. WS 134–5, 142–3, 145, 147, 149, 151–2, 156–7, 167, 171
Dervishes 103–20
Desaix, Gen. Louis 14, 18
Disraeli, Benjamin 77–8, 80–3
Djemal Kuchuk 130, 132, 240–1, 245
Djemal Pasha 125, 129–32, 162, 166, 185–6, 189, 200, 207–8, 211–12, 214, 218, 220–1, 225, 231
Djezzar Pasha 15–17
Dobbie, Brig. Gen. 144–5
Dobell, Lt. Gen. Sir Charles 207, 209, 211–13
Dost Mohamed 41–3, 47–9, 52, 55, 57, 59, 65, 68, 77
Douglas, Maj. Gen. Sir William 191
Duckworth, Adm. 30–2
Duff, Sir Beauchamp 137
Duhamel, Gen. 67
Duke of York 19–20
Duncan, Maj. Gen. 44
Dundas, Henry 6, 19–21, 28
Dunsterville, Maj. Gen. LC 229, 235–7, 246

Earle, Maj. Gen. William 108

Eastern question 29–34, 60–6, 78–80, 93–122
  definition of 29
Egypt 1, 5–33, 60–7, 78–80, 93–123, 127–32, 140, 162, 164–7, 186, 189–90, 192–4, 205–6, 216, 250
  Aboukir Bay 8, 11–13, 18, 22, 32
  Army 98, 103, 105, 111, 192, 194, 205–6, 216
  British occupation of 97–103
  as British protectorate 110, 129
  First World War 127–32, 162, 165–6
  and France 1, 5–31, 60, 64, 66, 79, 93–6, 100, 110, 131–2
  rule by the Porte 28, 31, 33, 94–5, 103, 110
  Suez Canal 66–7, 78–80, 93, 95–6, 99–100, 102, 111, 128, 131, 140, 162, 164–7, 186, 189–90, 192–3, 205, 250
Egyptian Expeditionary Force 192, 194, 205–6, 216
Elgin, Lord 18–19, 21, 28
Ellenborough, Lord 54, 57–8
Elphinstone, Maj. Gen. William 53, 55–7, 59, 88
England, Brig. Richard 58
Enver Pasha 125, 129–30, 136, 140, 162, 164, 184, 186, 197, 204, 220, 229, 231, 244, 248
Ethersey, Capt. Dick 69–70, 74

Faiz Mohamed 83–4
Fakhri Pasha 188
Fane, Gen. Sir Henry 43, 45–6, 53
Federal Republic of Trans-Caucasian Peoples 229
Feisal (son of Grand Sherif of Mecca) 163, 186, 188–9, 194, 214–16, 225–6, 230, 238, 241, 244–5
Fevzi Pasha 220–1, 223, 234
Firman, Lt. HOB 184
Foley, Capt. Thomas 12–13
Fortescue, the Hon. John 19–20, 28, 43, 48, 59
Fox, Gen. 30–1
France 5–31, 34–5, 37, 60–1, 64, 66, 79, 93–6, 98, 100, 110–11, 120–3, 131–2, 161–2, 165, 232, 245
  and African possessions/ambitions 111, 120–1
  and Egypt 1, 5–31, 60, 64, 66, 79, 93–6 100, 110, 123, 131–2
  and India, designs on 6, 13, 15, 18, 20, 28–30, 34–5, 37, 111
  Lebanon 161, 245
  and Persia 34–5

as protector of Latin Church within
Ottoman Empire 162
and Syria 15–17, 161–2, 165, 232, 245
see also Napoleon Bonaparte
Franco-Prussian War 98
Fraser, Maj. Gen. Mackenzie 31–4
French, Sir John 165, 206
Friant, Gen. Louis 22–4
Fry, Brig. Gen. 137, 142–3, 151–2

Ganteaume, Adm. 26–7
Gardanne, Gen. 35–6
Gatacre, Maj. Gen. 116
Georgia 229, 235–7
Germany 123–59
Turco-German *jihad* 123–59
Drang nach Osten 123
see also individual German
commanders
Ghazban, Sheikh 139
Gladstone, William Ewart/cabinet of 89,
91–2, 94–6, 102, 107–10
Gordon, Maj. Gen. Charles 103–9,
111–13, 120–1
Gorringe, Maj. Gen. George 139, 141,
144, 147–50, 177, 180–5
Gorst, Sir Eldon 127
Gough-Calthorpe, Vice-Adm. 248
Graham, Maj. Gen. Gerald 101, 106,
108
Great Game, the 29, 33–60, 65–92
121–2
area covered by 33
definition of 29

Haig, Sir Douglas 114, 120, 165
Haines, Gen. Sir Frederick 82, 84,
89–91
Halil Bey 155, 173–4, 177, 180–1,
183–5, 197, 200–2, 204–5, 220, 227
Hamilton Gen. Sir Ian 140, 156–7, 171
Hamilton Lt. Walter 85
Hamley, Lt. Gen. Sir Edward 99–101
Hardinge, Lord 133, 144, 153–4
Hartington, Lord 107
Hassan Bey 16–17
Havelock, Brig. Gen. Henry 71, 74–5
Hicks, Col. William 104
Hodgson, Brig. Gen. HW 207
Hoghton, Brig. Gen. 156–7, 171–2
Hunt, Capt. GH 75
Hunter, Maj. Gen. 116
Husrev Pasha 60
Hussein ibn Ali, Grand Sherif of Mecca
127, 160, 162, 185–6, 188–9, 193
sons of: Abdullah 161, 188
Ali 186, 188–9

Feisal 163, 186, 188–9, 194, 214–16,
225–6, 230, 238, 241, 244–5
Zeid 188
Hussein Kemal, Sultan of Egypt 129
Hutchinson, Maj. Gen. Hely 20, 24,
26–8

Ibrahim (son of Mehemet Ali) 60–1,
63–4
Ignatiev, Count Nikolai 77–8
India 6, 13, 15, 28–30, 34–5, 37, 39, 41,
50, 53, 59, 76–7, 82, 111, 161, 250
East India Co. 6, 29, 34–5, 39, 41, 50,
53, 59, 76
French designs on 6, 13,15, 28–30,
34–5, 37, 111,
Government/Army 127, 132, 134–51,
165–85, 194, 197–205, 230–1,
236–41, 244–6
Indian Mutiny, 1857 76
Moslems 161
see also Great Game, the
Ismaïl, Khedive 78–9, 93, 98, 103
Ismaïl Hakki Bey 247
Izzet Pasha 125, 248

Jaafar Pasha 162–3, 225, 244
Jervis, Adm. 7–8, 14, 18
Jevad Pasha 231, 234, 239–40
Jewish Legion 233
Jones, Sir Harford 35–6

Kara Bekr Bey 197, 200–2, 204–5
Kaufman, Gen. Konstantin 77, 79–81,
85
Keane, Gen. Sir John 45–50, 58, 89
Keary, Maj. Gen. 175, 177–9, 182–3
Keith, Adm. Lord 18–20, 22
Kemal, Mustapha 140, 220, 234,
239–40, 245, 248
Kemball, 173–4, 177–9
Keppel, Commander 113, 116–17, 121
Khairi Bey 186, 188
Khalifa, the 110–11, 113–14, 116–20
Kipling, Rudyard 66, 92
Kitchener, Horatio Herbert 95, 109–21,
127, 129, 141, 150, 154–5, 161,
164–5, 193, 206
Kléber, Gen. Jean-Baptiste 18–19
Kuwait, Sheikh of 134

Lake, Gen. Sir Percy 169–70, 176–7,
179–80, 182, 184–5
Lawrence, Maj. Gen. the Hon. HA 191
Lawrence, TE 161, 186–7, 189, 206,
214–17, 225–6, 237–9, 241–2,
244–5

Lean, Brig. Gen. 139, 144
Lebanon, the 61–4, 161, 230, 242–3, 245
Leeke, Sir Henry 69–70, 74
Lewis, Brig. Gen. 115–16, 118–19
Lindsay, Lt. Henry (later Maj . Gen. Sir Henry Lindsay-Bethune) 36
Lloyd George, David 165, 193–4, 199, 205–6, 219, 225, 230, 232, 242, 249
Lowe, Maj. Gen. Drury 101–2
Lyttleton, Brig. Gen. 115–16, 118–20
Lytton, Lord 78, 80–7, 89, 91–2

Macdonald, Brig. Gen. Hector 112, 114–16, 118–20
MacMunn, Maj. Gen. Sir George 195, 202, 204
Macnaghten, Sir William 40–1, 45–7, 49–57, 59, 81, 84–6, 102
Mahmud, Amir of Metemmeh 113–14
Mahmud II, Sultan 60
Malcolm, Brig. John (later Sir) 34–6
Malet, Sir Edward 102
Mamelukes 9–11, 14–17, 25, 27, 31–4
  Ibrahim Bey 11, 14–15
  Murad Bey 11, 14, 18
Maronites 62–3
Marshall, Maj. Gen. Sir WR 196–201, 204, 228–30, 232, 235, 246, 248
Martin, Col. RM 116, 119
Massy, Brig. Dunham 88
Maude, Maj. Gen. Sir Stanley 167, 176–7, 180–3, 185, 192–5, 197–205, 209, 219, 227–8
Maxwell, Lt. Gen. Sir John 115–16, 118–20, 128, 130, 161–6, 220
Mahon, Sir Henry 129, 160–2, 167, 186, 189
Mahon Agreement 161–2, 250–1
McNeill, Sir John 38–9
Mecca, Grand Sherif of
  see Hussein ibn Ali
Mehemet Ali 31–4, 60–2, 64–5, 103
Melliss, Maj. Gen. 139, 142–4, 149, 156–7, 171
Menou, Gen. Jacques-François 19, 22, 24–8
Middle East, importance of 38
Miller, Capt. Ralph 16, 18
Milne, Gen. (later Field Marshal, the Lord Milne) 248
Minto, Lord 35–6
Missett, Maj. 31–4
Mohamed Shah 38
Mohammerah, Sheikh of 133–6
Money, Maj. Gen. AW 195
Moore, Maj. Gen. John 19–20, 23–8, 31

Moslem extremism 250
Murad Bey 11, 14, 18
Murray, Lt. Gen. Sir Archibald 165–7, 189–94, 205–7, 209, 211–14, 216–17, 219
Murray, Charles 67, 75
Murray, Col. John 27
Mustapha Pasha 18

Napier, Gen. Sir Charles 59, 61–5
Napoleon Bonaparte 5–15, 17–22, 26, 28, 30–1
  and Egypt 5–22, 31
  and India 6, 13, 15, 28
  Marengo 20
  and Peninsular War 30
  in Syria 15–17
Napoleonic Wars 29
Nasir, Sherif 215–16
Nelson, Adm. Horatio 7–14, 18, 22, 30
Newcombe, Lt. Col SF 214, 218, 222–3
Nicholas, Grand Duke 166
Nicolls, Sir Jasper 53, 57
Nixon, Gen. Sir John 141–2, 144–50, 153–5, 157–8, 167–71, 195
Norris, Commodore DT 236–7
Northcliffe, Lord 78
Nott, Maj. Gen. William 47, 50–1, 53, 55–6, 58–9
Nunn, Capt. W 145–9, 151, 202
Nur-ud-Din 150–5, 157–9, 172–3
Nuri Bey 162–3, 235

Osman Digna 105–6, 113–14, 119–20
Ottoman Empire/Turkey 1–2, 4–34, 38, 60–7, 76, 78–80, 93–235, 238–5
  Arab population/Arab irregulars 134–9, 143–4, 147, 159–63, 169, 185–7, 188–9 193–4, 202, 206, 213–17, 225–6, 230, 237–9, 241–5, 249–51
  Baghdad, capture of 203–5
  Damascus, Beirut and Aleppo, capture of 242–6
  disintegration and collapse of Empire 227–49
  Egypt – *see* Egypt
  Gallipoli campaign 140–1, 149, 160, 162, 164–6
  Lebanon, the 61–4, 161, 230, 242–3, 245
  Megiddo, Battle of 1, 227, 233–4, 237–41, 250
  Mesopotamian Campaign 133–59, 164–85, 194–205, 220, 232, 246–9
  Palestine campaign 205–27, 230–5,

237–46, 249–50
pan-Turks and pan-Islamics 129–30,
    220, 229–30, 235, 237
railway construction 123
and Russia 67 78, 125, 136, 148, 166,
    180, 235
Syria 15–17, 60–5, 161–2, 165, 185,
    232, 242–6
Turco German *jihad* 123–59
Turkish Army, capitulation of 248
Turkish Army, toughness of 125–6
Turkish theatre of war, 1914–18 124
Young Turk revolution, 1908
    125
Outram, Lt. Gen. Sir James 71–5, 133

Palmerston, Lord 43, 60, 64–5, 69
Peel, Sir Robert 53–4, 57
Peninsular War 30
Perovski, Count 44, 52
Persia 34–9, 65, 67–8, 160, 172, 185,
    228–9, 235, 248
  Anglo-Persian relations 36
  Anglo-Persian War, 1856–57 133
  British operations in N.W. Persia, 1918
    228
  and France 34–5
  oilfields/oil interests 126, 128–9,
    132–4, 139–40, 144, 148, 160,
    164, 193, 195, 205
  Persian Gulf 68–75, 127, 132–3
  and Russia 35, 38, 67, 160, 172, 185
  Turkish withdrawal from Persian
    territory 248
Peyton, Maj. Gen. WE 163
de Phélypeaux, Col. R 6, 16, 18
Picot, Georges 162
Pitt, William, the Younger 6, 19–21
Pollock, Maj. Gen. George 57–9, 84
Ponsonby, Lord 60–1, 64–5
Pottinger, Sir Eldred/Pottinger family
    38–9, 44–5, 56
Pottinger, Sir Henry 45
Primrose, Lt. Gen. 89–91

Rennie, Commodore John 74–5
Ripon, Lord 89–91
Roberts, Maj. Gen. Frederick ('Bobs')
    84–9
Robertson, Sir William 165–6, 176, 185,
    192–5, 198–200, 202–3, 205, 209,
    211–13, 219, 225, 230
Royal Air Force (RAF) 239–40
Russia 29, 34–9, 43–4, 46, 51–2, 59,
    65–8, 76–92, 125, 128–9, 136, 148,
    160, 166, 172, 180, 185, 209,
    227–8, 235–6

and Afghanistan 35, 43–4, 46, 91–2
and Caucasia 35–6, 38, 128–9, 166,
    235–6
and Central Asia 35, 37, 51–2, 59,
    66–7, 76–8, 91
Crimean War 67–8, 78
and Great Game 29, 34–9, 43–4,
    51–2, 59, 66–8, 76–92
Orthodox Christians 78–9
and Ottoman Empire 67, 78, 125,
    136, 148, 166, 180, 235
and Persia 35, 38, 67, 160, 172, 185
Provisional Government, 1917 209,
    227–8
Russo-Turkish War 79–80

Sa'id Pasha 66, 79, 94
Sale, Brig. Gen. Sir Bob 48–50, 52–9
Sale, Lady 54, 57, 59
Salisbury, Lord 77, 111–13
Salmond, Maj. Gen. Geoffrey 239
Sayed Amed, the Grand Senussi 162
Senussi, the 162–3, 205, 225
Seymour, Adm. Sir Beauchamp 95–6,
    98–9
Shah Shuja 41, 43–7, 49–57, 84–5, 90
Shakespear, Richmond 51
Shea, Maj. Gen. 225
Shelton, Col. John 54, 57
Sher Ali, Amir 78, 81–9
Shuja
  see Shah Shuja
Sikhs 50, 59
Simonich, Count 38
Sind 41, 46, 50, 59
Singh, Jemadar Jewand 86
Singh, Ranjit 41, 43–4
Singleton, Lt. Mark 147
Sirkesheck-chee Bashi 74–5
Slavery in Sudan 103–4, 106, 111
Smith, Charles 7, 15, 18
Smith, Brig. Gen. Sir Charles 63–4
Smith, Sir Sidney 7–8, 14–19, 21–3,
    26–8, 62, 64–5
Smuts, Gen. Jan (later Field Marshal)
    213, 230
Spencer, Lord 8
Stalker, Maj. Gen. Foster 69–71, 73–4
Stewart, Lt. Gen. Donald 84, 86,
    89–91
Stewart, Col. Hamill 106
Stewart, Maj. Gen. Sir Herbert 108–9
Stewart, Brig. William 32
Stoddard, Charles 51–2
Stolietov, Count 81, 83, 85
Stopford, Brig. Gen. 70
Stopford, Gen. Sir Frederick 140

Stopford, Adm. Sir Robert 61–5
Sudan/Sudanese 103–22
  Mahdi rebellion/Mahdi'ism 13–20
  Omdurman, Battle of 115–20
  recognition of as Anglo-Egyptian
    condominium 121
  slavery in 103–4, 106, 111
Sulaiman Askari Bey 139, 142–3
Sultan of Turkey/Caliph of all Islam
    126–7, 162
Sykes, Sir Mark 162
Sykes, Sir Percy 36
Sykes-Picot Agreement 162, 244–5, 251
Syria 15–17, 60–5, 161–2, 165, 185,
    232, 242–6
  Syrian campaign 1840–1 60–5

Tewfik, Khedive 93–5, 102–4, 107, 110
  Anglo-French support for 94–5
Thomson Maj. 46, 48–9
Tiller, Maj. 209, 211
Townshend, Maj. Gen. Charles 141–2,
    145–7, 150–5, 157–60, 167–8,
    170–3, 175–7, 179–85, 197, 199,
    201–2, 248
  Kut, surrender of 184–5
Turkey
  see Ottoman Empire

United States' growing interests in
    Middle East 250

Vitkevich, Capt. 43
von der Goltz, Col. (later Field Marshal
    Freiherr Colmar) 123, 155, 168,

172–4, 183, 185
von Falkenhayn, Field Marshal 220–1,
    223–4, 231
von Kressenstein, Col. Freiherr Kress
    130–1, 162, 166, 186, 189–92,
    207–12, 218–1, 221–3, 231
von Lettow-Vorbeck 213
von Oppen, Col. 220, 232, 240
von Sanders, Gen. Liman 123, 125,
    130–2, 140–1, 231–2, 234–5,
    238–42, 244, 248
von Stotzingen, Freiherr 186

Wallace, Maj. Gen. A 163
Wapshare, Brig. Gen. 141
Wauchope, Maj. Gen. Patrick 32
Wauchope, Brig. Gen. 115–16, 118–20
Wavell, Field Marshal Lord 192, 194,
    217, 219, 227
Wilson, Maj. Gen. A 130, 132
Wilson, Col. Sir Charles 109
Wilson, Sir Henry 232
Wilson, Woodrow 250
Wingate, Maj. 120
Witts, Capt. FVP 197, 200–1
Wolseley, Gen. Sir Garnet 80–1,
    95–101, 103, 106–10
Wood, Maj. Gen. Evelyn 103, 105–6

Yakub Khan 85, 87, 91
Younghusband, Maj. Gen. George 150,
    155, 167–8, 171–7, 182–4
Yussef, Grand Vizier 21, 24, 26–8

Zaman Shah, Amir 34